THE COMPETITION LAW OF THE E.E.C.

A PRACTICAL GUIDE

James P. Cunningham
B.Com.(Lond.)
of the Middle Temple, Barrister-at-Law

SUPPLEMENT

to
September 13, 1975

Kogan Page

First published 1975 by
Kogan Page Limited
116a Pentonville Road, London N1 9JN

Printed in Great Britain by
Redwood Burn Limited
Trowbridge and Esher

ISBN 0 85038 440 0

TABLE OF CONTENTS

PART 4 MERGERS AND ABUSES OF DOMINANT POSITIONS

APPENDICES

PREFACE

My book *The Competition Law of the EEC – A Practical Guide* was written during the Summer of 1972. Since then, some three years have elapsed, years which have seen considerable developments in Community competition law – judgments by the European Court, decisions by the Commission in Brussels, further Community regulations, and also judgments by national courts in the Member States.

The judgments by the European Court have included that in *Continental Can*, holding that a merger can constitute an abuse of dominant position under Article 86 merely by extending that position. Refusal to supply was also held to be an abuse within Article 86, in the *Zoja* judgment. In *Centrafarm* and *Hag*, the Court ruled upon major issues in patent and trade-mark fields. And in *SABAM* and *Brasserie de Haecht (No.2)*, it dealt with the jurisdiction of national courts; the validity of notified agreements was the subject of a ruling in the latter. The *Transocean (No.2)* judgment was significant for its attitude to the Commission's procedure.

Among the decisions by the Commission, that in *European Glass Manufacturers* is of importance in relation to agreements to exchange price and other information. In *European Sugar Cartel*, very substantial fines were imposed. The *Advocaat Zwarte Kip* and *Sirdar/PHILDAR* decisions were concerned with trade marks; the latter is subject to an appeal to the Court, and may give rise to another important ruling.

Following the Court's judgment in *Continental Can*, a draft regulation to provide Community control of mergers was submitted by the Commission to the Council, but has not yet been adopted. The Regulations dealing with the block exemption for specialisation agreements and with the limitation of actions, the drafts of which appeared in the book as Appendices O and N, have now been made; the texts are given in Appendices Q and S of this Supplement, new letters and new marginal numbers being adopted to avoid confusion with the drafts. The authentic English texts of Regulations made prior to the 1st January, 1973, the date of accession of Denmark, Ireland, and the United Kingdom, have become available, in a Special Edition of the Official Journal; for ease of reference, both when using the book and the Supplement, they have been reproduced as Appendices to this Supplement using the same letters (B, E, F, etc.) as in the book, and the same marginal numbers. It has proved necessary to reproduce additional Articles from the Rome Treaty itself. The relevant provisions are reproduced as Appendix A to the Supplement, using the same marginal numbers as in the book for Articles which appear in both works – where new Articles have been introduced between consecutive marginal numbers, they are denoted by the addition of capital letters at the end of the numbers. I am indebted to H.M. Stationery Office for permission to include these.

Together, the book and this Supplement state Community competition law, except for the special fields of agriculture and transport, as at 13th September, 1975. Where I have felt that a Court judgment or a Commission decision is open to question, I have sought to indicate first what its impact is as a statement of Community law, and then to give my criticisms separately, in some instances as Annexes to the relevant chapter (Chapters 8 and 15).

The word "block" has now become accepted usage, as in "block exemption". I have, therefore, adopted it in place of "bloc" as used in the book. In spelling "specialisation" I have adopted "s" instead of "z", to conform to the relevant regulations, and similarly in "standardisation".

Finally, I would like once again to acknowledge my debt to Delyth Hale-Stephens, who has achieved the not-inconsiderable feat of turning my illegible holograph into an acceptable typescript.

James P. Cunningham

1 Temple Gardens,
Temple,
London, E.C.4.

HOW TO USE THIS SUPPLEMENT

The purpose of this Supplement is to bring up to date my book *The Competition Law of the EEC – A Practical Guide*. It should be used as an adjunct to the book, rather than as something for separate, narrative, reading.

This Supplement is divided into the same Parts and chapters as the book, and uses the same system of marginal numbers. Thus, to check whether there has been any development in a subject covered by any part of the text of the book, all that is required is to note the relevant number in the margin of the book – any new material will appear in the Supplement under the same number. For example, the book discusses notification of standard-form agreements under marginal number 6-46. Number 6-46 in the Supplement brings the discussion up to date with a note of the relevant aspects of the European Court's judgment in *Brasserie de Haecht (No. 2)*.

Where the new material is extensive or represents something which falls between two consecutive marginal numbers in the book, I have adopted the practice of using the first of the two numbers and adding capital letters. Thus 6-65A *et seq.* in the Supplement represent new material which logically falls between 6-65 and 6-66 in the book. But where the new material comes at the end of a chapter in such a way that the numbering can be continued, I have merely carried the numbers on, as in the case of 15-24 *et seq.* in the Supplement which follow on from 15-23 in the book.

To facilitate use of this Supplement, it has its own Table of Cases and Index.

TABLE OF CASES

The references are to marginal numbers.
C.M.L.R. = Common Market Law Reports
O.J. = Official Journal of the European Communities (prior to 1/1/73 the references are to the Journal Officiel = J.O.)

PART 1
GENERAL PRINCIPLES

CHAPTER 1

Competition and Restraints upon Competition

3. Monopoly – Dominant Position

1—05 The question whether containers made of tin-plate, glass, or plastics form one market or separate markets played a cardinal role in the appeal in the *Continental Can* case. The Commission had held that Continental Can, through its subsidiary Schmalbach, had a dominant position in three markets – open-top tins for meat, open-top tins for fish, and metal lids for glass containers. The Court annulled the Commission's decision, on the ground that the Commission had not shown "in detail the peculiarities which distinguish these three markets from one another and therefore necessitate their separate treatment. Nor is it stated by what peculiarities these three markets are distinguished from the general market for light metal containers, especially the market for metal containers for canned fruit and vegetables, condensed milk, olive oil, fruit juices and toilet preparations."[1] Later, reference is made to "containers made of other materials".[2] In considering the alleged dominant position of Schmalbach, "the delimitation of the market concerned is of crucial importance, for the possibilities of competition can only be considered in the light of the characteristics of the products in question, which reveal them to be particularly suited to satisfying a constant demand and interchangeable with other products only to a small extent."[3]

[1] [1973] C.M.L.R. p.226.
[2] *Ibid.* p.227.
[3] *Ibid.* p.226.

1–05A In *Kali und Salz/Kali Chemie*, the Commission refused exemption to the agreement on the ground that it enabled the parties to eliminate competition. The two companies were the only German producers of untreated potash fertiliser, but Kali Chemie specialised in production of a compound potash fertiliser. The agreement allowed Kali Chemie to supply its surplus untreated potash to Kali und Salz for re-sale. The Commission, in effect, regarded untreated potash as a separate market. The European Court, on appeal, annulled the Commission's decision. The Court pointed out that that decision showed that there was some competition between untreated and compound potash. Their prices and performance differed. Even though purchases of compound potash had increased, untreated potash was still used – some customers bought the one or the other at different periods. In effect, the Court regarded the relevant market as being wider than untreated potash, and as including compound potash.

4. Restrictive Trade Practices

Cartels

1–16 The relevance of countervailing power was recognised by the Commission in its *Rank/Sopelem* decision. Between them, Rank and Sopelem had some 20% of the trade in the E.E.C. in the relevant market – lenses and lens controls for cameras. But the camera manufacturers represented a specialised market, and were in direct touch with the lens manufacturers. The Commission therefore considered that the camera manufacturers were "well placed as regards scope for choice and bargaining power *vis-à-vis* Rank, Sopelem and their competitors".[4]

5. Control of Private Restraints upon Competition

Forms of Control in the Six E.E.C. Member States

1–38 *Germany* Legislation passed in 1973 gave the Bundeskartellamt power to deal with "arrangements", i.e. informal understandings which do not rank in law as agreements.

Forms of Control in the Three New Member States

1–39 *United Kingdom* The Fair Trading Act, 1973, gave power to

[4] Official Journal L29. 3.2.73. p.22.

extend to services cartels the registration and investigation procedure applicable to cartels relating to the supply of goods.

1–40 There are, therefore, nine national systems of control, systems of competition law, one in each Member State, in addition to Community law. There may, therefore, be simultaneous application of two systems to one agreement – for example; if the agreement is unlawful under, say, United Kingdom law and also under Article 85.1 of the Treaty, both United Kingdom law and Community law will apply to it. There is, therefore, the possibility of conflict. In that event, Community law prevails. As the European Court put it in *Wilhelm v. Bundeskartellamt:*

> "Consequently, conflicts between the Community rule and the national rules on competition should be resolved by the application of the principle of the primacy of the Community rule.
>
> It follows from the foregoing that in the case where national decisions regarding an agreement would be incompatible with a decision adopted by the Commission at the end of the proceedings initiated by it, the national authorities are required to respect its effects."[5]

M. Borschette, the Commissioner responsible for competition matters, speaking in the European Parliament on the 12th February, 1973 referred to that judgment. He continued:

> "To fulfil this obligation, Member States must first of all refrain from ordering, encouraging or authorising practices by undertakings that are prohibited either by **Article 85(1)** or by **Article 86**; secondly, Member States must refrain from prohibiting agreements which, pursuant to an individual decision or a regulation of the Commission, are covered by the exemption provided for in **Article 85(3)**."[6]

1–41 In its *Second Report on Competition Policy,* the Commission referred to two instances where both it and the German authorities had instituted proceedings, i.e. the proceedings against the dyestuffs manufacturers and the investigation into an agreement between the European and Japanese fibre manufacturers. Noting that no specific legal difficulties had arisen, the Commission said it was considering the desirability of

[5] [1969] C.M.L.R. p.119.

[6] Debates of the European Parliament. Sitting of Monday 12th February, 1973. p.13.

a regulation or directive under Article 87.2(e) of the Treaty, to deal with cases of simultaneous application of Community and national law. In its *Third Report on Competition Policy* the Commission again referred to the point. The complex legal problems which arose were to be discussed at a meeting of national experts during 1974. Difficulties might be averted by some procedural rules or by close co-operation and exchange of information between the national authorities and the Commission. The Commission's *Fourth Report on Competition Policy* refers to the meeting of national experts, which was held in December, 1974. The Commission and the governments of Member States felt that a regulation or a directive under Article 87.2(e) was unnecessary; instead, exchange of information between the Commission and the competent national authorities would be improved, and mutual consultation and harmonisation of competition policies should reduce risks of conflict between Community and national competition laws.

CHAPTER 2
The European Economic Community – The "Common Market"

2. The Common Market

2–02 Article 30 of the Treaty forbids not only quantitative restrictions on imports in trade between Member States but also "measures having equivalent effect". In the *Dassonville* case, the European Court held that an obligation to produce a certificate of authenticity may be such a measure in certain circumstances. In that case, the Dassonville firm imported Scotch whisky into Belgium, not directly from Scotland, but indirectly, from France. Under Belgian law, such imports had to be accompanied by a British customs certificate. The Dassonville imports were not accompanied by a certificate, although the bottles bore a reference to it. The Belgian authorities instituted criminal proceedings against the firm, which pleaded that the requirement to produce a certificate in the case of indirect imports was a measure having an effect equivalent to a quantitative restriction, and was therefore prohibited by Article 30. The Belgian court referred the point to the European Court. The United Kingdom government indicated to the Court that a customs certificate could be obtained for a small fee even after the goods had been exported from the United Kingdom. The Court held that a requirement by a Member State of a certificate of authenticity in respect of indirect imports (i.e. where the goods had been put on the market first in another Member State) is a measure having an effect equivalent to a quantitative restriction if the certificate is less easily obtainable by the indirect importer than by a direct importer (i.e. one importing directly from the country of origin), and is therefore contrary to Article 30.

2–02A The *Dassonville* judgment was given on the 11th July, 1974. On the 16th September, 1974, the Commission, in a reply to a written question in the European Parliament, dealt with a different aspect of documentation in respect of indirect imports.[1] The reply dealt with goods from a non-Member which are the subject of quantitative restriction or voluntary restraint under an agreement between a Member State and the non-Member, in conformity with the Treaty. In such cases, where the goods are imported indirectly into the Member concerned, after having first been put into circulation in another Member, the Member concerned may require the importer to produce the same sort of information as would be required in the case of direct imports. The Commission's view was that an import licence should normally be issued within eight working days, or within twelve working days if notification to the Commission is required.

In a reply given in December, 1973,[2] the Commission recognised that border formalities still presented difficulties for traders importing from one Member to another. These formalities arose from permissible national provisions, such as excise duties and laws for the protection of health relating to humans, plants, and animals, for the protection of public safety and morality, etc. The Commission was seeking harmonisation of national laws to reduce obstacles to inter-Member trade. In one instance, the requirement by the French authorities of a licence for import of tinned fish, the Commission had suggested to the French government that this practice was incompatible with Article 30, with the result that importers were no longer required to hold a licence.

4. The Institutions

2–05 The Assembly is now more usually referred to as "the European Parliament". Questions are put to the Commission by members on a wide range of subjects. In some instances the answers are useful in that they indicate the Commission's thinking on the particular subject.

The European Court

Constitution

2–05A For the constitution and procedure of the Court, reference has to

[1] Official Journal C121. 11.10.74. p.15.
[2] Official Journal C8. 31.1.74. p.2.

be made to three sources: first, Articles 164 to 188 of the E.E.C. Treaty, as amended by Articles 17 to 19 of the Act annexed to the Treaty of Accession; second, the Protocol on the Statute of the Court of Justice of the European Economic Community dated 17th April, 1957, as amended by Article 20 of the Act annexed to the Treaty of Accession; and third, the current Rules of Procedure of the Court issued by the Court on the 4th December, 1974.[3]

2–05B The Court consists of eleven judges, with partial replacement every three years – at one tri-ennial replacement six retire, and the next, five. The Court is assisted by three Advocates General; again there is tri-ennial replacement, first one retiring, and two at the end of the next three years. Retiring judges and Advocates General are eligible for re-appointment.

The President of the Court is elected by the judges.

The Court is divided into two Chambers, each with its own President. The allocation of judges and Advocates General to each Chamber is decided by the Court. When an application is lodged with the Court originating a case, the President of the Court assigns the case to one of the Chambers, and designates a judge from that Chamber to act as Rapporteur and also designates the Advocate General to be concerned with the case.

Procedure

2–05C The procedure before the Court falls into two parts. There is first the *written* procedure, i.e. the written pleadings and documents put in by the parties. When that stage is complete, there is the *oral* procedure, i.e. hearing the parties' agents and lawyers and the submissions by the Advocate General, and also any witnesses or experts. There is also provision for a *preparatory inquiry,* i.e. where the Court considers that there are issues of fact to be investigated. The Court may carry out the preparatory inquiry itself, or may assign it to the Chamber to which the case was allocated. If there is a preparatory inquiry, it takes place between the written and the oral procedure.

2–05D So far as competition law is concerned, there are two types of case of particular interest: appeals to the Court against decisions by the Commission, and references to the Court by national courts. The Court hears appeals by virtue of Article 173 of the

[3] Official Journal L350. 28.12.74. p.1.

Treaty (17-16), and references from national courts by virtue of Article 177 (17-17).

Appeals against Commission decisions

2–05E By Article 173 of the Treaty, the proceedings must be commenced within two months of the publication of the decision, or of its notification to the applicant, or of the day he first had knowledge of it. The proceedings commence with the *application* lodged with the Registrar of the Court (Rules, Article 38). It must be signed by the applicant's lawyer. It must identify the parties, i.e. the applicant and the Commission, and state the subject matter of the dispute, the form of order sought by the applicant, and the nature of the evidence on which he intends to rely (Article 38). A copy of the application is served on the defendant, the Commission, and one month is allowed for lodging the *defence* (Articles 39 and 40). Thereafter, there may be a *reply* from the applicant and a *rejoinder* from the defendant (Article 41). The time limits specified in each Rule apply only to parties habitually resident in Luxembourg. For others, they are extended as follows: Belgium, by two days; Federal Germany, and the European territories of France and Holland, by six days; Ireland, Italy, United Kingdom, and European territories of Denmark, by ten days; other European countries, by two weeks; and the rest of the world, by one month (Rules, Annex II).

Articles 44 to 54 of the Rules make provision for the preparatory inquiry, where the Court decides to have one, including the summoning of witnesses and experts, payment of their expenses, etc.

2–05F The oral procedure is opened by the President of the Court. The report by the Judge Rapporteur is read. Then the agents and lawyers of the parties are heard – the Commission is represented by its agent, and any Member States taking part are represented by their agents. The President and other judges, and the Advocate General, may put questions to the agents and lawyers (Rules, Article 57). The oral procedure ends with the Advocate General's submissions.

References under Article 177

2–05G Where the reference is concerned with the application of principles established by previous cases, it may be assigned by the Court to one of the Chambers (Rules, Article 95). The proceedings commence with the notification to the Court of the decision of the national court making the reference (Protocol, Article 20). The Registrar then notifies the Commission, the parties, and the Member States, and also the Council where the reference concerns a Council act or regulation. The Commission, parties, etc., have two months in which to submit statements of case or written observations to the Court. In effect, that constitutes the *written* procedure.

Thereafter, the provisions relating to the preparatory inquiry, if any, and the oral procedure apply, as outlined above.

Languages

2–05H The language of the case must be Danish, Dutch, English, French, German, Irish, or Italian (Rules, Article 29) i.e. one of the official languages of the Community. The applicant chooses the language. Article 29 provides that, where the application is against a Member State or a resident in a Member State, the official language of that State must be used. The Court may authorise the use of another official language if asked by either or both parties (but such a request cannot be made by the Commission or by any of the other Community institutions alone).

Where the case is a reference under Article 177, the language to be used is the language of the national court which made the reference (Rules, Articles 29 and 103). Where the case is an appeal against a Commission decision, the language will follow the language of that decision.

General comments on some of the Court's judgments

2–05I Since the beginning of 1973, there have been several significant judgments by the Court, in particular *Brasserie de Haecht (No. 2), SABAM v. Fonior, Zoja, Continental Can, Centrafarm,* and *Hag.* These judgments are examined critically in the appropriate places in this Supplement, and certain aspects of them have been found to be open to serious criticism. In some instances, these judgments either extend or modify principles previously laid down by the Court. This has enabled those principles to be considered more fully, and their validity – or lack of it – to be tested.

2–05J The criticisms which can be levelled at the Court's judgments may be summarised as follows.

Statements of the law have *not been sufficiently thought through.* For example, the clear statement of provisional validity for notified agreements in *Portelange* has been modified and restricted in *Brasserie de Haecht (No. 2)* and *SABAM v. Fonior* (*v.* paragraphs 4-26 and 4-07 *et seq.)* Moreover, it is doubtful if the Court's comments in *SABAM v. Fonior* are sound in so far as they suggest that national courts have no competence to hold an existing agreement notified in due time to be outside Article 85.1 (*v.* paragraph 4-07B(i)).

There is also *uncertainty* and *lack of clarity* in the language used. The *Zoja* and *Continental Can* judgments are instances (*v.* paragraphs 5-37B, and 3-95 and 5-40).

There is a *tendency to vague generalisation* where clear, cogent, thinking is to be expected. An illustration is the passage from the *Continental Can* judgment, beginning "The purpose of . . .", quoted in paragraph 15-32, with its "it cannot be supposed that" and its false antithesis between Article 85 (covering agreements, etc.) and Article 86 (which is alleged to cover only "unilateral activity").

Mention must also be made of the introduction of a *subjective, value opinion*, in the *Sirena* judgment, in which the Court deemed the object of other intellectual-property rights to be "often more important and worthy of greater protection" than the object of trade-mark rights (cf. paragraph 8-94).

2–05K Some, though by no means all, of these defects may spring from the Court's attempts to lay down general principles upon the facts of a particular, individual, case. The individual case does not normally give an opportunity to consider all the diverse possibilities, all the aspects of a question, which ought to be explored before a valid general principle can be stated. It is much sounder to restrict to the ambit of the particular case any principle based upon the facts of that case. Any comment outside that ambit can then be regarded as an *obiter dictum.*

2–05L There is a further charge which can be levelled against the Court's judgments. In some instances the Court has *over-stretched* (to use a charitable expression) the language of the Treaty in order to read into the Treaty something which is not there. This is to be seen in relation to intellectual-property rights in the *Centrafarm* and *Hag* cases, and merger control in the *Continental Can* case.

The Treaty, in Articles 222 and 36, indicates specifically that *bona fide* property rights are not prejudiced by the Treaty. The Court has evaded those provisions by ignoring Article 222 completely (*v.* paragraphs 8-93 *et seq.*) and by introducing the false distinction between the *existence* and the *exercise* of property rights (*v.* paragraphs 8-102 *et seq.*). National laws as regards patents and trade marks have been misrepresented, in the "specific object" doctrine (*v.* paragraphs 8-113 *et seq.*), and subjective value opinions introduced (as in the *Sirena* case).

As regards merger control, there is no specific provision in the Treaty conferring it. A comparison with the European Coal and Steel Community Treaty shows that its omission must have been deliberate. And Article 86, with its lack of provision for exemption, would not seem appropriate. But nevertheless, the Court by unconvincing arguments, some of which have been subsequently shown to be invalid (as by the comment in the draft mergers control regulation that exemption provision is necessary – 36-01), sought to prove that Article 86 did indeed give power to control mergers (*v.* paragraphs 15-29 *et seq.*).

2–05M By the methods referred to in the preceding paragraphs, the Court has arrogated to itself a law-making role. The functions of the Court under the Treaty are perfectly clear. Under Article 177 (17-17) its role is interpretative. Under Article 177 and Article 173 it is concerned with the validity and legality of acts of the Council and Commission – in effect, part of its role as interpreter of the Treaty. The Treaty is an agreement between the Member States. It affects, in direct and significant ways, the rights of citizens of the Member States. All the more reason why the provisions of the Treaty should be interpreted strictly – not over-stretched to include what is not there but what members of the Court consider should be there.

In its *Continental Can* judgment, the Court found it "necessary to resort to the spirit, structure and working of Article 86 and to the system and aims of the Treaty".[4] The lofty language should not obscure the fact that this means what the then members of the Court thought were the aims of the Treaty, etc., not what the parties to it intended to agree to. This is reminiscent of the "doctrine of public policy", as to which an English judge commented "I, for one, protest . . . against arguing too strongly upon public policy:- it is a very unruly horse, and when once you get astride it you never know where it will carry you. It may lead you from the sound law."[5] The "spirit, structure and working" of individual Articles and the "system and aims" of the Treaty are likely also to be unruly horses. The objection to interpretation by reference to unspecified "aims"

[4] [1973] C.M.L.R. p.223.
[5] Burrough J. in *Richardson v. Mellish* (1824) 2 Bing. 229. at p.252.

and "spirit" is that it gives too much freedom to the whim and fancy of the individual judge or judges concerned. At one time in England the branch of law known as Equity represented the powers of the Lord Chancellor, which he exercised according to his conscience – a situation which prompted a seventeenth-century commentator to suggest that adoption of the individual Chancellor's conscience as the criterion of Equity was just as sensible as taking the length of the individual Chancellor's foot as the standard measure of length.[6] Where the law can vary according to the opinion of the judges at the time, rather than being based upon a sound and strict interpretation of the texts, legal certainty disappears, and the role of the adviser becomes hazardous.

In the case of mergers and intellectual-property rights it would have been sufficient for the Court to have pointed to the fact that the Treaty does not provide any system of control for the former nor any means of reconciling, in the case of the latter, the conflict between the establishment of a common market and the retention of national intellectual-property rights. The Treaty provides in Articles 235 and 236 for action by the Members, through the Council in Article 235, to remedy any *lacunae.* In fact, despite the Court's efforts, this is what has become necessary in both instances. A draft mergers regulation has been put forward (*v.* paragraphs 15-24 *et seq.*). There are also the Draft Convention for a Community Patent (paragraph 8-11B) and the Draft Convention for a European Trade Mark (paragraph 8-52A).

It is to be hoped that the Court does not see itself with the same role and status as the American Supreme Court. The Supreme Court has had a life approaching 200 years to reach its present position, in a country which fought a Civil War to confirm and cement its unity. Consequently, the Federal Constitution of the United States is recognised as being something which the individual States have set up *above* them. That is not the case with the European Communities, to which the individual Members have *delegated* areas of activity, to be regulated by provisions agreed by the Members. While it is to be hoped that the European Community will be the means by which a politically united Europe will emerge, the Community is a very long way from that goal – the difference may be seen, for example, in the single currency and budgetary policy in the

[6] *Table Talk of John Selden* (ed. Pollock) Selden Society 1927. p.43.

United States as compared with the multiplicity of currencies and budgets in the Community.

2–05N It will be noted that the Court's function under Article 177 is to give "preliminary rulings". This prompts the question – who gives the final ruling? The final ruling may well be with the national courts. For example, the European Court may conceivably interpret the Treaty in such a way that there is an infringement of the basic national law of a Member – in which event, presumably, the national courts of that Member may refuse to enforce the Court's ruling. Say, for example, the Court ruled that the Treaty is irrevocable. Against that would be the United Kingdom doctrine that one Parliament cannot bind its successors. Thus, any subsequent Parliament of the United Kingdom is, by national law, free to take that country out of the Community. In the event of such a conflict, presumably national law would be effective.

Procedure

2–05O In the *Sirena* case, the Advocate General suggested that other intellectual-property rights are "often more important and worthy of greater protection" than trade-mark rights, a value judgment which the Court adopted (*v.* paragraph 8-94). In the *Centrafarm* case, the Advocate General excluded from the "specific object" of patent rights the ability to keep out of one country goods put on the market in another country by or with the consent of the patent owner, a view again adopted by the Court. To say the least, both propositions are open to grave doubt. The parties have no opportunity to comment before the Court upon the Advocate General's submissions. In so far as the Advocate General's submissions take the place of a hearing in a lower court, there is a defect in the procedure – on an appeal from a lower court, the parties are able to present to the appeal court their comments on the lower court's judgment. Consideration might be given to altering the procedure before the European Court to permit the parties an opportunity to comment on the Advocate General's submissions before the Court reaches its conclusions.

5. Competition Rules

2–07 Questions may arise as to the geographical area to which the competition rules apply. This is determined by Article 227, as amended by Article 26 of the Act annexed to the Treaty of

Accession (17-21). It is perhaps doubtful if Algeria is now within the purview of the Treaty.

Association and other agreements have now been negotiated between the Community and other states. Although the particular agreement may make provision for control over private restraints upon competition, that does not make the country concerned a part of the Common Market for the purposes of Articles 85 and 86.

CHAPTER 3
Cartels and Concerted Practices – Article 85

2. Article 85 Paragraph 1

Agreements, decisions by associations and concerted practices

"Agreements"

3–05A In the *Papiers Peints de Belgique* case, the parties had approved circulars setting out standard conditions of sale which the parties were to adopt. The Commission held that, while the approval of the circulars by the parties was a decision of an association of undertakings, there would be an agreement between undertakings whenever a customer of one of the parties accepted the standard conditions of sale as governing that customer's purchase. In so far as the standard conditions included resale price maintenance, i.e. in so far as the customer was under a restriction as to the prices he would charge, the agreement between the party and the customer incorporating the standard conditions would itself infringe Article 85.1. This follows the line adopted by the Commission in the *Kodak* case (*v.* paragraph 6-22). The parties have appealed against the Commission's decision in the *Papiers Peints* case.

In *WEA-Filipacchi*, the Commission held that an acknowledgment of receipt of a circular letter by signing and returning a copy would constitute an agreement between undertakings (*v.* paragraph 8-58A below).

An agreement within Article 85.1 need not, in the Commission's view, have all the characteristics of a civil law contract. In the *Franco-Japanese Ballbearings Agreement,* there was an exchange of letters between the French and Japanese trade bodies, as a result of which the Japanese undertook to raise their prices. This the Commission regarded as an agreement (*v.* 14-091 *et seq.*).

"Decisions by associations"

3–06 Instances of "decisions by associations" include *GISA*, in which the association constitution provided that any decision of a general meeting containing a provision that it must be observed by each member would be binding on all members. The decisions taken provided a comprehensive system of price fixing, including discounts and conditions of sale. In the *Papiers Peints* case, approval by the members of the circulars containing the standard conditions of sale constituted a "decision by an association".

"Concerted practices"

3–09 Other cases in which concerted practices were held to have operated were *Pittsburgh Corning* (*v.* 6-07 and 6-65A below) and *Marketing of Potassium Salts* (6-07 below).

3–09A The Commission concluded that a number of concerted practices had been operated in the *European Sugar Cartel* case.

One practice related to the supply of sugar to the Italian market. The French, Belgian, and German suppliers involved would sell only to certain Italian producers. Deliveries to other Italian buyers were made only at higher prices – the excess price to cover a margin for distribution and also a protection to the Italian producers. The Commission commented that "Normally, a producer is not interested in selling products in large quantities to one or more of his competitors."[1] (That may be so, but a manufacturer may supply his competitor in the event of a break-down of the competitor's plant, for two reasons – he may need help himself some day, and if the competitor can get such assistance it reduces the likelihood of the competitor installing additional capacity.)

In the Dutch market, the Belgian Raffinerie Tirlemontoise and the German Pfeifer & Langen sold large quantities of sugar to the two Dutch producers. Moreover, Tirlemontoise only sold direct to other Dutch buyers with the consent of the Dutch producers. The Commission regarded this as a concerted practice between the Belgian, German, and Dutch producers.

As regards the western part of Federal Germany, the

[1] [1973] C.M.L.R. p.D92.

Commission found that Tirlemontoise, having largely kept out of the market in 1968-69, increased its supplies in the following years but sold mainly to Pfeifer & Langen – sales to other customers were subject to Pfeifer & Langen's consent or made at prices corresponding to the latter's prices. Internal memoranda recorded the necessity to obtain Pfeifer & Langen's consent in one instance; in another, the price selected was that notified by Pfeifer & Langen to Tirlemontoise. The internal papers also revealed repeated references to a principle of "*chacun chez soi*". The Commission commented "All these measures would be incomprehensible if they were not based on a concerted action between the main sugar producers in the countries concerned."[2]

Similarly, the Commission regarded the increasing sales by two French sugar producers to two south German competitors as being a concerted practice. Numerous requests by other customers in south Germany were mostly made in vain.

During 1970 and 1971, a period of sugar surplus, the Community awarded subsidies for exports to meet the lower world prices. The subsidies were awarded as a result of tenders. The Commission concluded that certain French producers and Tirlemontoise had concerted their tenders.

In each case, the Commission regarded the practice as restricting competition.

3–12 The final text of the European Court's judgment on the appeal by the firms concerned in the *Aniline Dyes Cartel* case is now available. One of the grounds of appeal was that the Commission had failed to prove the existence of a concerted practice between the firms. The Court began its discussion of that ground with some general remarks "on the concept of concerted practice":

> "If **Article 85** distinguishes the concept of 'concerted practice' from that of 'agreements between enterprises' or 'decisions of associations of enterprises', this is done with the object of bringing under the prohibitions of this **Article** a form of co-ordination between undertakings which, without going so far as to amount to an agreement properly so called, knowingly substitutes a practical co-operation between them for the risks of competition.
>
> By its very nature, then, the concerted practice does not combine all the elements of an agreement, but may, *inter alia*,

[2] *Ibid.* p.D97.

result from a co-ordination which becomes apparent from the behaviour of the participants.

Although a parallelism of behaviour cannot by itself be identified with a concerted practice, it is nevertheless liable to constitute a strong indication of such a practice when it leads to conditions of competition which do not correspond to the normal conditions of the market, having regard to the nature of the products, the importance and number of the undertakings and the volume of the said market. Such is the case especially where the parallel behaviour is such as to permit the parties to seek price equilibrium at a different level from that which would have resulted from competition, and to crystallise the status quo to the detriment of effective freedom of movement of the products in the Common Market and free choice by consumers of their suppliers.

The question whether there was a concerting in the present case, therefore, can only be appraised correctly if the indications relied on by the challenged Decision are considered not in isolation but as a whole, having regard to the characteristics of the market in the products in question."[3]

The Court then turned to consider first the particular characteristics of the dye-stuffs market, and then the significant features of the three price rises in question. As to the dye-stuffs market, the Court noted that 80% of it was in the hands of 10 manufacturers, with different cost structures; substitutability between standard dye-stuffs was good, between non-standard items it was poor or non-existent; the cost of the dye-stuff was negligible in relation to the cost of the finished article, giving low elasticity of demand. The E.E.C. market for dye-stuffs was then (i.e. 1964-67) made up of five separate national markets (counting Belgium and Luxembourg as one), each with different price levels, the major supplier in each tending to be the price leader; in short, the overall market was compartmentalised, with fragmentation of competition. As to the three price rises in question, they indicated a progressive co-operation between the firms; in the second and third rises, the firms initiating them had announced the increases well in advance (two months ahead in the case of the 1967 increase), so making the extent of the rises transparent and eliminating competition; with 10 large firms the

[3] [1972] C.M.L.R. pp.622-3.

E.E.C. market for dye-stuffs was not oligopolistic, and the compartmentalisation of the five national markets made spontaneous, equal, price rises improbable on all national markets; it was, therefore, difficult to conceive spontaneous attainment of such parallelism as regards the timing of the rise, the national markets involved, and the particular products concerned. For example, as regards the 1964 increase, it was not plausible that increases in such separate markets as the Italian, the Dutch, and the Belgo-Luxembourg markets would be achieved spontaneously in 2-3 days. As to the 1965 and 1967 increases, by advance announcement of their intentions and the range of products involved, the firms had eliminated the risks of uncertainty. The general and uniform increases in the various markets was explicable only by "the convergent intention of these enterprises":

> "In these circumstances, having regard to the characteristics of the market in these products, the behaviour of the applicant, in conjunction with other undertakings against whom proceedings have been taken, was designed to substitute for the risks of competition, and the hazards of their spontaneous reactions, a co-operation which amounts to a concerted practice prohibited by Article 85(1) of the Treaty."[4]

The Court did, however, comment:

> "While it is permissible for each manufacturer to change his prices freely and to take into account for this purpose the behaviour, present and foreseeable, of his competitors, it is, on the other hand contrary to the competition rules of the Treaty for a manufacturer to co-operate with his competitors, in whatever manner, to determine a co-ordinated course of action relating to an increase in prices, and to ensure its success by the prior elimination of all uncertainty as to mutual behaviour relating to the essential elements of this action, such as rates, subject matter, date and place of the increases."[5]

—12A It would seem, therefore, that "conscious parallelism" on the one hand and "concerted practice" on the other are two distinct concepts. Where there is "parallelism of behaviour", that parallelism may result either from conscious parallelism or from

[4] *Ibid.* pp.627-8.
[5] *Ibid.* p.627.

concerted practice (or from an agreement or a decision by an association of firms). But, where the "parallelism of behaviour" leads to conditions which depart from what would be the normal conditions of the market, then that parallelism itself is evidence, a "strong indication", of a concerted practice. In the context of the *Aniline Dyes* case, the evidential nature of the parallelism of behaviour – evidence of a concerted practice – may have been reasonably clear, but in some circumstances the conclusions to be drawn may not be so clear. If firm A for the first time in the industry makes an advance announcement of a price rise one month ahead, and the other two firms, B and C follow, and then B, recognising the advantage of the practice, gives advance notice of another rise, adopted by the other two; and C then makes a price rise, at one month's notice, followed by the others; in those circumstances has there been only conscious parallelism, or have their actions amounted to a concerted practice? They have eliminated competition, the price level arrived at may not coincide with what competition would have given, they have avoided "the risks of competition" – but have they gone as far as "concerting" their actions? It is almost inevitable that conscious parallelism will lead to conditions which do not conform to the normal conditions of competition – if it did lead only to normal conditions, why adopt conscious parallelism (unless such parallelism is the competitive norm)? A clear answer on the point must await a ruling by the Court, but it would seem reasonable to assume that, without anything further, such conduct would be "conscious parallelism" and outside Article 85.1, not a "concerted practice" and therefore within 85.1. The important words are *"without anything further"*. Proof of parallelism of behaviour may present a difficult situation for the firms concerned. Do they then have to rebut any suggestion of concerted practice, and prove that they have not concerted their actions? That would mean proving the negative. Where the firms never meet, or have any inter-communication between themselves, proof of that may suffice. But where they belong to joint associations, even for such innocent, and proper, joint activities such as discussion of hygiene matters, or commenting on such things as draft Commission directives on labelling, etc., they may be in a difficult position. It could be that it is unwise for firms who adopt conscious parallelism to belong to trade "clubs" or associations. It would be wrong if the Commission, merely by proving the existence of parallelism of behaviour, could thereby shift the onus of proof onto the firms in question – it is for the Commission to prove the existence of concerted practice (or agreement, or decision), not for the firms to prove its absence. But firms would be well advised to be alert to the possible danger of parallelism of behaviour coupled with frequent meetings giving the opportunity for concerting of activities and practices – they may well find that they are charged with having gone beyond the opportunity and be charged with actually concerting their activities when indeed they have done no such thing.

"Undertaking"

"Enterprise entity"

3–18 The final text of the Court's judgment on the appeal by I.C.I. confirms the enterprise entity doctrine:

> "[132] The fact that the subsidiary has a distinct legal personality does not suffice to dispose of the possibility that its behaviour might be imputed to the parent company. [133] Such may be the case in particular when the subsidiary, although having a distinct legal personality, does not determine its behaviour on the market in an autonomous manner but essentially carries out the instructions given to it by the parent company. [134] When the subsidiary does not enjoy any real autonomy in the determination of its course of action on the market, the prohibitions imposed by **Article 85 (1)** may be considered inapplicable in the relations between the subsidiary and the parent company, with which it then forms one economic unit. [135] In view of the unity of the group thus formed, the activities of the subsidiaries may, in certain circumstances, be imputed to the parent company.
>
> [136] It is well known that the applicant held at the time the whole, or at any rate the majority, of the capital of these subsidiaries. [137] The applicant was able to influence, in a decisive manner, the sale price policy of its subsidiaries in the Common Market, and it in fact made use of this power on the occasion of the three price increases under discussion. [138] The telex messages relating to the 1964 increase, which the applicant had addressed to its subsidiaries in the Common Market, determined, in a manner binding on their addressees, the prices and other conditions of sale which they must impose in relation to their customers. [139] In the absence of

contrary indications, it must be assumed that on the occasion of the 1965 and 1967 increases the applicant did not act otherwise in its relations with its subsidiaries established in the Common Market.

[140] In these circumstances, the formal separation between these companies, arising from their distinct legal personality, cannot, for the purposes of application of the competition rules, prevail against the unity of their behaviour on the market. [141] Thus, it is indeed the applicant which carried out the concerted practice within the Common Market."[6]

Where the parent holds the majority of the shares in the subsidiary and determines the conduct of the subsidiary, they are regarded as "one economic unit" and the activities of the subsidiary may be imputed to the parent. (The Court's comment in the sentence numbered [139] is, to say the least, surprising — in what are, after all, quasi-criminal proceedings with the possibility of substantial fines, a high standard of proof should be essential; it should not be possible to shift the onus of proof so easily — how does one prove the negative?)

3—19 The European Court confirmed the application of the doctrine in its judgment on the appeal by Continental Can (*v.* paragraph 5-04 below), and also applied it in the appeal by Commercial Solvents (paragraph 5-04A below).

3—19A The doctrine has also been upheld by the European Court in *Centrafarm.* The *Centrafarm* case concerned parallel patents, i.e. patents in Holland and the United Kingdom held by the same concern, Sterling Drug Inc. Its subsidiary in the United Kingdom manufactured and sold in that country the drug protected by the patent, under licence from Sterling Drug. The United Kingdom subsidiary also supplied the Dutch sub-subsidiary which re-sold in Holland under licence. Centrafarm bought supplies on the market in the United Kingdom and re-sold them in Holland. The issue in the case was whether Sterling Drug could rely upon the Dutch patent to keep out the parallel imports (and also whether the Dutch sub-subsidiary could rely upon the trade-mark registration in Holland for the same purpose). One of the questions submitted to the European Court was whether Article 85 was applicable if any agreements or concerted practices involved were between undertakings in the same group. The Court ruled:

[6] *Ibid.* p.629.

"**Article 85** of the Treaty does not apply to agreements or concerted practices between undertakings belonging to the same group in the form of parent company and subsidiary, if the undertakings form an economic unit within which the subsidiary does not have real autonomy in determining its line of conduct on the market and if the agreements or practices have the aim of establishing an internal distribution of tasks between the undertakings."[7]

"Affect trade between Member States"

–20 The *Vereeniging van Cementhandelaren* case is relevant. The association (V.C.H.) comprised cement wholesalers. They had a system of fixed prices and conditions of sale for deliveries up to 100 tonnes. For deliveries of 100 tonnes and above, the prices were recommended, but the members were under an obligation to make a provable profit. There were restrictions on sales to non-authorised dealers. The share of the Dutch market held by V.C.H. members was about 67.5% in 1969 (against 85% in 1966-67). The Commission condemned the pricing and other arrangements.

V.C.H. appealed to the European Court on the ground that a purely national agreement, limited to Dutch territory, which did not apply to imports or exports, could not affect inter-Member trade – there were substantial imports of cement into Holland and many suppliers not in membership of the association, and therefore no risk of inter-Member trade being influenced. The Court rejected the argument. An agreement which extends to the whole of a Member State has, by its very nature, the effect of partitioning off the national market, so hindering the economic inter-penetration at which the Rome Treaty aims. In the particular case of V.C.H., the restrictive obligations on its members, such as the prohibition on sales to non-authorised dealers, made the penetration of the Dutch market by firms in other Members more difficult. (One would have thought that it would have had the opposite effect – as non-authorised dealers could not buy from the members, such dealers would have a greater incentive to seek supplies elsewhere, from suppliers in other Member States!)

–20A The following cases illustrate the types of impact upon inter-Member trade which the Commission has held to exist.

[7] [1974] 2. C.M.L.R. pp.507-8.

In *GISA*, the members had to reserve a minimum percentage of their purchases for the Dutch manufacturers, clearly affecting inter-Member trade. The price-fixing obligations applied both to home-produced and imported goods, including those imported from other Members. The Commission argued "Therefore, although these obligations only bind undertakings established in Holland, their effects also relate to trade between the member States".[8] Finally, as the obligations extended to the whole of Holland and applied to 75% of the sales in that country of the products in question, they provided protection for the Dutch manufacturers and made the economic inter-penetration aimed at by the Treaty more difficult.

In *Cementregeling voor Nederland,* Dutch, Belgian, and German cement manufacturers had established a system of delivery quotas in Holland. The Commission held that the system affected the free export of Belgian and German material to Holland.

One of the parties to the Cementregeling was Cimbel, the Belgian cement cartel. In the *Cimbel* case, the Commission held that there were a variety of effects on inter-Member trade. The quota agreement covered all the Common Market countries and therefore affected inter-Member trade. The prices fixed for the Belgian market discriminated against importers in, for example, West Germany and France who had to pay a higher price than Belgian wholesalers. The equalisation of receipts for sales covered sales in all the Member States, in effect subsidising exports; moreover, the export receipts were calculated on a single free-at-frontier price, thus eliminating any effect due to geographical situation. The obligation to notify increases in capacity and the restriction on transfer of production capacity (the transferee had to accept the cartel arrangements) helped to maintain the quota agreement, and therefore affected inter-Member trade. They also put obstacles in the way of acquisition of plants by non-Belgian concerns. Finally, the special discount given to public undertakings in Belgium prejudiced manufacturers in other Members.

In the Belgian *Gas Water-Heaters* case, the parties to the arrangement included three Belgian manufacturers and two importers. The agreement allowed sales to be made only to certain categories of buyers, and also provided for aggregate

[8] [1973] C.M.L.R. p.D133.

rebates. This meant that the importers were restricted as to their outlets. Moreover, as their sales represented 18.5% and 1.5% of the total Belgian sales, the aggregated rebates involved them in allowing substantial additional discounts. Although it did not say so specifically, it would seem that the Commission regarded the aggregate rebate as impeding penetration of the Belgian market by suppliers in other Members.

In *Nederlandse Cement,* certain German cement manufacturers had a joint sales company in Holland. They could not make direct deliveries into that country or Belgium or Luxembourg. They had a system of quotas, and their sales through the joint company were made on uniform prices and conditions. These arrangements jeopardised, in the Commission's view, freedom of trade between Germany and those three countries.

There was an aggregate-rebate scheme in *Papiers Peints de Belgique,* which applied to imported wallpaper sold by the members. The Commission regarded this as hindering imports into Belgium, although it did not spell out how. The Commission also regarded the members' general arrangements (which included such things as price fixing and resale price maintenance, standard conditions of sale, discounts, etc.) as affecting inter-Member trade as they also applied to imported wallpaper sold by the members. The Commission cited the Court's decision in *Vereeniging van Cementhandelaren* to justify the proposition that, as the arrangements extended to the whole of Belgium, they reinforced the compartmentalisation of markets at the national level, and therefore prevented the inter-penetration of markets. It may be significant that the Commission did not explain how the members' refusal to supply two Belgian dealers affected inter-Member trade. The members have appealed to the European Court against the Commission's decision.

"Appreciable effect"

3–23 In the fifth line, "Grasfillex" should read "Grosfillex".

Restraint upon competition

3–29 In *WEA-Filipacchi,* the company argued that its circular letter to its distributors, which had been accepted by some by signing and returning a copy, represented only an *attempt* to infringe Article 85.1. The Commission rejected the argument, holding that:

"The violation is already complete when an agreement has the object of restricting competition, even if it has not yet had that effect."[9]

This view seems clearly to be within the wording of 85.1.

3–30A The following cases illustrate some of the practices which have been held, by the Commission or the Court, to restrict competition.

(a) *Price fixing* Price fixing has been a feature in a variety of cases, such as *GISA* and *Papiers Peints.*

In *Papiers Peints* there was also fixing of resale prices — the standard conditions of sale imposed upon members at one time required their customers to adhere to the fixed resale prices.

In *Nederlandse Cement,* the parties had agreed to the adoption of uniform prices by their joint sales company.

(b) *Recommended prices* The Court specifically ruled in *Vereeniging van Cementhandelaren* that recommended prices were within the prohibition in Article 85.1. Recommended prices enabled the parties to foresee with reasonable certainty what their competitors would charge. The Commission followed the same reasoning in *Papiers Peints* — even if prices are not imposed as fixed prices but given only as a guide, they give competitors foreknowledge of their rivals' prices.

(c) *Delivered prices* One of the restrictions in the *European Glass Manufacturers* case was that the parties would charge only delivered prices.

(d) *Discounts and rebates* There was a comprehensive system of agreed discounts in *Gas Water-Heaters,* and also in *Papiers Peints.* In *Cimbel,* there were special discounts for public enterprises.

Where there are agreed discounts, there will frequently be found agreed classification of buyers, as, for example, in *Gas Water-Heaters* and *Papiers Peints.*

Aggregated rebates were condemned in *Gas Water-Heaters, Papiers Peints,* and *German Flat Glass.* The last-mentioned case concerned an agreement between the German subsidiaries of the two largest glass firms, St. Gobain/Pont-à-Mousson and Boussois-Souchon-Neuvesel. The agreement provided for their rebates to be aggregated. In the Commission's view this attracted orders to them and so helped to strengthen their position in the industry. The agreement was terminated at the Commission's instigation.

Loyalty discounts were condemned in *European Sugar Cartel.*

[9] [1973] C.M.L.R. p.D46.

(e) *Price equalisation* There was equalisation of prices in *Cimbel*, condemned by the Commission.
(f) *Standard conditions of sale* Standard or uniform conditions have been condemned in a number of cases, including *GISA*, *Papiers Peints*, *Gas Water-Heaters*, *Cimbel*, etc.
(g) *Quotas* Quota systems featured, and were condemned, in *Cimbel*, *GISA*, *Nederlandse Cement*, and *Cementregeling voor Nederland*. The programming of deliveries in *Preserved Mushrooms* was a form of market sharing through quotas, and was condemned.
(h) *Refusal to supply* The Commission condemned the refusal by the parties to supply two concerns, in *Papiers Peints*. In *European Sugar Cartel*, the practices included selling only to competitors and selling to third parties only with the consent of the competitor established in that market. Obligation to supply only certain categories of buyers implies refusal to sell to other buyers (*Gas Water-Heaters*).
(i) *Restrictions on transfers* In *Cimbel*, the parties were obligated not to transfer production capacity except to transferees who accepted the agreement provisions.
(j) *New capacity* In *Cimbel*, the parties were obliged to notify increases in capacity, and could not erect new cement works without approval.
(k) *Price notification* Obligations to publish or notify prices were condemned in *European Glass Manufacturers* and *Dutch Sporting Cartridges*.
(l) *Common sales agents* The use of common sales agents was condemned in *Marketing of Potassium Salts* and *Nederlandse Cement*.
(m) *Prohibition on selling outside the Common Market* The agreement in *Goodyear Italiana* precluded the distributor, Euram, from selling outside the E.E.C. The Commission regarded this as distorting competition within the Market because outside firms could not buy from Euram for re-sale within the Market. But that effect on competition was not likely to be appreciable, because such purchase and re-sale would not have been great because of the accumulation of profit margins, etc.

3–31A Even though firms are not actually competing, they may be potential competitors, so that an agreement between them containing restrictions may be regarded as restricting competition. That was the view taken by the Commission in *Rank/Sopelem*. Both parties made lenses and lens controls for cameras. Rank had specialised mainly on large lenses, and Sopelem in small and medium-sized lenses. But each, because of its experience and research facilities, was capable of extending its production to cover the whole range. The Commission consequently regarded them as potential competitors, and held their agreement, which provided for co-operation between them, to be within Article 85.1 – but exemption was granted under Article 85.3.

3–32 The supply of information as to prices was specifically condemned in the *European Glass Manufacturers* case.

Appreciable effect

3–37 In *WEA-Filipacchi,* the Commission ruled that the May 1970 Notice did not apply because the turnover of the group to which the company belonged was well in excess of 15 million units of account.

In *Advocaat Zwarte Kip,* the parties were held by the Commission to have connections with large groups. Moreover, although the actual imports from Holland into Belgium were small, the Commission argued that the obstacles to inter-Member trade which trade-mark rights could create were considerable, in that exercise of those rights might prevent large quantities of goods being imported. The *potential* restriction of competition was therefore considerable.

Particular types of agreement, etc., prohibited by Article 85.1.

3–39 In the *Vereeniging van Cementhandelaren* (V.C.H.) case, the association had recommended prices for transactions involving over 100 tonnes (of cement). The association appealed to the Court against the Commission's decision that the recommended prices were contrary to Article 85.1. The Court pointed to paragraph (a) of 85.1, and ruled that the recommended price system was just as contrary to 85.1 as a system of fixed prices. Recommended prices were not entirely devoid of effect in that they permitted parties to foresee with reasonable accuracy what their competitors' prices were likely to be, especially as the V.C.H. arrangements included provisions such as an obligation to make a profit.

Recommended prices were condemned by the Commission in *Papiers Peints.*

Standard conditions of sale have been condemned in a number of cases (cf. paragraph 3-30A).

–40 In EUMAPRINT, only concerns established or having an agent in the country in question could take part in a national exhibition, according to Eumaprint's regulations. Consequently, invitations already sent to certain firms located outside Italy, to take part in GRAFITALIA '73, were withdrawn. On the Commission's intervention the rules were changed.

An interesting case is the *Belgian Central Heating Agreement.* On the termination in 1962 of an exclusive-dealing agreement between manufacturers, wholesalers, and installers, a new agreement was entered into between the manufacturers and the installers. A "homologation" committee was to issue certificates of approval for equipment. One of the conditions of approval was an obligation to sell only to registered installers. In return, the installers' association undertook that its members would give preference to the equipment of manufacturers who have accepted the conditions of approval. The agreement was condemned by the Commission.

The various systems for controlling deliveries adopted in the *European Sugar Cartel* exemplify methods of market control. They included deliveries to competitors, and making deliveries to third parties dependent upon the consent of the competitor in whose area the third party was located.

–41 Quotas have featured in a number of agreements (*v.* paragraph 3-30A).

–44 Price equalisation was a feature, and also condemned, in *Cimbel.*

In the *Rank/Sopelem* case, the parties had originally adopted a provision under which sales by one in the other's territory would have involved a lump sum payment. This was removed at the Commission's instigation.

3. Article 85 Paragraph 2

–45 One of the issues in *Brasserie de Haecht (No. 2)* was the date from which nullity in pursuance of Article 85.2 took effect. The agreement in that case was one which was not subject to compulsory notification – the Brasserie de Haecht sent in a voluntary notification. In such circumstances, the European Court was asked, did nullity operate from the date it was first alleged, or from the date of an adverse decision? The Court's ruling was that "The nullity provided for in Article 85.2 has retroactive effect."[10] In other words, once Article 85.1 has been

[10] [1973] C.M.L.R. p.304.

held to apply to a term in an agreement or decision (and in the absence of any exemption under 85.3 or action by the Commission under Article 7 of Regulation 17) that term must be deemed to have been void *ab initio,* or from the date Regulation 17 came into effect (13th March, 1962), whichever is the later – in the case of agreements to which Article 85 applies "by virtue of accession", the accession date (1st January, 1973) is substituted for 13th March, 1962 (18-26).

Private suit

3–56 In *SABAM v. Fonior,* the issue related to the validity of agreements assigning copyright, in particular whether the agreements conferring upon SABAM the right in the words and music in a song were vitiated by alleged abuse by SABAM of its dominant position in Belgium. The European Court ruled that national courts were competent to decide such an issue of validity (even though the Commission had initiated but not completed an investigation into SABAM's activities). In a sense, this illustrates the use of Article 86 – and by analogy, Article 85 – as a sword, as a weapon to invalidate the other party's title. But the use of either Article to found an action for damages based solely on breach of the Article has not yet been seen.

3–57 In *Application des Gaz v. Falks,* the defendant was sued for breach of copyright. After the United Kingdom had joined the Common Market on 1st January, 1973, the defendant sought to amend his defence so as to claim that the plaintiff's case was vitiated by breach of both Article 85 and Article 86. In interlocutory proceedings, the English court of first instance and Court of Appeal allowed the amendment. In his judgment, Lord Denning, Master of the Rolls, referred to the European Court's decision in *SABAM v. Fonior.* He continued:

> "Put into English, that judgment of the European Court shows that **Articles 85** and **86** create rights in private citizens which they can enforce in the national courts and which the national courts are bound to uphold. Furthermore, on 27 March 1974 the European Court held that it is for the national courts to assess the facts so as to see whether they amount to an infringement.
>
> So we reach this important conclusion: **Articles 85** and **86** are part of our law. They create new torts or wrongs. Their names are 'undue restriction of competition within the

Common Market', and 'abuse of dominant position within the Common Market' ".[11]

The other two judges in the Court of Appeal did not venture so far.

It will be seen that Lord Denning's comments go further than the view of the group of jurists mentioned in paragraph 3-56. They took the view that entitlement to damages for breach of Article 85 (and Article 86) depended upon national law. Lord Denning's remark suggests that entitlement is conferred by Community law, i.e. that infringement is a tort actionable in English law. It would seem that, so far as his remarks go further than the admissability of infringement of Articles' 85 and 86 as a defence, they may have to be regarded as *obiter dictum.* Pending further clarification, they should be regarded with reserve.

4. Article 85 Paragraph 3

Improving the production or distribution of goods or promoting technical or economic progress

Improving the production of goods

3–61 The agreement in *Prym/Beka* was held by the Commission to have improved production. Costs of the "Standard" quality had been reduced by 20%.

Fair share for consumers

3–74 The Commission argued that consumers would share in the benefits from the *Prym/Beka* agreement because the pressure of competition in the needle market would ensure that the benefits of rationalisation were passed on to them.

No elimination of competition

3–78A In *Kali und Salz/Kali Chemie,* the two companies were the only German producers of potash. Kali Chemie specialised in the production of a compound potash fertiliser. The agreement between the two companies, made in 1970, allowed Kali Chemie to supply its surpluses of straight (untreated) potash to Kali und Salz for the latter to distribute. The companies notified the agreement, but the Commission refused to grant exemption, on the ground that the agreement gave the parties the possibility of

[11] [1974] 2. C.M.L.R. p.84.

eliminating competition in respect of straight potash fertiliser. The companies appealed to the European Court. The Court held that the agreement did not enable the parties to eliminate competition as regards a substantial part of the market. The Commission's decision showed that there was competition between compound potash and untreated potash. There were price and other differences between them. Although there had been a considerable increase in the use of compound potash fertiliser this had not eliminated untreated potash from the market – some buyers bought the untreated product at some periods and the compound product at others. The Commission's decision was annulled.

Block exemptions

3–85 The block exemption in respect of specialisation agreements has now been made – Regulation 2779/72. The Regulation is reproduced at Appendix K, and discussed in Chapter 12 (12-05A *et seq.* below).

3–87 The block exemption in respect of intellectual-property agreements is still awaited.

5. Conflict of laws

3–93 The different views held by the Commission and the United Kingdom government might have caused difficulty after the United Kingdom entry into the Common Market on 1st January, 1973. Prior to that date, under United Kingdom law, firms in the United Kingdom which were party to restrictive agreements having effects within the Common Market were not acting unlawfully so long as the agreement and any relevant actions took place in the United Kingdom. If, after 1st January, 1973, such firms notified their agreements to the Commission, they might have been exposed to fines.

That point was raised at a Conference in London on 5th October, 1972, when Dr. Schlieder gave such firms some re-assurance:

> "Even if we find out that illegal agreements exist in the new member states, it is unlikely that we shall come up with any fines; initially we intend to be strict only with those companies who know they are violating the provisions of the Treaty of Rome."[12]

[12] *The Times*. November 10th, 1972.

3–95 In its decision in the *Continental Can* case, the Court has gone some way towards confirming that the "effects" principle is part of Community law. When dealing with Continental Can's plea that the Commission had no jurisdiction over it, the Court relied upon the doctrine of enterprise entity to connect Continental Can and Europemballage (*v.* paragraph 5-04 below). It then went on:

> "Community law is applicable to such an acquisition which affects the market conditions within the Community."[13]

Prima facie, these words import the effects principle. But the purchase of the shares in Thomassen would probably have been equally subject to Community law on the "territorial" principle, in that the purchase of the shares would presumably have taken place in Holland. It may, therefore, be that the effects principle has not yet been finally confirmed as part of Community law, especially as the Commission's decision was annulled, on other grounds.

The Court's judgment in *Continental Can* was dated 21st February, 1973. It may be significant that the Court's judgment in *Zoja*, given over a year later on 6th March, 1974, followed its decision on the appeals in the *Aniline Dyes* case – Commercial Solvents was implicated because it and Istituto Chemioterapico were to be treated as one economic unit.

[13] [1973] C.M.L.R. p.222.

CHAPTER 4

Cartels and Concerted Practices (contd) – Regulation 17

2. Termination of Infringements

4—07 The roles of the Commission and of the national authorities have been clarified in two Court judgments.

In *Brasserie de Haecht (No. 2),* the agreement had been notified and the Commission had sent an acknowledgment. In proceedings brought in the Belgian court to enforce the agreement, it was argued that notification brought provisional validity, and that Article 9 of Regulation 17 conferred exclusive competence on the Commission in the sense that the national court had no jurisdiction, as the Commission had initiated a procedure. The Court ruled that a mere acknowledgment of notification did not constitute an initiation of a procedure by the Commission. Initiation requires an official act (*acte d'autorité*), whereas acknowledgment was a mere administrative formality. (In practice, the Commission usually writes to the parties concerned saying that it is initiating a procedure, and asking formally for information.)

As to the jurisdiction of national courts, the Court distinguished between "existing" (or, as it called them, "old") agreements notified in due time and "new agreements" (*v.* paragraphs 4-31 *et seq.*). As to duly notified existing agreements, only the Commission has competence to grant exemption under Article 85.3. Consequently, the Court argued, a national court cannot rule upon such an agreement until the Commission has taken a decision. But as regards new agreements, until the Commission has decided, they can be operated only at the risk of the parties. Even though a Commission decision may take some time, that does not relieve the national court of its duty to give a ruling if the validity of the agreement under Article 85 is in question. The court may, if it wishes, adjourn the proceedings pending the Commission's decision; but the court may hold that, for example because of absence of appreciable effect upon competition or inter-Member trade, the agreement is outside Article 85.1. (From the Court's use of the word "notified" and also on the basis of its reasoning, it would seem that its view that the national court should not rule upon existing agreements duly notified applies only where *exemption* has been sought, i.e. the view does not apply where only an application for negative clearance has been made.)

–07A The issue also arose in *SABAM v. Fonior.* Litigation had been instituted in the Belgian courts to determine a question as to copyright rights. It was alleged that SABAM's title was defective, because of infringement of Article 86. The Commission had already initiated an investigation into SABAM's activities. SABAM argued that the proceedings in the Belgian courts should be stayed, under Article 9.3 of Regulation 17, pending the Commission's decision.

The Court decided that Articles 85.1 and 86 confer direct rights on individuals which the national courts must safeguard. The reference to "authorities of the Member States" in Article 9.3 of Regulation 17 referred to the authorities deriving competence from Article 88 of the Treaty – in other words, what might be called the 'competition-law enforcement' authorities (the Court does not spell this out clearly, but that seems to be the drift of the judgment). In some countries those authorities may include courts (perhaps the Court had in mind the Restrictive Practices Court in the United Kingdom). But that did not mean that, what might be called, the ordinary civil courts dealing with civil actions between subjects were debarred by Article 9.3 from giving judgment. Such a court could, if it wished, stay judgment pending the Commission's decision; or, if there were no doubt that Article 85.1 did not apply (e.g. because of absence of appreciable effect on competition or inter-Member trade) or that Article 86 did not apply, the court should generally allow the proceedings to continue.

–07B The position is still by no means clear, but would seem to be as follows.

As regards direct enforcement of Articles 85.1 and 86, the national competition-law enforcement authorities would appear to be free to act, provided the Commission has not formally initiated a procedure. (It would normally be unlikely for the national authorities to want to take over the Commission's functions!)

As regards civil proceedings involving the application of Article 85.1:

(i) *"Existing" agreements notified in due time*

Where it is clear that the agreement is within Article 85.1, i.e. so that the issue is whether exemption will be given or not, the national court has no jurisdiction (it will be noted that the word used in *Brasserie de Haecht (No. 2)* is "notified", i.e. where exemption is sought).

Where it is clear that the agreement is outside Article 85.1 (e.g. because of absence of appreciable effect upon competition or inter-Member trade) the position is uncertain. The Court's ruling in *Brasserie de Haecht (No. 2)* would seem to exclude the national court from competence, but that may have been by inadvertence, *per incuriam.*

(ii) *All other agreements*

(a) notified agreements (i.e. where exemption is sought) – the national court may adjourn proceedings pending the Commission's decision, if the agreement is clearly within Article 85.1. If the agreement is clearly outside the Article, the court should continue to hear and decide the case, even though the Commission may have initiated its procedure.

(b) other agreements (i.e. where negative clearance has been sought, or no notification made) – the national court has jurisdiction to try the issue, even though the Commission may have initiated a procedure, e.g. started its own investigation.

In the Dutch *Stoves and Heaters* case, the agreement was an "existing" agreement notified in due time. Two members were being sued by the central office responsible for administering the agreement – they had failed to pay fines imposed upon them under the agreement for breaches of its terms (exclusive dealing and resale price maintenance). The Dutch civil court adjourned its proceedings pending the Commission's decision.

4–07C In its *Second Report on Competition Policy,* the Commission referred to two cases in which parallel proceedings had been instituted by the Commission and by the German authorities. Noting that no specific legal difficulties had arisen, the Commission indicated that it was considering whether a regulation or directive under Article 87.2(e) of the Treaty was needed to deal with instances of simultaneous application of Community and national law (*v.* paragraph 1-41 above).

4–09 The sector inquiry into the brewery industry showed a small volume of intra-Community trade. The Commission felt that this was due to large differences in drinking habits, reflected in differences in laws relating to the constituents and production of beer, and to brewery contracts which hampered inter-Member trade by limiting access to markets. The latter were under consideration by the Commission.[1]

Apparently the Commission has a list of sectors, on which it keeps a systematic watch for "concentration", i.e. mergers, take-overs, etc. between firms which would reduce consumers' freedom of choice. The Commission stated that the list did not indicate any presumption of infringement of the Community rules on competition.[2]

According to its *Fourth Report on Competition Policy,* the Commission commenced an inquiry into the oil sector following the shortage of supplies of crude oil at the end of 1973 and in early 1974, one of the objects being to see if the activities of any of the oil companies during the crisis infringed Community competition law.

4–10 Complaints from firms to the Commission appear to be increasing. For example, complaints were received in the *Papiers Peints* and *FRUBO* cases. Following the 1973/74 oil crisis, the Commission received several complaints that independent oil distributors had either been refused supplies or been charged excessive prices.

The situation in the Dutch *Stoves and Heaters* case was unusual. The agreement was between manufacturers, importers, wholesalers, and retailers of coal, oil, and gas heating appliances in Holland, covering some 90% of Dutch sales of the relevant equipment. The listed retailers could buy only from listed suppliers, and the latter could sell only to listed retailers. Listed retailers were obligated to sell only to consumers and not to other

[1] Cf. Reply to Written Question in European Parliament, 8th June, 1973. Official Journal C57. 17.7.73. p.23.

[2] Reply to Written Question in European Parliament, 14th September, 1973. Official Journal C85. 13.10.73. p.12.

dealers, and only at the suppliers' prices, i.e. resale price maintenance. There was provision for fines to be imposed upon members who broke the rules. Two members were fined for breaches, under those provisions. They refused to pay the fines, and were sued in the civil court. The court adjourned the case pending the Commission's decision upon the agreement, which had been notified. Meanwhile, the two members had laid complaints with the Commission. The agreement was terminated by the parties, but the Commission held that its contents, including the exclusive dealing provisions and the arbitration provisions, infringed Article 85.1. The Commission required the association to cease attempting to recover the fines in the civil court.

The Commission has now introduced a form, Form C, for use by persons wishing to lay complaints, i.e. asking the Commission to investigate possible infringements of Article 85 (or Article 86). The Form is reproduced in Appendix I, Part II.

4–13A By virtue of Article 191 (17-19), decisions must be notified to the addressee and take effect upon such notification. In the *Aniline Dyes* case, Imperial Chemical Industries submitted that the decision had not been formally notified to it; the Court, on appeal, held that any irregularity had been immaterial (*v.* paragraph 3-17).

The question of notification also arose in the appeal in the *Continental Can* case. Continental Can argued that the decision should have been served through diplomatic channels. The Court said:

> "A decision is duly served within the meaning of the Treaty if it is communicated to its addressee and the addressee has been enabled to take notice of it."[3]

3. Negative Clearance

Individual Negative Clearance

4–16 In view of the judgments by the European Court in *Brasserie de Haecht (No. 2)* and *SABAM v. Fonior,* it would now seem that national courts, when dealing with civil proceedings between subjects, can give rulings upon agreements, etc., even though the Commission is in process of investigating the particular

[3] [1973] C.M.L.R. p.221.

agreement, at least where it is clear that the agreement is not within Article 85.1 (cf. paragraphs 4-07 *et seq.* above).

4—17 This has been confirmed by the European Court's judgments in *Brasserie de Haecht (No. 2)* and *SABAM v. Fonior* (*v.* paragraphs 4-07 *et seq.* above).

4—18 Article 2.1 of Regulation 27/62 required seven copies to be submitted to the Commission of each application for negative clearance. With the accession of the New Members, that requirement has now been increased to ten copies, by Regulation 1699/75 – *v.* Appendix V.

4. Notification for individual exemption

4—25 The previous requirement, under Article 2.1 of Regulation 27/62, was that seven copies of each notification had to be sent to the Commission. Now that there are nine Members, ten copies of each notification must be submitted, as required by Regulation 1699/75 – *v.* Appendix V.

Status of notified agreements, etc.

4—26 The ruling by the European Court in *Portelange v. Smith Corona* was quite clear and unlimited:

> "The agreements envisaged in **Article 85(1)** of the Treaty, which have been duly notified under Regulation 17/62, are fully valid as long as the Commission has not given a ruling under **Article 85(3)** and under the provisions of Regulation 17."[4]

From the Court's judgments in *Brasserie de Haecht (No. 2)* and *SABAM v. Fonior* it is now clear that provisional validity is enjoyed only by "existing" agreements notified in due time, and not by "existing" agreements notified out of time or new agreements whenever notified (*v.* paragraphs 4-07 *et seq.* above). Admittedly, the notified agreement in the *Portelange* case was an "existing" agreement notified in due time. But the Court is open to criticism for giving a clear, specific, ruling which went much wider than the instant case and which may well have created problems for many concerns.

4—26A A new aspect of the provisional validity question arose in the Dutch *Stoves and Heaters* case. Two parties to the agreement were alleged to have infringed its terms, including those relating to exclusive dealing and resale price maintenance. Under the

[4] [1974] 1 C.M.L.R. p.419.

arbitration and appeal provisions of the agreement, they were required to pay fines. As neither of them paid the fines, they were both sued in the Dutch civil courts. The court adjourned its proceedings pending the Commission's decision on the agreement, which was an "existing" agreement notified in due time. The two parties had independently complained to the Commission under Article 3 of Regulation 17. The agreement was terminated voluntarily, so that the Commission's decision dealt only with those aspects relevant to the civil proceedings in the Dutch courts. Those aspects (exclusive dealing, resale price maintenance, and arbitration) were condemned as contrary to Article 85.1. The Commission specifically required the central office to desist from attempting to recover the fines.

Where then is the provisional validity? If the agreement was valid when its provisions were infringed by the two parties and the fines imposed, then surely the fines should have been paid? Of course, the dilemma is clear. If the Commission had not required the central office to desist, that would have amounted to allowing the enforcement of an agreement held to be contrary to Article 85.1. But if that is not what provisional validity means, what does it mean? It may be that a duly notified "existing" agreement can be enforced up to the time when it is condemned. Thereafter, it cannot be enforced, even in respect of pre-condemnation breaches. That may seem reasonable in relation to simple penalties for infringement, as in the instant case; but it may result in hardship where the agreement is one between two private parties, e.g. assigning a part of a business for payment, with an undertaking not to compete.

4—27 The question of standard-form contracts also arose in *Brasserie de Haecht (No. 2)*. The Court then ruled:

> "Notification duly effected of a standard-form contract is to be taken to be notification of all agreements having the same content, even previous ones, made by the same undertaking."[5]

The Court made clear that, in the case of an agreement made before the notification, the notification operated only from the date it was effected – a notification effected in 1969, and therefore outside the time limits in Articles 5 and 7 of Regulation 17, could not turn the agreements in question into "existing" agreements even though they may have been made before those time limits expired.

[5] [1973] C.M.L.R. p.304.

—28 The immunity from fines conferred by notification is illustrated by *Pittsburgh Corning Europe.* The concerted practice was held by the Commission to have operated from 1st October, 1970, to 1st June, 1972. But a request for negative clearance and exemption had been made on 6th January, 1971. The fine imposed was in respect of the period before that request.

The immunity relates only to activities within the notification. In *Papiers Peints* there had been notification, but the collective boycott by the members of two traders in Belgium was held by the Commission to be outside the notification, and a fine was imposed in respect of it. An appeal is pending before the European Court.

In the *Papiers Peints* case, the Commission regarded the notification made in 1962 as being incomplete. In its decision, in relation to the determination of the fine, the Commission commented:

> "The Commission leaves open the questions as to whether or not the *Groupement* acted in good faith in notifying the agreements and restrictive decisions or attempted to conceal the full implications of their market arrangements by providing vague statements and by not disclosing the existence of agreements and written decisions."[6]

The full implications of these remarks remain to be explored. It may be that immunity is obtained only by a *bona fide* notification, in the sense that anything not clearly within the notification may attract a fine – vague statements may be construed strictly, against those party to the notification.

An instance of an agreement where the Commission took a decision after only a preliminary examination is *Sirdar/PHILDAR* (*v.* paragraphs 8-58 *et seq.*).

"Existing" agreements, etc.

In relation to the original Members

—32 *Brasserie de Haecht (No. 2)* confirms that only the Commission has competence to determine that an "existing" agreement notified in due time is void under Article 85 (*v.* paragraphs 4-07 *et seq.* above)

In the *Belgian Central Heating Agreement* case, the parties had asked for application of Article 7 of Regulation 17. Exemption

[6] Official Journal L237. 29.8.74. p.10.

under Article 85.3 was refused, and so also was a declaration under Article 7.

In relation to new Members

4–34 In respect of "existing" agreements notified in due time, only the Commission is competent to rule that the agreement, etc., infringes Article 85.1 *(Brasserie de Haecht (No. 2)* – *v.* paragraphs 4-07 *et seq.* above).

In *Sirdar/PHILDAR,* the agreement was made in 1964 between a French and a United Kingdom company. Each was precluded from selling goods under its particular trade mark in the other's country. Sirdar, the United Kingdom company, notified the agreement in June, 1973. The Commission ruled that the agreement did not qualify for treatment under Article 25 of Regulation 17 as an "accession" agreement. In the Commission's view, the agreement was intended to prevent Sirdar's wool from being imported into France from the United Kingdom or any other Member. On that basis, the agreement restricted competition in the Common Market and affected inter-Member trade from the date it was made, 1964, and should have been notified then.

"By virtue of accession"

4–40 From the Court's comment in Continental Can's appeal against the Commission's decision, it would at least seem that the Court favours the "effects" principle (*v.* paragraph 3-95 above).

New agreements, etc.

4–44 The advisability of incorporating what might be called a "Henkel/Colgate" clause postponing operation of an agreement until after a favourable decision by the Commission has been confirmed by the Court's reasoning in the *Brasserie de Haecht (No. 2)* case. Following that reasoning, it would now appear that notification of a new agreement does not give any provisional validity. The national courts are competent to give a decision where the question of application of Article 85.1 arises in civil proceedings between subjects, even though a Commission investigation may be in train (*v.* paragraphs 4-07 *et seq.* above). Where the court considers that Article 85.1 does not apply it can so rule; if the Article is held to apply, the court may adjourn the proceedings pending the Commission's decision on the application or not of Article 85.3 (i.e. exemption).

In this context, the *Brasserie de Haecht (No. 2)* case does not make all that much difference. In the case of new agreements there is no possibility of a declaration under Article 7 of Regulation 17 to protect the parties where exemption is refused, so that the parties operate a notified new agreement at their peril – it is better to postpone operation until the Commission's decision is known.

Procedure

–47 The exemption runs from the date the agreement qualifies for exemption, if that date is later than notification, i.e. where the agreement has been modified to qualify for exemption. In the case of "existing" agreements notified in due time, the Commission can exercise its power under Article 7 (18-08) and grant a declaration to cover the period prior to amendment. This is what happened as regards the standard agreements for appointing distributors used in the *Bayerische Motoren Werke* case. The original notified agreements were "existing" agreements and were notified before 1st February, 1963, in due time. The amendments to satisfy Article 85.3 took effect from 1st January, 1973. A declaration under Article 7 of Regulation 17 was incorporated in the Commission's decision taking the original agreements outside the prohibition in Article 85.1 for the period 13th March, 1962 (when Regulation 17 came into effect) until 1st January, 1973. For other agreements, there is no such power. For example, the *Goodyear Italiana* agreement was notified on 7th November, 1973, but did not qualify for exemption until 7th August, 1973, so that the exemption could run only from the latter date (*v.* paragraph 6-44A).

5. Relief from the obligation to notify

–51 In its *GISA* decision, the Commission condemned the price-fixing and quota arrangements operated by GISA, the Dutch plumbers' merchants' association. The price fixing had operated from 1961 onwards, and the quota arrangements from 1963 to 1970. There had been no notification, but no fines were imposed. It may be that the Commission regarded the arrangements as coming within Article 4.2(1).

In the *European Sugar Cartel,* the main suppliers in the western part of Federal Germany were Westdeutsche Zucker and Pfeifer & Langen. Their agreements with their distributors, who in many cases acted for both, prohibited the sale of sugar from other sources without the consent of the principals. The Commission regarded these agreements as falling outside Article 4.2(1) as they controlled imports and exports.

Status of agreements, etc., within Article 4.2

4–54 It would now appear that the immunity applies only to "existing" agreements notified within the time limits set out in Articles 7 and 25 of Regulation 17. For all other agreements, it would seem that a national court may decide on the application of Article 85.1 in civil proceedings between subjects, with the possibility of adjourning proceedings pending a Commission decision whether to grant exemption or not (*v.* paragraphs 4-07 *et seq.* above).

6. Ancillary provisions

Procurement of information

4–64 In *Optische Werke Rodenstock,* the original request for information was made towards the end of 1969. A further request was made in February, 1971. The formal request for information was not made until September, 1972. In *Misal,* the first request was made in the fourth quarter of 1969, the second in March, 1971, and the final, formal, request in September, 1972.

It would seem that in September, 1972, the Commission had reviewed outstanding requests for information, because similar formal requests were then sent to some 60 other concerns. By March, 1973, satisfactory replies had been received from 51 of the 62 undertakings involved.[7]

Investigations by and on behalf of the Commission

Professional privilege

4–79A Some trade associations have their legal advisers present at association meetings. If, in the course of a meeting, legal advice is given by the advisers and recorded in the minutes, that part of the minutes will be protected by professional privilege, but not the remainder of the minutes. Of course, the mere fact that legal advisers were present throughout the meeting does not mean that

[7] Reply to Written Question in European Parliament, 27th March, 1973. Official Journal C29. 12.5.73. p.8.

anything said at the meeting and *any* record of it is privileged – privilege applies only to any legal advice which may have been given.

In some instances, associations follow a practice of having an outside lawyer as the independent chairman. In those situations, the same rules apply. If and when the lawyer chairman acts as legal adviser, his advice is privileged. When he acts purely as chairman, he is acting as agent for the association, and privilege does not apply.

In *Papiers Peints,* lawyers sent the notification to the Commission, on behalf of the members. In that situation, the lawyers would seem to have been acting purely in an executive capacity. Apparently the notification was incomplete, and the members explained this on the basis that in 1962 there was uncertainty as to what particulars were required. It would seem that the Commission suggested that the lawyers who prepared the notification might attend to give an explanation, but that suggestion was not taken up.

Hearings

—82 The obligation to give the parties notice of objections raised extends to conditions which the Commission puts in an exemption. In *Transocean Marine Paint Association (No. 2),* the extension of the exemption was allowed by the Commission but on condition that the parties informed the Commission without delay of any links (by way of common directors or managers or by financial participation) between a member and an outside company. The members appealed against this condition, on the ground that it was too wide and had not been communicated to them so as to enable them to deal with it in their submissions. The Court upheld the appeal, annulled the condition, and referred the case back to the Commission.

The Court held that Regulation 99/63

> "applies the general rule that a person whose interests are perceptibly affected by a decision taken by a public authority must be given the opportunity to make his point of view known. This rule requires that an undertaking be clearly informed, in good time, of the essence of the conditions to which the Commission intends to subject an exemption and it must have the opportunity to submit its observations to the Commission. This is especially so in the case of conditions

which, as in this case, impose considerable obligations having far-reaching effects."[8]

Fines and penalties

4–90 It would appear that, although there may be parallel proceedings, there should not be double fines. In *Boehringer (No. 2),* the Court distinguished between fines imposed under the laws of Member States and those imposed under the laws of non-Members. As regards the former:

"The Commission is under a duty, in fixing the amount of a fine, to take into account the sanctions already imposed on an undertaking in respect of the same act, in cases of sanctions for infringements of the antitrust law of a member-State which are therefore breaches of laws committed in the territory of the Community."[9]

M. Borschette, the Commissioner responsible for competition matters in the Commission, expressed his view in the following terms:

"This means in practical terms that national authorities must refrain from imposing a financial penalty if the Commission has already imposed a fine on the same grounds. Conversely, the Commission is obliged to set off against the fine it intends to impose any financial penalty imposed earlier by a national authority."[10]

It is important that the penalty should be imposed "on the same grounds", or, as the Court put it "in respect of the same act". In the *Boehringer* appeal, the Court commented that the Community fine took account only of those acts which "were likely to affect trade between the member-States and to distort competition within the Common Market".[11] Consequently, it would seem that a fine imposed by a national authority for acts which did not affect inter-Member trade would not have to be taken into account by the Commission in fixing the Community fine.

4–91 As mentioned in paragraph 4-90 above, the Court in the *Boehringer* appeal distinguished fines imposed by non-Members:

"The question as to whether the Commission can also be under a duty to set off a sanction imposed by authorities of a

[8] [1974] 2 C.M.L.R. p.477.
[9] [1973] C.M.L.R. p.887.
[10] Debates of the European Parliament. 12th February, 1973. p.13.
[11] [1973] C.M.L.R. p.887.

nonmember-State, need only be determined if the acts alleged in the case against the applicant by the Commission on the one hand and by the American authorities on the other are identical."[12]

In that case, although the actions arose from the same agreements, they were distinct as to their purpose and also their territorial effect. The Community fines were for dividing up the domestic markets in the Common Market, etc. The United States fines were for other actions, including the acquisition and sharing out of the American stockpile and the maintenance of abnormally high selling prices in the United States. Consequently, the Court refused to reduce the Community fine of 180,000 units of account by reason of the United States fine of $80,000.

The Court also commented that, contrary to the argument urged before it, the mischief lay, not in the cartel agreements themselves, but in their execution.

–91A It should be noted that the substantive fines imposed by the Commission have been increasing. The fines imposed in the *European Sugar Cartel* decision totalled 9,000,000 units of account (say £3,750,000) – appeals are pending before the Court.

In *Papiers Peints,* the Commission complained that the infringement had started in October, 1971 and had continued up to the date of the decision, July, 1974, despite the adverse decision by a Belgian court in March, 1973 and the statement of objections issued by the Commission itself in October, 1973 – the Commission regarded this continuance of the infringement as an "aggravating circumstance". (However, it would seem that there the Commission had in mind the collective boycott, and the Commission did not show how that affected inter-Member trade – an appeal is pending before the European Court.) The fines on the four members totalled 358,500 units of account (say £150,000).

In *WEA-Filipacchi,* the infringement was held by the Commission to be "deliberate". Some dealers who had received the circular letter had drawn the attention of WEA-Filipacchi to the fact that export prohibitions violated Article 85.1, but nevertheless that company persisted. A fine of 60,000 units was imposed (say £25,000).

In *Pittsburgh Corning Europe,* the concerted practices were

[12] *Ibid.*

operated by Pittsburgh and Hertel on the one hand and Pittsburgh and Formica Belgium on the other. But they were at the instigation and for the exclusive benefit of Pittsburgh, and the fine was accordingly imposed on that company, amounting to 100,000 units (say £40,000).

In the *Deutsche Philips* case, there were two opposing considerations. Export bans constitute a severe infringement of Article 85.1, in the Commission's view, and Deutsche Philips was an important concern in the electrical appliance industry. On the other hand, the infringement had arisen from negligence. The fine was 60,000 units.

No fines were imposed in *European Glass Manufacturers.* The Commission explained in its *Fourth Report on Competition Policy* that it had refrained from imposing a fine because the restrictions involved in that case had not previously been dealt with in a Commission decision and it was not obvious to the parties that their conduct infringed Community competition law.

4–93 *Unit of account* The unit of account represented, when it was fixed, the gold equivalent of one American dollar, i.e. the pre-Smithsonian dollar. Gold was then $35 to the ounce, at the official price. The market price is now nearer $150.

The Community does not now relate its unit of account to the value of gold. For the purposes of the Common Agricultural Policy, the exchange rates to be taken for the currencies of the Member States are defined, and changed, from time to time. For the purpose of budget contributions from the Members, and for calculating fines imposed under Regulation 17, the old official parities of the currencies are still being used. This means that the £ sterling is still regarded as being equivalent to 2.4 units of account. A unit of account based on a "standard basket" of the nine Member currencies is expected to be proposed by the Commission when the opportunity arises.

Limitation of actions

4–101 The Council Regulation specifying limitation periods was made in November 1974, taking effect from 1st January, 1975. It is Regulation 2988/74, and is reproduced at Appendix S. It is mainly on the same lines as the draft, but there have been some changes of substance, as well as drafting amendments.

The limitation period in respect of infringements relating to requests for information is three years, and for other infringements five years (35-02). The limitation period is interrupted and starts running again in certain circumstances, but cannot exceed more than twice the original limitation period, ignoring periods when time is suspended by reason of proceedings pending before the Court (35-03). The limitation period for enforcement of fines, etc., is five years (not three as in the draft), as specified in Article 4 of the Regulation (35-05). There is provision for the limitation period to be interrupted and to start running again (35-06) and for suspension (35-07).

6A. Appeals

—102A The validity of Commission decisions can be tested by appeal to the European Court, under Article 177(b) of the Treaty. An instance of a successful appeal was that by Transocean against the condition imposed by the Commission in respect of the extension of the exemption under Article 85.3 *(Transocean Marine Paint Association (No. 2)).* The parties in the *Papiers Peints* case also appealed.

An appeal does not automatically suspend the decision appealed against, but the Court can order suspension if it thinks fit (Article 185 – 17-18A).

—102B The Court also has power under Article 172 of the Treaty (17-15D) and Article 17 of Regulation 17 to review fines and penalties.

7. Conclusion

—103 It is worth noting that in cases of urgency, the Commission can act quickly. In one instance involving a major public floatation on the London Stock Exchange, the Commission was able to clear the proposed terms within two months.

—106 Another instance of the Commission's practical approach is the Business Co-operation Centre ("The Marriage Bureau"). This began operation on 1st May, 1973 under the title and address: Bureau de rapprochement des entreprises, 15-17 rue Archimède, 1040 Brussels, Belgium. Its aim is to help small and medium-sized concerns seeking links with other concerns. In its first year, the Centre had been approached by over 1,800 concerns, about half from Germany (545) and the United Kingdom (427).[13]

[13] Reply to Written Question in European Parliament, 5th July, 1974. Official Journal C95. 13.8.74. p.21.

CHAPTER 5

Monopolies and Dominant Positions—Articles 86 and Regulation 17

2. Article 86

"One or more undertakings"

5–04 The question of enterprise entity arose on the *Continental Can* appeal to the European Court. The company argued that it was not within the jurisdiction of the Commission or of the Court for two reasons: first, its seat lay outside the Community, and, second, the alleged unlawful conduct was attributable to Europemballage not to Continental Can. The Court disposed of these points as follows:

"The applicant companies maintain that according to the general principles of public international law, as an undertaking with a seat outside the Community, Continental Can is not subject to the jurisdiction of the Commission or the Court of Justice; that the Commission therefore had no power to issue the challenged decision against Continental Can or to address to it the demand contained in Article 2 of the decision; and that furthermore the unlawful conduct in respect of which the Commission took proceedings was not directly attributable to Continental Can but to Europemballage.

The applicant companies cannot deny that Europemballage, set up on 20 February 1970 by Continental Can, is a subsidiary company of Continental Can. The fact that the subsidiary has its own legal personality cannot rule out the possibility that its conduct may be imputed to its parent company. This is particularly the case where the subsidiary does not determine its market behaviour autonomously but mainly follows the instructions of the parent company.

It is established that Continental Can caused Europemballage to make an offer to buy to the Thomassen & Drijver-Verblifa shareholders in Holland and provided the necessary funds for this purpose. On 8 April 1970 Europemballage bought the Thomassen & Drijver-Verblifa shares and bonds offered to it on that date. Therefore this transaction on the basis of which the Commission adopted the decision in question must be attributed not only to Europemballage but also and mainly to Continental Can. Community law is applicable to such an acquisition which affects the market conditions within the Community. The fact that Continental Can does not have a seat in the territory of one of the member-States does not suffice to remove it from the jurisdiction of Community law."[1]

The appellants had also argued that there was an error in the form of the decision, in that the text in the Official Journal was entitled "Continental Can Company" whereas the French version of the decision, the only binding version, had "Europemballage Corporation". The Court disposed of the point by saying:

"However, in view of the economic and legal relations between Continental Can and Europemballage this fact cannot impair the validity of the challenged decision."[2]

—04A The identity of parent and subsidiary company also arose in the *Zoja* case. If Commercial Solvents and Istituto did not form one economic unit, the latter would not be fixed with the dominant position held by the former. The Commission held that Commercial Solvents and Istituto Chemioterapico "should be treated as forming, in their relations with Zoja and for the purposes of application of Article 86, only one single and identical undertaking or economic entity."[3] The grounds adduced by the Commission for so doing were several. First, Commercial Solvents held 51% of the share capital in Istituto. Next, five of the ten members of the latter's management board came from the former, including the chairman who was also president of Commercial Solvents; of the six members of the executive committee of Istituto, three were representatives of Commercial Solvents. And the prohibition on re-sale of nitropropane and aminobutanol for manufacture of ethambutol imposed

[1] [1973] C.M.L.R. pp.221-2.
[2] *Ibid.* p.220.
[3] [1973] C.M.L.R. p.D57.

by Commercial Solvents on its distributors followed the failure of the merger talks between Istituto and Zoja.

When the point came before the Court, that tribunal, in its judgment, referred to the Commission's grounds for treating Commercial Solvents and Istituto as one. It also pointed out that, when the former decided no longer to sell nitropropane and aminobutanol, it made an exception in favour of Istituto which produced ethambutol and specialities based on that product. Moreover, Istituto bought up quantities of nitropropane which were still available on the market and sold them for re-sale only for paint manufacture and not for pharmaceutical purposes outside the Common Market. The Court continued:

> "As regards the market in nitropropane and its derivatives the conduct of Commercial Solvents Corp. and Istituto, has thus been characterised by an obviously united action, which, taking account of the power of control of Commercial Solvents Corp. over Istituto, confirms the conclusions in the decision that as regards their relations with Zoja the two companies must be deemed an economic unit and that they are jointly and severally responsible for the conduct complained of. In these circumstances the argument of Commercial Solvents Corp. that it did not do business within the Community and that therefore the Commission lacked competence to apply Regulation 17 to it must likewise be rejected."[4]

5–05 Where the dominant position is held, not by one undertaking alone, but by several a convenient phrase might be "multi-firm" dominant position as against "single-firm" dominant position.

A comment by the Court in its judgment on the *Continental Can* appeal supports the view that Article 86 does apply to a multi-firm dominant position:

> "**Article 85** concerns agreements between undertakings, decisions by associations of undertakings and concerted practices, whereas **Article 86** covers unilateral activity on the part of one or several undertakings."[5]

Prima facie, this would suggest that Article 86 cannot apply where there is an agreement between the undertakings concerned. Admittedly, if there were an agreement and the consequent action came within Article 86, the agreement would also

[4] [1974] 1. C.M.L.R. p.344.
[5] [1973] C.M.L.R. p.224.

normally be within Article 85. But, pending a specific ruling on the point, it would seem to be more prudent to take the wording of Article 86 at its face value, and to regard it as applying not only to unilateral acts but also to consensual action in multi-firm dominant positions.

5—06 Block exemption for specialisation agreements was given by Regulation 2779/72 (Appendix O).

"Dominant position"

5—08 The definition of a "dominant position" put forward by the Commission was not challenged in the appeal to the Court. It was followed by the Commission in its decision in the *European Sugar Cartel,* with references to the market shares of the undertakings involved and their ability to act independently.

In *Eurofima,* the Commission did not go to the stage of a formal decision, in that the proceedings were terminated informally. In its press release, the Commission merely said that Eurofima held a dominant position within the Common Market because it was "the most important buyer of the type of rolling stock concerned".[6] The *Third Report on Competition Policy* gives some more information. Eurofima was set up by sixteen European railway administrations, and the invitation to tender for standard passenger carriages was issued on behalf of six administrations.

5—16 One of the grounds of the appeal in the *Continental Can* case was that the market shares alleged to be held by Schmalbach in the cans for meat and for fish and in metal lids did not establish a dominant position in the market for all light metal containers. The exclusion of containers made of other, substitute, materials such as plastics and glass was not justified.

The Court, first, pointed out that the Commission had not shown why the markets for "light containers" for meat, "light containers" for fish, and "metal closures for the canning industry apart from crown corks" should be distinguished from each other or distinguished from the general market for light metal containers (for example, for canned fruit and vegetables, condensed milk, fruit juices, etc.). The Court took the view that merely to show that the products in question were used for packaging different products was not sufficient to make them

[6] [1973] C.M.L.R. p.D218.

separate markets – it would also have to be shown that they had special production characteristics. A dominant position in light metal containers for meat or for fish would not be conclusive in the absence of proof that competitors in light metal containers for other products could not enter the market in strength by adapting their production methods.

The Court also mentioned that some of the points made by the Commission in its decision suggested that the three products in question were parts of a larger market. The Commission had referred to a German concern with a bigger share of the market for light metal containers for canned fruit and vegetables than the share held by Schmalbach, and to another concern with about 40% of the German demand for crown corks – suggesting that metal cans for other purposes and crown corks were relevant in considering the markets for cans for meat and fish and for metal closures.

The Court referred to other contradictions in the Commission's decision. As regards the economic limits of transport, the figures quoted by the Commission conflicted with the argument that German buyers could not draw supplies from producers in countries bordering Germany. The Commission had also not disposed of the potential competition from other concerns in Belgium and Germany which produced cans for their own use and sold any excess production on the market.

For these reasons, the Court concluded that the Commission's decision had to be annulled.

5–16A Three instances of dominant position were identified by the Commission in its *European Sugar Cartel* decision.

Raffinerie Tirlemontoise produced about 50% of the Belgian sugar output. In addition, through majority holdings or marketing contracts, it controlled the output of other firms, so that it controlled some 85% of the sugar market in Belgium and Luxembourg (the latter country having no sugar producers and being supplied from Belgium). In addition, the company had financial interests in other large European sugar producers, particularly in France, and was possessed of substantial technical know-how. Because of its strong position in Belgium, the company influenced other Belgian sugar producers, who usually followed the same sales policy in relation to the Belgian wholesalers as did Tirlemontoise. Tirlemontoise had a "capacity .... for independent action which enables it to act without having to take its competitors' activity into account to any appreciable extent".[7] That capacity, and its size, gave Tirlemontoise a dominant position in the Belgian and Luxembourg sugar market.

In Holland there were only two sugar producers, Suiker Unie and Centrale Suiker. They co-operated very closely in their activities, with joint buying of raw materials, a quota system for sales, joint market research and advertising, and unified ex-works prices and sales conditions. In relation to other concerns, such as wholesalers, their uniform conduct, in the Commission's view, made them appear as a single entity. Together they produced 85% of the Dutch requirements, and in addition were able to control almost all the imports of sugar into Holland. Their market position and capacity to act independently enabled them "to act without having to take their competitors into account to any appreciable extent".[8] They had a dominant position in the Dutch sugar market. This is an instance of a multi-firm dominant position.

Südzucker Verkaufs had a dominant position in the southern part of Federal Germany. It handled almost all the output of its members, and any separate sales by the latter were usually made through the same distributors. Südzucker fixed its own prices and sales policy. Sales in its territory by producers in other parts of Federal Germany or France were negligible, so that Südzucker was estimated to have at least 90-95% of the market. "This position gives it the opportunity of behaving independently, which enables it to act without having to take its competitors' activities into account to any appreciable extent."[9]

It will be observed that, in all three instances, the Commission has adopted the same "capacity to act independently" approach as it did in its Continental Can decision (*v.* paragraph 5-08).

5–16B In *Zoja,* the situation was in some ways more simple, in others more complicated. In brief, nitropropane was the raw material for making aminobutanol, which in turn was the raw material for making ethambutol, a drug used in the treatment of pulmonary tuberculosis. The Commission held that Commercial Solvents and Istituto Chemioterapico, treating both as constituting one economic entity, had a world monopoly of the production of nitropropane and aminobutanol and that, therefore, they had a

[7] [1973] C.M.L.R. p.D103.
[8] *Ibid* p.D105.
[9] *Ibid.* p.D106.

dominant position for those materials in the Common Market. And there was no other material available on an industrial scale which could be used to make ethambutol. The Commission also regarded ethambutol as constituting a market by itself; admittedly, that drug was used in association with other anti-tuberculosis drugs, but that meant that it complemented, rather than competed with, the other drugs – the maintenance of sales of ethambutol at a high level, despite the appearance of new drugs and the fact that the demand for anti-tuberculosis drugs was not an expanding one, confirmed that the possibility of replacing ethambutol by these alleged competitors was negligible.

As part of their appeal, the companies disputed that they had a world monopoly of nitropropane and aminobutanol; they also claimed that a separate market for ethambutol did not exist, and that, therefore, there could not be a separate market in its raw material. To support the first allegation they said that another Italian company produced ethambutol from other raw materials, and that it could be made from thiophenol; that a third Italian company made aminobutanol from butanone, and that it could be made from three other materials without using nitropropane; and, finally, that a French company was producing nitropropane independently, and that it could be made without using the processes used by Commercial Solvents. The Court was not impressed by these arguments. Production of ethambutol by the Italian company from other materials was only on a modest scale and solely for its own consumption; and production from thiophenol was too vague and uncertain for serious consideration. Production of aminobutanol from butanone by the other Italian company was also on a modest scale and to meet its own needs, and would require considerable expenditure for Zoja to adopt it; the alleged other alternative methods of production had not been proved on an industrial scale and would involve uneconomic prices. Finally, the production of nitropropane by the French company was still only on an experimental scale; and the other methods of making it had still to be proved on an industrial scale and would involve uneconomic prices. To show that Commercial Solvents did not have a dominant position it would be necessary to prove the presence on the market of some other raw material which could be substituted without difficulty for nitropropane/aminobutanol – not the existence of experimental processes, or alternatives requiring adaptation of Zoja's manufacturing methods. In fact, the three main producers of ethambutol,

Commercial Solvents, American Cyanamid, and Zoja, all used raw materials made by Commercial Solvents. The Court held that Commercial Solvents' dominant position in the raw materials had been established.

As to the question of markets, the Court held that the market in the raw materials and the market for the finished product could be distinguished. It was possible to hold that a dominant position existed in the former alone, without having regard to the latter. But in considering the effects of abuse of the dominant position in the raw-material market, the consequences felt in the market in which the finished product was sold, including restriction of competition in that market by eliminating one competitor, could be taken into account even though the finished product did not constitute a market in itself.

—16C A narrow view of the relevant market was taken by the Commission in *General Motors Continental.* Belgian law required all motor vehicles used on the public highway to satisfy certain technical requirements. To achieve this, each type of vehicle had to be approved; and each vehicle of each type had to have a certificate of conformity with the type approval, and also a type-shield to be affixed to the vehicle. After 15th March, 1973 the Belgian state testing stations would not accept for testing vehicles which had been registered abroad for less than six months. Consequently, since that date the manufacturer's agent in Belgium had the sole responsibility for issuing a certificate of conformity for such vehicles.

General Motors Continental (G.M.C.), a Belgian company, was the Belgian agent for the General Motors group, and obtained general approval for vehicles made by member companies of the group, including Opel cars and also cars manufactured by group companies in the United States. After 15th March, 1973, persons importing Opel and other General Motors group cars into Belgium – that is, private individuals and dealers who did not buy through G.M.C., i.e. parallel imports – were dependent upon G.M.C. to obtain type approval (if the model in question had not already been approved) and to supply certificates of conformity and type-shields, where the vehicle had been registered in some other country less than six months previously. Between the 15th March, 1973 and the 31st July, 1973, G.M.C. charged, in five cases, B.fr. 5,000, plus B.fr. 900 VAT for the issue of certificates and shields, the same charge as was made for American models. In June and July, 1973, in other cases of parallel imports of Opel vehicles only B.fr. 1,000 was charged, including VAT. From 1st August, 1973 onwards, its charges were B.fr. 1,250 on cars made by General Motors group companies in Europe and which had already been type-approved, with charges of B.fr. 5,300 and above for models made in America. Later, some part of the charges was re-imbursed in the five cases, in two B.fr. 4,500 was returned and in three B.fr. 4,425. G.M.C. ascertained that the costs for obtaining type approval for Opel cars was only B.fr. 123 as against B.fr. 3,654 for American models, per vehicle. Other Belgian firms approached by the Commission had charged B.fr. 2,500 or less for the same service in respect of parallel imports of other makes of vehicle, and the government testing stations charged B.fr. 1,140.

The Commission held that G.M.C. had a dominant position, by reason of the legislative requirements, in connection with obtaining type approval and the supply of certificates of conformity and type-shields, both in respect of new models and of vehicles registered in another country less than six months previously. That dominant position was in Belgium, 'a substantial part of the Common Market'. In the Commission's view G.M.C. had abused that dominant position in two ways. First, G.M.C. had charged excessive prices in respect of parallel-import vehicles in the period 15th March, 1973, to 31st July, 1973. Second, by discriminating against dealers who wished to import direct, and not through G.M.C., who would have been required to pay that excessive price.

The Commission imposed a fine of 100,000 units of account (say £40,000). In arriving at that figure, the Commission took into account the short duration of the offence and the reimbursement of part of the charges in the five cases.

5–18 The statement in this paragraph – that Article 86 requires both a dominant position and also an abuse of that position – which seemed eminently reasonable in the light of the clear wording of the Article, may now have to be treated with some caution, in the light of the Court's remarks in the *Continental Can* appeal. Two sentences are significant:

"There may therefore be abusive behaviour if an undertaking in a dominant position strengthens that dominant position so that the degree of control achieved substantially obstructs competition, i.e., so that the only undertakings left in the market are those which are dependent on the dominant undertaking with regard to their market behaviour.

Such being the meaning and the scope of **Article 86** of the EEC Treaty, the question raised by the applicant companies of the causal connection which in their view must exist between the dominant position and the abusive exploitation is irrelevant, for the strengthening of the position of an undertaking may be abusive and prohibited by **Article 86** of the Treaty, regardless of the means or the methods whereby it has been achieved, if it has the effects described above."[10]

In short, in the Court's view there can be an abuse of a dominant position even if that position has not been abused! Merely to strengthen a dominant position can be an abuse of it!

"Within the Common Market or in a substantial part of it"

—21 In *European Sugar Cartel,* the Commission regarded Belgium and Luxembourg together, Holland, and the southern part of Federal Germany, each to be a substantial part of the Common Market. In *General Motors Continental,* Belgium alone was considered by the Commission to be a substantial part.

In *Zoja,* the Court held that the dominant position was in the world market.

"Abuse"

—24A In *General Motors Continental,* the abuse, in the Commission's view, was two-fold. There was a charging of excessive prices. And the excessive prices discriminated against dealers who wished to import independently of General Motors Continental.

—24B Refusal to supply, i.e. cutting off supplies, was the abuse in the *Zoja* case. Zoja had been Istituto's main customer for aminobutanol from 1966 onwards. Merger talks between the two in 1968 and 1969 broke down at the end of 1969. In 1970, raw material was available at lower prices from other suppliers, and Zoja negotiated a cancellation of its order on Istituto. By the end of 1970, supplies from other sources had dried up. Istituto had bought up some nitropropane supplies, and re-sold them to paint manufacturers on the condition that they would not be re-sold again for pharmaceutical use. In November, 1970, Zoja sought supplies of aminobutanol from Istituto, and the latter replied that Commercial Solvents had told it not to sell aminobutanol. The Commission held that Commercial Solvents/Istituto had abused their dominant position by refusing to supply raw materials to

[10] [1973] C.M.L.R. p.225.

one of the principal users, so tending to eliminate one of the principal producers of ethambutol in the Common Market, limiting competition in and the production of that product. Commercial Solvents' production was such that it could have supplied Zoja, whose requirements represented only about 5-6% of Commercial Solvents' production of nitropropane.

Before the Court, Commercial Solvents argued that it was Zoja which had discontinued supplies, by cancelling its contract with Istituto. By the time Zoja had changed its mind and wanted to buy again, Commercial Solvents had changed its policy, having decided not to supply the intermediate products or the raw materials, but to supply only the finished product. The Court continued:

> "However, an undertaking being in a dominant position as regards the production of raw material and therefore able to control the supply to manufacturers of derivatives cannot, just because it decides to start manufacturing these derivatives (in competition with its former customers), act in such a way as to eliminate their competition which, in the case in question, would have amounted to eliminating one of the principal manufacturers of ethambutol in the Common Market. Since such conduct is contrary to the objectives expressed in **Article 3(f)** of the Treaty and set out in greater detail in **Articles 85** and **86,** it follows that an undertaking which has a dominant position in the market in raw materials and which, with the object of reserving such raw material for manufacturing its own derivatives, refuses to supply a customer, which is itself a manufacturer of these derivatives, and therefore risks eliminating all competition on the part of this customer, is abusing its dominant position within the meaning of **Article 86.**"[11]

This is a remarkable doctrine. It would seem that once a firm in a dominant position has started to supply a competitor, it cannot refuse to supply (presumably, unless there is some other ground, such as failure to pay, increasing credit risk, etc. – but the latter might be met by requiring cash before delivery). Does this mean that the customer is guaranteed supplies for ever? Or is it purely a question of motive?

The Court also said:

> "It is also unnecessary to examine, as the applicants have

[11] [1974] 1. C.M.L.R. pp.340-1.

asked, whether Zoja had an urgent need for aminobutanol in 1970 and 1971 or whether this company still had large quantities of this product which would enable it to reorganise its production in good time, since that question is not relevant to the consideration of the conduct of the applicants."[12]

In other words, the supplier cannot argue that the customer had enough stocks to carry him over until he could make other arrangements! This does seem to be an unnecessarily high degree of feather-bedding! The whole basis of competition policy is that firms should be self-reliant, the weak and incompetent going to the wall to make way for the efficient and competent. It is a system of natural selection (cf. 16-04K below).

—24C According to its *Fourth Report on Competition Policy,* the Commission is considering an alleged case of refusal to supply in the oil industry. Following the oil crisis in 1973/74, the Commission received several complaints from independent oil distributors that they had difficulty in obtaining supplies. After investigation, the Commission sent statements of objections to seven large suppliers in the Netherlands on the ground that they had abused their collective dominant position by refusing to supply an independent network in that country.

—33 Although it allowed the appeal on factual grounds, i.e. that the Commission had not established that light metal containers for meat and fish and metal closures were each a separate, distinct, market, the Court in its judgment in the *Continental Can* appeal did indeed confirm the Commission's interpretation of Article 86, that the extension of a dominant position by a merger which reduced competition could be an abuse of a dominant position. The Court's reasoning is considered in detail in Chapter 15. In outline, the Court said that Article 85 prohibited decisions of associations of undertakings which only restricted competition without necessarily eliminating it, and it could not, therefore, be supposed that Article 86 would allow mergers between undertakings which might eliminate competition altogether. "There may therefore be abusive behaviour if an undertaking in a dominant position strengthens that dominant position so that the degree of control achieved substantially obstructs competition. . ."[13]

The words of Article 86 are reasonably clear to any objective

[12] *Ibid.* p.341.
[13] [1973] C.M.L.R. p.225.

interpreter, "Any abuse. . . of a dominant position . . . shall be prohibited. . ." means "any misuse. . . of a dominant position". If the dominant position is not misused or abused, Article 86 should not apply. Merely extending a dominant position without misusing it, would not seem to be within the Article. One cannot help feeling that the Court has fallen into the error of confusing the normative and the positive, of confusing what the Court thinks *ought to be* with what is.

It is, to say the least, remarkable that, if the Court's interpretation of Article 86 was the correct one, neither Regulation 17 nor anything done in the eleven years between that Regulation and the *Continental Can* judgment had provided for it! The Commission lost no time. The Court's *Continental Can* judgment is dated 21st February, 1973, and in five months, on 20th July, 1973, the Commission submitted to the Council a draft regulation on the control of mergers – Appendix T. This is discussed in Chapter 15.

5–33A The abuses held by the Commission to have been committed in the *European Sugar Cartel* did involve use of the relevant dominant position. In effect, the dominant concern or concerns used its position to bring pressure to impose what the Commission held to be improper conditions.

Raffinerie Tirlemontoise was held to have brought economic pressure on two wholesalers, Exportation de Sucre and Hottelet, to compel them to re-sell only to certain customers and for certain uses. The economic pressure took the form of refusing to supply if the sugar was used for non-permitted uses. In the absence of alternative sources of supply, the wholesalers had, in the Commission's view, to accept the conditions.

The two Dutch producers, Suiker Unie and Centrale Suiker, had brought economic pressure to bear on the three Dutch wholesalers. The pressure consisted, as the Commission saw it, in threats to cut off the wholesalers' trade with the Dutch dairy industry. The purpose of the pressure was to get the wholesalers to agree not to sell their 1969 and 1970 imports of French sugar at prices much below the Dutch producers' prices, to sell some of those imports to the Dutch producers, and not to make any more imports without the producers' consent.

Südzucker Verkaufs was held to have compelled its distributors not to handle sugar from other sources without its consent. At first sight, this would seem to be inconsistent with Regulation 67/67, which permits the distributor to agree to buy only from the principal. In the *Sugar Cartel* case, however, the Commission regarded the imposition of such a term to be an abuse when the principal held a dominant position – perhaps the distinction lies in the possession of a dominant position which enables the principal to impose the condition.

–33B There was a second, somewhat different, abuse held by the Commission to have been committed by Südzucker. This was a loyalty discount of 3DM per tonne if the purchaser bought all his requirements from Südzucker. The Commission regarded it as an abuse for a concern in a dominant position to give a loyalty discount with the object of strengthening and extending that position. The buyers were, in any event, partly dependent upon Südzucker for supplies, so that loss of the discount for a small quantity purchased outside could, in the Commission's view, be a serious disadvantage. Another way of putting the Commission argument would seem to be – "if you do buy from other sources, you will be forced to pay a higher price for the supplies which you have to draw from us".

–33C In *Eurofima,* the Commission regarded it as unreasonable for a buyer inviting tenders for the development of passenger railway-carriages to require the successful tenderer to concede to it an unlimited right to use any patented inventions resulting from the development, without any further payment to the successful tenderer.

As explained in paragraph 16-01A below, the information available is not sufficient to judge the validity of the Commission's attitude. If the successful tenderer was to be paid all the costs of the development, it would seem not unreasonable for Eurofima to have required all rights in the inventions to be assigned to it – it had borne the cost. But if the tenderer was to be paid only for the carriages actually supplied, then the Commission's view would seem to be justified.

Effect upon inter-Member trade

–35 The requirement that there must be an effect upon inter-Member trade must now be regarded in the light of the Court's comments in the *Zoja* case – *v.* 5-37B below.

–37 In its judgment on the *Continental Can* appeal, the Court pointed to an inconsistency in the Commission decision. On the one hand, the Commission regarded Schmalbach and Thomassen as potential competitors, and, on the other hand, it argued that competition between Continental Can's licensees was restricted by reason of the "so-called market information procedure".[14]

5–37A In *European Sugar Cartel,* the Commission regarded the pressure brought by Raffinerie Tirlemontoise and the two Dutch producers, Suiker Unie and Centrale Suiker, on their respective wholesalers as affecting inter-Member trade, in that it limited and in some instances prevented the import of sugar from one Member to another. As regards Südzucker, the Commission merely stated that the ban on distributors handling sugar from other sources without consent and the loyalty discount were capable of affecting inter-Member trade, without explaining how. However, there would presumably have been some effect on that trade, in so far as purchases from producers in other Members were impeded. But some explanation of why that effect was regarded as appreciable should have been given – it does appear that there were other wholesalers who could have imported, and if the producers who were members of the cartel would have refused to sell the prohibition and discount alone might have had little or no effect.

5–37B In *Zoja*, the Commission pointed to exports by that company to France and Germany. There was, therefore, actual and potential inter-Member trade. American Cyanamid had patents in most Members, but those patents had been challenged in Germany and held invalid in France. In those circumstances, cutting off raw material supplies to Zoja could affect inter-Member trade.

On appeal to the Court, the appellants argued that, even if there had been abuse of a dominant position, it would not fall within Article 86 because there was no effect on inter-Member trade. The absence of such effect was, it was submitted, due to two things: first, Zoja sold 90% of its production outside the Common Market, which was becoming less important as a market as tuberculosis became less prevalent; and, second, patents held by American Cyanamid and other companies prevented Zoja selling specialities based on ethambutol. Without dealing with the latter point, the Court rejected the arguments. In so far as it referred to the actual exports by Zoja from Italy to France and Germany, it may be that the Court was right to reject the argument. But in the course of its reasoning the Court made some comments which indicate that the requirement that there must be an effect on inter-Member trade need not be construed narrowly.

[14] *Ibid.* p.228.

The first comment is:

> "This expression is intended to define the sphere of application of Community rules in relation to national laws. It cannot therefore be interpreted as limiting the field of application of the prohibition which it contains to industrial and commercial activities supplying the member-States."[15]

The first sentence may be correct. There has to be a dividing line between Community and national law. If inter-Member trade is not affected, there would seem to be no *locus* for Community law to interfere. Some effect upon inter-Member trade is, therefore, a reasonable pre-requisite for the application of Community law. But the requirement of some effect on inter-Member trade does go beyond defining the sphere of Community law. It does indicate where Community law does not apply. In the absence of any effect upon inter-Member trade, Article 86 is inapplicable. If that is how the first sentence should be interpreted, the second sentence is unobjectionable. Article 86 is not limited to cases of actual supply to other Members. There can be indirect, as well as direct, effects on inter-Member trade.

The Court then continued, and identified impact upon "the competitive structure within the Common Market" as a possible, indirect effect:

> "The prohibitions of **Articles 85** and **86** must in fact be interpreted and applied in the light of **Article 3(f)** of the Treaty, which provides that the activities of the Community shall include the institution of a system ensuring that competition in the Common Market is not distorted, and **Article 2** of the Treaty, which gives the Community the task of promoting 'throughout the Community harmonious development of economic activities'. By prohibiting the abuse of a dominant position within the market in so far as it may affect trade between member-States **Article 86** therefore covers abuse which may directly prejudice consumers as well as abuse which indirectly prejudices them by impairing the effective competitive structure as envisaged by **Article 3(f)** of the Treaty.
>
> The Community authorities must therefore consider all the consequences of the conduct complained of for the competitive structure in the Common Market without distinguishing between production intended for sale within the

[15] [1974] 1 C.M.L.R. p.342.

market and that intended for export. When an undertaking in a dominant position within the Common Market abusively exploits its position in such a way that a competitor in the Common Market is likely to be eliminated, it does not matter whether the conduct relates to the latter's exports or its trade within the Common Market, once it has been established that this elimination will have repercussions on the competitive structure within the Common Market."[16]

This statement of Community law may be valid, provided it is to read as being subject to the qualification that the repercussion on the competitive structure is one which may appreciably affect inter-Member trade, as required by Article 86. But if the repercussion on competitive structure is such that there can be no appreciable effect on trade between Member States, then, on its clear wording, Article 86 cannot apply. If the change in the competitive structure were to eliminate some minor firm in the west of Ireland or Scotland, say, which had never exported and was not likely to export, then Article 86 could not apply.

5–38 In *General Motors Continental*, only five instances of excessive charging were involved. It might have been thought that this would not have been considered likely to have an "appreciable effect" on inter-Member trade. It may be that there was thought to be an effect wider than the particular instances, in the sense that other parallel imports might have been prevented. Or it may be that, in cases where there is held to be an actual abuse of a dominant position, the "appreciable effect" doctrine will not be applied strictly.

Conflict of laws

5–40 As noted in 5-04 above, in its appeal Continental Can argued that it was outside the jurisdiction of the Commission on two grounds. First, its seat was outside the Community; and second, the acts in question were those of its subsidiary, Europemballage. The Court held that the acts of the subsidiary could, in the circumstances, be attributed to the parent, and dismissed that aspect of the appeal. In doing so, however, it delivered itself of the following, typically oracular, remark:

"Community law is applicable to such an acquisition which affects the market conditions within the Community."[17]

[16] *Ibid.*
[17] [1973] C.M.L.R. p.222.

It is not clear what this means. It might be an attempt to confirm the "effects" principle. Or it might mean that it was the change in the market conditions within the Community which attracted Community law. The point is that Europemballage itself was an American company, incorporated in Delaware. Europemballage had an office within the Community and may have been considered to have been within Community law on that ground, or the purchase of the Thomassen shares by Europemballage may have been considered to have taken place within the Community. The vital step, why Europemballage was held to be within Community law, is not dealt with. Consequently, whether the "effects" principle is Community law or not remains uncertain.

-40A The "effects" principle does not appear to have been raised in the *Zoja* appeal. The refusal to supply was by Istitute itself, which was established within the Community. The question of enterprise entity arose because if Commercial Solvents and Istituto did not form one unit, the latter by itself would not have had a dominant position, so the argument ran.

Miscellaneous

-42 Following the Court's decision in *SABAM v. Fonior*, it appears that parties can plead unlawfulness under Article 86 in private litigation before national courts (*v.* 3-56 above). Whether breach of Article 86 itself is sufficient to form the base of a suit for damages remains to be seen.

As regards the United Kingdom, the comment by Lord Denning, Master of the Rolls, has to be kept in mind (*v.* 3-57 above).

-43 It is significant that one of the considerations suggested as calling for a special regulation to deal with mergers was the need for some exemption procedure. The power to grant exemption in cases where mergers may be held to be incompatible with the Community is specifically referred to in the recitals in the draft regulation (*v.* 36-01). This demonstrates how far the interpretation of Article 86 given by the Court in the *Continental Can* appeal departs from the clear "abuse" character of Article 86.

43A One of the issues in *SABAM v. Fonior* was whether SABAM, a private organisation, came within the terms of Article 90(2) of the Treaty (17-14). The Court held that the Article applies only where the state itself in the Member country has entrusted its functions to the body in question. Consequently, SABAM did not come within the Article – in effect, the functions performed by SABAM had been assumed by the body itself or granted to it by its members under its standard terms of membership.

3. Regulation 17

5–45 The fact that the national courts in Member States must enforce Article 86 was made clear in *SABAM v. Fonior*. The dispute was whether SABAM or Fonior held the rights in the words and music of a song. One issue was whether the assignments through which SABAM had acquired its rights from the author and the composer were tainted by breach of Article 86. SABAM was a private professional body set up to enforce the rights of those authors, composers, etc., who joined it – under the terms of membership they had to assign their rights in current and future compositions, SABAM being able to retain those rights for up to five years after termination of membership. It was suggested that the standard terms of membership constituted an abuse of SABAM's dominant position in Belgium. The Commission had already instituted an investigation into SABAM.

The Court ruled that:

> "If abusive practices are exposed, it is for the national court to decide whether and to what extent they affect the interests of authors or third parties concerned, with a view to deciding the consequences with regard to the validity and effect of the contracts in dispute or certain of their provisions."[18]

The court had power to proceed despite the fact that the Commission had instituted its own investigation (*v.* paragraphs 4-07A *et seq.* above).

Termination of infringements

5–46A The abuse in the *Zoja* case was refusal to supply. In its decision the Commission ordered Commercial Solvents and Istituto:

(a) to make an immediate supply of 60,000 kg. of nitropropane or 30,000 kg. of aminobutanol to Zoja at a price no higher than the maximum then being charged by them for those materials;

and (b) to submit within two months proposals for future supplies to Zoja.

In each case, there would be a penalty of 1,000 units per day in the event of failure to comply.

[18] [1974] 2 C.M.L.R. p.285.

On appeal to the European Court, Commercial Solvents and Istituto submitted, first, that the Commission had no power to order specific supplies in this way, and, second, that the supplies ordered went beyond Zoja's requirements for its E.E.C. trade, corresponding rather to the requirements for its world trade.

As regards the first submission, the Court referred to Article 3 of Regulation 17, giving the Commission power to require termination of the infringement. The Court held that this conferred power to require specific acts to be performed, or proposals to be put forward to procure conformity with the requirements of the Treaty. The Commission was, therefore, entitled to order specific supplies.

As regards the second submission, the Court did not consider that the words in Article 86 referring to effect upon inter-Member trade meant that only that effect could be taken into account in defining the infringement or its consequences. If Commercial Solvents/Istituto were ordered to give Zoja only sufficient supplies for its E.E.C. trade, its cost level would be affected. In the circumstances, the Commission could take into account the extent to which the need to maintain the competitive structure, i.e. the maintenance of Zoja as an effective competitor, necessitated the ordering of supplies. The submission was rejected.

It is clear, therefore, that in appropriate cases specific supplies can be ordered.

-46B The Commission has introduced a form, Form C, for use by persons asking the Commission to investigate alleged infringements of Article 86. The form is reproduced in Appendix I.

-49 Article 191 of the Treaty (17-19) requires decisions of the Commission to be notified to the persons to whom they are addressed. They take effect only upon such notification.

In the *Aniline Dyes* case, Imperial Chemical Industries appealed, one of the grounds being that the Commission's decision had not been notified to it, but had been sent to its German subsidiary, which did not have authority to accept service of the decision. The Court held:

> "Irregularities in the procedure of notificiation of a Decision are external to the legal act and therefore cannot vitiate it."[19]

Irregularities might prevent time from beginning to run under Article 173 of the Treaty (17-16), but the Article provided for

[19] [1972] C.M.L.R. p.620.

time to run from when the addressee had knowledge of the decision. In the case of I.C.I., it had knowledge of the decision, and had acted upon it. The grounds of appeal were dismissed.

In the *Continental Can* appeal, it was argued that the decision had reached that company by post, whereas it should have come, so it was suggested, through the diplomatic bag. The Court held that a decision is duly served if it is communicated to the addressee and the latter has been enabled to take notice of it. Those requirements were satisfied as regards Continental Can.

5–50 The decision may also require the parties concerned to supply specific quantities of raw materials, and these are not necessarily limited to the amount needed solely for E.E.C. trade (*v.* paragraph 5-46A above).

In its *GEMA (No. 2)* decision, the Commission varied its first decision in that case, so as to allow the association to introduce a different form of resignation from membership.

5–52 Fines totalling 9,000,000 units of account were imposed by the Commission in the *European Sugar Cartel* case. These were partly in respect of infringements of Article 86. Appeals are pending before the Court.

In *Zoja,* the Commission had imposed a fine of 200,000 units of account. On appeal, the Court reduced it to 100,000 units. The Court agreed that the seriousness of the infringement called for a heavy fine, but the duration of the infringement, about two years, would have been less if the Commission had acted more expeditiously – the Commission had been advised by Zoja within six months of the first refusal of supplies by Commercial Solvents/Istituto. Moreover, supplies had been made available as ordered.

Negative clearance

5–53 The draft mergers regulation (Appendix T) envisages a form of clearance. Below given levels, notification is unnecessary.

Procurement of information

5–58 The comments as regards professional privilege in paragraph 4-79A above should be noted.

Investigations by and on behalf of the Commission

5–61 The comments as regards professional privilege in paragraph 4-79A above should be noted.

Hearings

5–63 Reference is made to paragraph 4-82 above.

Fines and penalties

5–64 Reference is made to the comments in paragraph 5-52 above.

4. Limitation of Actions

5–68 The regulation regarding limitation has now been made. It is Regulation 2988/74 (Appendix S). Under Article 1, the limitation period for procedural infringements is three years, and five years for substantive infringements. The period in respect of enforcement of sanctions is five years – Article 4. There are provisions governing the suspension of the limitation periods, and their interruption.

5. Appeals

5–69 Appeal from a Commission decision lies to the European Court, under Article 177(b) of the Treaty (17-17). By Article 185 (17-18A), appeals do not have suspensory effect, but the Court may order the decision to be suspended, in whole or in part, if it thinks fit.

By virtue of Article 172 of the Treaty (17-15D) and of Article 17 of Regulation 17 (18-18), the Court has power to review fines and penalties imposed by the Commission.

5–70 In *Continental Can* the appeal was successful. The Court held that the Commission had not shown that there was any dominant position in that it had not established that the three commodities in question (light metal containers for meat and for fish, and metal closures) formed separate markets.

In *Zoja*, the appeal as to the substantive issues was unsuccessful, but the Court did reduce the fine from 200,000 to 100,000 units of account.

PART 2
VERTICAL AGREEMENTS

CHAPTER 6
Distribution Agreements

2. Application of Article 85.1

-07 Although it may be unusual for the entire relationship between a principal and a distributor to be in the form of a concerted practice, nevertheless a concerted practice may come into existence as something collateral to the distributorship agreement. In *Pittsburgh Corning Europe,* Pittsburgh Corning Europe S.A., a Belgian company, manufactured cellular glass in Belgium, which was marketed through its distributors Formica Belgium in Belgium and Hertel & Co. in Holland and through its German subsidiary, Deutsche Pittsburgh Corning, in Germany. The prices charged in Germany were considerably higher than those in Belgium and Holland, up to 40% higher. As a result, parallel imports were made, from Belgium and Holland into Germany, estimated to amount to some 11,000 cubic metres in 1970 out of total sales of cellular glass in Germany of about 93,000 cubic metres. To deal with this situation, Pittsburgh Corning Europe prevailed upon Formica Belgium and Hertel to introduce new pricing systems, in 1970. The "normal" price was increased substantially, so that parallel exports to Germany became uneconomic; but a discount of 20% was granted where it could be shown that the glass was to be used on a site in Belgium or Holland respectively. The Commission pointed out that it was inconceivable that Formica Belgium and Hertel would have independently arrived at identical systems and identical prices, nor was the discriminatory pricing system in the interest of either. The Commission ruled that the discriminatory price system was a concerted practice carried out by Pittsburgh Corning Europe and Formica Belgium in the one case, and

Pittsburgh Corning Europe and Hertel in the other. A fine of 100,000 units of account (about £40,000) was imposed upon Pittsburgh Corning Europe for the period prior to notification and application for exemption, about 3 – 4 months. As the system had been introduced at the instigation of and to the advantage of Pittsburgh Corning Europe only, no fine was imposed upon Formica Belgium or Hertel.

Concerted practices in connection with distribution agreements were held by the Commission to obtain in relation to the *Marketing of Potassium Salts.* Kali und Salz had a *de facto* monopoly in Federal Germany and Société Commerciale des Potasses et de l'Azote (S.C.P.A.) a legal monopoly in France. Kali und Salz and S.C.P.A. each appointed the same distributor in Holland (Nederlandse Kali-Import) and the same distributor in Italy (Sali Potassici). S.C.P.A.'s agent in Federal Germany was Henri Vallette, a sub-subsidiary of Kali und Salz. Given the substantial size of Kali und Salz and S.C.P.A., the fact that they had each appointed the same distributors in Holland and Italy necessarily implied an acceptance that they would not compete with each other in those countries; for two such undertakings which should normally be competitors so to eliminate competition between them was a concerted practice. Similarly, Vallette when acting as distributor for S.C.P.A. in Federal Germany could not be expected to follow a sales policy which would conflict with the interests of the group to which it belonged, i.e. to the Kali und Salz group; the appointment of Vallette as S.C.P.A.'s distributor therefore consituted a concerted practice between S.C.P.A. and Kali und Salz.

"Between undertakings"

"Trade representatives"

6–13 It is understood that the Commission has under consideration a draft Directive to Member States aimed at harmonising national laws relating to contracts between agents and their principals. A commercial agent would be defined to include legal persons (companies, etc.,) as well as natural persons. The principal would have to indemnify the agent in respect of legal proceedings relating to royalties, patents, or trade marks applying to the goods or services in question (apparently irrespective of whether the litigation arose from something done by the agent himself or not). If he was to handle payment for the goods or services, the agent would have to be paid a special commission; and an additional commission if he acted as *del credere* agent. The agent would have to be given a commission statement at not more than three-monthly intervals and have the right to inspect the principal's books to check its accuracy. If the principal availed himself of the agent's services to a lesser extent than the "agent could reasonably expect", the agent would have to be paid compensation. The period of notice to terminate the agreement should not be less than two months, rising to twelve months after ten years. Upon termination, the agent "or his heirs" would be entitled to compensation as "clientele allowance", in effect a payment for the goodwill created by the agent. Any term restricting the agent from competing with the principal after termination of the agency relationship could not exceed eighteen months, and during the restriction the agent must be paid compensation.

The main argument for the Directive seems to be that goods must be traded in on the same conditions throughout the Common Market. The legal basis for the Directive is claimed to be Article 57.2 (which relates to pursuit of activities by self-employed persons) and Article 100 (which provides for harmonisation of national laws which affect the establishment or functioning of the Common Market). It may be questioned whether the proposed action is necessary at all, and whether it is valid under the Treaty certainly as regards agents which are corporate bodies. Freedom of action is one element in competition – regulation and regimentation can be just as detrimental when it is governmental as when it is private. Unnecessary, remote, legislation is one of the arguments used by opponents of the Common Market and it is to be hoped that too much ammunition will not be placed in their hands.

—16 The *European Sugar Cartel* case illustrates the Commission's view that the decision whether a distributor is a "trade representative" or not is a question of fact, a question to be decided not by the way the distributor is described in the relevant agreement but by the functions he actually performs. In the western part of Federal Germany some eleven sugar producers were grouped in Westdeutsche Zucker, the largest of the eleven being Pfeifer & Langen. Both Westdeutsche Zucker and Pfeifer & Langen had negotiated commission and agency agreements with the same distributors. They argued that these agreements did not infringe Article 85.1, in that the agents were not autonomous but formed part of the sales organisation of the respective principal. The 1962 Notice therefore applied.

The Commission ruled that the fact that the distributors were described in the agreements as agents or commission-agents did not decide the issue – the real economic function of the distributors had to be considered. In fact, the distributors in question did not work for a single principal. They acted for Westdeutsche Zucker and Pfeifer & Langen (and also other suppliers in some cases); they also sold in the world market, acting more as independent wholesalers. Consequently, they could not be regarded as being integrated into the enterprise of a principal, so as to exclude the operation of Article 85.1. (Instances of distributors acting for two or more principals supplying the same products are discussed in paragraphs 6-07 and 6-650.)

A similar decision, to disregard the words of the contract and to be guided by the economic facts, was taken by the Commission in the *Pittsburgh Corning Europe* case. Pittsburgh Corning in other E.E.C. countries sold through "concessionaries", i.e. independent traders. In Belgium, however, its agreement with Formica Belgium provided that for an initial period the latter would act as an agent only, but on the date when Belgium introduced value added tax, Formica Belgium was to cease being an agent and become an independent trader, i.e. it would trade on its account in Pittsburgh Corning's product. During the initial period the formal consequences of Formica's position as agent were followed – invoices were issued in Pittsburgh's name and Formica was remunerated by a commission. The Commission rejected an argument that, as regards the initial period, the 1962 Notice applied. The position as agent was given to Formica, not as a trial period of training or probation, but for fiscal considerations arising out of the introduction of value added tax; the main part of Formica's turnover during the so-called agency period derived from sale of goods of its own manufacture and of goods which it re-sold under concessions from other suppliers (i.e. in which it acted as a merchant or independent trader). Moreover, Formica was associated with such substantial groups as American Cyanamid and De La Rue, and therefore sufficiently independent and powerful *vis-à-vis* Pittsburgh Corning to have taken an independent line. The Commission concluded that it was impossible to regard Formica Belgium as having an auxiliary function or as being integrated into Pittsburgh Corning's own distribution system.

"Affect trade between Member States"

-21 Examples of agreements and concerted practices relating to principal-distributor relationships are the *Deutsche Philips* and *Pittsburgh Corning* decisions. Deutsche Philips operated resale price maintenance in Germany for its products such as electric shavers and domestic appliances. It had agreements with its distributors at various levels (wholesalers, retailers, etc.) in Federal Germany under which the goods in question could be sold to consumers only at the Federal German r.p.m. price, whether the sale was in that country or in some other E.E.C. country. Moreover, the resale price obligation applied not only to goods bought from Deutsche Philips direct or from its distributors in Federal Germany but also to those bought from foreign suppliers. The agreements were held to affect inter-Member trade.

In the *Pittsburgh Corning* case, the Pittsburgh Corning Europe's distributor in Holland, Hertel, introduced a new price system, a new, increased, "normal" price, but with a reduction of 20% where it was shown that the goods would be used in Holland. The Belgian distributor, Formica Belgium, introduced a similar system for Belgium. The Commission held that the new systems resulted from concerted practices by Pittsburgh Corning Europe with Hertel as regards Holland and with Formica Belgium as regards Belgium. The concerted practices had the object and effect of preventing goods bought in Holland or Belgium from being shipped to and resold in Federal Germany, i.e. parallel imports were effectively stopped.

An illustration of the operation of Article 4.2(1) of Regulation 17 is to be found in *European Sugar Cartel.* Westdeutsche Zucker and Pfeifer & Langen had distribution agreements with the same distributors. The latter were obliged to sell only in their respective territories and to particular customers. They could not handle sugar from other sources without the permission of the other party to the contract, Westdeutsche or Pfeifer & Langen. The Commission regarded this prohibition on handling other sugar as restricting imports and exports, and therefore as taking the agreements outside Article 4.2(1). This seems to be an extension of the Article from agreements, etc., which "relate" to imports or exports, to agreements, etc., which "affect" – but it may be that the agreements in question did specifically refer to imports and exports (the decision is not clear on the point).

-22 In the *Deutsche Philips* case, there was an export ban. Distributors in Federal Germany were prohibited by their agreements with Deutsche Philips from exporting electric shavers. Because export bans "constitute a severe infringement of Article 85", a fine of 60,000 units of account (say £25,000) was imposed, even though Deutsche Philips had not committed the infringement deliberately but through negligence. The Commission's *Third Report on Competition Policy* described this as "(o)nly a relatively small fine" because the Commission was able to regard "the retention of the export ban as a negligent oversight rather than deliberate policy."[1] Another provision in the agreements prevented the German distributors from supplying dealers in other Member States; the German wholesalers could sell to non-German dealers only with permission from Deutsche Philips, and the German retailers could sell only to consumers and could not advertise in publications addressed to other retailers. The Commission regarded these provisions as having the same effect on inter-Member trade as export bans.

"Appreciable effect"

6–25 In the *Pittsburgh Corning* case, the volume of parallel imports into Federal Germany which was stopped by the discriminatory price systems introduced by Hertel and Formica Belgium amounted to about 10% of the total sales of cellular glass in Germany. The companies concerned were substantial. In view of the size of the trade involved and the "flagrant character of the restriction, the latter should be regarded as particularly noticeable, whatever the respective shares of the market of any other comparable products."[2] It would seem that the required degree of effect upon inter-Member trade may be inversely proportional to the gravity of the offence, a more serious infringement requiring a lower effect upon inter-Member trade to be "appreciable" and *vice versa* for a less serious infringement.

"Prevent, restrict or distort competition"

6–27 Several of the provisions in the agreements between Deutsche Philips and its distributors in Federal Germany were held by the Commission to restrict competition. Clearly the export ban on electric shavers, and the requirement that the German r.p.m. price should be observed even on sales outside that country, did so. The re-import price-fixing (i.e. requiring the r.p.m. price to be

[1] Commission of the European Communities. *Third Report on Competition Policy*. Brussels 1974. p.17.

[2] [1973] C.M.L.R. p.D9.

applied to goods bought outside and re-imported into Germany) prevented competition between German retailers.

3. Exemptions

"Block exemption"

-33 The block exemption granted by Regulation 67/67 was extended for ten years, from 31 December, 1972, to 31 December, 1982, by Regulation 2591/71 (*v.* Appendix R).

An example of a distributor agreement which did not qualify for the block exemption is to be found in *Garoche v. Striker Boats.* The parties had entered into an exclusive dealing agreement under which Garoche had the exclusive right to distribute Striker's boats in France and Monaco. Striker sold two boats to a buyer in Monaco through an Italian dealer. Garoche sued for damages in the French courts for breach of the exclusive sales concession. The Cour de Cassation upheld a ruling by the Court of Appeal that the exclusivity clause in the agreement, which had not been notified, did not qualify for exemption under Regulation 67/67 and was null and void under Article 85.

The fact that an exclusive distributor agreement is between parties in the same Member State and concerns only re-sale in that Member does not preclude it from affecting inter-Member trade, as is shown by the *Goodyear Italiana* agreement (*v.* paragraph 6-44A). In that case individual exemption had to be given.

-33A The view taken by the Commission in the *Duro-Dyne* case is important. That exclusive distributor agreement covered the whole Common Market, i.e. Duro-Dyne appointed Europair as its sole distributor in the nine Member States (and also Switzerland and South Africa). The Commission held that the agreement was not within the block exemption granted by Regulation 67/67, as the agreement did not relate to re-sale "within a specific part" of the Common Market.

-34 An example of a distribution agreement between competing producers was that in *Kali und Salz/Kali Chemie.* They were the only two potash producers in Federal Germany. Under the agreement Kali und Salz was to buy and distribute Kali Chemie's output less any quantities required by the company for its own use in the production of compound fertilisers. It appears to have been accepted that the agreement, made in 1970, fell outside Regulation 67/67.

6–38 Articles 4.1 and 5 of Regulation 67/67 dealt with "existing" agreements, i.e. those in existence on 13th March, 1962. Provided the agreement had been notified by 1st February, 1963 and amended before 2nd August, 1967 to comply with the conditions contained in the Regulation, and provided the amendments were notified to the Commission by 3rd October, 1967, the exemption applied not only to the period after amendment but also to the period before amendment. In the case of "accession" agreements, amendment had to be made by 30th June, 1973 (Article 5 as amended).

For all other agreements, i.e. "new" agreements, Article 4.2 applies – exemption runs only from the date the agreement complied with the conditions of the Regulation and in any event not earlier than the date of notification where the agreement was subject to notification. Thus, if an agreement had been made in, say, June 1962 and duly notified when made, and had then been appropriately amended in, say, June 1967, then the block exemption would have applied from June 1967. But, upon an adverse decision by the Commission in respect of the period from June 1962 to June 1967, the parties would have been unprotected and exposed to private suit.

6–39 Similarly, if the agreement confers absolute territorial protection on the distributor, it is outside the exemption. In the *Misal* case, an exclusive distributorship agreement had been notified; in its decision formally requiring the firm to supply information about the agreement, the Commission noted that Regulation 67/67 did not apply because of the absolute territorial protection granted by the agreement. Similar decisions were addressed to 45 other concerns. The same ground for excluding the block exemption figured in the *Optische Werke Rodenstock* decision; similar decisions were issued in relation to 15 other undertakings. In all these instances the Commission was seeking information as to turnover, *inter alia*. It would seem that agreements conferring absolute territorial protection will be condemned, unless there are grounds, other than Regulation 67/67, for holding them to be outside the prohibition in Article 85.1 (for example, because the turnover is so small as to make the agreement of no appreciable effect – *v.* 6-23 – 6-26).

Individual exemption

6–42 The importance of distribution agreements is indicated by the fact that of the 4,353 cases pending on 31st December, 1974, distribution agreements constituted about 39%, the second largest group after licensing agreements (some 50%), according to the *Eighth General Report on the Activities of the European Communities.*

–42A It is noteworthy that three recent Commission decisions granting individual exemption to distribution arrangements use similar language in describing the benefits arising from the arrangements. The *Bayerische Motoren Werke* decision is dated 13th December, 1974, and deals with the standard form of agreements used by B.M.W. with its distributors. B.M.W. undertook not to make direct sales to consumers (with certain exceptions) in its distributors' territories. The Commission considered that "this allows B.M.W. to concentrate its marketing activity, and relieves B.M.W. of the need to maintain a multitude of business relationships".[3] The *Duro-Dyne* decision dealt with an exclusive distribution agreement, in which Duro-Dyne made Europair its sole distributor in the nine Member States (and Switzerland and South Africa) for its products, accessories for use in heating and air-conditioning installations. Europair also made and sold heating and air-conditioning equipment. The Commission commented: ". . . . in this way Duro-Dyne can consolidate the distribution of its production. It is not obliged to maintain numerous business contacts with distributors in the various Member States. . .".[4] In *Goodyear Italiana*, the exclusive distributor agreement related to Italy; Goodyear Italiana was "not obliged to maintain business relations with a large number of intermediaries and buyers".[5] The *Duro-Dyne* and *Goodyear Italiana* decisions are both dated 19th December, 1974.

It does seem that the Commission recognises that the balance of advantage – economic, commercial, and managerial – can in some situations lie against the firm setting up its own selling and distribution system. The balance can be in favour of using some other firm to handle detailed distribution. In effect, this is why, in some trades, distribution is handled by wholesalers who buy in bulk from the manufacturers, and then deal with buyers who require smaller quantities.

–43 The Commission has published in its *Third Report on Competition Policy*[6] some information on the working of the Omega

[3] Official Journal L29. 3.2.75. p.7.
[4] Official Journal L29. 3.2.75. p.12.
[5] Official Journal L38. 12.2.75. p.12.
[6] Brussels 1974. pp.22-3.

Brandt distribution arrangements. Omega appointed only one "general agent" in each country, and each general agent agreed to nominate only a limited number of retailers. There were, therefore, quantitative limitations on the number of distributors, as well as qualitative limitations, i.e. requirements as to professional standards and service. The justification for the quantitative limitations was that removal of the limitation on numbers would so reduce the turnover of each dealer in Omega watches as to make uneconomic the stocking of a wide range of models and active sales promotion. In the three years from the decision in 1970, the differences between the highest and lowest retail prices in each country had narrowed. The price ranges in 1970 lay between 33% and 50%; in 1973 they had dropped to between 4% and 21%.

6–44 Sopelem is party to an agreement with Rank to which the Commission has given exemption. The agreement provides for the relevant products to be sold under two trade marks, "MONITAL" for Sopelem's products and "VAROTAL" for Rank's products. Sopelem is the exclusive distributor of "MONITAL" and "VAROTAL" goods in certain countries, and Rank the exclusive distributor in other countries. Neither party can promote sales or maintain stocks of the relevant products in the other's exclusive distribution countries, and each must forward to the other inquiries and orders from countries in which the latter is the exclusive distributor. But within Common Market countries each can fulfil unsolicited orders from the other's exclusive territory. The whole arrangement is based upon joint research and production, and is discussed in more detail under Chapter 9.

6–44A Because Regulation 67/67 does not apply where the agreement is between firms in the same Member State and concerns only re-sale within that Member, individual exemption had to be given in *Goodyear Italiana*. On 1st May, 1963, Goodyear Italiana entered into an exclusive sales agreement with Euram Italia. The agreement was notified on 7th November, 1963. In its original form, Euram was prohibited from exporting outside Italy, and Goodyear could not sell in Italy either the agreement products or products likely to compete with them. The agreement was later modified so that:

(i) Euram was granted exclusive selling rights in Italy for the product (plastic film under the trade mark "Vitafilm" for packaging foodstuffs) and Goodyear was not to sell the products directly in Italy;

(ii) Euram was not to sell competing goods;
(iii) Euram was to buy certain minimum quantities;
(iv) Euram was not to sell outside the Common Market, but could sell in other Member States;
(v) Euram would not engage in active sales policy, e.g. by advertising or opening branches, in other Member States;
(vi) Euram was free to fix its resale prices.

The Commission regarded (ii) and (v) as having an appreciable effect upon competition. Not only was Euram's freedom restricted but also that of potential suppliers to Euram (affected by (ii)) and of dealers and consumers in other Members who would face limited availability of the product (because of (v)). The effect was appreciable because of Euram's leading position as a supplier of packaging film for foodstuffs, having some 30% of the Italian Market. Inter-Member trade was affected because, without the agreement, trade might have developed differently. The prohibition in (iv) distorted competition within the Common Market, because firms outside the E.E.C. could not buy from Euram for re-sale within the E.E.C. – but this was not likely to be an appreciable effect, because of extra profit margins, etc. Consequently, because of (ii) and (v), the agreement fell within Article 85.1.

As to Article 85.3, Goodyear Italiana operated mainly in the tyre market. Euram marketed a whole range of complementary packaging materials, so that the agreement enabled Goodyear's product to reach an expanding consumer demand without Goodyear having to set up an organisation to deal with a large number of buyers for "Vitafilm". Items (ii) and (iv) would encourage Euram to concentrate on and develop its own territory, and were indispensable to achieving the main advantage, improvement of distribution. Consumers would reap a fair share of the benefits, because Euram would have to take account both of "Vitafilm" reaching Italy from other suppliers and also of competing products. Because the modifications to the agreement to bring it within Article 85.3 were not completed until 7th August, 1973, the exemption operated only from that date, running until 31st December, 1982.

-44B The Commission refused to grant exemption to the agreement between the two companies in *Kali und Salz/Kali Chemie* on the ground that it gave them the possibility of eliminating competition in straight (untreated) potash fertiliser. The two companies were the only German producers of untreated potash, but Kali Chemie specialised in producing compound potash fertiliser, and the agreement permitted it to supply its surplus untreated potash to Kali und Salz for re-sale. The companies appealed, and the European Court annulled the Commission's decision. That decision showed that there was competition between untreated and compound potash. The prices differed, and although sales of compound had increased, untreated fertiliser was still bought – some customers switched from the one to the other and back again. The basis for refusing exemption, elimination of competition, was not justified.

Standard-form agreements

6–46 The *Parfums Marcel Rochas* case was concerned with an "existing" agreement in standard form notified in due time, i.e. by 1st February, 1963. The European Court ruled upon the position of standard-form agreements where the notification was later, in *Brasserie de Haecht v. Wilkin(No. 2).* In that case the agreement was made in 1963 in the standard form used by Brasserie de Haecht but the standard form was not notified until 1969. The European Court held that notification of a standard-form contract operates as notification of all agreements in that form made by the same undertaking, even of those entered into before the notification. But the notification effected in 1969, i.e. outside the time-limits in Articles 5.1 and 7.2 of Regulation 17, could not confer the benefits of those Articles on "existing" agreements not otherwise notified. In short, it may be said that notification of a standard-form contract is good notification for all agreements in that form by the same undertaking, but that the notification operates only from the date it is made, in respect of agreements made prior to notification.

4. Condemned Agreements

Market insulation

6–49 An attempt at market insulation was struck down in *Garoche v. Striker Boats.* Striker had given Garoche an exclusive sales concession for Monaco, France, and other countries. The agreement required Striker not to sell in the concession countries, either directly or indirectly, nor to allow any sales therein on its behalf. Two of Striker's boats were sold in Monaco through an Italian agent, and Garoche sued Striker for damages. The French

Cour de Cassation rejected the appeal by Garoche against the dismissal of its claim. The block exemption under Regulation 67/67 did not apply; the parties had sought to make it difficult for buyers to obtain supplies from other distributors, so that Article 3 applied and excluded the benefit of the exemption. As the Court pointed out, the agreement had resulted in the isolation of the French market and Garoche's prices were not subject to competition. The agreement was prohibited by Article 85.1, and null and void under Article 85.2.

Parallel imports

6–55 An example of an agreement falling outside the block exemption given by Regulation 67/67, because of the operation of Article 3(b) is to be found in the *Garoche v. Striker Boats* case (*v.* 6-49).

Freedom for parallel imports is specifically preserved under Regulation 2779/72, which confers block exemption on specialisation agreements complying with its conditions. By Article 2.1(d) (33–03) exclusive distribution rights may be accorded to the other parties to the agreement provided they do not restrict the possibility of parallel imports.

Where a distributorship agreement merely authorises the distributor to exploit, or does not prohibit him from exploiting, a national requirement in a Member State calling for a certificate of authenticity in respect of imported goods, the agreement is not thereby rendered null and void even if the certificate is less easy to obtain in respect of imports from Member States other than the State of origin. This principle was laid down by the European Court in the *Dassonville* case. The Dassonville firm imported Scotch whisky into Belgium from France. By Belgian law, such imports had to be accompanied by a British customs certificate. The Dassonville imports bore, on the bottles, a reference to the appropriate certificate, but were not accompanied by it. Civil proceedings by the authorised distributors for the brands of whisky in question, and also criminal proceedings, were instituted against the Dassonville firm, which pleaded that the Belgian law was a measure having an effect equivalent to a quantitative restriction on imports (cf. Article 30 – 17-06) and therefore prohibited by the Rome Treaty. The Belgian court referred the question to the European Court, and the United Kingdom government represented to the Court that customs certificates could be obtained, for a small fee, even after the goods had been exported from the United Kingdom. The Court ruled that, where the certificate of authenticity is less easily obtainable for indirect imports from other Member States than for direct imports from the State of origin, the requirement to produce such certificates does constitute a measure having an effect equivalent to a quantitative restriction, and is prohibited by the Treaty. But, as noted above, provided the distributorship agreement goes no further than authorising the distributor to use, or does not prohibit him from using, the national requirement, it does not become null and void thereby.

Pittsburgh Corning Europe case

6–65A The object of the concerted practice in the *Pittsburgh Corning Europe* case was to prevent parallel imports from Belgium and Holland into Germany. Pittsburgh Corning Europe S.A. sold its cellular glass in West Germany through its German subsidiary. Sales in Belgium and Holland were handled by its distributors in those countries. The prices in Germany were up to 40% higher than in Belgium and Holland, with the result that parallel imports occurred from those countries into Germany, amounting in 1970 to some 10,000 cubic metres out of total German sales of about 93,000 cubic metres. To prevent these parallel imports, Pittsburgh Corning Europe prevailed upon its Belgian and Dutch distributors to introduce new, discriminatory, pricing arrangements. Much higher, "normal", prices were introduced such that, with transport costs, imports into West Germany would be uneconomic. But a discount of 20% was granted where it was shown that the glass was to be used in Belgium or Holland.

The object of the concerted practices was to prevent import into and re-sale in West Germany. A fine of 100,000 units of account (about £40,000) was imposed on Pittsburgh Corning Europe.

Deutsche Philips case

6–65B N.V. Philips Gloeilampenfabrieken, of Eindhoven, the Dutch parent company, and its subsidiaries operated standard conditions of sale which included an export ban. Following action by the Commission, the parent company wrote to the Commission, in 1968, saying that the export ban had been deleted so far as exports to Member States were concerned. The West German subsidiary, Deutsche Philips, sent its new terms to the Commission in 1968, in which the export ban related only to exports outside the Common Market. There were, however, other conditions which Deutsche Philips was operating which were not notified to the Commission. These conditions were mainly concerned with protecting the resale price maintenance system in Germany. In respect of electric razors, export from Germany was prohibited. In relation to electric razors and other goods there was re-import price-fixing – goods bought outside and imported into Germany had to be sold at the German r.p.m. prices. There were bans on horizontal trading – wholesalers in Germany were to supply only specialised retailers, and the retailers could supply only consumers.

As regards the re-import price-fixing, the Commission recognised that German retailers could buy outside Germany at lower prices, but this would only increase their profit, because their agreements prevented them from selling below the German r.p.m. price – at the retail stage, the effect was the same as export or re-import bans. The exclusion of horizontal trading prevented wholesalers and retailers in Germany supplying dealers in other Member States, having the same effect as an export ban. A fine of 60,000 units of account (say £25,000) was imposed in respect of the export ban on electric razors from Germany. It will be noted that the other terms – re-import price-fixing and ban on horizontal trading – were regarded as impeding parallel imports and exports in the same way as the export ban itself.

4A. Particular Practices

–65C When explaining the law, it is usually more convenient to start with the law itself, i.e. the explanation follows the lines taken by the law. But the system adopted by the law is not necessarily the system adopted in the business world, and an explanation which is systematic and logical when viewed from the point of view of the law may appear unsystematic and chaotic when approached from the opposite direction, from the particular practices adopted in business. The object of the following paragraphs is to work backwards to the law from particular practices dealt with in the cases.

Collective agreements

–65D These are agreements between a number of independent undertakings by which the parties ordain a distribution network. They may be *unilateral,* where the parties are all at the same level in the economic chain, for example where the parties are all manufacturers of the products in question – a *horizontal* agreement. They may be *reciprocal,* where the parties are at different levels in the economic chain, for example where a group of manufacturers makes an agreement with a group of wholesalers. Reciprocal collective agreements are both *horizontal* and *vertical* – the parties at each level have agreed with each other and with the parties at the other level or levels.

Unilateral agreements

6–65E The Belgian *Gas Water-Heaters* case concerned a unilateral agreement. The parties were three Belgian manufacturers and two importers, having between them over 70% of the Belgian market. The agreement came into force in 1966; for the preceding twenty years there had been a reciprocal exclusive agreement with the Belgian distributors. The agreement prescribed the conditions of sale and the terms on which the members were to sell. Supply on 'sale or return', guarantees for more than one year, and aftersales service on other than the agreed terms, were all forbidden. Buyers were divided into five classes: approved wholesale distributors, having a minimum turnover and minimum floor area; approved distributors of bottled gas; gas and petrol companies supplying bottled gas and appliances; recognised installers; other customers such as builders and contractors. The agreement fixed the basic discount to each class of buyer; in addition, the distributors, gas and petrol companies, and fitters were granted delivery discounts varying with the quantity taken at each delivery; the distributors and gas and petrol companies were also given aggregated rebates increasing with their total annual purchases from all sources (from members as well as non-members). Members were not allowed to sell to dealers other than those in the five classes of customer.

In its decision, the Commission pointed out that the agreement restricted and distorted competition within the Common Market. The members could not supply other dealers, such as large shops, co-operatives, or chain stores. The distributors and gas and petrol companies in the distribution network, as well as the members, were obliged to comply with the allowed discounts and standard conditions of sale – thereby preventing competition through each fixing his own terms and conditions. The aggregated rebate system attracted particular criticism. The level of rebate was not related to any service supplied by the buyer. Moreover, any non-member, such as a manufacturer in another Member State, who wished to enter the Belgian market would have to more than match the discounts allowed by the members in order to interest dealers (the decision does not deal with the possibility of a non-member supplying a dealer excluded from the distribution network). The aggregated rebate system not only distorted competition on the Belgian market but also affected inter-Member trade. The members were required to terminate the standard discounts and conditions of sale, and the aggregated rebate system.

It would seem that agreement by manufacturers upon the technical standards necessary for dealers, distributors, and installers, may not necessarily be ruled out, provided the standards are technically necessary and are applied without discrimination.[7] It may also be that some recognition of the services provided by dealers, etc., may be permitted in the level of discount, where the discount is fixed in relation to the service provided – but it would call for individual exemption under Article 85.3.

Reciprocal agreements

–65F Reciprocal collective agreements usually take the form of obligations on the member manufacturers or importers to supply only the member distributors, and on the member distributors to buy only from the member manufacturers or importers. The Commission in its *Premier Rapport sur la Politique de Concurrence*[8] pointed out that a reciprocal collective agreement of this type forms a closed system of distribution. It divides the market artificially into two parts; on the one hand there is the closed system of the member manufacturers and importers and the member distributors dealing exclusively with each other, and on the other hand the non-member manufacturers and non-member distributors. This division of the market becomes more detrimental where, as is usually the case, the member manufacturers represent the greater part of the national supply and the member distributors the greater part of the national distribution network. By the closed distribution system the greater part of the national market would be closed to manufacturers in other Member States, and buyers would have their freedom of choice limited. Both in that Report and in its *Third Report,*[9] the

[7] Cf. *Third Report on Competition Policy.* p.21.
[8] Brussels 1972. p.36.
[9] At p.21.

Commission referred to the *Convention Faïence* agreement, between a manufacturers' association and a dealers' association. The reciprocal supply and purchase obligations formed a closed system aimed more at securing outlets for the manufacturers than at improving the use and distribution of the products.

The Commission reached a similar conclusion in relation to the Dutch *Stoves and Heaters* agreement, which included manufacturers, importers, wholesalers, and retailers, and related to coal, oil, and gas appliances. The members handled about 90% of the Dutch sales of the agreement appliances. The central office issued lists of approved suppliers and approved retailers. The latter could buy only from the former, and the former could supply only to the latter. The approved retailers could sell only to consumers, i.e. horizontal dealing was prohibited. The retailers were also bound to charge the suppliers' fixed prices, i.e. there was collective resale price maintenance. Fines were imposed for breaches of the agreement, through a system of arbitration hearings and appeals. The agreement, which had been notified in 1962, was terminated, following complaints from two members who were being sued in the civil courts for recovery of fines imposed on them for breaches of the agreement. The Commission formally condemned those parts of the agreement relevant to those civil proceedings, in effect the exclusive dealing and r.p.m. provisions, and also the arbitration provisions. The Commission required the central office to desist from its attempts to recover the fines.

6–65G The *Belgian Central Heating Agreement* was concerned with a system for according approval to central-heating boilers and radiators, with exclusive supply and purchase aspects. The agreement was between the Central Heating Association, representing the manufacturers and sellers of the equipment, and U.B.I.C. representing the installers, and provided for a committee to issue certificates of approval. The conditions for approval included an obligation to sell only to registered installers (some 70% of the market). In return, U.B.I.C. undertook that its members would give preference to the equipment of manufacturers who had accepted the conditions for approval.

The Commission held that the agreement restricted competition by preventing the approved manufacturers from selling to distributors in Belgium, and by preventing non-approved manufacturers from selling to the 70% of installers who were registered. Inter-Member trade was also affected. To procure approval, manufacturers had to submit to regulation by a private organisation, and to overcome artificial obstacles and delays and discriminatory practices. Exemption under Article 85.3 was refused, because the standards to which the approval committee worked were the normal standards of the Belgian Standards Institute, and the qualifications for installers were those already laid down in Belgian legislation.

–65H The association of Dutch wholesalers of sanitary and plumbing ware (GISA) had an agreement with the Dutch manufacturers' association, Fabrisan. The manufacturers undertook to sell their production solely to the GISA members and to non-members who accepted the same conditions; in return, the GISA members had to take a minimum proportion of their requirements from the Fabrisan members, varying from 25% to 75% depending upon the product. Although the GISA/Fabrisan agreement had already been terminated, the Commission condemned the obligation on the GISA members to take minimum percentages of their requirements from the Fabrisan members.

GISA had, however, continued its own price-fixing arrangements. GISA fixed the selling price for each type of article sold by its members, applying a "conversion factor" to the manufacturer's price. The conversion factor increased with the classification of the item into "high turnover", "normal turnover", "low turnover", and "luxury" – the "luxury" group having the highest factor. If the item had been imported and GISA fixed a conversion factor for it, and if that did not bring the selling price up to the price of the equivalent Dutch product, the price of the latter was taken as the selling price – from May 1971 this provision applied only to imports from non-E.E.C. countries. GISA also fixed the conditions of sale for its members, including the discounts to be allowed, including trade, quantity, and purchase discounts; an extra of 10% had to be added to the price where the sale was to a buyer other than the installer. Members had to send to GISA copies of price lists, price circulars, and quotations. These arrangements were all condemned. The GISA price regulation system, and the agreement with Fabrisan, had been adopted by decision of its members in general meeting.

It is interesting to note that, although the GISA price regulation system and the GISA/Fabrisan agreement were in operation after 1962, and had not been notified, no fines were imposed. The Commission commented in its decision that the system and agreement fell within Articles 4.1 and 5.1 of

Regulation 17, but there is no reference to the question of fines. It would seem that they came within Article 4.2(1), and were relieved from the obligation to notify.

6–65I Another reciprocal collective agreement was the *Dutch Sporting Cartridges Agreement.* This was between the suppliers of .22 sporting ammunition and cartridges (the only local manufacturer and some eleven importers) and some 150 retailers. There was also a price notification scheme operated between the suppliers, and a resale price maintenance system operated by the retailers, both of which the Commission considered restricted competition.

Selective distribution net-works

6–65J A selective distribution net-work is one in which the supply of goods or services is confined to certain selected distributors – the goods or services are not allowed to be handled by all distributors who wish to deal in them. The criteria adopted as the basis for selection may be quantitative or qualitative. In the *Omega Brandt* case both quantitative and qualitative criteria operated. The main distributor in each country was to nominate only a limited number of concessionaires, according to the expected turnover in each area, so that each concessionaire should have an adequate level of business to justify carrying stocks – a quantitative limitation. To be appointed, concessionaires had also to satisfy certain objective professional standards – a qualitative limitation.

Such limitations are likely to be held contrary to Article 85.1 as restricting competition. Where the criteria cannot be objectively justified, they will be condemned. In the Belgian *Gas Water-Heaters* case (6-65E), dealers such as large shops, co-operatives, and chain stores were excluded; in the *Convention Faïence* case, general contractors and public authorities were both excluded from the types of customers who could be approved. These were both collective agreements, and were condemned.

Because of the conditions in the perfumery industry, the Commission took the view that the amended agreements in the *Perfumery Manufacturers* case did not call for action under Article 85.1. The case concerned two manufacturers, Parfums Christian Dior and Lancôme. Each manufacturer had its own selective distribution network based on exclusive franchises. Each firm had an exclusive franchise contract with its general agent in each country, each general agent in turn making distribution contracts with the retailers in his area. The approved retailers were limited on a qualitative basis (professional qualifications, class and siting of shop, etc.) and partly on a quantitative basis to adapt the number of outlets to the size and purchasing power in the vicinity. But the two manufacturers concerned accounted for only relatively small market shares in each of the E.E.C. countries. There were also a large number of competing concerns. On this basis the Commission concluded that there was no need to intervene, but the two manufacturers were told that the Commission would check to make sure that the admission or exclusion of qualified retailers from each distribution system was not based on arbitrary decisions nor a disguised means of reducing competition in intra-Community trade. Obligations on the retailers to maintain resale prices even for re-imported or re-exported articles, to supply only ultimate customers, and to obtain supplies only from the general agent in their country, were removed at the Commission's request.

-65K Exemption under Article 85.3 or negative clearance has been given to a number of selective distribution systems adopted by individual manufacturers. The *Omega Brandt* case has already been mentioned. In the *Kodak* case, the conditions of sale required that the goods should be sold only by trained personnel and on suitable premises – provided the retailer satisfied the requirements, neither Kodak nor the wholesaler could refuse to supply; negative clearance was given.

The Commission proposed to adopt a favourable decision (presumably individual exemption under Article 85.3) in respect of the *SABA* distribution system. SABA was a West German supplier of radio and television receivers, etc. It had concessionaires in each of the three Benelux countries, with each of whom it had an exclusive agreement; it also had agreements with its wholesalers, in Germany, and its retailers, throughout the whole of the Common Market. Under the agreements, each SABA concessionaire and wholesaler could supply any other SABA dealer and any consumer, except that, because of the German r.p.m. system, the German wholesalers were prohibited from selling to consumers. The retailers could supply, on their national markets, only consumers, but could supply any other SABA dealer in other Member States. Retailers could become SABA retailers if they satisfied certain qualitative requirements – an establishment specialising in the products in question, maintenance of a range of SABA products, willingness to enter into the standard SABA agreement, ability to give technical advice and guarantees with after-sales service, etc.

The Commission granted exemption under Article 85.3 to the *Bayerische Motoren Werke* (B.M.W.) distribution system. This had both quantitative and qualitative aspects. The system was based on standard forms of contract between B.M.W. and its selected distributors, under which the latter were required to conclude standard-form agreements with retailers selected by B.M.W. As each distributor and retailer was the sole appointee in his territory, there was a quantitative limitation. Each dealer (using that term to include both distributors and retailers) was obliged not to operate depots or branches or seek business in the territory of any other dealer, and also not to handle competing products without B.M.W.'s consent. The qualitative requirements on all dealers included the following – standard of equipment, management, service department, and after-sales service, all to be to B.M.W.'s requirements, maintenance of sufficient stocks, and grant on re-sale of the appropriate guarantee. Each dealer had to supply B.M.W. with information as to sales trends, etc. On its side, B.M.W. undertook to supply its goods to its dealers, to guarantee those goods, and not to sell or deliver directly in their territories (with certain excepted categories such as public authorities and fleet operators, etc.). The Commission regarded the system as improving sales and servicing and granted exemption for five years, up to 31st December, 1977.

A somewhat different situation obtained in the *Duro-Dyne* case. Duro-Dyne Corporation of New York made accessories such as valves, couplings, electric welding equipment, etc. for heating and air-conditioning installations. Europair, in Belgium, not only manufactured but also imported and exported heating and air-conditioning equipment. Duro-Dyne appointed Europair its exclusive general distributor for the nine Member States (and also Switzerland and South Africa). Europair bought and re-sold on its own account, and was free to fix its own re-sale prices. It had to maintain an adequate stock and ensure satisfactory sales service. Europair distributed its goods (including the Duro-Dyne products) through exclusive dealers in each Member State – these agreements the Commission regarded as coming within the block exemption given by Regulation 67/67. The Commission did not regard the Duro-Dyne/Europair agreement itself as coming within Regulation 67/67, because it covered the whole of the Common Market, not a "specific part" of the Market. But the Commission granted individual exemption under Article 85.3. The items handled constituted a wide range of technical products, small accessories for heating and air-conditioning installations. The Duro-Dyne range complemented and supplemented the Europair production. The agreement improved distribution of the products in the Common Market. There remained sufficient outside competition to ensure that consumers received a fair share of the benefits; and, although direct exports by Duro-Dyne to the E.E.C. had to be through Europair, indirect exports to the E.E.C. were not precluded (i.e. imports into the E.E.C. of supplies sold by Duro-Dyne to firms outside the Common Market, and re-sold by them).

In these three cases it would seem that the benefits of selectivity outweighed the disadvantages.

-65L In the *Deutsche Philips* case, the element of selectivity appeared to have been aimed, not at improved distribution, but at maintenance of the r.p.m. system in Germany. Deutsche Philips' wholesalers and retailers in West Germany were forbidden to export Philips' electric shavers. The wholesalers were obliged to confine their supplies of large domestic appliances, television sets, and shavers to specialised retailers, and the retailers could sell only to consumers – i.e. there was a ban on horizontal trading both at the wholesale and retail levels. Wholesalers could not sell direct to consumers – ban on direct sales. And retailers could not sell to wholesalers – ban on reverse trading. To the extent that they applied to inter-Member trade, these restrictions were condemned by the Commission as falling within Article 85.1, i.e. both restricting competition and affecting inter-Member trade.

Merger of distribution net-works

-65M In the *SHV/Chevron* case, the agreements were between Chevron-Oil Europe and Steenkolen ("SHV"). A joint company, Calpam N.V., was set up in Holland, each party holding half of the capital. Through Calpam N.V., joint subsidiaries were established in Germany, Denmark, and the Benelux countries. The independent distribution systems of each party in those five countries were transferred to Calpam, so that for the products in question the parties' distribution systems were merged.

The Commission granted negative clearance. Neither party held a dominant position, so that Article 86 did not apply. As to Article 85, the agreement contained no clause restricting competition between Chevron and SHV in areas other than those covered by the joint subsidiaries. In those areas, the parties had agreed not to compete with each other without the other's consent. But

SHV would disappear as an independent distributor of the products, and Chevron would have no industrial or commercial incentive to compete with companies in which it held 50% of the capital. There was a provision that Chevron would fix the price of asphalt sold by the Calpam subsidiaries, but only Chevron of the two parties had previously sold asphalt. The Commission therefore concluded that the agreement did not infringe Article 85.1 – presumably because there was in fact no restriction of competition by virtue of those provisions of the agreement.

Distribution through competitors

6–65N Distribution through competitors has been condemned in two cases. In *Marketing of Potassium Salts*, the French Société Commerciale de Potasses et de l'Azote appointed Henri Vallette as its agent in West Germany, Vallette being a subsidiary of Kali und Salz. This the Commission held to be a concerted practice, and required the parties to terminate it. Similarly, the agreement by which Kali und Salz marketed the available supplies of potash from Kali Chemie was also condemned by the Commission but allowed by the Court on appeal – the agreement had not permitted the parties to eliminate competition, and it therefore qualified for exemption under Article 85.3.

In the *European Sugar Cartel* case, the Commission found that the Italian producers bought supplies of sugar direct from the French, Belgian, and German producers. The deliveries were allocated between the suppliers on a quota basis. Deliveries by the suppliers to other purchasers in Italy were only made at higher prices. This had the effect of eliminating from the Italian market all competition by the French, Belgian, and German producers – without the concerted practice, in the Commission's view, they would have sold their sugar separately in Italy through their own separate channels. For this, and other activities, the Commission imposed substantial fines. An appeal to the European Court is pending.

A different view was taken by the Commission in the *Duro-Dyne* case, an exclusive distributor agreement covering the whole of the Common Market. Duro-Dyne, an American company, making valves and other accessories for heating and air-conditioning installations, appointed Europair its sole distributor for the nine Member States (and also Switzerland and South Africa). Europair also made heating and air-conditioning equipment. The products were technical items, and the

Commission considered that the agreement improved distribution, Europair's range being complemented and supplemented by Duro-Dyne's range of several hundred varied articles.

Distribution through joint agents

–650 Situations where competitors have sold their products through joint agents have also been condemned. Just as a man cannot serve two masters, God and Mammon, so no agent can compete with himself and sell for two principals. Whereas in the Biblical context he would love the one and despise the other, in the commercial context he might serve the interests of both by suppressing competition. And no competitor, if he were seeking to compete with his rival, would entrust the marketing of his goods to that rival's agent.

The *Nederlandse Cement-Handelmaatschappij* (N.C.H.) was a joint company set up in Holland by a number of German cement manufacturers. Those manufacturers and 12 other German cement manufacturers marketed their products in Benelux through N.C.H. There was a bilateral common-form agreement between N.C.H. and each of its suppliers. The agreement appointed N.C.H. as the exclusive distributor for the suppliers in Benelux, and required N.C.H. to market the supplies at uniform prices and conditions of sale. N.C.H.'s total sales were allocated between the 36 suppliers according to agreed quotas – each supplier was both entitled and obliged to meet his quota. In effect, N.C.H. was the joint distributor for its 36 principals. The Commission argued that, underlying the bilateral agreements, were three unwritten 'base' agreements – first, an agreement between the suppliers not to apply different prices and conditions, second, an agreement as to the quotas, and third, an agreement not to make direct sales in Benelux. These agreements, and the restrictions in the bilateral agreements, were held to restrict competition and affect inter-Member trade. Exemption was refused, and the agreements and restrictions condemned.

In the *European Sugar Cartel* case, some of the distributors worked both for Westdeutsche and Pfeifer & Langen. The agreements bound the distributor to sell only in his area and to particular customers, and not to handle sugar from other suppliers except with the consent of the principal, i.e. imports and exports were prohibited. The distributors could not be regarded as trade representatives under the Notice relating to Sole Agency Contracts (Appendix C), and as imports and exports were controlled, the relief from the obligation to notify given by Article 4.2(1) of Regulation 17 (18-05) was not available. The agreements were condemned because of the restrictions on imports and exports.

In *Marketing of Potassium Salts,* the Commission found that Kali und Salz and Société Commerciale des Potasses et de l'Azote had each appointed the same distributors both in Holland and in Italy. The Commission regarded the joint appointment of the same distributor as implying an agreement between the principals not to compete, having the same effect as a concerted practice to prevent or restrict competition. The principals were required to cease selling through the same distributors.

To sum up – in the absence of special circumstances, where competitors use the same distributor the Commission will hold that there is either an implied agreement or a concerted practice to restrict or prevent competition. Given that the effect on competition is appreciable, and that there is also an appreciable effect on inter-Member trade, the agreement or concerted practice will be considered to come within the prohibition in Article 85.1.

Absolute territorial protection

6–65P Attempts to create absolute territorial protection, i.e. to prevent all parallel imports, have fallen foul of Article 85.1. The classic case was *Grundig/Consten,* in which the French trade-mark registration was, by agreement, in Consten's name, so that Consten could bring proceedings against other importers for infringement of the "GINT" mark. The restrictions on parallel imports were struck down by the Commission and the European Court. In the *Béguelin* case, the Court, on a reference from the French court, held that a distributorship agreement would fall within Article 85.1 if the distributor could prevent parallel imports.

In *Pittsburgh Corning Europe,* the attempt to provide absolute territorial protection for its German subsidiary – by arranging for its distributors in Belgium and Holland to charge discriminatory higher prices for export sales – resulted in a fine of 100,000 units of account (say £40,000) on Pittsburgh Corning. Because of the clauses in the distributorship agreement conferring absolute territorial protection, Garoche was unable to sue Striker Boats for breach of contract because of deliveries in the territory assigned to Garoche (*Garoche v. Striker Boats*).

On account of the absolute territorial protection which they granted, the Commission held some 62 exclusive distributorship agreements to fall outside the block exemption in Regulation 67/67 (*Misal* and *Optische Werke Rodenstock* decisions). These concerned a wide range of industries, including foodstuffs, aircraft construction, film equipment, electrical equipment, watches and clocks, and industrial vehicles.[10]

Export bans

–65Q Prohibition of exports to other Member States strikes at the very essence of the Common Market. The Commission will object to them in distributorship and other agreements unless there are grounds for granting exemption. For example, total bans on exports in the agreements in the *Bayerische Motoren Werke* and *Goodyear Italiana* cases were amended so as to allow exports to other Member States.

The fact that the export ban is ancillary to a resale price maintenance scheme is not sufficient to protect it. The export bans in *Du Pont de Nemours (Deutschland)* on photographic equipment and in *Deutsche Philips* on electric shavers were included in the standard conditions of sale as part of the r.p.m. systems, but were removed in the former, and condemned in the latter, case. An export ban was included in Sperry Rand's agreement with its German distributors as part of the resale price maintenance arrangements for Remington razors, electric clocks, etc. It was removed at the Commission's request.

In the *AEG-Telefunken* case, that company had prohibited its German distributors from selling domestic electric appliances in Holland, on the ground that appliances for sale in Germany did not conform to the safety requirements in Holland. But as all domestic electric appliances sold in Holland had to conform to the safety regulations and other legal standards in force there, no matter where the appliance in question was manufactured, the ban on exports by the German distributors was removed, at the Commission's request.

Exclusive dealing

–65R The disallowance of absolute territorial protection and export bans is aimed at removing impediments against parallel imports. But it is quite permissible for the parties to provide for exclusive dealing *as between* themselves. Regulation 67/67 recognises this in Article

[10] *Second Report on Competition Policy.* p.51.

1 – the principal can undertake to supply only the distributor, and the distributor to buy only from the principal, in the agreement territory (23-02). In the *Goodyear Italiana* case, Goodyear was prohibited from selling directly in Italy; and in the *Bayerische Motoren Werke* case, B.M.W. undertook, *vis-à-vis* its distributors, not to sell directly in their areas (except for certain customers such as fleet operators, etc.), and the distributors undertook, *vis-à-vis* the retailers, not to appoint any other retailers in their areas.

Prohibition on seeking business

6–65S Although a ban on the distributor exporting outside his territory is unlikely to be allowed, it is permissible to prohibit him from actively seeking business outside it, and from establishing branches and depots. Article 2.1(b) of Regulation 67/67 makes this clear.

In the *SABA* case, the exclusive distributors in the Benelux countries were under an obligation not to carry out any publicity or establish any subsidiary or distribution depot outside their respective territories. Similarly, B.M.W.'s distributors and retailers could not advertise or operate a branch or depot outside their respective territories. And in the *Goodyear Italiana* case, while Euram was free to sell anywhere in the Common Market, it was not to engage in an active sales policy outside Italy, by advertising or setting up branches or depots. In *SABA*, the Commission proposed to take a favourable decision; in the other two, exemption was given.

It would seem that, although a prohibition on the distributor seeking business outside his territory will be regarded as a restriction of competition, the Commission may regard it favourably as encouraging the distributor to concentrate his efforts in his territory.

Prohibition on handling competing products

6–65T He can, however, be bound not to handle competing products. Such a term is permissible in an agreement within the block exemption under Regulation 67/67 (*v.* Article 2.1(a)). The B.M.W. retailers were required not to sell competing products, but that did not prevent the Commission from granting exemption – the dealers were thereby forced to concentrate in their own areas. In the *Goodyear Italiana* case, however, the obligation on Goodyear not to make direct sales in Italy of products similar to, and likely to compete with, the agreement products was modified so as to relate only to the agreement products themselves.

Ban on direct supplies

—65U In some cases, the distribution system has included prohibition of direct supplies, e.g. by a wholesaler to a consumer, bypassing the retailer. This was the situation in *Deutsche Philips* where there was, under Deutsche Philips r.p.m. and distribution arrangements, a ban on supplies by wholesalers to consumers. The Commission held that the ban infringed Article 85.1 to the extent that it affected inter-Member trade.

It would seem, therefore, that such a prohibition is in order where it is confined to trade within the Member. The *SABA* arrangements provided that, in Germany, the wholesalers only had the right to sell to retailers, because of the r.p.m. system. The Commission apparently did not object to this. In the *Sperry Rand* case, which also concerned an r.p.m. system in Germany, the German wholesalers were not allowed to supply *any other* wholesalers nor any ultimate customers, without consent; the Commission objected to those terms, presumably because the restriction was not confined to Germany.

Ban on horizontal dealings

—65V Distribution arrangements have included prohibitions on horizontal dealings, i.e. by wholesaler to wholesaler, and retailer to retailer. These were present in the *Deutsche Philips* case. The wholesalers could supply only specialised retailers, so that they could not sell to other wholesalers or intermediate dealers. Similarly, the retailers could sell only to consumers, preventing them from selling to wholesalers. Both prohibitions were held by the Commission to infringe Article 85.1 to the extent that they affected inter-Member trade. There had been similar bans on horizontal dealings in the *Du Pont de Nemours (Deutschland)* case, but these were removed on representations from the Commission, and also in *Sperry Rand*.

It would seem, however, that such terms are permissible where they apply only within one Member State, as in such circumstances there would be no effect upon inter-Market trade. For example, the *SABA* retailers were required, within their own national market, to sell only to consumers, although there was no restriction on their sales in other Member States.

Ban on reverse dealing

—65W A ban on reverse dealing is, for example, one which prevents a retailer selling to a wholesaler. There was such a ban in the *Deutsche*

Philips case, held by the Commission to infringe Article 85.1 in so far as inter-Member trade was concerned. In *Sperry Rand* and *Perfumery Manufacturers,* the retailers were obligated to sell only to ultimate consumers, without restriction; the Commission regarded these as equivalent to indirect export bans and required their deletion, presumably because the retailers were not free as regards sales in other Members.

But if the ban does not affect inter-Member trade, it appears to be permissible. In *SABA,* the retailers could sell, in their national markets, only to consumers, i.e. ruling out reverse dealing; but they were free to sell to any buyer in other Members.

Price fixing

6–65X In the *Deutsche Philips* case, the company operated an r.p.m. system in Germany, and its price-fixing and distribution agreements bound dealers to re-sell only at the prices fixed by the company. In so far as it affected inter-Member trade, this was held to infringe Article 85.1.

Of course, where the distributor is truly the *agent* of the principal, i.e. selling on behalf of, and for the account of, the principal, the latter may fix the selling price. In this situation there is no re-sale by the agent – the goods remain the property of the principal until the agent sells them for the principal, when the property passes to the buyer.

Re-import price fixing

6–65Y The price-fixing provision in the *Deutsche Philips* case applied not only to supplies bought in Germany, but also to supplies re-imported into Germany. That aspect of the price fixing was condemned as infringing Article 85.1. A similar provision was eliminated from the standard conditions in the *Du Pont de Nemours (Deutschland)* case.

Maintenance of stocks

6–65Z In the *Duro-Dyne* and *Bayerische Motoren Werke* cases, there were obligations on the distributors to maintain sufficient stocks. In *SABA,* the obligation was to maintain as full a range as possible of SABA products. The Commission accepted these terms.

Professional standards

6–65AA Obligations as to technical competence, provision of adequate premises, etc., have been accepted by the Commission in a number of cases. In *Bayerische Motoren Werke*, the equipment, layout, and technical and commercial management had to be to B.M.W.'s requirements. In *SABA*, the requirements related to the size and character of the premises, ability to give technical advice, etc.

It is important, however, that such requirements should not be applied in a discriminatory manner, i.e. all distributors wishing to become distributors and having the requisite standards should be equally free to enter the system (unless there is some quantitative limit on numbers, in which case individual exemption will be required as in *Bayerische Motoren Werke*).

After-sales service, guarantees

-65BB In the *SABA* and *Bayerische Motoren Werke* cases, the distributors were obliged to provide after-sales service, including service under the relevant guarantees. The Commission allowed these terms in the latter case, and seems prepared to do so in the former.

A different aspect of after-sales service figured in *Constructa.* Constructa GmbH. was a subsidiary of the German Siemens company. On the Commission's intervention, Constructa arranged that Siemens S.A. in Brussels would service Constructa domestic appliances wherever bought if the owner could not obtain servicing elsewhere in Belgium or Luxembourg.

Supply of information

-65CC There were obligations on the distributors to supply information to the principal in the *Duro-Dyne* and *Bayerische Motoren Werke* cases. The information to be supplied included sales quantities, number of customers, sales trends, market situations, stocks, expected demand, etc. No objection was raised by the Commission to these terms.

CHAPTER 7
Resale Price Maintenance

2. Application of Article 85 to r.p.m.

7–10 Where there is no effect upon inter-Member trade, a re-sale price maintenance system will be outside Article 85.1. For example, in the *SABA* case, so far as Germany was concerned, the wholesalers were allowed to sell only to the retailers, i.e. not directly to consumers, as part of the r.p.m. system. But for sales outside Germany, they were free to sell to consumers. Similarly, the retailers in Germany (and also in other countries) were allowed to sell only to consumers, so preventing them from selling to other retailers or wholesalers – but that restriction applied only as regards sales in their national markets, they being free in other countries to sell to anyone. These restrictions applying only within Member States were apparently acceptable to the Commission, which proposed to take a favourable decision on the SABA agreements. The Dutch court enforced a re-sale price obligation between a Dutch importer and a Dutch retailer in the *Melitta* case. The retailer was re-selling the absorbent paper below the fixed price. There was no evidence of effect on inter-Member trade, and the court ordered the retailer to stop selling below the r.p.m. price. Conversely, in the *Deutsche Philips* case, the agreements between Deutsche Philips and its German retailers bound the latter to apply the fixed re-sale prices to all sales, whether within Germany or in other Members. The price-fixing obligation was condemned in so far as it affected inter-Member trade.

In short, the fact that r.p.m. is permissible and legally enforceable in a Member State does not mean that actions to support the r.p.m. system, but which infringe Article 85.1, are thereby justified. The Deutsche Philips agreements required its

German retailers to apply the fixed re-sale prices even to goods bought in other Members and re-imported into Germany. This re-import price fixing was condemned. In the *Du Pont de Nemours (Deutschland)* case, the company removed a re-import price-fixing obligation on representations from the Commission.

-12 The *ASPA* case was an instance of *collective* r.p.m., i.e. where the obligation is imposed, not *vertically* by the manufacturer imposing it on his distributors, but *horizontally* by agreement between manufacturers or between distributors. The ASPA agreement was between the manufacturers and distributors collectively. Similarly, in the *Dutch Sporting Cartidges* case, the agreements imposed a collective obligation on the Dutch retailers to maintain the prescribed minimum re-sale prices; the agreements were between the retailers, represented by their association, and the twelve cartridge suppliers who included one manufacturer in Holland and six in other Member States, so that inter-Member trade was affected. The agreements were terminated on the Commission's intervention.

CHAPTER 8
Intellectual Property

1. Introduction

8–04 The European Patent Convention was signed on the 5th October, 1973, but is not yet in force (*v.* 8-11A). A Draft Convention for a European Patent for the Common Market has also been prepared (*v.* 8-11B).

A Draft Convention for a European Trade Mark Law has been prepared by officials of the Commission, and was published in 1973 (*v.* 8-52A).

8–08 Since paragraph 8-08 was written, there have been a number of cases, the most important being *Hag* and *Centrafarm.* The lines of the European Court's approach have now become much more clear.

The first hurdle which the Court had to surmount was Article 222 of the Treaty – "This Treaty shall in no way prejudice the rules in Member States governing the system of property ownership" (17-20). Taken at its face value, that Article removes intellectual-property rights from the ambit of the Treaty and, therefore, of the Court. The Court avoided that difficulty by distinguishing between the *existence* of intellectual-property rights and the *exercise* of those rights. Thus, in the *Grundig/Consten* case, the Court argued that the Commission's decision, against which Grundig and Consten were appealing, did not affect the *grant* of trade-mark rights, but did limit their *exercise.* The distinction between the *existence* of intellectual-property rights, which is not affected by the Treaty, and the *exercise* of those rights, which is governed by the Treaty, was applied by the Court and further developed in the *Deutsche Grammophon, Sirena, Hag,* and *Centrafarm* cases.

Having thus brought the *exercise* of intellectual-property rights within the area governed by the provisions of the Treaty, the Court had no further problem as regards Article 85. Where the exercise of those rights involved an agreement (or a decision of an association, or a concerted practice) Article 85 could apply if the agreement, etc., fell within its scope. The trade-mark agreement between Grundig and Consten could, therefore, be struck by the prohibition in Article 85.1. In the wording adopted in the *Sirena* and *Centrafarm* cases, Article 85 may apply whenever the exercise of intellectual-property rights is "the object, the means, or the consequence, of an agreement".[1] Equally, Article 86 could apply to the exercise of intellectual-property rights if the conditions required by the Article were satisfied – this is implied by the Court's comments in the *Sirena* and *Deutsche Grammophon* cases.

However, there remained the possibility that intellectual-property rights might be exercised in situations where there was no agreement and no dominant position. For example, the same firm might own parallel patents, protecting the same invention, in both Member A and Member B; if the national patent laws of Member A permitted the firm to prevent imports into A of goods put on the market by the firm itself in Member B under the patent in Member B, the firm, by exercising its patent rights, could partition the markets in the two Members – without any question of an agreement or of a dominant position. And Article 36 would seem to preclude interference by Community law: "The provisions of Articles 30 to 34 shall not preclude prohibitions or restrictions on imports, exports or goods in transit justified on grounds of . . . the protection of industrial and commercial property. Such prohibitions or restrictions shall not, however, constitute a means of arbitrary discrimination or a disguised restriction on trade between Member States" (17-08). The Court overcame this obstacle by a pincer movement. First, it decided that Article 36 supports the view that intellectual-property rights are affected by the Treaty provisions, and that the Article protects only those rights which are the "specific object" of the intellectual property (*Deutsche Grammophon, Hag,* and *Centrafarm*). Secondly, it conjured up the principle of the "free movement of goods in the Common Market" to use the language of the *Deutsche Grammophon* and *Centrafarm* cases,[2] or the "free circulation of goods" in the *Hag* case.[3] In effect, the exercise of his rights by the

[1] [1971] C.M.L.R. p.274; [1974] 2 C.M.L.R. p.506.
[2] [1971] C.M.L.R. p.657; [1974] 2 C.M.L.R. p.504.
[3] [1974] 2 C.M.L.R. p.143.

owner of parallel patents to prevent parallel imports of goods put on the market by himself or with his consent, was not part of the "specific object" of his patent rights and would be incompatible with the principle of the "free movement" or "free circulation" of goods in the Common Market (*Centrafarm*). The same conclusion was reached as regards rights analogous to copyright (*Deutsche Grammophon*); and also as regards trade-mark rights where the trade marks in both Members derived from a common source (*Centrafarm* and *Hag*).

The reasoning adopted by the Court to reach these ends is anything but satisfactory, and is examined critically in the Annexe to this Chapter (8-91 to 8-149 below).

8–08A Despite the clear shortcomings of the reasoning by which the Court has arrived at its conclusions, the cases referred to in 8-08 above must, at least for the time being, be regarded as correctly stating Community law. In the light of those cases, the principles of Community competition law of general application to intellectual-property rights may be summarised as follows:

Abuse of dominant position

The position here has not changed. The mere holding of intellectual property does not of itself constitute a dominant position within Article 86. There must be the ability to prevent effective competition in a substantial part of the Common Market taking into account similar goods or substitutes (*Sirena, Deutsche Grammophon* cases).

The charging of a higher price for the protected article as compared with similar non-protected goods is not of itself proof of abuse within Article 86. But it may be proof of abuse if the price difference is substantial and cannot be justified objectively (*Parke Davis, Sirena, Deutsche Grammophon* cases).

Exercise of rights not involving agreement, etc., – parallel imports

This is the situation where the intellectual-property rights are being exercised in such a way that no agreement (or decision of association, or concerted practice) is involved – for example, the use of patent rights in one Member to keep out imports from another Member.

There are three separate possibilities – first, where the intellectual-property rights in both countries are held by the same person or group i.e. parallel rights; second, where they are held by different persons, i.e. they are not in the same hands; and third, where there are rights in the importing Member, but not in the exporting Member. The position is as follows:

(i) Parallel rights

The expression "parallel rights" relates to the situation in which the rights in the exporting Member and in the importing Member are held by the same person. Where the goods were put on the market in the exporting Member by the owner of the rights, or with his consent (e.g. by a licensee), he cannot use his rights in the importing Member to prevent those imports (parallel imports) – (*Centrafarm, Cinzano,* and *Castrol* cases). (In practice, that will be the usual situation – if the goods were put on the market in the exporting Member by a third person without the consent of the owner of the intellectual-property rights, there will usually be infringement of those rights.) Where the rights are held by different members of the same group, such as a parent company in one Member and its non-autonomous subsidiary in the other Member, it would seem that the same principle applies – the rights cannot be used to exclude the parallel imports; this is implied in the *Centrafarm* judgment, the imports can be kept out only where the owners of the rights are "legally and economically independent of each other"[4] – in effect, the enterprise-entity doctrine.

The use of the rights in the importing Member to prevent such parallel imports is not, in the Court's view, part of the "specific object" of the rights, and therefore not protected by Article 36. Consequently, where the national patent laws in the importing Member do not recognise the exhaustion of rights doctrine, to allow those laws to be used to stop parallel imports would be "incompatible with the rules relating to the free circulation of goods".

There is, however, the problem of imports from a non-Member (*v.* 8-08B).

[4] [1974] 2 C.M.L.R. p.503.

(ii) Rights separately owned

Where the rights in the exporting and the importing Member are held by different persons "legally and economically independent of each other", i.e. where the imported goods have not been put on the market by or with the consent of the owner of the rights in the importing Member, he can use any right given by the law of the importing Member to prevent the imports (*Centrafarm*).

But where, although the rights are separately owned, they share the same origin or source, i.e. they were once in common ownership from which the separate ownership has devolved, the rights cannot be exercised so as to stop the imports (*Sirena, Hag*). This is so even where ownership in one Member does not rest upon a chain of voluntary assignments, but is dependent upon a non-voluntary devolution, such as sequestration (*Hag*).

(iii) Rights in importing Member, none in exporting Member

Where the goods have been put on the market in the exporting Member by some third party, i.e. not by the owner of the rights or with his consent, he can exercise his right to prevent the imports (*Parke Davis, Centrafarm*). But where the goods were put on the market in the exporting Member by the owner of the rights, or with his consent, he cannot exercise his right to prevent the imports (*Deutsche Grammophon*).

Exercise of rights involving agreement, etc.

Whenever, in the exercise of intellectual-property rights, an agreement (or decision of association, or concerted practice) is involved, Article 85 will apply to the agreement, etc., if the conditions of the Article are satisfied (*Grundig/Consten, Sirena, Centrafarm, Sirdar/PHILDAR*).

But if the parties to the agreement are all members of the same group, i.e. parent and subsidiary companies, forming a single economic entity, where the subsidiary does not have real autonomy, the doctrine of enterprise entity will apply, and Article 85 will not apply to the agreement (*Centrafarm*).

—08B It must be recognised that the interpretation of the Treaty provisions as given by the Court, and summarised in the preceding paragraph, is deficient in many respects. For example, what is the position where the imports are, not from another Member, but from a non-Member? This was the position in the *Minnesota* case. Minnesota held parallel patents in the United States and the United Kingdom. The goods were manufactured in the United States under a licence under the United States patent. They were marketed in that country, bought by a third party, imported into the United Kingdom and sold there. The English court held that sale in the United States did not confer any rights under the United Kingdom patent, and granted an interlocutory injunction pending trial of the case. Can that decision be regarded as correctly indicating Community law? Would the result have been different if the goods had first been imported into a Member State where Minnesota did not have patent protection, put on the market there, and then imported into the United Kingdom?

Similarly, what is the position under Community law where the rights in one Member are in single ownership and in the other Member in joint ownership? Or where they are in joint ownership in the importing Member, there being no rights in the exporting Member, and manufacture and marketing in the latter is by one of the joint owners only? For example, the patent in Member X may be owned jointly by A and B, there being no patent in Member Y; if A alone manufactures and markets the goods in Member Y, can B exercise his rights in Member X to prevent import of goods marketed by A?

Community law, as interpreted by the Court, is completely unsatisfactory. A critical examination of the recent cases is to be found in the Annexe to this Chapter (8-91 to 8-149 below).

Exhaustion of rights

-09 The main West German case relating to the exercise of trade-mark rights in respect of imported goods is *Maja*. A Spanish soap manufacturer had registered the mark "Maja" in Germany. The court held that the mark indicated that soap carrying the mark originated from that manufacturer. Consequently, soap made by the manufacturer to which he had applied the mark and which he had put on the market in some other country, Spain or France, was genuine "Maja" soap, and its import and sale in Germany did not infringe the German registration. In effect, the "Maja" mark indicated a connection in the course of trade between the manufacturer and that particular soap; and the trade connection was just as genuine in the case of soap marketed by the manufacturer in some other country and imported into Germany by a third party as in the case of soap sold by the manufacturer in Germany through his sole distributors there. By putting the soap on the market in the other country he had "exhausted" his right to use the German registration to prevent its import.

8–09A The *Maja* decision was followed and extended by the Bundesgerichtshof (Federal German Supreme Court) in its *Cinzano* decision. The Italian parent company, Francesco Cinzano, had subsidiary companies in Germany and Spain. The German subsidiary imported the vermouth from Italy in bulk, and bottled and sold it in Germany. The Spanish subsidiary produced vermouth in Spain, and a French manufacturer produced it in France under licence from the Italian company. The Spanish and French wines differed from the Italian, being adapted to the local tastes. The court recognised that the Spanish subsidiary and the French licensee were legally autonomous persons. The trade mark "Cinzano" was registered in Germany by the German subsidiary and the Italian parent, and the German subsidiary marketed the Italian Cinzano vermouth in Germany under that mark, in a distinctive bottle. The Spanish and French wines were marketed in those countries under the same mark, but with an additional band around the neck of the bottle reading "Spanish Vermouth" or "French Vermouth". The defendant in the case had imported the Spanish and French wines and re-sold them in Germany.

The court held that the German registration did not entitle the German subsidiary to stop the import and re-sale by the defendant. The Spanish and French concerns derived their right to use the mark "Cinzano" from the Italian parent, as did the German company. The mark indicated origin of the vermouth from the one multi-national group. The mark on the goods imported by the defendant indicated a trade connection with the same group, and as those goods derived from the group, there was no deception. In effect, the goods imported by the defendant were "genuine goods".

8–09B The German court did, however, point out that the expression "exhaustion of rights" is somewhat misleading. What is meant is that the owner of the mark cannot use his registration to prevent the re-sale of what are genuine goods. But his rights are not completely extinguished by his marketing the goods – for example, he may be able to prevent subsequent sale under the mark if the goods have been altered.

This is akin to the English "passing-off" cases, where old or second-hand goods have been sold as new. In *Wilts United Dairies Ltd v. Thomas Robinson, Sons & Co. Ltd,* the defendants sold old stock of the plaintiff's condensed milk – condensed milk began to deteriorate after six months, and the old stock sold was at least twenty months old. The tins of old and new were not distinguishable, and it was held that the defendants had represented that the goods were fresh stock.

–09C In essence, the purpose of a trade mark is to indicate a connection in the course of trade between the marked goods and the owner of the mark. If the owner of the mark is carrying on business in goods bearing the mark, the marked goods will become identified with him. Thus, cases of honest concurrent user can arise, where two separate and independent enterprises have each been using the same mark on goods of the same class in the same country. But if a trade-mark owner is not carrying on business in the goods, he cannot acquire the reputation of being associated with goods bearing the mark. This is illustrated by the cases mentioned below in paragraphs 8-48A *et seq.*

Thus, in any particular trade-mark case it is possible and relevant to pose the question – is the object solely to protect the legitimate interests of the trade-mark owners? or is the object to divide up the market between competing enterprises in a manner inconsistent with competition law and policy? This is discussed further in paragraphs 8-12A, 8-15, 8-48F, 8-54C and 8-126.

–09D Considerations such as these – the inability of the trade-mark owner to prevent re-sale of genuine goods, the possibility of honest concurrent user, etc., – point to the difference between trade-mark rights and patent rights. The trade-mark owner has the exclusive right to attach his mark to goods. But he does not thereby acquire a monopoly of the sale of goods bearing the mark. He cannot prevent re-sale by other persons of genuine goods bearing the mark.

Some national patent systems, however, do indeed confer upon the patent owner the exclusive right to exercise the invention protected by the patent, i.e. a monopoly. Thus, the United Kingdom patent grants "to the said patentee by himself, his agents, or licencees, and no others" the right to "make, use, exercise and vend the said invention". Consequently, there is infringement if somebody else, without the permission of the patentee, express or implied, sells the patented goods in the United Kingdom, even though those goods may have been made or marketed by or with the consent of the patentee. Hence, in the *Minnesota* case, a licence under the United States patent was held not to confer any rights under the United Kingdom patent held by the same patentee, and an interlocutory injunction was granted to prevent import and sale in the United Kingdom of goods made under the United States licence. Equally, it would seem, from the *Centrafarm* case, that Dutch patent law recognised the patent owner as having a similar monopoly in the Netherlands under the Dutch patent.

In such circumstances, the patent rights permitted the patentee legally to divide up the exercise of the invention. He was free to give one licensee exclusive rights either generally or in a particular sector. He could license a licensee to use a patented machine to produce one class of articles but not another, or to use the machine but not to sell it. Within the limitations imposed by the national patent law, he was free to divide up his monopoly as he wished, and was outside the reach of competition law. By contrast, the trade-mark owner does not have such a monopoly.

It is regrettable, therefore, that the European Court has tended to treat patent rights and trade-mark rights as being *ejusdem generis* from the point of view of competition law. There are significant differences in those rights as will be seen from the discussion in the following sections, and they should be treated separately. (Admittedly, the Advocate General and the Court did distinguish between patents and trade marks in the *Sirena* case, considering the former "economically and humanely more respectable" and "often more important and worthy of greater protection", but these are unfounded value judgments as to the subject matter of the rights, not a reasoned distinction between the rights – *v.* paragraph 8-94.)

Statistics

8–10 It is interesting to note that, of the 39,000 agreements notified up to 31st December, 1973, 4,035 were outstanding, and of the latter 2,026 were licensing agreements[5] (i.e. about 50%). At the 31st December, 1974, 4,353 cases were outstanding, and again licensing agreements accounted for roughly 50%, the largest group (distribution agreements coming next with 39%), according to figures given in the *Eighth General Report on the Activities of the European Communities.*

2. Patents

8–11 As mentioned in paragraph 8-09D above, there is a valid distinction

[5] Reply to Written Question No. 480/74. Official Journal C8. 11.1.75. p.1.

to be drawn between patent rights and trade-mark rights. Some national patent systems, such as those in the United Kingdom and in Holland, confer upon the owner of a patent a legal monopoly as regards the exercise of the invention protected by the patent (subject to any restriction contained in the patent law). Thus, United Kingdom cartel law (i.e. the Restrictive Trade Practices Acts and the Fair Trading Act) has special provisions recognising the extent to which the patent owner can exercise his rights outside the cartel law. As will be seen from the account of the Draft Convention for a Community Patent (paragraph 8-11B below), the recognition by the governments of the Member States of the monopoly rights of patentees has given rise to a fundamental disagreement with the Commission.

In the light of developments since paragraph 8-11 was written, it will now be more convenient to discuss the impact of Community competition law on patent rights under the following headings:

(i) the European patent, and the Community patent;
(ii) the existence, and the exercise, of patent rights;
(iii) exercise of patent rights not involving any agreement;
(iv) agreements relating to patent rights;
(v) clauses in agreements relating to patent rights.

There has been no change or development in Community competition law as regards abuse of dominant position, so that there is nothing to be added to paragraph 8-14.

The European patent, and the Community patent

–11A The situation at present is that each Member State, in common with other countries in Europe and the rest of the world, has its own patent system and grants its own patents. There are considerable differences between the methods of obtaining these national patents, the methods of maintaining them in existence, and the rights attaching to them. In some countries, such as Federal Germany and the United Kingdom, there is a detailed prior technical search of other patents and provision for hearing oppositions by interested parties, in an attempt to ensure that the invention for which a patent is sought is novel. In other countries, such as Belgium and Italy, the patent is issued on application without any prior search. Once a patent has been granted, in some countries no further payment is required throughout its life; in others, renewal fees have to be paid, in some places increasing with the age of the patent. The life span of the patent can also vary from country to country.

The inventor seeking patent protection must pursue an application in each country in which he wishes to have protection. In an attempt to introduce some degree of rationalisation, a Convention on the Grant of European Patents was signed in Munich on 5th October, 1973, by representatives of the nine Member States and of other European countries. The Convention provides a simplified system for obtaining patents in the adherent countries. The inventor has the choice of either applying separately for a national patent in each country as at present, or of applying for a "European patent". Application for a European patent will involve only one search, and when granted the patent will confer the same rights in each adherent country as would a national patent in that country.

8–11B The European Patent Convention is not yet in force, and its entry into force may be considerably delayed by the proposal to have a "Community patent". This proposal is to be found in the Draft Convention for the European Patent for the Common Market. This Draft Convention modifies the European Patent Convention in its application to Member States in an important respect – when granted, a European patent will operate for the Community as a whole and not in respect of some of the Member States, or of one of them, only. In short, the inventor, within the Common Market will find, if the Draft Convention comes into force, that his European patent when granted will operate as a Community patent, i.e. one patent applying throughout the whole of the Community.

There are two provisions in the Draft Convention which are of significance from the point of view of competition law. Article 32 provides for the exhaustion of the rights attaching to a Community patent. Under Article 32, once the proprietor of the patent has put the product protected by the patent on the market in one of the Member States, he has exhausted his rights in the goods so marketed. And the same exhaustion applies where the goods have been so marketed by a licensee. Article 78, paragraph (1), applies the principle of exhaustion of rights to national patents. Once the proprietor has put the products on the market in *any* Member State, he has exhausted his rights under the national patent granted in any Member State in the products so marketed. Paragraph (2) of Article 78 extends paragraph (1) to cover the situation where the marketing is not by the proprietor but by a person who has "economic connections" with the proprietor. "Economic connections" are deemed to exist between two persons where "one of them is in a position to exert a decisive influence on the other, directly or indirectly, with regard to the exploitation of a patent, or where a third party is in a position to exercise such an influence on both persons". In effect, this is the doctrine of enterprise entity.

However, so far as the Commission is concerned, the sting of the Draft Convention lies in its tail. Appended to the Draft Convention is a Draft Protocol. According to the latter, the effect of Articles 32 and 78 is to be suspended during a transitional period. During that period, the Community patent would rank as a national patent in each Member, and the national rules would apply – so that in those Members whose national patent systems do not recognise exhaustion of rights, the national patent systems would apply, and the patent owner would be able to prevent parallel imports even though the imported products were marketed by him or with his consent. The transitional period would be for five years in the first instance, running from the date the Draft Convention came into force, with a possibility of extension for up to a further five years.

The Commission on 4th April, 1974 issued an Opinion addressed to all Member States.[6] The Commission argued that the Protocol was incompatible with the free movement of goods under the Treaty, and based itself on the European Court's decision in the *Deutsche Grammophon* case. Signature of the Protocol would, therefore, amount to a variation of the Treaty without complying with the procedure for amendment set out in Article 236 of the Treaty. The Commission expressed itself as being against adoption of the Protocol.

The Draft Convention and the Draft Protocol were to have been considered at a Community Patent Conference in Luxembourg from the 6th to 28th May, 1974. At the request of the United Kingdom government, that Conference was postponed indefinitely.
–11C It is quite clear that the governments of the Member States do not share the views of the Commission and of the European Court that the Treaty restricts the exercise of patent rights. As will be seen from the discussion in paragraphs 8-98 *et seq.* of the *Centrafarm* and other cases, the Court's reasoning and rulings do not bear critical examination. The view taken by the governments of the Member States is in strict accordance with the Treaty – the Treaty does not affect patent rights, which are preserved by Articles 36 and 222, so that any variation of those rights required to bring them into line with the aims of the Treaty is something which remains to be done, either under the Treaty itself (Articles 235 or 236) or by

[6] Official Journal L109. 23.4.74. p.34.

separate action. In fact, the governments have opted for separate action, under the Draft Convention and the Draft Protocol.

It is clearly better to recognise a *lacuna* where it exists, and to put it right by appropriate action – as the governments of Member States are proposing to do – rather than to abuse and torture language into an interpretation which the language does not bear, as the European Court has sought to do.

The existence, and the exercise, of patent rights

8–12 In the *Parke Davis* case, the Court recognised that Article 85 applies only where there is an agreement (including in that word a decision of an association or a concerted practice), and Article 86 only where there is abuse of a dominant position. The grant of patent rights by a national legal system involved neither an agreement nor such an abuse, so that the *existence* of patent rights was not affected by those two Articles. But the *exercise* of patent rights could fall within the Articles if there were a relevant agreement or abuse. However, in that case, the exercise by Parke, Davis of its rights to prevent infringing imports into Holland of drugs made and marketed by an independent Italian manufacturer involved neither such an agreement nor abuse. In effect, Parke, Davis could exercise its patent rights.

In the *Centrafarm* case, again there was no agreement or abuse, just an exercise of rights under the Dutch patent. But there was an important difference – the imported goods had been manufactured and marketed in the United Kingdom, not by an independent third party, but by a subsidiary company operating under a licence under the United Kingdom patent.

Centrafarm B. V. v. Sterling Drug Inc. and Winthrop B. V.

8–12A The facts of the *Centrafarm* case are simple. Sterling Drug Inc., an American company, held parallel patents in Holland and the United Kingdom in respect of a drug. It had granted to its United Kingdom subsidiary, Sterling-Winthrop, a licence under the United Kingdom patent to manufacture and to sell the drug. Sterling-Winthrop supplied the drug to its subsidiary in Holland, Winthrop B.V. to which Sterling Drug had granted a sales licence under the Dutch patent. The drug was sold in both countries under the trade mark "Negram", held in the United Kingdom by Sterling-Winthrop, and in Holland by Winthrop B.V.

Because of the government price-control regulations, the price of the drug was much lower in the United Kingdom than in Holland,

and Centrafarm took advantage of that situation by buying in the former country supplies put on the market by Sterling-Winthrop and re-selling them in the latter country. Sterling Drug sued Centrafarm for infringement of its Dutch patent, and Winthrop B.V. sued for infringement of its exclusive right to use the "Negram" trade mark. The Dutch Court of Appeal decided in favour of Sterling Drug and Winthrop, and Centrafarm appealed to the Hoge Raad. The latter submitted eight questions, as to the patent aspects of the case, to the European Court. The questions are set out in full in paragraph 8-98, but may be summarised as follows:

I As to the rules concerning the free movement of goods:

(a) Do the rules in the Treaty concerning the free movement of goods preclude a patentee in a Member State from exercising the rights given to him to prevent imports from another Member of goods put on the market in the latter by his licensee?

(b) If the answer to (a) is in the negative, do the rules preclude his exercising his rights if the object is to partition national markets from each other?

(c) Does it make any difference if the patentee and the licensee belong to the same group, or not?

(d) Can the patentee exercise his rights to prevent the imports if they are occasioned by government price regulation in the exporting Member?

(e) Can the patentee exercise his rights to prevent the imports in order to protect the public where the goods in question are pharmaceuticals?

(f) Does Article 42 of the Act Concerning the Conditions of Accession prevent the rules of the E.E.C. Treaty relating to the free movement of goods from applying to exports from the United Kingdom to Holland until 1st January, 1975?

II As regards Article 85:

(a) Where a holder of parallel patents has granted parallel licences in different Member States, is there an agreement or concerted practice prohibited by Article 85, so that action by the patentee to prevent parallel imports must be treated as unlawful?

(b) Does Article 85 apply if all the concerns involved belong to the same group?

Question I(b) is of interest. The Dutch court seems to have had in mind some distinction on the lines suggested in paragraph 8-09C above. If a patent (or trade-mark) owner is permitted to exercise any right he may have to keep out parallel imports, is he free to do so only where he is acting in legitimate defence of his intellectual-property rights and is not seeking to divide up markets contrary (so it would be alleged) to competition policy? If that was the reasoning behind question I(b), it overlooks the fact that the intellectual-property rights may legitimately include a legal monopoly, i.e. legal right to partition the market (cf. paragraph 8-126 below).

8–12B It is significant that neither the Advocate General in his submissions nor the European Court in its judgment bothered to consider Article 222 of the Treaty. That the property in the patent rights was outside the reach of the provisions of the Treaty does not appear to have been argued. It may have been tacitly assumed that Article 222 protected only the existence of the property, leaving its exercise to be governed by whichever provisions of the Treaty were relevant.

Exercise of patent rights not involving any agreement

8–12C Having apparently accepted that the exercise of patent rights could be governed by the provisions of the Treaty, and there being no question of any agreement or abuse of dominant position to which Article 85 or Article 86 might apply, the Court based its judgment upon what might be called "the doctrine of the free movement of goods in the Common Market".

Doctrine of the free movement of goods in the Common Market

8–12D In order to deal with questions I(a) and I(b), the Court referred to "the provisions of the Treaty on the free movement of goods" and particularly Articles 30 and 36. The English translation of its reasoning is set out in paragraph 8-100 in full, but may be summarised briefly. Article 30 prohibits measures restricting imports between Member States, and measures having equivalent effect. Article 36 preserves intellectual-property rights, i.e. Article 30 does not affect the existence of "the rights which constitute the specific object of such property".

As regards patents, the "specific object" is the exclusive right to use the invention by manufacture and first putting the product into circulation. Rights granted by national patent laws to prevent imports may be exercised where the imported goods have been manufactured by third parties without the patentee's consent or where the patentees are not connected. But to allow a patentee to use such rights to prevent the import of goods put on the market by the patentee himself or with his consent "would be incompatible with the rules of the E.E.C. Treaty relating to the free movement of goods in the Common Market".

Given the reply to question I(a), question I(b) did not arise. Nor did it make any difference whether the enterprises involved belonged to the same group or not (question 1(c)).

–12E Put like that, the reasoning does not seem objectionable. It is suggested, however, that the reasoning does not stand up to critical scrutiny – a critical examination of the Court's judgment is to be found in paragraphs 8-117 *et seq.* below. However, pending further developments, the judgment must be regarded as setting out Community law on the point, at least for the time being, although perhaps as being subject to some reservation.

"Specific object" of patent rights

–12F It will be observed from paragraph 8-12D that the Court has construed Article 36 of the Treaty as protecting only those rights "which constitute the specific object of" the particular intellectual property. This construction is examined critically in paragraphs 8-113 *et seq.* below.

In effect, the construction introduces an important gloss on the existence/exercise distinction. There now seems to be a distinction between what might be called the "substance" of the rights – "the specific object" of the rights – and the remainder of them. Article 36 would seem to protect the substance, but not the rest.

Parallel imports

–13 By applying its doctrine of the "free movement of goods in the Common Market", the Court was able to arrive at a conclusion precluding Sterling Drug from keeping the parallel imports out of Holland. In short, Sterling-Winthrop in the United Kingdom could continue to export its patented product to Holland and distribute that product there through its subsidiary Winthrop B.V., but the group could not prevent the parallel imports by Centrafarm of goods bought by Centrafarm in the United Kingdom.

–13A A similar case, also involving parallel imports from the United Kingdom into Holland, was *Castrol v. Tunbridge Tyre Services Ltd.* The plaintiff company held patents in the United Kingdom and Holland covering lubricants. The defendants bought Castrol lubricants in the United Kingdom and re-sold them in Holland.

Castrol sought an injunction against the defendants to stop them re-selling the lubricants in Holland. In its decision, in October, 1973, the Dutch court refused an injunction, basing its view on the decision of the European Court in the *Deutsche Grammophon* case.

8–13B *Government price controls* It will be recalled that the price situation of which Centrafarm took advantage arose from the prices freeze imposed by the United Kingdom government. The English company, Sterling-Winthrop, had to keep its prices at such a level that they became lower than the prices charged by Winthrop B.V. in Holland. Consequently, Centrafarm could buy at the lower United Kingdom prices and re-sell at a profit in Holland. Question I(d) in the *Centrafarm* case asked whether the patent-holder could prevent imports where prices were lower in the exporting country because of governmental measures.

The Court's answer was that one of the tasks of the Community is to eliminate such situations which are likely to distort competition. But that should be achieved by harmonisation of price-control measures in the Member States. The introduction by Member States of "measures incompatible with the rules on the free movement of goods" is not a permissible remedy.

8–13C *Protection of the public* Question I(e) in the *Centrafarm* case dealt with the situation where the patent relates to pharmaceutical products – can the patent-holder keep out imports with the object of protecting the public?

The Court recognised that protection of the public health was one of the grounds under Article 36 authorising Member States to depart from the "rules on the free movement of goods". But that departure from the "rules" should be by public-health measures "not by way of a misuse of the rules on industrial and commercial property".[7] Whether the proposed exercise by Winthrop B.V. of its rights under Dutch patent law was an "abuse" of industrial property is discussed in paragraphs 8-98 *et seq.* The Court went on:

> "Besides, the specific object of the protection of industrial and commercial property is distinct from the object of the protection of the public and any responsibilities that can imply."[8]

(Perhaps, but both are within, and given equal protection by, Article 36!) The Court's formal answer was:

> "The holder of a patent for a pharmaceutical product could

[7] [1974] 2 C.M.L.R. p.505.
[8] *Ibid.*

not evade the Community rules on the free movement of goods in order to control the distribution of the product for the protection of the public against defective products."[9]

-13D *Act Concerning the Conditions of Accession – Article 42* Article 42 of the Act required quantitative restrictions on imports and exports between the original Members and the New Members to be abolished from the date of accession, i.e. 1st January, 1973. But "measures having equivalent effect" did not have to be abolished until 1st January, 1975. Question I(f) in the *Centrafarm* case asked whether the rules on the free movement of goods therefore allowed, prior to 1975, the exercise of patent rights to exclude imports from the United Kingdom.

In its judgment, the Court argued that the transitional period allowed by Article 42 could apply only to those types of "measures having equivalent effect" to which the transitional period in Articles 30 and 32 to 35 of the E.E.C. Treaty applied. Therefore, Article 42 did not apply to import restrictions based on national patent rights.

This argument is defective on two counts. First, Articles 30 and 32 to 35 do not apply, when properly interpreted, to the proper exercise of patent rights, such exercise being protected by Articles 36 and 222 (*v.* paragraphs 8-118 *et seq.* below). Second, even if Articles 30 and 32 to 35 do apply to the exercise of patent rights, there is nothing in them to suggest that such rights were outside the transitional period. There is, of course, nothing in those Articles to suggest that patent rights came within the transitional period provisions, because, except for the exception in the second sentence of Article 36, patent rights were, and are, outside the scope of the Articles, on a proper and objective construction of the Articles.

13E Since paragraph 8-13 was written there has been not only the *Centrafarm* case but also the *Hag* case (*v.* 8-54B *et seq.* below). Open to criticism though the Court's judgments in those cases may be, until the law as laid down in them has been changed, they must be taken as stating Community law as it now stands, albeit with some reserve. As they stand, those cases confirm the position as regards parallel imports as set out in paragraph 8-13.

For convenience, the statement of the position as regards parallel imports given in paragraph 8-13 has been revised to conform with that part of the summary in 8-08A above dealing

[9] *Ibid.* p.507.

with the exercise of rights not involving any agreement. There are the three possibilities referred to in 8-08A: first, patent rights in both countries held by the same person or group – parallel patents; second, patent rights in both countries but held by different persons; third, patent rights in importing Member but none in exporting Member. To these must be added the further possibility; imports from a non-Member.

(i) *Parallel patents*

This is the situation where there are patents in the exporting and the importing Member, both owned by the same person. Where the goods were put on the market in the exporting Member by the patent owner or with his consent, as by a licensee, he cannot use his patent rights in the importing Member to prevent import of those goods (*Centrafarm* and also *Cinzano* and *Castrol*). In practice it is unlikely that the goods can be put on the market without the patent-owner's consent, as that would normally constitute infringement of his patent.

Where the patents are held by different companies in the same group, for example by one subsidiary in one Member and by another subsidiary in the other Member, it would seem that the same principle applies. This would follow from the enterprise entity principle. In the *Centrafarm* judgment the Court indicated that imports can be excluded only where the owners of the patents are "legally and economically independent of each other".[10]

(ii) *Patents held separately*

Where the patent in the exporting Member is owned by one person, and that in the importing Member by another person, and the two persons are "legally and economically independent of each other", the right given by the patent in the importing Member to prevent the imports can be exercised (*Centrafarm*) – it being understood that the imported goods have not been handled by the owner of the patent in the importing Member.

But where the patents in the two Members

[10] *Ibid.* p.503.

derive from a common origin, having once been in common ownership and then assigned separately, it would seem that the right to exclude imports may not be exercisable (on the basis of the *Sirena* and *Hag* cases). This would apply even if devolution of ownership was based on sequestration, not voluntary assignment (on the basis of the *Hag* case).

(iii) *Patent in importing Member, none in exporting Member*
Provided the goods have been manufactured and put on the market by some independent third party, i.e. not by or with the consent of the patent owner, he can use his rights to prevent imports (*Parke Davis*, *Centrafarm*).

(iv) *Imports from non-Member*
On the principles in *Parke Davis*, and *Centrafarm*, it is clear that imports can be stopped where the goods were put into circulation in the exporting country by some independent third party.

Provisionally, it may be taken that direct imports from a non-Member country can be stopped, even though the goods were put into circulation in the exporting country by or with the consent of the owner of the patent in the importing Member (*Minnesota*). As it was a decision of an English court, this cannot be taken as final, but *prima facie* it would seem to be sound – the so-called "rules relating to the free movement of goods in the Common Market" cannot, presumably, apply to goods in a non-Member. There remains the problem of such goods being brought first into a Member where there is no patent, and then exported to the Member where patent protection has been taken out.

The comments above in relation to the position where the goods were put into circulation in the exporting Member by a person unconnected with, and without the consent of, the patent owner are confirmed by the answer given by the Commission on 10th June, 1974, to a question in the European Parliament:

"... the Commission feels that the marketing of infringing goods by a person unconnected with the proprietor of a patent, or acting without his consent, undermines the very existence of patent rights. In such cases exercise of rights attaching to a patent to prevent importation of infringing goods constitutes neither arbitrary discrimination [nor] disguised restriction or [sic] trade between Member States."[11]

Agreements relating to patent rights

8–15 Given that Article 222 protects only the existence of patent rights, not their exercise, the Court has held that Article 85 can apply to agreements relating to the exercise of those rights, provided the requirements of the Article are satisfied. Using the form of words which has become standard, the Court in the *Centrafarm* case said, in answer to question II(a), that the way in which patent rights are exercised may be within the prohibition in Article 85 "whenever the exercise of such a right appears as the object, means or consequence of an agreement".[12]

This was not a direct answer, but only an oblique answer, to the question put. Admittedly, the question was not a model of clarity. It asked, in effect, whether parallel licences granted by a holder of parallel patents implied agreements or concerted practices prohibited by Article 85, so as to make unlawful any attempt by the patent owner to prevent parallel imports. It may be that the Dutch court had in mind the sort of distinction mentioned in paragraphs 8-09C and 8-12A above – if patent rights can be exercised to keep out parallel imports, is that right lost if the patent owner has attempted to divide up markets by parallel licences. In the circumstances, as the patent owner cannot exercise his rights to keep out such imports (on the Court's ruling), the question does not arise.

8–15A Question II(b) in the *Centrafarm* case asked whether, given that Article 85 applied to patent agreements, the fact that the parties belonged to the same group, or economic unit, would make any difference. This did elicit a straight reply, which is worth quoting in full:

"**Article 85** does not apply to agreements or concerted practices between undertakings belonging to the same group in the form of parent company and subsidiary, if the undertakings form an economic unit within which the subsidiary does not have real autonomy in determining its line of conduct

[11] Official Journal C90. 29.7.74. p.10.
[12] [1974] 2 C.M.L.R. p.506.

on the market and if the agreements or practices have the aim of establishing an internal distribution of tasks between the undertakings."[13]

-16 The *Kabelmetal* licence was not protected by Article 4.2(2)(b) of Regulation 17. It had terms not concerned with restricting the user of patent rights – an obligation to assign ownership of improvements, and a prohibition on challenging the validity of the patents.

Clauses in agreements relating to patent rights

Terms relating to area

-30 *Manufacturing licence* In *Kabelmetal*, the German Kabelmetal company gave an exclusive manufacturing licence in France to Luchaire. The Commission regarded the exclusivity as restricting competition. But the agreement promoted economic and technical progress by introducing a new manufacturer, and exemption was granted.

Ban on exports

-32 The *Kabelmetal* licence originally precluded the licensee, Luchaire, from selling in certain parts of the Common Market, but that restriction was removed.

-32A The possibility of admitting export restrictions in patent licences was discussed at the meeting of Commission and government experts in December, 1974 (*v.* paragraph 8-47) and is referred to in the Commission's *Fourth Report on Competition Policy.* The meeting recognised that there are arguments in favour of and against allowing such provisions in licensing agreements.

In favour of permitting restrictions of direct export by the licensee were three considerations. If his rewards were reduced to unacceptable levels, the patent owner might be deterred from granting licences. Small licensors may need protection against swamping of their reserved territory by large licensees. And any considerable discouragement of licensing could induce large enterprises to keep patented inventions to themselves – the "keep it in the family" argument. But against these considerations could be put such arguments as the power of the licensor to decide whether to grant licences, the royalties he obtains, and the advantages in time and cost he may enjoy. Moreover, exemption might be given under Article 85.3 in appropriate cases.

[13] *Ibid.* pp.506-7 and 507-8.

As regards export bans to protect the licensee from direct imports into his territory either by the licensor or other licensees, the basic argument was that the licensee needed some protection for his investment in production and promotion of the product. Again, this argument might be met by exemptions under Article 85.3 in appropriate cases. The Commission considered it improbable that restrictions to protect licencees' rights could be regarded as relating to the *existence* (as against the *exercise*) of patent rights as those rights were vested in the patentee and were "not property rights of licensees" – in other words they clearly fell within Article 85.

8–32B The Commission's comments in its *Fourth Report* were confined to *direct* imports. Basing itself upon the Court's judgment in *Centrafarm,* the Commission pointed out that the licensor could not protect his reserved territory by binding his licensees to impose export restrictions on their customers. This means, of course, that licensees' territories cannot be protected against such indirect imports, either.

One cannot refrain from asking – in such circumstances, what is the value of protection against direct imports when that protection can be so easily evaded? The licensee or licensor who is himself precluded from making direct exports has only to find a willing collaborator – perhaps an associate company – to buy the goods at a small handling charge and export them. They then become indirect exports, and must be permitted! This does illustrate the absurdities to which a doctrinaire, obsessive, adherence to an invalid principle can lead.

Terms relating to the product or process

8–33 *Restrictions on the method of exploitation* In its *Fourth Report on Competition Policy,* the Commission expresses the view that a licence agreement may include field-of-use restrictions. Where the invention is capable of different applications, the licensor may, in the Commission's view, limit a licence to a particular field of use, and each of several licensees may be given a different field. But the Commission considers that Article 85.1 might apply if the field-of-use restrictions were a means of implementing an agreement to eliminate competition between the licensees.

The latter is a remarkable doctrine. The legal quality of what is done depends, not upon the nature of what is done, but the purpose or motive for which it is done! A restriction upon competition is acceptable if the intention is not to restrict competition!

-34 *Quantitative obligations* According to its view expressed in the *Fourth Report on Competition Policy,* the Commission considers that Article 85.1 applies to an obligation in a licence restricting the licensees' production to a specified quantity. The Commission argued that the normal effect of such a term would be to prevent the licensee from increasing his output, thus making him less effective as a competitor. On a number of licensees, such quantitative restrictions might, the Commission argued, have the same effect as export bans.

But the patent owner has a legal monopoly to stop other people producing any quantity by the patented invention. That is his property right. Is it no less his property right if he says to the licensee "You, who are not in a position legally to make any of these goods, are hereby given permission to make 1,000 and only 1,000"? By what authority under the Treaty is the Commission given power to say that every licence must be for an unlimited quantity? Where now are the property rights protected by Article 222 of the Treaty? Are patent owners likely to be encouraged to grant licences if those licences must be without quantitative limit?

-38 *Prohibition on competing products or processes* A non-competition provision in a licence agreement could, in the Commission's view as expressed in its *Fourth Report on Competition Policy,* so tie up a licensee that he might have to go out of business when the licensed technology became obsolete. Such prohibitions could strengthen the patent owner and weaken competition from manufacturers of substitutes. The Commission therefore regarded such restrictions as coming within Article 85.1, although exemption under Article 85.3 might be available in appropriate cases.

There seems to have been no thought given by the Commission to the possibility of the licensee being engaged in unrelated products, or to the possibility that the patent owner may not be prepared to put the licensee into a position to avoid the patent and any liability to pay royalty by using information supplied by the patent owner to make goods which fell outside the patent. Nor does the Commission appear to envisage that the restriction on the licensee might stimulate non-licensees to enter the market.

Terms as to the relations between the grantor and the licensee

39 *Life of the licence* Where the life of the licence does not exceed the life of a single licensed patent, the Commission does not consider Article 85.1 to apply, according to the view expressed in

the *Fourth Report on Competition Policy*. But whether a licence which applies to more than one patent can be given a life which continues after the expiry of the first patent to expire, is regarded by the Commission to be still an open question.

This is, to say the least, surprising. If a licence confers on the licensee rights under two patents, he may still wish to enjoy rights under the patent which expires later even though the earlier may have expired. Is he to be debarred from having those rights, or is he to enjoy them without payment or royalty or other obligation? If the latter, then patent owners, when granting licences, will have to confine each licence to one patent only. It will bring Community law into disrepute, and will benefit only those who prepare fair copies for signature!

8–42 *Rights in improvements* The licence in the *Kabelmetal* case, in its original form, required the licensee, Luchaire, to transfer the ownership of improvements to Kabelmetal. That provision was removed by the parties, and was replaced by an obligation to grant a non-exclusive licence.

Conclusion

8–47 The block exemption regulations under Regulation 2821/71 have still not been issued. The comment in the *Third Report on Competition Policy,* covering the year 1973, suggested that finding the right policy to adopt in relation to patent licensing and know-how agreements was not proving easy:

> "One of the most important current tasks of competition policy is the scrutiny of patent licensing and knowhow agreements. The Commission has had previous opportunity to express its views on a number of aspects of this subject. The main problems arising from an analysis of cases now under review concern assessment, in the light of Article 85(1) and (3), of the various aspects of the allocation of markets and production between parties to agreements. The points at issue include:
>
> (a) the territory or technical application which the holder of the patent may reserve to himself as against his licensees;
>
> (b) the territory or technical application which each licensee can protect as against the patent holder and the other licensees;
>
> (c) the mutual protection of the parties which may be provided for under cross-licences.

> The foregoing may be achieved by export bans, restrictions on the sale of the protected products for given uses or measures having similar effect."[14]

That inference is confirmed by the Commission's comments in its *Fourth Report on Competition Policy.* The Commission referred to the Court's distinction between the existence and the exercise of patent rights necessitating the appraisal of individual licensing provisions so as to differentiate between those provisions "germane" to the existence of the patent rights and those relating to the exercise of the rights – a differentiation which remained to be fully worked out by the Court (*v.* paragraph 8-149). A conference had been held in December, 1974, attended by representatives of the Commission and by government experts from the Member States, to exchange views on certain common types of patent licence provisions, i.e. prohibition of exports, field-of-use restrictions, quantitative restrictions, prohibitions on competition, and licence duration. These are discussed above under marginal numbers 8-32A and B, 8-33, 8-34, 8-38 and 8-39 respectively.

The Commission, according to the *Fourth Report,* was still considering a block exemption, but there still remained the difficulties of arriving at appropriate criteria which might reconcile the principal conflicting issues, the legitimate exercise of the monopoly rights conferred by patents, on the one hand, and the requirements of a unified market on the other. In order to expedite the examination of licensing agreements, a special Industrial Property Rights Division has been set up in the Directorate General for Competition.

47A In the Commission's view, Article 85 applies to patent-licence agreements which contain provisions restricting competition, such as exclusivity clauses, and provisions which may, indirectly, affect competition such as prohibitions on challenges to the validity of the patent. At the same time, it is clear from the rulings of the European Court in the *Centrafarm* case that Article 85 does not apply to parent and subsidiary companies within the doctrine of enterprise entity.

To practical businessmen it will be obvious that the best policy is, wherever possible, to keep inventions protected by patents "within the family", i.e. to give licences only to non-autonomous subsidiaries. By this means, even though parallel imports cannot

[14] Brussels 1974. p.23.

be stopped, they will have been put into circulation by the group, so that the original selling prices in each Member can be controlled and price disruption prevented. Moreover, there is no question of passing the related know-how to independent third parties who might then attack the validity of the patent.

Of course, the whole object of patent systems is to procure the publication of information and the dissemination of know-how. A flexible licensing system, permitting the parties to determine freely how they will divide the patent monopoly between themselves and to accept restrictions accordingly, will contribute significantly to the spread of know-how – the owner of the know-how is more likely to disclose it to an independent third party if he has enforceable legal rights to control its use and to prevent it being used against him. The attitudes adopted by the Commission and the Court are in truth militating against the very objectives which patent systems have been designed to achieve.

Furthermore, where a patent owner and his licensees are keeping the exercise of the patented invention to themselves, partitioning national markets between them, there is a greater incentive for other enterprises to discover new methods of manufacture outside the patent protection.

It is to be hoped that those concerned with making Community law and policy will reconsider their attitudes – a less doctrinaire, more practical, approach, might yield greater benefits to the Community and the consumer in the long run.

3. Trade Marks

8–48 It is important to keep in mind the true nature, the function, of a trade mark. Its function is to indicate a connection in the course of trade between the goods bearing the mark and the owner of the mark. The implications, and limitations, of this "trade connection" concept can be illustrated by individual cases.

8–48A As the function is to indicate a trade connection, it is relevant to establish with whom the goods bearing the mark are connected – or, to put it another way, to whom does the reputation in the trade mark belong? In *Imperial Tobacco Company of India Ltd v. Bonnan,* British American Tobacco ("B.A.T.") manufactured "Wills 'Gold Flake'" cigarettes. The business of importing and selling those cigarettes in India had been transferred to the plaintiffs. There was at the time no trade-mark registration system in that country. The defendant, Bonnan, had bought surplus canteen stocks of "Wills 'Gold Flake'" cigarettes, made by

B.A.T., imported them into India and re-sold them there. The plaintiffs brought proceedings in the Indian courts to prevent Bonnan from re-selling in India. The Indian courts and the United Kingdom Privy Council, on appeal, held that the reputation in the goods belonged to B.A.T. as the successors of W. D. & H. O. Wills. That reputation did not belong to Imperial Tobacco Company of India. The cigarettes sold by Bonnan originated with B.A.T., as did those re-sold by Imperial Tobacco, so that Bonnan was not "passing off" his cigarettes as something which they were not. In effect, one might say they were "genuine goods", i.e. genuine "Wills 'Gold Flake'" cigarettes made by B.A.T.

In the "*Radiation*" case, the registration was held by the parent company, Radiation Ltd. That company did not manufacture or sell any goods. Manufacturing and sale were carried on by the subsidiaries, who applied the mark to the goods. But the parent company had power to control the subsidiaries and to select the goods to which the mark was to be applied. The use by the subsidiaries was use by the parent. The trade mark was the "house mark" of the group.

The "*Bostitch*" case was analogous, involving use by an agent. The United Kingdom registration was held by the American manufacturer. The machines and staples sold under the mark were made by the American manufacturer in the United States and distributed in the United Kingdom by the agent. During the 1939-45 War, because of supply difficulties, the agent began manufacture in the United Kingdom, with the assistance of the American principal. The court found that the reputation in the goods was with the American manufacturer, even when the goods had been made in the United Kingdom by the agent. The American manufacturer was able to prevent the United Kingdom agent from using the mark against the wishes of the American company.

-48B Because the question is "To whom are the goods connected – who has the reputation in the goods?", it is possible for two separate persons to be connected with the mark, i.e. honest concurrent user. In *Ingenohl v. Wing On,* Ingenohl had established before 1914 factories in Manila in the Philippines and in Hongkong making cigars under trade marks registered in various countries. The Manila factory, together with the goodwill of that part of the business and the trade marks, was seized by the American Custodian of Alien Property, and sold to Olsen & Co. After the end of the 1914-18 War, Olsen continued to carry on the Manila business, using the same trade marks. The defendants, Wing On, in Shanghai bought and re-sold there some of the cigars made in the Manila factory. The plaintiff, Ingenohl, sued for infringement of his trade-mark rights in Shanghai. On appeal, the United Kingdom Privy Council held that Olsen was entitled to use the marks. Consequently, there was no infringement by the sale of the Olsen products in Shanghai provided there was no representation that the Olsen goods were connected with the plaintiff.

8–48C The *Ingenohl* case can be compared with two sequestration cases arising out of the 1939-45 War. In *Reuter v. Muhlens,* the United Kingdom registration and rights in the mark "4711" in respect of eau de Cologne had been vested in the Custodian of Enemy Property, who had assigned them to the plaintiffs. After the War, the defendant, who owned the German rights in the mark wrote letters bearing the mark to addressees in the United Kingdom. At that time the defendant was not carrying on any business in the United Kingdom. It was held that the plaintiff was validly registered as the holder of the mark in the United Kingdom, and that as the defendant was not then carrying on any business in the United Kingdom he could have no rights in the mark – in other words, as he had no trade in the United Kingdom there could be no trade connection there between the defendant and goods bearing the mark.

Similarly in *Adrema Ltd v. Adrema-Werke GmbH,* Adrema-Werke ("A.W.") had set up Adrema Ltd ("A. Ltd") in the United Kingdom before the 1939-45 War. A. Ltd had always held the United Kingdom registration for the mark "Adrema", and distributed A.W.'s products in that country. The shares in A. Ltd, and the trade-mark registration, were vested in the Custodian of Enemy Property, and assigned by him after the War. It was held that A. Ltd had the exclusive right to use the mark "Adrema" in the United Kingdom.

8–48D The same question of reputation in the mark arose in the *Löwenbräu* case. Löwenbräu München had been selling their beer in the United Kingdom under the Löwenbräu mark since 1872, with breaks during the two Wars. The court held that the word "Löwenbräu" in the United Kingdom indicated their beer. The defendants, Grunhalle Lager, owned a brewery in Bavaria, and started to brew a lager in the Channel Islands which they sold in the United Kingdom under the name "Grunhalle Löwenbräu". Despite the fact that the plaintiffs did not have the exclusive use of the mark "Löwenbräu" in Germany, the court held that that mark in the United Kingdom indicated the plaintiffs' beer, and that use of the word "Löwenbräu" by the defendants would cause confusion. The requirements for a "passing off" action appeared, therefore, to be satisfied and the court granted an interlocutory injunction to restrain the defendants from passing off their beer as that of the plaintiffs by using the mark "Löwenbräu".

The defendants sought to rely upon Community law, on the basis that the plaintiffs could not stop the defendants using the "Löwenbräu" mark in Germany, and therefore should not be able to do so in the United Kingdom. The court considered Articles 3, 5, 9, 30 to 37, 85, 86, and 222 of the Treaty, as well as the *Grundig/Consten, Sirena,* and *Deutsche Grammophon* cases. The court pointed out that the plaintiffs were not trying to stop import of their own beer into the United Kingdom. They were only seeking to exercise their Common Law rights to stop the defendants' beer being passed off as the plaintiffs' beer, by the defendants' using the mark "Löwenbräu" which in the United Kingdom indicated only the plaintiffs' product. The court ruled that there was no necessity to make a reference under Article 177 to the European Court, and granted an interlocutory injunction.

-48E However, where the goods are genuine goods in the sense that there is in fact a connection between them and the owner of the trade mark as indicated by the trade mark, re-sale of the goods by a person other than the owner of the mark or his licensee does not infringe the mark. This is the doctrine of "exhaustion of rights". In the *Imperial Tobacco Company of India* case, the cigarettes re-sold by the defendant were genuine "Gold Flake" made by B.A.T. (*v.* paragraph 8-48A above). In *Heidsieck Monopole v. Buxton* (8-09) the champagne bought by Buxton in France and re-sold in the United Kingdom was genuine Heidsieck champagne. In neither case was re-sale prohibited.

Similar principles have been applied by the German courts. In *Maja,* the German trade mark indicated soap originating from the Spanish manufacturer. Soap bearing the same mark put on the market in Spain or France by the same manufacturer was, therefore, genuine in that it was connected with the owner of the German mark. The German mark could not be used to prevent imports of that soap. In the *Cinzano* case, the parallel imports consisted of "Cinzano" vermouth made in Spain by a subsidiary and in France by a licensee. Even though the Spanish and French wines differed from the Italian product marketed by the parent company and its subsidiary in Federal Germany under the German mark, the court held that the parallel imports could not be kept out, the mark was "an indication of origin in the multinational concern" (this is comparable with the "house mark" concept in the "*Radiation*" case – 8-48A above).

In the *Cinzano* case, the German court did recognise that the expression "exhaustion of rights" is misleading. Although the owner of the mark, by putting the goods in circulation or consenting to their marketing with his mark applied to them, has exhausted his right to stop re-sale in that condition, his rights have not been completely extinguished. For example, he may be able to sue if the goods were subsequently altered without his consent but nevertheless sold under the mark so as to be passed off as genuine original goods. This was the situation in the *Wilts United Dairies v. Robinson* case. Robinson sold off old stock of the plaintiffs' condensed milk – stock at least twenty months old, when condensed milk began to deteriorate after six months. This was held to be passing off old stock as new goods.

8–48F From this account of trade-mark practice, it will be clear that there are situations in which the owner of the mark in one country can genuinely seek to exercise his rights to prevent import of goods legitimately marked by somebody else in another country. Equally, there may be situations where there is honest concurrent user. It may, therefore, be possible to distinguish between a valid exercise of trade-mark rights as against an exercise which is directed towards market division contrary to competition policy. This may have been what was in the mind of the Dutch court in posing question I(b) in the *Centrafarm* trade-mark case (*v.* paragraphs 8-54C and 8-126 below). It may be necessary, in this context, to distinguish between a valid assignment, where the transferor is genuinely parting with control, and assignment where he is keeping control, perhaps where the assignment is not 'outside the family' so that the mark still remains the mark of the group, the "house mark".

8–48G Similarly, it will be clear that there are vital differences between patent rights and trade-mark rights. In many national systems, the patent confers a legal monopoly, which its patent holder is at liberty to divide up as he wishes without reference to competition law. The owner of the trade mark does not have such a monopoly. He cannot prevent re-sale of genuine goods bearing the mark, in the absence of a material alteration or deterioration in the goods.

52 In the light of developments since Chapter 8 was written, it will be more convenient to discuss the impact of Community competition law upon trade-mark rights under the following headings:

(i) the Draft Convention for a European Trade Mark;
(ii) the existence, and the exercise, of trade-mark rights;
(iii) exercise of trade-mark rights not involving any agreement;
(iv) agreements relating to trade-mark rights;
(v) clauses in agreements relating to trade-mark rights.

As to abuse of dominant position, there has been nothing to add to or to alter the account given in paragraph 8-57.

Draft Convention for a European Trade Mark

52A In 1973, the Commission published the draft of a Convention for a European Trade Mark. The draft provides for a "European trade mark" obtained by registration in a new "European Trade-Mark Office". There would also be a "European Trade-Mark Court". The European trade mark would apply throughout the whole of the territory of the countries party to the Convention, and could be transferred or extinguished only for the whole of that territory. National trade-mark systems would continue to exist, parallel with the European mark. The owner of a European trade mark would not be able to object to its use upon goods put into circulation by him or with his consent or put into circulation by or with the consent of a person "economically connected" with him. Persons would be deemed to be "economically connected" if one could exercise over the other an important influence as regards the use of the mark, or some third person could exercise such influence on both. Where a national mark is held by the owner of a corresponding European mark or by a person "economically connected" with such owner, or is used with the consent of such an owner or of a person "economically connected" with such an owner, it would not be permissible to use the national mark to object to the use of the corresponding European mark on goods put into circulation by or with the consent of the owner of that European mark or put into circulation by or with the consent of a person "economically connected" with him. The owner of the national mark would not be able to object to its use simultaneously with a different European mark, in the same circumstances, i.e. where the same person owned both marks, where the national mark was used with the consent of the owner of the European mark, where both were "economically connected", or where both marks were used with the consent of a person "economically connected" with the owner of the European mark.

The existence, and the exercise, of trade-mark rights

8–54A In *Grundig/Consten*, the Court argued that Articles 36 and 222 of the Treaty did not prevent the provisions of the Treaty from applying to the exercise of trade-mark rights. Article 222 is not referred to in the *Sirena* judgment, but Article 36 was – although that Article might protect the existence of trade-mark rights, it could not preclude their exercise from falling within Article 85 (and 86) in the appropriate circumstances, i.e. if there were an agreement, etc., on which the Article could bite. Similarly, in *Hag* and *Centrafarm*, the Court held that, while Article 36 might protect the existence of trade-mark rights, their exercise could, according to the particular circumstances, be affected by the prohibitions in the Treaty.

Van Zuylen Frères v. Hag A.G.

8–54B The facts in the *Hag* case were as follows. Hag A. G. held patents for de-caffeinising coffee. In 1907 and 1908 it registered the word "Hag" as a trade mark for its coffee in Germany and in Belgium and Luxembourg. In 1927 it set up a subsidiary in Belgium, and in 1935 transferred to the subsidiary the Belgian and Luxembourg marks. During the 1939-45 War, the shares in the Belgian subsidiary were sequestrated, and eventually sold to persons not connected with Hag A.G. In 1971, the Belgian company transferred its marks to Van Zuylen Frères. Thereafter, although the Belgian company continued to produce de-caffeinised coffee, it did not sell to the public but only to the trade, and Van Zuylen bought supplies from the company, presumably for re-sale under the mark.

In the meantime, Hag A.G. had sought to re-enter the Belgo-Luxembourg market using the mark "Decofa", but without success. In 1972 it began to deliver in Luxembourg coffee from its German factory bearing the "Hag" mark. Van Zuylen Frères instituted proceedings for infringement in Luxembourg. Setting out in general terms a hypothetical case based on the *Hag* facts, the Luxembourg court referred two questions to the European Court (the full text of the questions is given in paragraph 8-133 below):

(1) In the given circumstances would Article 85 and/or the rules for the free circulation of goods within the E.E.C., in particular Articles 5 and 30 *et seq.*, especially Article 36, allow a person in the same position as Van Zuylen Frères to use his trade-mark rights to resist the import of the infringing goods?

(2) Would the answer be different if the infringing goods were sold in the importing Member, not by the holder of the mark in the exporting Member, but by a third person who had bought the goods in the exporting Member from the holder of the mark there?

The Court excluded Article 85 from consideration, presumably because no agreement was involved. It held, on the basis of Article 36, that although the Treaty did not affect the existence of trade-mark rights, its provisions could apply to the exercise of those rights. Its answer to question (1) was that it would be incompatible with the Treaty provisions requiring the free circulation of goods within the Common Market to allow trade-mark rights to be used to prevent imports where the trade-mark rights in the exporting and the importing Member shared the same origin. As to question (2), if the holder of the mark in the exporting Member could sell the goods in the importing Member, so could a third party who had bought the goods from him. (The relevant parts of the judgment are set out in paragraph 8-133 below.)

Centrafarm B.V. v. Sterling Drug Inc. and Winthrop B.V.

4C The facts in the *Centrafarm* case are set out in paragraph 8-12A above. The mark "Negram" was held in the United Kingdom by the British subsidiary and in Holland by its Dutch subsidiary, Winthrop B.V. Goods bearing the mark were bought in the United Kingdom on the market and re-sold in Holland. Winthrop B.V. sought to prevent the imports by relying on its Dutch trade-mark registration. The questions posed by the Dutch court to the European Court are set out in full in paragraph 8-98, but may be summarised as follows:

I. As to the rules concerning the free movement of goods:

(a) Can a company use its trade-mark rights in an importing Member to exclude imports into that country of goods, bearing the mark, put on the market in the exporting Member by another company in the group, holding the mark in the exporting Member?

(b) If the trade-mark rights can be so used, is the answer different if the object or effect of the exercise of the rights is to partition the markets in the respective Members?

(c) Can the owner of the mark in the importing Member rely upon the fact that prices in the exporting Member have been kept down by government action?

(d) Where the product is a pharmaceutical, can the owner of the mark in the importing country justify the exercise of his rights by the need to exercise control in order to protect the public in the event of defects appearing?

(e) Did Article 42 of the Act Concerning Conditions of Accession postpone the operation of the rules concerning the free movement of goods until 1st January, 1975?

II. In relation to Article 85:

Does the situation in question I(a) imply the existence of practices forbidden by Article 85, and does that Article therefore preclude the exercise of trade-mark rights in the circumstances set out in question I(a)?

Question I(b) is of interest, in that the Dutch court would seem to have had in mind a distinction between what might be called the *bona fide* exercise of trade-mark rights, and exercise to achieve a purpose inconsistent with competition policy (cf. paragraphs 8-09C and 8-48F).

Basing itself on Article 36, and without reference to Article 222, the Court held that the Treaty does not affect the existence of trade-mark rights but may affect the exercise of those rights. The answers to the various questions are given in more detail below, but in short the Court ruled that it would be incompatible with the free movement of goods within the Common Market to allow trade-mark rights to be used in the manner described.

Exercise of trade-mark rights not involving any agreement

8–54D Neither the *Hag* nor the *Centrafarm* case involved an agreement – both cases were concerned with the unilateral exercise of trade-mark rights. Having decided that the Treaty could apply to such exercise, which provisions could so apply, given that there was no agreement on which Article 85 could bite? The Court answered this question by reference to the "rules relating to the free movement of goods in the Common Market", to use the wording in the *Centrafarm* judgment – the *Hag* judgment uses the expression "free circulation". Even so, the Court had to overcome the obstacle presented by Article 36, which *prima facie* protects trade-mark rights from the provisions of the Treaty, except in the case of "arbitrary discrimination" or "disguised restriction". The Court held that the protection of Article 36 extends only to the "specific object" of the trade-mark rights.

Doctrine of the free movement of goods in the Common Market

-54E In the *Hag* judgment, the Court said:

> "Since the application of **Article 85** is excluded in such circumstances, the question should be examined solely in the light of the rules relating to the free circulation of goods.
>
> The provisions of the Treaty relating to the free circulation of goods, in particular **Article 36,** have the effect that measures restricting imports and all measures of equivalent effect are prohibited between member-States."[15]

Consequently, given that Article 36 protected only the "specific object" of the trade-mark rights, the Court continued:

> "Therefore, to prohibit trading in one member-State in a product which lawfully bears a trade mark in another member-State, for the sole reason that an identical mark, sharing the same origin, exists in the first State is incompatible with the provisions laying down the free circulation of goods within the Common Market."[16]

On that basis, the answer was that the trade-mark owner could not prevent the imports in the circumstances in questions (1) and (2) (*v.* 8-54B).

The reasoning in the *Centrafarm* case was similar:

> "The effect of the provisions of the Treaty on the free movement of goods, particularly **Article 30,** is to prohibit between member-States measures restricting imports and all measures of equivalent effect.
>
> By **Article 36** these provisions do not, however, prevent

[15] [1974] 2 C.M.L.R. p.143.
[16] *Ibid.* p.144.

> prohibitions or restrictions on imports justified on grounds of protection of industrial and commercial property."[17]

But Article 36 protected only the "specific object" of the trade-mark rights, so that:

> "The question should therefore be answered to the effect that the exercise by the holder of a mark of the right given him by the laws of a member-State to prohibit the marketing in that State of a product bearing the mark put on the market in another member-State by such holder or with his consent would be incompatible with the rules of the EEC Treaty, relating to the free movement of goods in the Common Market."[18]

The answer to question I(a) was therefore "No", and consequently question I(b) did not arise.

The Court's reasoning in relation to "the rules on the free movement of goods in the Common Market" is open to criticism. It is discussed critically in paragraphs 8-117 *et seq.* below.

8–54F There remains to be considered the Court's views as regards the "specific object" of trade-mark rights.

"Specific object" of trade-mark rights

8–54G It will be more convenient to deal with the *Centrafarm* case first. In it, the Court's logic seems reasonably clear:

> "As regards trade marks, the specific object of commercial property is *inter alia* to ensure to the holder the exclusive right to utilise the mark for the first putting into circulation of a product, and to protect him thus against competitors who would take advantage of the position and reputation of the mark by selling goods improperly bearing the mark."[19]

But to allow trade-mark rights, in Members where the exhaustion of rights doctrine did not operate, to be used to keep out goods marketed by or with the consent of the trade-mark owner would be an obstacle to the free movement of goods, which would not be justified. It would seem that the Court was treating Winthrop B.V. in Holland and Sterling-Winthrop in the United Kingdom as being one person, presumably on the enterprise entity basis, the former being a subsidiary of the latter.

It will be seen that the Court has arrived, in the *Centrafarm*

[17] [1974] 2 C.M.L.R. p.503.
[18] *Ibid.* p.509.
[19] *Ibid.* p.508.

case, at the same conclusion as would have been reached on the reasoning in the *"Radiation"* and *Cinzano* cases, i.e. the mark was the mark of the group of companies, so that the imports were "genuine goods" and therefore did not infringe the local trade mark.

54H In the *Hag* judgment, the Court started from the basis that "**Article 36** only allows derogations from the free circulation of goods in so far as such derogations are justified by the protection of the rights which constitute the specific object of such property".[20] This would justify use of the trade-mark rights to protect the lawful owner of the mark against infringement by any person "lacking any legal title". But, as trade-mark rights could be used to partition markets and prevent the free circulation of goods:

> "It could not therefore be accepted that the exclusiveness of the trade mark right, which can be the consequence of the territorial limits of the national laws, should be relied upon by the holder of a mark with a view to prohibiting trading, in one member-State, in goods lawfully produced in another member-State under an identical mark which has the same origin."[21]

The reader of the judgment is left to discern how the common origin prevents the trade-mark rights from being used to exclude imports of infringing goods. It will be recalled that, in the *Sirena* case, the marks shared a common origin, but there the Court ruled that Article 85 could apply as the rights to use the mark had devolved through agreements – there was no reference to this 'doctrine of common origin'. The *Hag* reasoning is examined critically in paragraphs 8-133 *et seq.* below.

Bearing in mind the judgment in the *Centrafarm* case, it may be that the doctrine of common origin of the trade mark will be used to cover cases where the mark is in the hands of the same person, or of the same group of companies (the same economic entity), or derives from the same person.

54I It will be interesting to see if the doctrine of common origin is relied upon in an English case recently referred to the Court, *E.M.I. Records Ltd v. C.B.S. United Kingdom Ltd.* Apparently the mark "Columbia" used on records had at one time been in the same ownership in the United States and the United Kingdom, having been in the hands of the C.B.S. group. For some

[20] [1974] 2 C.M.L.R. p.143.
[21] *Ibid.* pp.143-4.

time, however, the mark in the United Kingdom had been held by E.M.I., and in the United States by C.B.S. E.M.I. sought to restrain the sale of "Columbia" records in the United Kingdom by C.B.S. The court granted an interlocutory injunction to prevent further sales by C.B.S. pending the result of a reference to the European Court. The question referred asked, in effect, whether the trade-mark rights in a Member State could be used to keep out imports from a non-Member of goods bearing the mark and lawfully put into circulation in that non-Member by a person not connected with the owner of the rights in the Member, given that the rights in the Member and the non-Member shared a common origin. The same issue arose in Denmark (E.M.I. Records *v.* C.B.S. Grammafon).

Parallel imports

8–55A The decision in the *Centrafarm* case was that parallel imports, i.e. imports of goods put into circulation by or with the consent of the owner of the mark in the importing Member (treating a group of companies as one owner), could not be excluded by the use of trade-mark rights. The *Hag* case, in effect, decided that, where the trade marks in the two Member States derive from a common origin, the imports are to be treated as parallel imports.

The *Centrafarm* judgment also excluded government price controls and protection of the public from being used as justification for exercise of trade-mark rights.

8–55B *Government price controls* Following the same reasoning as that which it had adopted on the patent side of the *Centrafarm* case (8-13B), the Court answered question I(c) on the trade-mark side to the effect that government price-control measures did not justify the exercise of trade-mark rights to keep out parallel imports.

8–55C *Protection of the public* As to question I(d) on the trade-mark side of *Centrafarm,* the use of trade-mark rights to exercise control over pharmaceutical products to prevent circulation of defective goods and so to protect the public was not justified. The specific object of intellectual property was not the protection of the public, which was a matter for public-health control (cf. 8-13C).

8–55D *Act Concerning the Conditions of Accession – Article 42* Question I(e) as regards trade marks in the *Centrafarm* case received the same answer as I(f) on the patent side – *v.* paragraph 8-13D.

-56 Taking account of developments since paragraph 8-56 was written, the exposition given there of the impact of Community competition law on the exercise of trade-mark rights in relation to parallel imports can be re-stated:

(i) *Parallel trade marks*

This is the situation where the marks in the importing and exporting Member States are both owned by the same person. Where the goods were put into circulation in the exporting Member by or with the consent of the owner of the marks, he cannot use his rights in the importing Member to prevent imports (this may be deduced from the patent side of the *Centrafarm* case, and from *Castrol*; it is also the principle in *Cinzano*).

Where the trade marks are held by different members of the same group, for example subsidiaries of a common parent, the same principle applies *(Centrafarm).*

(ii) *Trade marks in separate ownership*

Where the mark in the exporting Member is owned by a person "legally and economically independent" of the owner of the mark in the importing Member, the latter can apparently stop imports of goods bearing the mark, provided he did not put them into circulation or consented to their marketing *(Centrafarm).*

But, where the marks derive from a common origin, the owner of the mark in the importing Member cannot prevent the import of goods put into circulation in the exporting Member by the owner of the mark there (*Hag* and *Sirena*). The same principle applies even if the title to the mark is derived through an involuntary transfer, such as sequestration (*Hag*).

(iii) *Trade mark in importing Member, but not in exporting Member*

This situation is unlikely to arise. Even though the mark may not be registered in the exporting Member, the question arises only where the imported goods bear the mark – for example, where the mark is an unregistered mark. The principles set out in (i) and (ii) apply.

(There is the possibility of the goods being imported unmarked, the mark being applied after import. If the goods did not originate, either directly or indirectly from the owner of the mark in the importing Member, this would clearly be an infringement. But if the goods did derive from him, directly or indirectly, what then? It would presumably be an infringement of his trade-mark rights, of his exclusive right of "first putting into circulation" (to use the words in *Centrafarm*)[22].)

(iv) *Imports from non-Member*

Where the goods were put into circulation in the non-Member by a person "legally and economically independent" of the owner of the mark in the importing Member, presumably he can exercise his rights to prevent imports.

Where the goods were put into circulation in the non-Member by or with the consent of the owner of the mark in the importing Member (members of the same group being treated as one owner), then the decision whether imports can be stopped or not would seem to depend upon the principle applied. If the relevant principle is "the free movement of goods in the Common Market", presumably direct imports can be stopped, as they would not have been legitimately in circulation in the Common Market (on the *Minnesota* principle). But what would be the position of indirect imports, where the goods were first sold in a Member where the trade mark was not registered or used? If the relevant principle is one of "genuine goods" or "house mark of an international group", then imports cannot be stopped, whether direct or indirect. If such a case arose, the Court would have to decide whether it was basing itself on national trade-mark law or upon Community law.

Finally, there is the possibility that the marks in the non-Member and in the Member might have a common origin. Both the "free movement of goods in

[22] [1974] 2 C.M.L.R. p.503.

the Common Market" and the "genuine goods" principles would suggest that imports could be stopped. The "free movement of goods in the Common Market" principle would not be applicable in the case of direct imports, as the goods would not have been put legitimately into circulation in the Market, so that the imports could be stopped. On the "genuine goods" approach, the goods would not be "genuine", but would derive from some other person, so that again the importation could be stopped. It is not clear what the position as regards "free movement of goods within the Common Market" would be if the goods were first marketed in a Member State in which the goods could be lawfully sold, and then imported into the Member where the exclusive right to use the mark was in other hands. It will be interesting to see what conclusion the Court comes to on the *E.M.I. Records* case.

Agreements relating to trade-mark rights

–58 In its *Advocaat Zwarte Kip* decision, the Commission dealt with an agreement relating to trade-mark rights but containing market-division provisions. The mark "Advocaat Zwarte Kip" was registered by a Dutch concern, Van Olffen, in Holland, Belgium, and Luxembourg. In 1938 the rights in the mark in Belgium and Luxembourg were assigned and eventually, by a series of agreements, came into the hands of Cinoco. The partition of markets was confirmed in various letters between Olffen and Cinoco, in particular in a letter from the former dated 13th October, 1971, saying "We assure you that we will do everything possible to prevent delivery of our Advocaat from the Netherlands to Belgium."[23] Some of the Advocaat marketed by Cinoco in Belgium and Luxembourg was made for it by Olffen, although to a formulation different from that used by Olffen for the Advocaat marketed under its brand. A third party bought some of Olffen's "Advocaat Zwarte Kip" in Holland and imported and re-sold it in Belgium. Cinoco sued for infringement of its mark.

The Commission argued that the drink produced by the original Dutch owner of the mark and imported into Belgium could not be regarded as "spurious products". There was nothing

[23] Official Journal L237. 29.8.74. p.13.

to stop Cinoco using its trade-mark rights to stop truly spurious goods, so that "the substance of the trade mark is not put in issue".[24] But the agreement was intended to partition the market and continued to have that effect, and came within Article 85. The Commission added:

> "Thus the present Decision is not directed at the agreement in so far as the latter assigns a trade mark from one undertaking to another, but only at the agreement for the partitioning of markets included therein."[25]

The Commission required the parties to refrain from hindering the free movement between Holland, Belgium, and Luxembourg of products bearing the "Advocaat Zwarte Kip" mark.

The decision is unsatisfactory in a number of respects. It claims to be based in part on the Court's decision in the *Grundig/Consten* case. That may be so in so far as Cinoco was distributing Advocaat made by Olffen. But in so far as Cinoco drew its "Advocaat Zwarte Kip" from some other supplier, the *Grundig/Consten* case would not be analogous. Equally, the Commission said that Olffen Advocaat could not be a "spurious product" in Belgium. But in so far as Cinoco drew on other suppliers, it would be spurious. The Commission does not seem to have asked the relevant questions – was the 1938 transfer a genuine transfer of the mark and the associated business and goodwill, or was it a market-sharing operation? was the reputation of the mark in Belgium and Luxembourg associated with Cinoco or with Olffen?

8–58A The *WEA-Filipacchi* decision by the Commission was also concerned with restraint of exports. WEA-Filipacchi in France was part of the Warner Brothers group (Warner, New York, held 51% of the shares and Bank Rothschild held 39%). It had exclusive distribution rights in France and various other countries, including Germany, in certain trade marks relating to "pop" music, such as "Rolling Stones", etc. In February, 1972, WEA-Filipacchi sent a circular letter to its principal distributors in France drawing their attention to the trade-mark situation, and explaining that it must ensure that no exports (from France) took place. The recipients were asked to acknowledge receipt by signing and returning a copy of the letter. Eighteen of the recipients did so. The Commission held that signature and return

[24] *Ibid.*
[25] *Ibid.* p.15.

of the copy implied acceptance of the contents, constituting agreements between each of the eighteen and WEA-Filipacchi. The object of those agreements was to prevent export of the relevant records to other Member States, particularly Germany. Article 85 therefore applied, and the Commission imposed a fine of 60,000 units of account (say £25,000) on WEA-Filipacchi.

Sirdar/PHILDAR case

-58B The agreement in *Sirdar/PHILDAR* is quite different. In most countries there is a system of registration for trade marks, goods being divided for this purpose into various classes. Where a firm seeks to register a new mark which is not in any way like any existing registered mark, there is no difficulty. But if the new mark is confusingly similar to an existing mark, the proprietor of the latter may be in a position to object to the registration of the new mark. If the parties cannot resolve the problem between themselves, there is usually provision for a decision to be obtained by litigation. Of course, if the goods on which the new mark is to be used are quite distinct from those on which the existing mark is used and where the goods are traded in on different markets, so that there is no risk of confusion, the owner of the existing registered mark may agree not to oppose the application to register the new mark upon the applicant undertaking not to use the latter on the type of goods on which the former is used. This is not an agreement to restrict competition – it is a sensible settlement of the problem. But what if both marks are for use on the same type of goods? It may be that the owner of the existing registration is not in fact using the mark on that type of goods (he may be using it on other goods), in which case he may not seek to oppose the new registration. That leaves the situation where the proprietor of the existing registered mark is using it on a particular type of goods, and the applicant wishes to use, on the same type of goods, the new mark which is either the same as or confusingly similar to the existing mark.

If it is the *same* mark, there will usually be no problem, as the authorities are not likely to allow it to be registered (the purpose of a mark is to identify the goods with the owner of the mark, so that two different owners cannot normally be allowed to use the same mark on the same type of goods where buyers will be confused). But what about a mark which is not the same but is a confusingly similar mark? This raises the question whether the new mark is confusingly similar to the old. It is not merely a matter of visual impact, viewing the marks side by side. Account must be taken of the aural impact – the ear must be considered as well as the eye. Words which look quite different may sound alike. A trade mark is used to identify goods, e.g. so that a buyer can make his requirements known, conveniently, efficiently, and without risk of confusion. If the buyer is himself a trader in that market, e.g. a retailer, he will usually be *au fait* with the various brands used on the range of goods he deals in, and he is unlikely to make mistakes – although mistakes are possible between similar names in telephone conversations, etc. But where the buyer is not *au fait* with the market, he may have in his mind only a rough, rather than a precise, idea of the mark identifying the goods he wishes to buy. This is the problem of "imperfect recollection". In deciding whether two marks are, or are not, confusingly similar, regard must be had to the possibility of confusion by such a buyer who has only an imperfect recollection of the mark on the goods he is seeking. On the basis of the possibility of imperfect recollection, the United Kingdom House of Lords held that "RYSTA" should not be allowed to be registered because of its close phonetic resemblance to "ARISTOC" (*Rysta Ltd's Application*). In English, the first syllable of a short word tends to be more important, as it is that syllable which is usually accented, but with short foreign, or invented words, such as a two-syllable word, both syllables may be equally accented and equally important, or the last syllable may be stressed.

The question whether or not two marks are confusingly similar can be decided only in the light of the particular circumstances of the case, and of the visual and aural impact of the marks. Litigation can be uncertain in outcome, but certain to be costly and lengthy. In such a situation, it is sensible for the parties to arrive at a compromise. The problem usually arises where the proprietor of the existing registered mark is established in, say, country A and his mark is well known to consumers there, and the applicant who seeks to register his mark in that country has already established it in his own country, say B, where it is equally well known to consumers. In such circumstances, the parties may agree not to seek to register their marks in the other's country. This does not prevent them registering completely different marks – it only stops them registering confusingly similar marks.

8–58C That was the situation in *Sirdar/PHILDAR.* The English company

Sirdar had been using the mark "SIRDAR" in the United Kingdom since its registration in 1898, for knitting wool; in 1973 its turnover in the United Kingdom was about £9 million, exports represented only some £500,000. The French company, Mulliez, had been using its mark "PHILDAR" in France since 1945, also on knitting wool; its turnover in 1973 in France was equivalent to about £9.5 million, exports representing some £6.4 million. In 1962, Mulliez sought to register "PHILDAR" in the United Kingdom in class 25 for clothing and in class 23 for knitting yarn. As regards the class 25 application, no objection was raised by the proprietors of the "PHILDON" and the "PHILDORA" marks, nor by Sirdar which had "SIRDAR" registered in that class. But Sirdar did object to the class 23 application, because of the confusing likeness between "PHILDAR" and "SIRDAR" which was registered in that class, although the proprietor of "PHILDORA" did not oppose the application. As a result of Sirdar's opposition, Mulliez and Sirdar entered into an agreement, under which Mulliez agreed not to use "PHILDAR" in the United Kingdom for knitting wools nor to use any other mark which could be confused with "SIRDAR", nor any mark including the termination "DAR" or one likely to be confused with it; Sirdar agreed not to use "SIRDAR" in France on knitting wools, or any other mark which could be confused with "PHILDAR", etc. Each party agreed not to authorise anybody else to register the forbidden marks without the consent of the other party. And each agreed not to oppose renewal by the other of its mark in its own or any other country except that Sirdar could oppose an application in respect of "PHILDAR" in the United Kingdom, and Mulliez could oppose an application in respect of "SIRDAR" in France. In effect, each party accepted that the other had established its mark in its own country, and each undertook not to use its mark in the other's country.

With the accession of the United Kingdom to the Common Market, Mulliez considered that the agreement was nullified by Articles 85 and 30 to 36, and sought to register "PHILDAR" in the United Kingdom in class 23. Sirdar opposed the application. Mulliez also sought to sell knitting wool in the United Kingdom under the mark "PHILDAR". Sirdar instituted proceedings against it for breach of the agreement, for infringement of the "SIRDAR" registration, and also for passing off the Mulliez goods as Sirdar goods.

Sirdar had notified the agreement in June, 1973. The

Commission, after a preliminary examination, held that the agreement infringed Article 85.1 and did not qualify for exemption under Article 85.3. The Commission argued:

(a) That the object of the agreement was to restrict competition, in that its object was to prevent Sirdar and dealers from selling "SIRDAR" wool in France and Mulliez and dealers from selling "PHILDAR" wool in the United Kingdom.

(b) That for Mulliez to use a different mark in the United Kingdom would deprive it of the impact of its "PHILDAR" advertising.

(c) That it would be financially impossible for Mulliez' distributors in the United Kingdom to change the labels.

(d) The argument that the marks were similar and confusing did not justify the restriction or what the Commission considered to be "market sharing".

As grounds for refusing exemption under Article 85.3, the Commission said:

(e) The agreement did not improve distribution, but rather hindered it.

(f) The agreement harmed consumers by denying the British consumers the French knitting wool.

The Commission's decision prompts a number of comments. The failure by the proprietors of "PHILDON" and "PHILDORA" to oppose the Mulliez application to register "PHILDAR" in the United Kingdom may have been due to the fact that the proprietors were not trading in the goods in question – the decision does not deal with this point. The argument that the object of the agreement was to restrict competition overlooks the facts as set out in the decision. The decision makes clear that Mulliez were not selling wool under the "PHILDAR" mark in the United Kingdom. Therefore, to get that mark known to the British consumers would need a promotional campaign. Such a campaign could have been mounted just as easily for any other mark which Mulliez could have adopted under the agreement. Moreover, even if Mulliez' distributors could not have changed the labels, presumably Mulliez itself could have packed some of its production for the United Kingdom market – this would have been necessary anyway because of language differences. It could be argued, therefore, that there was in fact no, or no appreciable, restriction of competition.

Of course, the basic issue in the case is whether "SIRDAR" and "PHILDAR" are confusingly similar in practice. Will consumers, who are accustomed only to the former mark, be confused and buy goods they do not wish to buy if the latter mark is allowed to be used? Thus, in judging the likely effect of introducing the latter mark into the United Kingdom, where the former mark appears to be in widespread use, experience in other countries where both marks may circulate and consumers be accustomed to both marks may not be relevant. Essentially, of course, such trade-mark issues tend to be subjective – does the tribunal itself find the marks confusingly similar or not. Where the marks are confusingly similar, an agreement between the parties may be to the benefit of consumers, by avoiding confusion and preventing consumers from being misled into buying goods they do not wish to have. The Commission could therefore, find itself in the difficult position of having to decide fine trade-mark issues – whether two marks are or are not confusingly similar – in attempting to determine whether Article 85.3 should be applied or not.

3–58D Sirdar has appealed to the European Court. If the Court upholds the Commission's decision, parties to trade-mark conflicts such as that which faced Sirdar and Mulliez will have no alternative but to fight their battles through the trade-mark tribunals, with all the waste of time and effort that will entail. Only the lawyers will gain. It will not be open to the parties to arrive at sensible trade-mark arrangements which in fact do not restrict their capacity to compete effectively.

Enterprise entity

3–60A Question II on the trade-mark side of the *Centrafarm* case asked, in effect, whether the existence of parallel marks held in different Member States by different companies in the same group implied a concerted practice prohibited by Article 85, so that exercise of those rights would be prohibited if the object was to keep out parallel imports. The Court did not give a direct answer to either part of the question, but applied itself to the question of enterprise entity:

> "**Article 85** of the Treaty does not apply to agreements or concerted practices between undertakings belonging to the same group in the form of parent company and subsidiary, if the undertakings form an economic unit within which the subsidiary does not have real autonomy in determining its line

of conduct on the market and if the agreements or practices have the aim of establishing an internal distribution of tasks between the undertakings."[26]

The answer given is, therefore, that *if there were* a concerted practice, it would not be within Article 85 as it would not be "between undertakings". But, on the facts of that case, would the parallel holding of trade marks constitute a concerted practice? That remains uncertain.

8–60B From the "*Radiation*" (8-48A) and *Cinzano* (8-09A and 8-48E) cases, it will be seen that the national courts, at least in the United Kingdom and in Germany, had recognised, as part of trade-mark law, that a mark might come to be connected with a group of companies. This is a more practical approach than the "enterprise entity" principle. It asks whether the mark is associated in the minds of the trade and purchasers with one member of the group only, or with the group as a whole.

5. Copyright, Performing Rights, and Analogous Rights

8–67 The variety of situations which can arise is illustrated by three recent cases, all concerned with copyright.

In *Lerose Ltd v. Hawick Jersey International Ltd*, the subject matter was a fabric design. The plaintiffs prepared their own original designs, and then made up fabrics to those designs. They claimed that the defendants had infringed their copyright in one such design by making up a fabric to conform to that design, i.e. by copying the design. The judge held that there was nothing in Community law to inhibit the proceedings.

In *SABAM v. Fonior,* the original issue was who held the right to produce and sell records of a song.

Tins for holding camping gas were the subject matter of *Application des Gaz S.A. v. Falks Veritas Ltd.* The plaintiffs claimed that the defendants had infringed the plaintiffs' copyright in a particular form of tin. The defendants counter-claimed, denying infringement and alleging breaches of Articles 85 and 86.

6. Know-how

Clauses in know-how agreements

8–89 The "block" exemption to be issued under Regulation 2821/71 is referred to under 8-47 above.

[26] [1974] 2 C.M.L.R. p.511.

Annexe to Chapter 8

1. Introduction

91 The purpose of this Annexe is to consider objectively the judgments in the *Centrafarm* and *Hag* cases, to test the validity of the reasoning contained in them.

Those two judgments were preceded by four other judgments by the European Court in intellectual-property cases. In chronological order these were: *Grundig/Consten* (judgment dated 13th July, 1966), *Parke, Davis* (29th February, 1968), *Sirena* (18th February, 1971), and *Deutsche Grammophon* (8th June, 1971). The facts in these cases will be found in the book. In the following paragraphs the relevant parts of the judgments will be referred to, as a preliminary to consideration of the *Centrafarm* and *Hag* cases.

Grundig/Consten

2 In this judgment, the Court dismissed Article 222 of the Treaty quite simply:

> "**Articles 36, 222** and **234** of the Treaty, invoked by the applicants, do not oppose every impact of Community law on the exercise of national industrial property rights. **Article 36,** which limits the scope of the rules on the liberalisation of trade contained in Title 1, Chap. 2 of the Treaty, cannot limit the field of application of **Article 85. Article 222** is limited to stating that the 'Treaty shall in no way prejudice existing systems and incidents of ownership' in the member-States. The injunction in Article 3 of the *dispositif* of the attacked decision not to use national law relating to trade marks to obstruct parallel imports, without touching the grant of those

> rights, limits their exercise to the extent necessary for the attainment of the prohibition deriving from **Article 85(1).**"[27]

The Court here, relies upon the distinction between the *existence* of intellectual-property rights, protected by Article 222, and their *exercise,* which is not so protected and which is within Article 85 in so far as there may be an agreement, etc. It will be noted that Article 36 is not relied upon for the distinction, and any conflict between 36 and 85 is dismissed by the mere assertion that the former "cannot limit the field of application" of the latter.

That is the last occasion in these cases that the Court refers to Article 222. Thereafter it is ignored.

Parke Davis

8–93 The first question submitted by the Dutch court to the European Court in this case (could a holder of a patent exercise his rights against imports from a Member in which there were no patent rights?) referred specifically to Articles 36 and 222. The Court noted that:

> "The national rules relating to the protection of industrial property have not yet been the subject of unification within the Community. In the absence of such unification, the national character of the protection of industrial property and the variations between the different laws on the subject are liable to create obstacles both to the free circulation of the patented products and to competition within the Common Market.
>
> In the field of provisions relating to the free circulation of products the prohibitions and restrictions of importation justified for reasons of protection of industrial property are allowed by **Article 36,** but subject to the express qualification that they 'shall not amount to a means of arbitrary discrimination nor to a disguised restriction on trade between member-States'. For similar reasons, the exercise of the rights flowing from a patent granted under the laws of a member-State does not, of itself, involve breach of the rules of competition fixed by the Treaty."[28]

and concluded:

> "1. The rights granted by a member-State to the holder of a patent are not affected as regards their existence by the prohibitions of **Articles 85(1)** and **86** of the Treaty.

[27] [1966] C.M.L.R. p.476.
[28] [1968] C.M.L.R. p.58.

> 2. The exercise of those rights would not in itself fall under **Article 85(1)** in the absence of any agreement, decision or concerted practice referred to in that provision, or **Article 86** in the absence of any improper exploitation of a dominant position."[29]

In the judgment only one reference is made to the "provisions relating to the free circulation of products", quoted above. The existence/exercise distinction is accepted but not argued. And no reference is made to Article 222 in the reasoning in the judgment, despite its being mentioned in the question.

Sirena

94 In this case, the Court relies, for the first time, on Article 36 to justify the distinction between the existence and the exercise of intellectual-property rights:

> "In the sphere of the free movement of goods **Article 36** permits prohibitions and restrictions on imports justified on the grounds of the protection of industrial and commercial property, on condition, however, that they do not constitute 'a means of arbitrary discrimination or a disguised restriction on trade between member-States'. Although **Article 36** forms part of the chapter concerning quantitative restrictions in trade between the member-States it stems from a principle that may well apply in competition law in the sense that, although the rights granted by the legislation of a member-State in respect of industrial and commercial property are not *per se* affected by **Articles 85** and **86** of the Treaty, their exercise may nevertheless come within the prohibitions laid down in these provisions.
>
> . . . .
>
> . . . .
>
> The exercise of trade mark rights is particularly liable to contribute to the division of markets and therefore to prejudice the free movement of goods between States which is essential for the Common Market. Trade mark rights are distinguished from other industrial and commercial property rights in so far as the object of the latter is often more important and worthy of greater protection than the object of the former."[30]

Again, there is a reference to the free movement of goods, but absolutely no mention of Article 222, nor is there any mention of

[29] *Ibid.* p.60.
[30] [1971] C.M.L.R. p.273.

the "specific object" of intellectual-property rights which first appears in the *Deutsche Grammophon* case. The completely unjustified and unsupported value judgment will be noted, that other intellectual-property rights are "often more important and worthy of greater protection" than trade-mark rights! This derives from a similar comment in his submissions by the Advocate General. Both he and the Court appear to be unaware that the vast majority of, for example, patents are for inventions which are never worked. A well-known trade mark which enables consumers to identify readily and to procure without waste of time the goods they want is infinitely more valuable socially than some un-used patented invention. The function of the Court is to interpret the Treaty, not to make unjustified value judgments.

Deutsche Grammophon

8–95 This is the first case in which the Court, seeking to hold that the Treaty provided for the restriction of intellectual-property rights, did not have any agreement available upon which to bring in Article 85:

> "Nevertheless, if such an exercise of rights does not fulfil the requirements of the definition of an agreement or concerted practice under **Article 85** of the E.E.C. Treaty, to answer the question it must further be decided whether the exercise of the protection right in issue conflicts with other provisions of the Treaty, in particular those relating to the free movement of goods.
>
> For this purpose reference must be made to the principles for the realisation of a uniform market among the member-States which are laid down in the Title 'The Free Movement of Goods' in the second part of the Treaty devoted to the 'Foundations of the Community' and in **Article 3 (f)** of the Treaty which provides for the establishment of a system to protect competition within the Common Market against distortions.
>
> Although the Treaty otherwise permits prohibitions or restrictions on the movement of goods between member-States laid down in **Article 36,** it nevertheless sets clear limits to these prohibitions or restrictions by providing that these exceptions may not amount 'either to a means of arbitrary discrimination or to a disguised restriction on trade between the member-States'.
>
> According to these provisions, in particular **Articles 36, 85**

and **86**, it must therefore be considered to what extent the marketing of products imported from another member-State may be prohibited in exercise of a national protection right similar to copyright.

Article 36 mentions among the prohibitions or restrictions on the free movement of goods permitted by it those that are justified for the protection of industrial and commercial property. If it be assumed that a right analogous to copyright can be covered by these provisions it follows, however, from this **article** that although the Treaty does not affect the existence of the industrial property rights conferred by the national legislation of a member-State, the exercise of these rights may come within the prohibitions of the Treaty. Although **Article 36** permits prohibitions or restrictions on the free movement of goods that are justified for the protection of industrial and commercial property, it only allows such restrictions on the freedom of trade to the extent that they are justified for the protection of the rights that form the specific object of this property.

If a protection right analogous to copyright is used in order to prohibit in one member-State the marketing of goods that have been brought onto the market by the holder of the right or with his consent in the territory of another member-State solely because this marketing has not occurred in the domestic market, such a prohibition maintaining the isolation of the national markets conflicts with the essential aim of the Treaty, the integration of the national markets into one uniform market. This aim could not be achieved if by virtue of the various legal systems of the member-States private persons were able to divide the market and cause arbitrary discriminations or disguised restrictions in trade between the member-States.

Accordingly, it would conflict with the provisions regarding the free movement of goods in the Common Market if a manufacturer of recordings exercised the exclusive right granted to him by the legislation of a member-State to market the protected articles in order to prohibit the marketing in that member-State of products that had been sold by him himself or with his consent in another member-State solely because this marketing had not occurred in the territory of the first member-State."[31]

[31] [1971] C.M.L.R. pp.656-8.

Again, it will be noted, Article 36 is used to justify the existence/exercise distinction, without explanation as to how it does so. For the first time Article 36 is held to protect, not all the property rights, but only those which "form the specific object" of the property in question. No justification is given – all we have is the mere *ipse dixit* of the Court. There is no discussion as to what the specific object of the rights conferred upon the record manufacturer by German law are, merely an assertion that to use those rights to prevent the import of records marketed by the manufacturer into Germany would conflict with the free movement of goods. Once again, Article 222 – "This Treaty shall in no way prejudice the rules in Member States governing the system of property ownership" – is completely ignored.

8–96 Some aspects of these decisions can now be brought together:

(i) Article 222, having been lightly dismissed in *Grundig/Consten* was ignored thereafter, despite its specific mention in the first question in *Parke, Davis.*

(ii) The distinction between *existence* and *exercise,* which in *Grundig/Consten* was at large, in *Sirena* and *Deutsche Grammophon* has, without explanation, become a derivative of Article 36.

(iii) The "free circulation of products" in *Parke, Davis* has developed, through *Sirena,* into the "provisions regarding the free movement of goods in the Common Market" in *Deutsche Grammophon.*

(iv) The "specific object" of intellectual-property rights, and the limitation to it of the protection given by Article 36, first sees the light of day in *Deutsche Grammophon,* when no other principle was available upon which to rule against the exercise of intellectual-property rights.

These do not suggest a steady adherence *ab initio* to some clear and well-founded principles – rather, an uncertain, confused, groping.

8–97 Against that background, the judgments in the *Centrafarm* and *Hag* cases can be viewed in perspective.

2. Patents

8–98 Apart from *Parke, Davis,* the only relevant case involving patents is *Centrafarm.* The facts in *Centrafarm* are set out in paragraph 8-12A above. The patent aspect of *Centrafarm* formed Case 15/74 (the trade-mark aspect Case 16/74). The questions submitted by the Dutch court to the European Court on the patent aspect were:

"In Case 15/74:

I. As regards the rules concerning the free movement of goods:

(a) Assuming that:

1. a patentee has parallel patents in several of the countries belonging to the EEC,
2. the products protected by those patents are lawfully marketed in one or more of those countries by undertakings to whom the patentee had granted licences to manufacture and/or sell,
3. those products are subsequently exported by third parties and are marketed and further dealt with in one of those other countries,
4. the patent legislation in the last-mentioned countries gives the patentee the right to take legal action to prevent products thus protected by patents from being there marketed by others, even where these products were previously lawfully marketed in another country by the patentee or by the patentee's licensee;

do the rules in the EEC Treaty concerning the free movement of the goods, notwithstanding what is stated in **Article 36**, prevent the patentee from using the right under 4 above?

(b) If the rules concerning the free movement of goods do not under all circumstances prevent the patentee exercising his rights under 4 above, do they however so prevent him if the exercise of that right arises exclusively, or partially, from an attempt to partition national markets from each other for products protected by the patent, or at any rate has such partitioning as an effect?

(c) Does it make any difference to the reply to the questions under (a) and (b) above that the patentee and the licensees do or do not belong to the same concern?

(d) Can the patentee, for the purpose of justifying his aforementioned right, successfully rely upon the fact that the price differences in the respective countries, which make it worthwhile for third parties in one country to market products originating in another country, and give the patentee an interest in taking action against such practices, are the consequence of governmental measures that result in the price level of these goods being lower in the exporting country than would have been the case in the absence of those measures?

(e) At any rate where the patent relates to pharmaceutical products, can the patentee for the purpose of justifying the exercise of his patent right successfully rely upon the fact that the circumstances described under (a) above prevent him from controlling the distribution of his products, such control by him being considered essential for the purpose of taking measures to protect the public where defects manifested themselves?

(f) Is it a consequence of **Article 42** of the Treaty of Accession that if the rules of the EEC Treaty relating to the free movement of goods prevent the exercise of a patent right as before mentioned, it is until 1 January 1975 not possible in Holland to rely upon these rules in relation to such goods originating in the United Kingdom?

II. As regards **Article 85**:

(a) Does the fact that a patentee owns parallel patents in different countries belonging to the EEC and that he has in those countries granted to different undertakings associated with the patentee licences to manufacture and sell (assuming that all of the agreements entered into with such licensees are exclusively or in part designed to regulate differently for the different countries the conditions on the market in respect of the goods protected by the patent) mean that this is a case of agreement or concerted practices of the type prohibited by **Article 85** of the EEC Treaty, and must an action for breach as referred to under I (a) above – to the extent that this must be regarded as the result of such agreements or concerted practices – for that reason be treated as unlawful?

(b) Is **Article 85** also applicable if, in connection with agreements or concerted practices as there referred to, it is only undertakings belonging to the same concern that are involved?"[32]

-99 The questions fall into two groups. Those in I relate to the exercise of patent rights where no agreement, etc., is involved. Those in II concern the exercise of rights where some agreement is involved.

Exercise of patent rights not involving any agreement

Question I(a)

-100 The basic issue is whether the provisions of the Treaty affect the mere exercise of patent rights, where that exercise does not involve any agreement, etc., upon which Article 85 might bite. The Court's conclusion is embedded in its answer to question I(a):

> "*As to question I (a)*
>
> [4] In this question the Court is asked to say whether, in the circumstances given, the rules of the Treaty on free movement of goods prevent a patentee opposing the marketing by other persons of a product protected by the patent.
>
> [5] The effect of the provisions of the Treaty on the free movement of goods, particularly **Article 30**, is to prohibit between member-States measures restricting imports and all measures of equivalent effect.
>
> [6] By **Article 36** these provisions do not, however, prevent prohibitions or restrictions on imports justified on grounds of protection of industrial and commercial property.
>
> [7] But it appears from that same **Article**, particularly from its second sentence, as well as from the context, that while the Treaty does not affect the existence of the rights in industrial and commercial property recognised by the law of a

[32] [1974] 2 C.M.L.R. pp.485-6.

member-State, the exercise of such rights may nonetheless, according to circumstances, be affected by the prohibitions in the Treaty.

[8] In so far as it makes an exception to one of the fundamental principles of the Common Market, **Article 36** allows derogations to the free movement of goods only to the extent that such derogations are justified for the protection of the rights which constitute the specific object of such property.

[9] As regards patents, the specific object of industrial property is *inter alia* to ensure to the holder, so as to recompense the creative effort of the inventor, the exclusive right to utilise an invention with a view to the manufacture and first putting into circulation of industrial products, either directly or by the grant of licences to third parties, as well as the right to oppose any infringement.

[10] The existence, in national laws on industrial and commercial property, of provisions that the right of a patentee is not exhausted by the marketing in another member-State of the patented product, so that the patentee may oppose the import into his own State of the product marketed in another State, may constitute an obstacle to the free movement of goods.

[11] While such an obstacle to free movement may be justifiable for reasons of protection of industrial property when the protection is invoked against a product coming from a member-State in which it is not patentable and has been manufactured by third parties without the consent of the patentee or where the original patentees are legally and economically independent of each other, the derogation to the principle of free movement of goods is not justified when the product has been lawfully put by the patentee himself or with his consent, on the market of the member-State from which it is being imported *e.g.*, in the case of a holder of parallel patents.

[12] If a patentee could forbid the import of protected products which had been marketed in another member-State by him or with his consent he would be enabled to partition the national markets and thus to maintain a restriction on the trade between the member-States without such a restriction being necessary for him to enjoy the substance of the exclusive rights deriving from the parallel patents.

[13] The plaintiff has argued along these lines that because of the variations between the national laws and practices there are no truly identical or parallel patents.

[14] On that it should be noted that in spite of the variations in the national rules on industrial property resulting from lack of unification, the essential element for the judge to decide in the notion of parallel patents is the identity of the protected invention.

[15] The question should therefore be answered to the effect that the exercise by a patentee of the right given him by the laws of a member-State to prohibit the marketing in that State of a product protected by the patent and put on the market in another member-State by such patentee or with his consent would be incompatible with the rules of the EEC Treaty relating to the free movement of goods in the Common Market."[33]

On that basis, the Court ruled:

"1. The exercise by a patentee of the right given him by the laws of a member-State to prohibit the marketing in that State of a product protected by the patent and put on the market in another member-State by such patentee or with his consent would be incompatible with the rules of the EEC Treaty relating to the free movement of goods in the Common Market."[34]

101 Courts command respect by the cogency of their judgments – in free societies, it is the acceptance of the law by the majority which makes enforcement of the law possible. Cogency derives from clarity. It cannot be claimed that the Court's reasoning, as set out above, is a model of clarity – rather, it is an example of inspissated obscurity. It calls for deeper examination.

Distinction between "existence" and "exercise" of patent rights

102 Paragraph [7] quoted above argues that the second sentence of Article 36 and also the context support the view that the provisions of the Treaty affect the *exercise* of patent rights, although they do not affect the *existence* of those rights. There is

[33] *Ibid.* pp.503-4.
[34] *Ibid.* p.507.

absolutely no explanation, no reasoning – just the mere assertion. On examination, neither the second sentence nor the context supports that conclusion.

8–103 The second sentence of Article 36 reads:

> "Such prohibitions or restrictions shall not, however, constitute a means of arbitrary discrimination or a disguised restriction on trade between Member States."

What is there there to suggest a distinction between the existence and the exercise of patent rights? Absolutely nothing!

It cannot seriously be suggested that the effect of the second sentence is to preclude a patentee from imposing a quantitative restriction on a licensee who is an importer, whereas such a restriction can be imposed on a domestic licensee. That would be absurd.

8–104 The second sentence of Article 36 is a qualification of the first sentence. The construction of the second therefore depends upon the construction of the first sentence. That leads, in turn, to a consideration of the "context" of the Article.

8–105 Article 36 qualifies Articles 30 to 34. The latter deal with quantitative restrictions on imports and exports and measures having equivalent effect, quotas being the subject-matter of 32 and 33. It is clear that these Articles are concerned with restrictions, etc. imposed by governmental authorities, i.e. restrictions of a public nature. This is borne out by the references to "Member States" in Articles 31, 32, 33, and 34.2. It is only public authorities which can impose restrictions on imports and exports. Private individuals and companies can seek to achieve the same result, but this must be by other means, such as cartel agreements, etc. – where they affect inter-Member trade, such activities are within Articles 85 and 86.

That Articles 30 to 34 are concerned with public, governmental, activities is also borne out by consideration of the four groups of factors mentioned in the second sentence of Article 36 which justify such restrictions. The first three groups are: public morality, public policy, and public security; protection of health and life of humans, animals, or plants; and protection of national treasures. These are all typical objects of action by public authorities. Private persons cannot impose restrictions to protect them. That suggests that the fourth group – protection of industrial and commercial property – relates to action taken by public authorities, that is public, governmental, restrictions aimed at protecting the intellectual-property rights conferred upon citizens of the state. An example of such a restriction is section 64A of the United Kingdom Trade Marks Act, 1938. Under that section, the proprietor of a registered trade mark can give notice to the customs authorities of the expected arrival of goods bearing a mark which will infringe the mark; the importation of the goods into the United Kingdom is then prohibited (except for the private and domestic use of the importer).

-106 The same conclusion is supported by asking "What is there disguised about a patentee exercising his patent rights?" And if his patent gives him a monopoly, as a United Kingdom patent does, he is free to exercise it in an arbitrary manner – but that does not make it an "arbitrary discrimination" in trade between Members. As Graham J. put it in the *Minnesota* case: "I do not see how the grant of an injunction in the present case could be said to constitute such a means having such an effect", i.e. a "means of arbitrary discrimination or disguised restriction, on trade between member-States."[35] (cf. paragraph 8-121)

-107 What the second sentence of Article 36 is aimed at is, as explained in paragraph 8-105, any system of intellectual property set up by a Member State deliberately to distort trade. For example, a Member might alter its patent laws so that a patent would be granted to any person first setting up a production plant to manufacture the product. That would not be a reward for publishing an invention, but a means of protecting domestic industry. Restrictions to protect that sort of intellectual property are not protected from the prohibitions in Articles 30 to 34. Another example would be non-essential requirements which prevented imports from one Member while leaving home production and imports from other Members uncontrolled.

108 From this consideration of Articles 30 to 34 and Article 36, the true position becomes clear. Articles 30 to 34 are concerned with the activities of governmental authorities. Private property rights in intellectual property are not affected. Indeed, they are taken outside the Treaty by Article 222. Because they are outside the Treaty, Article 36 became necessary, to implement Article 222 and to show, without doubt, that the prohibitions in Articles 30 to 34 do not apply to restrictions aimed *bona fide* at the protection of those property rights protected by Article 222. It is only in the case of sham, non-genuine, government action that the second sentence of Article 36 comes into play – "arbitrary discrimination or disguised restriction".

[35] [1973] C.M.L.R. p.264.

8–109 Against this background, it is significant that the Court has chosen to ignore, to omit from its reasoning any reference to, Article 222.

8–110 It is clear, then, that there is no support, neither in the second sentence of Article 36, nor in its context, for the suggestion that only the *existence* of patent rights is outside the provisions of the Treaty, not their *exercise*.

8–111 But further, the whole concept of the distinction between the *existence* and the *exercise* of rights is open to question.

The validity of the distinction may be tested by applying it to a different situation. Say the written constitution of a state guaranteed the liberty of the subject. And say the government of that state said to one of its citizens: "We recognise that the constitution confers upon you the right of liberty. We are not going to affect the *existence* of that right, we are only going to regulate your *exercise* of it – henceforward your exercise of the right of liberty shall be confined to one small room with bars on the windows."! Put like that, the distinction will be dismissed as hypocrisy, as a cheap semantic trick.

To take another hypothetical example. The rights conferred by ownership of land include the right to determine how that land shall be used, subject to non-interference with the rights of owners or occupiers of adjoining land, etc. Thus, the house owner can say how his garden is to be used, how it will be laid out, and so on, and he can keep other people out. But say the authorities take power to direct the garden owner as to how the garden will be laid out, how it shall be maintained, etc., and also to direct him to admit the public at all times. And say the authorities exercise those powers. They can truly say: "We have not interfered with the *existence* of your ownership of the garden – we have only affected the *exercise* of your rights." The owner still has the ownership and all the burdens of ownership, such as the cost of maintenance, etc., but the benefits of ownership have disappeared.

8–112 Considerations such as these demonstrate that the dinstinction between the *existence* of rights and their *exercise*, as drawn by the Court, is invalid. Their existence cannot be divorced from their exercise. On the contrary, the *existence* of rights lies in the capacity to *exercise* them.

"Specific object" of patent rights

8–113 Perhaps it was in anticipation of such a criticism that the Court, having ignored it in the *Grundig/Consten*, *Parke Davis*, and *Sirena* cases, conjured up the concept of "specific object" in the *Deutsche Grammophon* case (cf. 8-95 above).

In *Centrafarm*, the "specific object" of a patent is stated by the Court to be "*inter alia* . . . the exclusive right to utilise an invention with a view to the manufacture and first putting into circulation of industrial products". That statement echoes the comments by the Advocate General in his submissions:

> "An essential feature of the patent right is the exclusivity as to both the manufacture and the first marketing of the products manufactured. Such statutory monopoly, laid down in favour of an individual, necessarily implies the right to oppose the sale of the patented product if it has been manufactured by third parties or has been marketed without the consent of the patentee. For that reason the national laws can lawfully permit the patentee to oppose the importation of products manufactured or marketed without his agreement. But it would not be possible to justify the prohibition of importation into one State to protect the single holder of parallel patents in various member-States on the basis of the territorial limitation within the Common Market of the consent given by him to the sale. Such a limitation, which in the circumstances under consideration would have the sole function of permitting the patent holder to control the outlets of the product in the Community, cannot be considered part of the specific purpose of the patent right; and it is certainly not compatible with the fundamental principles of the Community system relating to the circulation of goods that a company, holder of parallel patents in the Community, which company has taken part through a company wholly controlled by it in the marketing of a given product in a member-State, should oppose its importation by third parties who have acquired it into another member-State, and thereby guarantee a commercial monopoly for another of its subsidiary companies."[36]

·114 It is clear from *Centrafarm*, and also from *Deutsche Grammophon*, that the rights which were held not to be part of the "specific object" were just those rights which were incompatible with the "rules relating to the free movement of goods in the Common Market". That is too facile an argument. The Court and the Advocate General have both conveniently overlooked the fact

[36] [1974] 2 C.M.L.R. p.493.

that patent systems, and patent rights, existed before the Treaty of Rome – whatever was the specific object of such rights before the Treaty could not have been altered by it, especially bearing in mind Article 222 (which the Court prefers to ignore).

Moreover, the "first putting into circulation" argument is clearly insufficient. It is possible to exercise some patented inventions without putting the product into circulation. Take, for example, a patent protecting a new machine for dry-cleaning clothes. The patentee, instead of selling the machines could grant licences only in respect of machines *hired* from him, and the hiring agreement could provide a short period of notice. The machines would not be "in circulation". One cannot help feeling that the reasoning, if such it may be called, of the Advocate General and the Court displays a lack of awareness of the complexities of patent situations.

8–115 The "specific object" concept is introduced in *Centrafarm* with the mere statement, without proof, that "Article 36 allows derogations to the free movement of goods only to the extent that such derogations are justified for the protection of the rights which constitute the specific object of such property." In fact, Article 36 contains no such limitation. Nor can it – Article 36 is there to implement Article 222, and Article 222 safeguards property rights from interference from the provisions of the Treaty.

However, the Court goes on: "As regards patents, the specific object is *inter alia* to ensure to the holder . . . the exclusive right to utilise an invention with a view to the manufacturer and the first putting into circulation of industrial products . . ." As a statement of fact, that may be correct, in so far as the words "*inter alia*" recognise that the "specific object" includes other things. The Court then goes on to state that the power given to the patent holder to prevent import into one State of products put on the market by him in another State may be an obstacle to the free movement of goods, and is not justified. Why not? The only argument advanced by the Court is that to allow the patent holder to prevent such imports would enable him to partition national markets and restrict trade between Member States "without such restriction being necessary for him to enjoy the *substance* of the exclusive rights deriving from the parallel patents" (emphasis added). In short, having admitted by the use of the words "*inter alia*" that the "specific object" of patent rights is not limited to "manufacture and first putting into circulation" the Court, quietly drops the "*inter alia*" and by that piece of verbal prestidigitation suggests that the "specific object" or "substance" of patent rights goes no further than, and is exhausted by, first putting into circulation! What has happened to the right to exclude imports given by United Kingdom and, apparently, Dutch law?

If there is a valid doctrine of "specific object" that doctrine requires adequate argument and logic to justify it. United Kingdom law grants to the patentee a monopoly in his invention, subject to the provisions of the Patents Act. His rights include the right to exclude goods made by him or his licensee under a patent in some other country, as recognised by the court in *Minnesota.* It would appear that Dutch law conferred the same right. Neither the Advocate General nor the Court have adduced any reason why those rights were changed by the Rome Treaty, bearing in mind Article 222. The mere *ipse dixit* of the Court is not sufficient to consitute Community, or any other, law, still less that of the Advocate General.

116 If there be such a concept as the "specific object" of patent rights, that object would be to give to the inventor an adequate reward for making his invention public. Views as to what is "adequate" in this context clearly vary from country to country. It is not the function of the Court to reconcile any divergent views in the Member States as to such adequacy. The Treaty already makes provision for any action that may be necessary, in such Articles as 235, 236, or 100 and 101.

"Rules relating to the free movement of goods"

117 It seems clear that the "specific object" concept was conjured up so that anything inconsistent with the "rules relating to the free movement of goods" could be held to be not part of the specific object. What are these "rules", where do they come from, do they really exist?

118 The phrase "rules relating to the free movement of goods in the Common Market" does not appear in the Treaty. "Free Movement of Goods" is the heading to Title I of Part Two of the Treaty, the Part dealing with "Foundations of the Community". "Title I – Free Movement of Goods" is divided into three parts: first, there are three Articles, 9-11, without any sub-heading; second, there is "Chapter 1 – The Customs Union"; and third, "Chapter 2 – Elimination of Quantitative Restrictions between Member States".

Article 9 states that the Community is based on: first, a

customs union which covers all trade in goods originating in Member States and imports from third countries in free circulation in Member States, and which involves the abolition of customs duties between Members "and all charges having equivalent effect"; and second, a *common customs tariff.* Article 10 makes clear what is meant by "in free circulation" – compliance with import formalities and payment of "any customs duties or charges having equivalent effect". Article 11 requires Members to take appropriate measures.

"Chapter 1 – The Customs Union" deals with the elimination of customs duties between Members and the establishment of the common customs tariff.

"Chapter 2 – Elimination of Quantitative Restrictions between Member States" comprises Articles 30 to 37 inclusive. Article 30 prohibits "quantitative restrictions on imports and all measures having equivalent effect" but *"without prejudice to the following provisions"* (emphasis added). Article 31 requires Members to refrain from introducing new quantitative restrictions or "measures having equivalent effect". Articles 32 and 33 deal with quotas and "measures having equivalent effect". Article 34 prohibits "quantitative restrictions on exports, and all measures having equivalent effect" between Member States. Article 35 provided for earlier removal of quantitative restrictions on imports and exports, i.e. earlier than the dates given in Articles 30 to 34. Leaving Article 36 on one side for the moment, Article 37 was concerned with state monopolies in Member States.

8–119 Article 36 (17-08) states categorically that the provisions of Articles 30 to 34 do not preclude prohibitions or restrictions on imports and exports justified on certain grounds, including "the protection of industrial and commercial property", with the proviso "Such prohibitions or restrictions shall not, however, constitute a means of arbitrary discrimination or a disguised restriction on trade between Member States." Article 36 is required, because Article 222 (17-20) makes it clear that the "Treaty shall *in no way* prejudice the rules in Member States governing the system of property ownership" (emphasis added). It is clear that Article 30, with its "without prejudice to the following provisions", is subject to Article 36, and Article 36, respecting the provisions of Article 222, safeguards prohibitions and restrictions on imports and exports justified on the ground of "protection of industrial and commercial property". But Article 36 disallows any attempt to abuse its provisions – for example, where prohibitions or restrictions justified on grounds such as public morality or security, public health, or protection of industrial and commercial property, etc., constitute arbitrary discrimination or disguised restriction on inter-Member trade.

120 Put in its context, Article 36 is quite clear. Given that the Community is based on a customs union, with no tariffs between Members, it was essential to make sure that measures having the same effect as tariffs were also eliminated, such as quotas, or modified, such as state monopolies. But because the Treaty leaves property intact, measures to protect industrial and commercial property had to be excluded from the prohibition of restrictions, etc., on inter-Member trade in goods. But those measures had to be *bona fide,* for the genuine protection of such property, and not hidden restrictions of the types prohibited by Article 30. For example, if Member A sought to prohibit imports of foodstuffs from Member B alleging danger to health, but did not apply the same rules to imports from Member C, that would be an "arbitrary discrimination" and forbidden by the second sentence of Article 36. Similarly, if a Member introduced a patent system granting patent protection to any person who first established within its territory a production unit for a particular product, that might be a "disguised restriction" on inter-Member trade.

121 That the true construction of Article 36 is quite clear to the unbiassed reader is demonstrated by the words of Graham J. in the *Minnesota* case:

> "The Common Market point, if I may so call it, which arises since this country's accession to the Treaty by virtue of the European Communities Act 1972 can be dealt with shortly. **Articles 30 to 34,** dealing with the 'Elimination of Quantitative Restrictions between Member States', are not, it is thought, on their wording prima facie apposite to cover measures such as the grant of an interlocutory injunction to protect patent rights. Even, however, if this view were wrong, **Article 36** makes it specifically clear that **Articles 30** to **34** do not preclude prohibitions or restrictions justified on the ground of protection of industrial and commercial property, subject to the general proviso that they do not constitute means of arbitrary discrimination or disguised restriction on trade between member-States. I do not see how the grant of an injunction in the present case could be said to constitute such a means having such an effect."[37]

[37] [1973] C.M.L.R. p.264.

Where the exercise of patent rights is *bona fide*, and not a colourable attempt to achieve "arbitrary discrimination" or "disguised restriction", Article 36, when properly interpreted, allows that exercise. To use the words of Graham J. again:

> "As I see it, all that is involved here is a straight-forward enforcement of rights under United Kingdom letters patent with no ulterior motives on the part of the defendants or the plaintiffs."[38]

Similarly, in *Centrafarm* there was nothing disguised about Sterling Drug's attempted exercise of its patent rights.

8–122 In short, it is clear that there are no "rules relating to the free movement of goods in the Common Market" in the sense that the Court seeks to imply. The title "Free Movement of Goods" is concerned only with tariffs and quotas on imports and exports between Members, and similar measures – tariffs, quotas, and measures of a public, governmental, nature. The Articles within Title I of Part Two do not interfere with intellectual-property rights, which are safeguarded by Article 222 implemented by Article 36.

Conclusion

8–123 This discussion of the Court's answer to question I(a) may be summed up as follows. The distinction between the *existence* and the *exercise* of patent rights is invalid, and is not supported in any way by Article 36. Neither does that Article justify the concept of the "specific object" of patent rights, narrower than the rights accorded by national law. On the contrary, Article 222, implemented by Article 36, protects all private property rights, including patent rights, from interference by the Treaty provisions. The so-called "rules relating to the free movement of goods within the Common Market" in the sense implied by the Court do not exist within the Treaty.

8–124 From this analysis of that part of the judgment in the *Centrafarm* case dealing with question I(a), it is clear that the Court has mis-interpreted the Treaty – it has twisted and tortured the language of the Treaty to arrive at a totally invalid conclusion.

It may well be that the Court has fallen into the trap of confusing *what should be* with *what is.* Perhaps, having found nothing in the Treaty to reconcile any inconsistency there *may* be between the Treaty's object of establishing a common market and

[38] *Ibid.* p.266.

the right given in some countries to exclude the import of patented products put into circulation by the patent owner in other countries, the Court may have felt it was incumbent upon it to find some solution in the Treaty at all costs. But in that event, the proper course for the Court was to point out the *lacuna,* the failure of the Treaty to deal with the situation. It would have been simpler to point out that Articles 222 and 36 preserve such patent rights, but that the exclusion of such imports *would seem* to be inconsistent with the concept of a common market. The Treaty already provides machinery for *lacunae* in its provisions to be remedied. The Council has some powers under Article 235 to take appropriate measures by unanimous decision, and the governments of Member States can amend the Treaty by common accord under Article 236. In fact, this is more or less what is happening with the Draft Convention for a Community patent. The Court does not have law-making powers under the Treaty, only interpretative functions. Where new laws are required, it is for the appropriate bodies to provide them, under Articles 235 or 236 if necessary, not the Court – if the solution lies in approximation of the existing laws of Member States, that is provided for in Articles 100 and 101.

125 In the preceding paragraph, in referring to a possible inconsistency between the object of setting up a common market and the preservation of patent rights, the words used are "*may*" and "*would seem*". This is deliberate. There is no necessary conflict between that object and that preservation. The policy underlying the grant of patent protection is to offer the inventor the inducement of a temporary monopoly as a reward for making the invention public. It does not necessarily follow from the Treaty that that reward is reduced – on the contrary, it is not only possible but also reasonable to envisage that, for making his invention known and ultimately available to all people within the Common Market, the inventor might be given a temporary monopoly within the whole of the Market with freedom to divide it up.

Question I(b)

126 In this question the Dutch court seems to be distinguishing between what might be called a valid exercise of patent rights and an invalid, i.e. anti-competitive, exercise. The answer given by the European Court followed from its answer to question I(a):

"As to question I(b)

This question was put should the Community rules not in

all circumstances oppose the patentee exercising the right conferred on him by the national law to prohibit the import of the protected product.

Question 1(b) has become without substance following the reply given to question I(a) above."[39]

It is suggested that the question is wrongly conceived. A patent in some countries gives the patentee a statutory monopoly. He can, therefore, lawfully exercise it in an anti-competitive manner if he so wishes.

Question I(c)

8–127 The Court's answer to this question was:

"As to question I(c)

By this question the Court is asked to say whether the reply to question I(a) varies according to whether the patentee and his licensees do or do not belong to the same group.

It follows from the reply given to question I(a) that the essential factor constituting a restriction in the trade between member-States is the territorial protection given in a member-State to a patentee against the import of the product which has been marketed in another member-State by the patentee himself or with his consent.

Thus the grant of a sales licence in a member-State has the result that the patentee can no longer oppose the marketing of the protected product throughout the Common Market.

It therefore makes no difference whether the patentee and the licensees belong to the same group or not."[40]

This answer conforms to patent law. Where the patentee is given a statutory monopoly, he may exercise it personally or through others.

Question I (d)

8–128 The Court's answer here was:

"As to question I(d)

By this question the Court is asked to say, in substance, whether the patentee may, notwithstanding the reply given to the first question, oppose the import of the protected products when there are price differences resulting from

[39] [1974] 2 C.M.L.R. p.504.
[40] *Ibid.* pp.504-5.

measures taken by the public authorities in the exporting country to control the prices of the goods.

The Community authorities have among their tasks that of eliminating factors which could be likely to distort competition between member-States, e.g. by the harmonisation of national measures for the control of prices and by the prohibition of aids incompatible with the Common Market, as well as by the exercise of their powers in competition matters.

The existence of such factors in a member-State, however, could not justify the maintenance or the introduction by another member-State of measures incompatible with the rules on the free movement of goods, *inter alia* relating to industrial and commercial property.

A negative reply should thus be given to this question."[41]

and

"It also makes no difference whether there exist between the exporting member-State and the importing member-State price differences resulting from measures taken by the public authorities in the exporting State with a view to controlling the price of the product."[42]

This answer would seem to be justified. Price controls, keeping prices down in the home market, would seem to be inconsistent with the Common Market and call for action under Article 100.

Question I(e)

129 The Court's answer was:

"As to question I(e)

By this question the Court is asked to say whether a patentee, in order to be able to control the distribution of a pharmaceutical product with a view to the protection of the public against risks from defective products, is authorised to exercise the rights conferred on him by the patent notwithstanding the Community rules on the free movement of goods.

The protection of the public against the risks from defective pharmaceutical products is a legitimate concern, and therefore **Article 36** of the Treaty authorises the member-States to derogate from the rules on the free movement of goods for reasons of protection of health and life of humans and animals.

[41] *Ibid.* p.505.
[42] *Ibid.* p.507.

However, the measures necessary to that end should be taken as part of the field of public health control and not by way of a misuse of the rules on industrial and commercial property.

Besides, the specific object of the protection of industrial and commercial property is distinct from the object of the protection of the public and any responsibilities that can imply.

A negative reply should therefore be given to this question."[43]

and

"The holder of a patent for a pharmaceutical product could not evade the Community rules on the free movement of goods in order to control the distribution of the product for the protection of the public against defective products."[44]

Given that a holder of a patent has a national monopoly he should be able to exercise his rights irrespective of the motive. Protection of the public would certainly seem to be a justifiable objective of the exercise of patent rights.

Question I(f)

8–130 The Court's answer was:

"*As to question I(f)*

By this question the Court is asked to say whether **Article 42** of the Act of Accession of the three new member-States implies that the rules of the Treaty on the free movement of goods cannot be invoked in Holland before 1 January 1975 in so far as the goods in question come from the United Kingdom.

Article 42 of the Act of Accession provides in paragraph 1 that quantitative restrictions on imports and exports between the Community as originally constituted and the new member-States shall be abolished from the date of accession.

Under paragraph 2 of the same **Article**, which is more particularly in mind in the question, 'measures having equivalent effect to such restrictions shall be abolished by 1 January 1975 at the latest'.

In its context this provision can apply only to those measures of equivalent effect to quantitative restrictions

[43] *Ibid.* p.505.
[44] *Ibid.* p.507.

which, as between the original six member-States, had to be abolished by the end of a transitional period under **Articles 30** and **32** to **35** of the EEC Treaty.

It follows therefore that **Article 42** of the Act of Accession has no effect on the import prohibitions resulting from national law on industrial and commercial property.

Such matter is therefore subject to the principle embedded in the Treaty and in the Act of Accession that the provisions of the Treaties instituting the European Communities regarding free movement of goods, particularly **Article 30**, are applicable to the new member-States as from the date of accession unless expressly provided otherwise.

It follows that **Article 42** of the Act of Accession could not be invoked to hinder the import into Holland, even before 1 January 1975, of goods put on the United Kingdom market by the patentee or with his consent in the circumstances set out above."[45]

and

"**Article 42** of the Act concerning the Conditions of Accession and the Adjustments to the Treaties could not be invoked to prevent the import into Holland, even before 1 January 1975, of goods put on the market in the United Kingdom by the patentee or with his consent."[46]

This reply has been discussed in paragraph 8-13D above.

Exercise of patent rights involving some agreement, etc.

Questions II(a) and II(b)

·131 The Court gave the following answers to these questions:

"As to questions II(a) and (b)

[38] By these questions the Court is asked to say whether **Article 85** of the Treaty is applicable to agreements and concerted practices between the holder of parallel patents in different member-States and his licensees, if the totality of the agreements and concerted practices has the aim of regulating differently according to country the market conditions for goods protected by the patents.

[39] While the industrial property rights recognised by the law of a member-State are not affected in their existence by

[45] *Ibid.* pp.505-6.
[46] *Ibid.* p.507.

Article 85 of the Treaty, the way in which they are exercised may be covered by the prohibitions set out in that **Article.**

[40] That may be so whenever the exercise of such a right appears as the object, means or consequence of an agreement.

[41] **Article 85**, however, does not apply to agreements or concerted practices between undertakings belonging to the same group in the form of parent company and subsidiary, if the undertakings form an economic unit within which the subsidiary does not have real autonomy in determining its line of conduct on the market and if the agreements or practices have the aim of establishing an internal distribution of tasks between the undertakings."[47]

It will be noted that the Court has adopted the existence/exercise distinction, but this time without any reference to Article 36. The distinction is no more valid here than it was in relation to question I(a) (*v.* paragraphs 8-102 – 8-112 above). The exercise of patent rights is protected by Article 222, and therefore outside Article 85. Of course, if an agreement relating to patent rights included a term outside those rights, that term could fall within the Article.

3. Trade Marks

8–132 Two cases deal with trade marks, *Hag* and the trade-mark side of *Centrafarm.* Chronologically *Hag* comes first, the judgment being dated July 1974.

Hag case

8–133 The facts in the *Hag* case are summarised in paragraph 8-54B above..

The Luxembourg court submitted two questions to the European Court:

"Should **Article 85** and/or the rules for the free circulation of goods within the EEC, in particular **Articles 5, 30** et seq., and especially **Article 36** of the Treaty be interpreted as meaning: that the present holder of a trade mark within a member-State (A) of the Community is entitled to resist, on the grounds of its rights in that trade mark, imports into the member-State (A) by the original holder of the same trade mark in another member-State (B) of goods from that member-State (B) bearing the same trade mark as the goods of the first member-State (A), when it is established that:

[47] *Ibid.* pp.506-7.

– the trade mark at issue was assigned by the original holder within a member-State (B) to its subsidiary, constituted within another member-State (A), pursuant to agreements which took effect before the coming into force of the Treaty;
– this subsidiary, which was sequestrated after the second world war by the Government of the State (A), was subsequently sold with the trade mark by that Government to a third party;
– the said third party in turn assigned the trade mark to the present holder in that State (A);
– there exists no legal, financial, technical, or economic link between the present holder and the original holder of the trade marks in States (A) and (B)?

2. Would the answer to question 1 be the same if the sale of the goods in member-State (A) was made not by the original holder of the trade mark in member-State (B), but by a third party, such as an importer, who had duly obtained the goods in member-State (B) from the original holder?"[48]

In its judgment, the European Court noted that as, in the circumstances, Article 85 was excluded "the question should be examined solely in the light of the rules relating to the free circulation of goods". It then continued:

"The provisions of the Treaty relating to the free circulation of goods, in particular **Article 30**, have the effect that measures restricting imports and all measures of equivalent effect are prohibited between member-States.

Under **Article 36**, these provisions do not, however, prevent prohibitions or restrictions on imports justified by reasons of protection of industrial and commercial property.

It appears, however, from that very **Article**, particularly in its second sentence, as well as from the context, that, while the Treaty does not affect the existence of the rights recognised by the laws of a member-State on industrial and commercial property, the exercise of those rights may nonetheless, according to circumstances, be affected by the prohibitions of the Treaty.

In so far as it applies an exception to one of the fundamental principles of the Common Market, **Article 36** only allows derogations from the free circulation of goods in

[48] [1974] 2 C.M.L.R. pp.129-30.

so far as such derogations are justified by the protection of the rights which constitute the specific object of such property.

Thus, in any case, the application of the laws on the protection of trade marks protects the lawful holder of a mark against infringement on the part of persons lacking in any legal title.

The exercise of the trade mark right is such as to contribute to the partitioning of the markets and thus to affect the free circulation of goods between member-States, all the more so in that, as opposed to other industrial and commercial property rights, it is not subject to temporal limits.

It could not therefore be accepted that the exclusiveness of the trade mark right, which can be the consequence of the territorial limits of the national laws, should be relied on by the holder of a mark with a view to prohibiting trading, in one member-State, in goods lawfully produced in another member-State under an identical mark which has the same origin.

In fact, such a prohibition, establishing the isolation of the national markets, would come into conflict with one of the fundamental aims of the Treaty, the fusion of the national markets into one single market.

While, in such a market, the indication of the origin of a trade-marked product is useful, informing consumers thereon can be done by means other than those which would affect the free circulation of goods.

Therefore, to prohibit trading in one member-State in a product which lawfully bears a trade mark in another member-State, for the sole reason that an identical mark, sharing the same origin, exists in the first State is incompatible with the provisions laying down the free circulation of goods within the Common Market.

In the second question it is asked whether the same would apply if the trading in the trade-marked product was carried out not by the holder of the mark in the other member-State but by a third party who had properly acquired the product in that State.

While the holder of a trade mark in one member-State may himself put the trade-marked product on sale in another member-State, the same applies for a third party who has lawfully acquired that product in the first State."[49]

[49] *Ibid.* pp.143-4.

and

"1. To prohibit trading, in one member-State, in a product which lawfully bears a trade mark in another member-State, for the sole reason that an identical mark, sharing the same origin, exists in the first State, is incompatible with the provisions laying down the free circulation of goods within the Common Market.

2. While [? If] the holder of a trade mark in one member-State may himself put the trade-marked product on sale in another member-State, the same applies for a third party who has lawfully acquired that product in the first State."[50]

134 Several points may be noted. First, Article 222 is again completely ignored.

Secondly, Article 36 is relied upon to justify the distinction between the *existence* of rights, which is not affected by the Treaty, and their *exercise* which may be affected by its provisions. The observations in paragraphs 8-102 – 8-112 above are relevant.

"Specific object" of trade-mark rights

135 Again it is asserted that Article 36 only protects those rights "which constitute the specific object" of the relevant property, entirely without proof of that assertion (cf. paragraphs 8-113 – 8-115 above). It is admitted in the judgment that the trade-mark rights can be used to protect the legal holder from infringement by persons lacking any legal title. But, as trade-mark rights could be used to partition markets, "it could not therefore be accepted" that they should be used to prohibit "trading, in one member-State, in goods lawfully produced in another member-State under an identical mark *which has the same origin*" (emphasis added). No justification is given, except that "to prohibit trading in one member-State in a product which lawfully bears a trade mark in another member-State, for the sole reason that an identical mark, *sharing the same origin,* exists in the first State is incompatible with the provisions laying down the free circulation of goods within the Common Market" (emphasis added).

136 Again, the Court has avoided saying what the specific object of the intellectual property in question, a trade mark, is. The Court

[50] *Ibid.* pp.144-5.

has proceeded, woodenly, on the same lines as before. The use of trade-mark rights to keep out the Hag A.G. imports would be "incompatible with the provisions laying down the free circulation of goods" etc., and – *Eureka* – that must be outside the "specific object"!

8–137 The validity of the reference to those "provisions" has already been discussed in paragraphs 8-117 to 8-122 above, and shown to be non-existent.

Principle of "common origin"

8–138 The Court has conjured up, in this case, another concept – that of "common origin". Again, there is no supporting argument, no justification – just the Court's mere *ipse dixit.*

It will not be overlooked, and surely is relevant, that this concept would have equally applied in the *Grundig/Consten* and *Sirena* cases. Why was it not referred to in them? Would it be too uncharitable to say that it had not been thought of?

The "common origin" concept overlooks two aspects of trade marks. First, a trade mark need not operate over a whole Member, still less over the whole of the Community. A trade mark on goods indicates a trade connection between those goods and the owner of the mark. If the goods circulate only within a small geographical area – say one county or one large town, in the United Kingdom – it is only in the eyes of the consumers in that area that the owner of the mark holds the reputation in the mark. It may be that exactly the same mark is used in a different area on the same type of goods by a different owner – the consumers in the second area associating the reputation in the mark with the second owner. In short, it is possible for two different owners to use the same mark on the same type of goods in different areas, without any confusion. A simple illustration from the field of services is the number of hotels operating under a similar name, e.g. "Grand", without confusion. If this concurrent user is possible in one country, it is even more possible in the much larger area of the Common Market.

Secondly, trade marks can be used or renewed over long periods of time. For example, Löwenbräu München had used their mark in the United Kingdom since 1872, over 100 years.

Putting these two aspects together, it will be seen that a trader in one country or part of a country finding that he no longer required his trade mark in another country because his trade there had fallen to nothing, might transfer the mark to a local trader in the second country. Thereafter, the mark might be used quite separately by both traders in their own areas without any confusion being caused, the consumers in each area associating the goods bearing the mark with the local trader in that area. If such separate use had continued for a long time – say 100 years – would it be right to deny one trader the right to keep out the goods of the other trader on the "common origin" principle? To do so would conform neither to justice, nor to equity, nor to common sense, nor to consumer protection.

-139 The principle of "common origin", it will be observed, denies one essential characteristic of property rights. If a trade mark cannot be used to protect its owner from infringement by goods bearing the same mark which shares a "common origin", that means, in effect, that a trade mark cannot be assigned. One of the inherent rights of property is the capacity to assign. It is now only too clear why Article 222 has been ignored!

Conclusion

-140 The Court has not shown in what way the action by Van Zuylen Frères was a "disguised restriction" or an "arbitrary discrimination". In fact, a little knowledge of trade-mark law and practice, and an absence of any doctrinaire obsession with competition law, would have indicated that the true purpose of a trade mark is to show a trade connection with the owner of the mark. In Luxembourg and Belgium the reputation in the "Hag" mark lay with Van Zuylen, not with Hag A.G. The latter, far from having any connection with the mark, had attempted to sell their product under the mark "Decofa". Therefore, on normal trade-mark principles, as exemplified in similar circumstances by the three cases referred to in paragraphs 8-48B and 8-48C (which also concerned titles derived from sequestration, not from voluntary transfers), Van Zuylen Freres should have been able to exclude the Hag A.G. product bearing the "Hag" mark – on the simple ground that, in the eyes of the purchasers, the "Hag" mark in Luxembourg and Belgium denoted the Van Zuylen concern, not Hag A.G. The latter would not, thereby, be prevented from competing – only from using a confusingly similar mark.

Centrafarm case

-141 The facts in the Centrafarm case are set out in paragraph 8-12A above. The trade mark used both in Holland and the United Kingdom was "Negram". The trade-mark side of the case was numbered 16/74. The questions submitted by the Dutch court on the trade-mark side were:

"*In Case 16/74:*

I. In relation to the rules concerning free movement of goods:

(a) Assuming that:

1. different undertakings in different countries belonging to the EEC forming part of the same concern are entitled to the use of the same trade mark for a certain product,
2. products bearing that trade mark, after being lawfully marketed in one country by the trade mark owner, are exported by third parties and are marketed and further dealt with in one of the other countries,
3. the trade mark legislation in one last-mentioned country gives the trade mark owner the right to take legal action to prevent goods with the relevant trade mark from being marketed there by other persons even if such goods had previously been marketed lawfully in another country by an undertaking there entitled to that trade mark and belonging to the same concern,

do the rules set out in the EEC Treaty concerning the free movement of goods, notwithstanding the provisions of **Article 36**, prevent the trade mark owner from making use of the right mentioned under 3 above?

(b) If the rules concerning the free movement of goods do not in all circumstances preclude the trade mark owner from exercising the right mentioned under (1) 3, is he precluded from so doing if the exercise of that right arises either exclusively or partially from an effort to partition the markets of the relevant countries from each other in relation to the said goods or at least has the effect of thus partitioning those markets?

(c) Can the trade mark owner successfully rely in

justification of the exercise of the above-mentioned right on the fact that the price differences in the relevant countries, which make it profitable for third parties to market products coming from one country in the other country, and give the trade mark owner in that other country an interest in taking action against such practices, are the result of governmental measures whereby in the exporting country the prices of those products are kept lower than would have been the case in the absence of those measures?

(d) Can the trade mark owner, at least if the relevant product is a pharmaceutical product, properly rely in justification of the exercise of his trade mark right in the manner mentioned on the fact that the state of affairs described under (a) limits his opportunities of controlling the distribution of the products, which control by him is considered necessary so that measures for protection of the public can be taken in the event of defects appearing?

(e) Does **Article 42** of the Treaty of Accession involve that, if the rules of the EEC Treaty relating to the free movement of goods prevent an exercise of a trade mark right as stated above, those rules cannot be involved in Holland until 1 January 1975 in so far as the relevant goods come from the United Kingdom?

II. In relation to **Article 85**:
Does the situation described under I (a) involve that practices of the kind forbidden by Article 85 of the EEC Treaty exist, and must an action for infringement as mentioned therein, in so far as it is to be regarded as a consequence of such practices, be held impermissible for this reason?"[51]

-142 The Court's answer to question I(a) was:

"*As to question* I(a)

[51] [1974] 2 C.M.L.R. pp.486-7.

[3] By this question the Court is asked to say whether, in the circumstances posited, the rules of the Treaty on free movement of goods prevent the holder of the mark opposing the marketing by other persons of a product protected by the mark.

[Paras. [4]-[7] are identical to paras. [5]-[8] of Case 15/74.] [52]

[8] As regards trade marks, the specific object of commercial property is *inter alia* to ensure to the holder the exclusive right to utilise the mark for the first putting into circulation of a product, and to protect him thus against competitors who would take advantage of the position and reputation of the mark by selling goods improperly bearing the mark.

[9] The existence, in national laws on industrial and commercial property, of provisions that the right of the trade mark holder is not exhausted by the marketing in another member-State of the product protected by the mark, so that the holder may oppose the import into his own State of the product marketed in another State, may constitute an obstacle to the free movement of goods.

[10] Such an obstacle is not justified when the product has been lawfully put, by the holder himself or with his consent, on the market of the member-State from which it is imported in such a way that there can be no question of abuse or infringement of the mark.

[11] If the holder of a trade mark could forbid the import of protected products, which had been marketed in another member-State by him or with his consent, he would be enabled to partition the national markets and thus to maintain a restriction on the trade between the member-States without such a restriction being necessary for him to enjoy the substance of the exclusive right deriving from the mark.

[12] The question should therefore be answered to the effect that the exercise by the holder of a mark of the right given him by the laws of a member-State to prohibit the marketing in that State of a product bearing the mark put on the market in another member-State by such holder or with his consent would be incompatible with the rules of

[52] *v.* paragraph 8-100 above.

> the EEC Treaty relating to the free movement of goods in the Common Market."[53]

and

> "1. The exercise by the holder of a trade mark of the right given him by the laws of a member-State to prohibit the marketing in that State of a product bearing the mark and put on the market in another member-State by such holder or with his consent would be incompatible with the rules of the EEC Treaty relating to the free movement of goods in the Common Market."[54]

143 This answer raises the same issues as regards the existence/exercise distinction and the so-called "rules relating to the free movement of goods in the Common Market" as did the answer to question I(a) on the patent side. These points have already been discussed in paragraphs 8-102 *et seq.* above.

144 The answer asserts that the "specific object" of a trade mark is "*inter alia*" the exclusive right of "first putting into circulation". As far as it goes, that is correct. The words "*inter alia*" preserve the other rights of the owner of the mark, for example to sue for passing-off sub-standard goods. It is significant, however, that in the remainder of its judgment, the Court bases itself upon the case of a holder of a mark who puts the goods into circulation himself, or allows them to be put into circulation, bearing the mark. If those had been the circumstances, the normal trade-mark principle of "genuine goods" would have applied. But there is no evidence that Winthrop B.V., the Dutch company, consented to the marketing of the goods in the United Kingdom by Sterling-Winthrop. So that, in so far as it is based on non-existent facts, the Court's conclusion falls.

But not only could the "genuine goods" principle have applied, given the appropriate facts, the "house mark" or "international concern" principles in the "*Radiation*" and *Cinzano* cases would have been equally applicable had some consideration been given to trade-mark law. And if Dutch law did not recognise these principles, then Article 222 of the Treaty should have preserved the rights of Winthrop B.V., and the Court could have pointed to the necessity for approximation of Members' trade-mark laws under Articles 100 or 101 or to the

[53] *Ibid.* pp.508-9.
[54] *Ibid.* p.510.

need for extension or amendment of the Treaty under Articles 235 and 236.

8–145 The answers to the other questions follow the answers given on the patent side, and do not call for further comment.

4. Conclusion

8–146 As a consequence of its obsessive concentration on competition considerations and its doctrinaire approach, the Court has completely mis-construed the Treaty. This is illustrated by its cavalier dismissal and ignoring of Article 222. The falsity of its conclusions based on Article 36 is shown by the complete absence of logical explanation, and its total reliance on mere assertion. The existence/exercise distinction has been shown to be fallacious.

In fact, the Court has departed from the role assigned to it by Article 177. So far as it is relevant, that role is "to give preliminary rulings concerning ... the interpretation of the Treaty". (It will be noted that the Court's ruling is "preliminary" – who gives the final ruling?) The Court has exceeded its function by indulging in irrelevant value judgments (for example, the alleged comparative value of patents and trade marks – *v.* paragraph 8-94), and by assuming the role of law-maker (for example, reading into the Treaty rules relating to the free movement of goods and restrictions upon the exercise of intellectual-property rights which do not appear in the Treaty). The Treaty is an agreement between the Members. It should be interpreted strictly and in precise accordance with its terms, so that its provisions are not distorted and extended beyond what the parties have agreed to. The Treaty is not the constitution of a new state, conferring law-making powers on its supreme court.

8–147 In some instances the Court may have been misled by remarks by the Advocate General in his submissions – for example, as to the comparative value of patents and trade marks (*v.* paragraph 8-94) and as to the nature of patent rights (*v.* paragraph 8-113).

It can be argued that the Advocate General in his submissions to some extent makes up for the absence of a lower court or courts in which the issues involved would have been analysed and discussed. But if there had been judgments by lower courts, the parties would have been in a position to comment on those judgments in presenting their cases to the Court itself. Perhaps consideration should be given to amendment of the Court's procedure so as to give the parties an opportunity to comment on the Advocate General's submissions.

-148 Finally, it is submitted that the Treaty, in its application to intellectual-property rights, is clear and unambiguous:

(1) By virtue of Article 222 intellectual-property rights are outside the Treaty, and are not affected by the Articles concerned with the "Free Movement of Goods" nor by Articles 85 and 86.

(2) The Articles concerned with the "Free Movement of Goods" apply only to prohibitions, restrictions, and similar measures of a public, governmental, nature. Even so, any *bona fide* prohibitions, etc., intended for the protection of intellectual-property rights are preserved by Article 36.

(3) There may be problems in that differences in national intellectual-property rights may result in inequalities in the conditions upon which concerns in different Member States compete with each other.

(4) If so, the solution of those problems should be sought in the application of the appropriate provisions of the Treaty, such as Articles 100 and 101 (approximation of laws of Member States) or Articles 235 and 236 (extension or amendment of the Treaty). Satisfactory, comprehensive, and internally consistent solutions will be found only by subjecting each item of intellectual property to separate treatment, taking account of its peculiar problems and of the accumulated experience of those legal systems which have had to find solutions to those problems over the years in conditions of actual trading and real life. The Member States are, indeed, already attempting to apply such an approach in the field of patents.

149 The problems created by the Court's approach to the application of the Treaty to intellectual property seem to have been recognised by the Commission in its *Fourth Report on Competition Policy:*

"On a legal plane, the Commission faces the problems of definition exposed by the Court of Justice in its distinction between the existence of nationally protected industrial property rights, which is not to be affected by Community law, and the exercise of these rights, which can be subject to the Treaty rules. Accordingly, any appraisal of particular patent licensing provisions requires prior differentiation between terms which are germane to the existence, and those which relate to the exercise, of patent rights, in order to establish upon which provisions the Commission may properly rule. While the differentiation remains to be more fully worked out by future decisions of the Court, it is clear that patent licensing agreements are not automatically within Article 85(1) if the agreements simply confer rights to exploit patented inventions against payment of royalties, but that questions of applicability of Article 85(1) arise if a grant is accompanied by terms which go beyond the need to ensure the existence of an industrial property right, or where the exercise of such right is found to be the object, means or consequence of a restrictive agreement."[55]

Only two questions need be asked. What terms are required in a patent licence "to ensure the existence" of that industrial-property right? How does a restriction in a patent licence be non-restrictive of competition if it is not related to a restrictive agreement but restrictive of competition if it is so related? If a patent owner agrees to permit a limited invasion of his monopoly by a licensee that is permissible, but it is not permissible if the object of the limitation is to preserve the rest of his monopoly!

The difficulties into which the Commission appears to have been led in attempting to apply the Court's approach to five common types of licence provisions are mentioned in paragraphs 8-32A and B, 8-33, 8-34, 8-38 and 8-39 above.

[55] Commission of the European Communities. *Fourth Report on Competition Policy*. Brussels 1975. p.20.

PART 3
HORIZONTAL AGREEMENTS

CHAPTER 9
Joint Research Agreements

3. Cases

Rank/Sopelem

19A The Commission granted individual exemption under Article 85.3 in respect of the Rank/Sopelem agreement. The agreement had originally contained certain provisions to which the Commission had raised objection. There had been clauses prohibiting either party exporting directly or indirectly outside the sales territory assigned to it by the agreement, in effect making it impossible for the parties to trade between France and the other Member States; as an alternative, the parties considered substituting a requirement that the exporting party must make a lump sum payment, but that was rejected as incompatible with Article 85.1. There had also been certain procedural provisions, restricting the right of each party to administer its own intellectual-property rights, particularly application for, and enforcement of, patent rights. An obligation on each party to refrain from using, after termination of the agreement, trade marks belonging to the other party which it had been using during the life of the agreement was also objected to, on the ground that the party concerned would thereby be put out of business.

The agreement in the form for which the Commission granted exemption established a system for close co-operation between the parties in research and development, production, and distribution in relation to lenses and lens controls. The main terms were as follows:

Research, development, manufacture

(a) By continuous contact between their research teams,

the parties were to co-ordinate their activities. Research and development programmes and production projects were to be allocated by joint agreement, information exchanged for this purpose to be kept secret even after the end of the agreement. Where each party had a substantial share in the development work, the results would be "joint products" protected by jointly-owned patents taken out and maintained by joint agreement. In any country in which one party had no interest, the other party would be free to take out patents at its own expense in the joint names of both parties. After termination of the agreement, both parties would be free to use all joint patents. Third parties would be allowed to use joint patents only where Sopelem and Rank both agreed.

(b) Each party remained free to carry out its own research and development in the joint fields, taking out patents in its own name. Distribution of products protected by such patents could be entrusted to the other party upon the agreement terms, but in return for a royalty in appropriate cases.

(c) Each party remained free to carry out sub-contract work for the other party, in parallel with such work for third parties, provided that no confidential information was disclosed.

Distribution

The agreement distinguished between:

Sopelem products, i.e. those in which the rights belonged exclusively to Sopelem, to be marketed under the trade name "MONITAL" created specifically for that purpose and belonging to Rank;

Rank products, i.e. those in which the rights belonged exclusively to Rank, marketed under the name "VAROTAL";

joint products, marketed either under "MONITAL" or "VAROTAL" depending upon whether manufacture was by Sopelem or Rank.

Both parties were to offer concurrently the entire range of joint products as well as their own products. The relationship of the parties was buyer and seller, each being free to fix its own prices and conditions. But each had to provide in its own territory the same after-sales service and on the same terms as the manufacturing party provided in the territory. On termination of the agreement Sopelem could take over the "MONITAL" mark for a reasonable price, subject to Rank's right to use it for two years.

The marketing territories were allocated as follows. Sopelem was the exclusive distributor of "MONITAL" products in the six original Member States plus twenty-one other countries, and of "VAROTAL" products in France and six African countries. Rank was the exclusive distributor of "MONITAL" products in Denmark, Ireland, and the U.K. and most of the rest of the world, and of "VAROTAL" in the Common Market (except France) and the rest of the world (except for the six African countries). In North America, Brazil, China, and COMECON countries, both parties could market "MONITAL" products.

Neither party could maintain stocks nor seek business in "MONITAL" or "VAROTAL" in the other's territory, and each had to forward to the other any inquiries relating to the latter's territory. But each was free to supply against unsolicited orders in any Member State in the other's marketing territory, subject to payment by the exporting party to the other of a sum strictly limited to the actual cost of providing free after-sales service.

In effect, the parties were free to allocate between themselves primary responsibility for research, development, and production, and – in the marketing territory of each – for distribution. No doubt the agreement was outside Regulation 2779/72 on account of the size of the parties, particularly Rank – exceeding the quantitative limits in Article 3.1 of the Regulation (33-04).

Between them, Sopelem and Rank represented some 20% of the E.E.C. trade in the products in question. But the products constituted only a small proportion of each party's turnover – 5%-6% of Sopelem's and 10% of Rank's. The agreement was considered to help improve production, distribution and technical progress. The joint range of products was wider, and each party had the advantage of the other's distribution network. Co-ordination of research and development had contributed to technical progress. Rank's sales in France had increased, and so had Sopelem's export sales to the rest of the world. Consumers benefited from the wider range of better-quality products offered by each party. There was also improvement in customer service.

CHAPTER 10

Joint Production, Selling and Purchasing

3. Joint Selling

No effect on inter-Member trade

10–07 Following the general trend towards mergers and concentration of industries, the Commission found that a number of central selling agencies had disappeared. One of those to go was the Comptoir Français de l'Azote (C.F.A.).[1]

10–08 Another case involving price equalisation was *Asybel.* Asybel S.C. was a joint selling organisation set up by the Belgian non-ferrous metal producers to market their output of by-product sulphuric acid. It re-sold both on the Belgian market and in export markets. The price equalisation system operated in such a way that, in respect of each financial year, the producers received a standard price for each tonne of acid calculated on the basis of Asybel's total income and deliveries. The Commission held that the arrangement fell within Article 85.1 because price competition was excluded, and advised the parties that exemption could not be granted.

10–08A The Dutch metallurgical producers sold their by-product sulphuric acid through a joint sales agency, N.V.C.P. – *Nederlandsche Verkoopkantoor voor Chemische Producten.* Unlike the corresponding Belgian organisation, Asybel (10-08), N.V.C.P. was concerned only with sales in Holland, and there was no price equalisation arrangement. It merely sold on behalf of each of its members that quantity which the member delivered to it. However, small and medium-sized Dutch re-sellers were required

[1] *Third Report on Competition Policy*. p.47.

to buy exclusively from N.V.C.P. The Commission pointed out that this prevented the re-sellers from importing from other Member States, and that it constituted an infringement of Article 85.1. That restriction was then terminated. Apparently the Commission did not regard the remaining N.V.C.P. arrangements as falling within Article 85.[2]

Exemptions

-14 Exclusive distribution arrangements figured in the *Rank/Sopelem* agreement for joint research, development, production, and marketing (*v.* 9-19A).

-14A The Commission announced that it was proposing to take a favourable decision on the agreement relating to *Nuclear Fuels.* This was an agreement between the British and French re-processers of uranium oxide fuels (B.N.F.L. and C.E.A. respectively), four large German chemical companies, and KEWA, a joint German company set up by the other parties. The agreement provided for the parties to set up a second joint company, United Reprocessers Gesellschaft (U.R.G.), with the main object of marketing fuel re-processing services. The parties undertook not to operate in the oxide fuel re-processing field except through U.R.G. In effect, U.R.G. would operate on behalf of B.N.F.L. and C.E.A. until their capacity was used up, at which stage KEWA was free to set up a plant. The KEWA plant could have a capacity of 1,500 tonnes, and B.N.F.L. and C.E.A. would not raise their own capacities above 800 tonnes a year without the consent of the other parties. Until their fill-up date, the British and French plants would share equally the fuel to be re-processed, after fuel from certain named power stations had been treated by the French plant.

The grounds upon which the Commission proposed to come to a favourable decision were not indicated, but presumably individual exemption was envisaged in the light of the special nature of the material in question.

Condemned agreements

-14B *Nederlandse Cement-Handelmaatschappij* N.C.H. was a joint company set up in Holland by 26 German cement producers to market their products. At the date of the decision it was operating in the whole of Benelux on behalf of 38 German

[2] *Ibid.* p.48.

producers. Each producer had entered into a bilateral agreement with N.C.H., granting the latter exclusive marketing rights in Benelux. The principal was prohibited from selling in Benelux, directly or indirectly, except through N.C.H. N.C.H. was to sell at uniform prices and on uniform conditions. The business was allocated between the principals on the basis of quotas.

The Commission held that there were, in addition to the written bilateral agreements, some three oral "base agreements" between the principals. The first was an agreement not to sell at different prices and conditions, limiting their and N.C.H.'s freedom to compete. The second was an agreement as to the quotas – the producers regarded the quotas both as a right and an obligation to deliver the quantity in question; the freedom of each to sell more, or less, in Benelux was thereby restricted. The third base agreement was to sell in Benelux exclusively through N.C.H., thereby restricting the producers in their freedom to offer cement in Benelux, and presenting the buyers there with only one seller in place of nearly 40. The Commission held the base agreements and certain provisions in the bilateral agreements (requiring N.C.H. to adopt uniform prices and conditions, requiring the principals to supply the quota quantities, etc.) to be infringements of Article 85.1, and the parties were required to terminate them.

4. Joint Purchasing

10–16 The Commission has now granted negative clearance in relation to an agreement setting up another SPAR company, *Intergroup*. Intergroup was set up by ten SPAR companies, eight of which were nationals of Member States. Intergroup was enpowered to undertake market research and negotiate purchase contracts for its clients, but without having exclusive rights.

CHAPTER 11
Standardisation Agreements

3. Cases

–07 In anticipation of the expiry of the exemption on 31st December, 1972, the Association applied in October, 1972, for an extension of the exemption. The number of members had increased to twenty with one in each of seven Member States (only Luxembourg and Ireland having no Association member). The total turnover of members in all marine paints had increased, mainly due to the accession of the Nippon Paint Group to the Association. The proportion of members' turnover represented by Transocean paint had risen from one-third in 1967 to about three-quarters in 1972. Nevertheless, the members' share of the world marine paint market amounted to only 5% to 10%, there being some eight important competitors in the market including International Red Hand with some 25% to 30% of the market.

Two of the Association members belonged to large industrial groups which had other interests in the marine paint field. The French member Astral was part of the AKZO group which included another marine paint manufacturer, Sikkens in the Netherlands; and the Spanish member Urruzola was part of the B.A.S.F. group, of which the German marine paint maker Glasurit was also part. However, AKZO and B.A.S.F. were not important in the marine paint market, a market quite distinct from that for other paints – some 80% of marine paints cannot be used for other purposes.

The Commission in *Transocean (No. 2)* considered that the co-operation between the Association members enabled them to compete more intensively with other makers of marine paints, and decided to extend the exemption in exercise of its powers under Article 8.2 of Regulation 17. In consideration of the fact that the members included companies in the AKZO and B.A.S.F. groups, both having strong positions in the general paints markets, the extension was for a fixed period, up to 31st December, 1978.

The Commission did object to two provisions in the Association arrangements which it had previously accepted. These were, first, the restriction on supplying Transocean paint in the territory of another member, or to a ship registered in that territory – such supplies could be made only against payment of a commission to the member to whom the territory had been allocated; and, second, the need to seek a member's consent before supplying non-Transocean paints in his territory. The Commission had regarded some degree of territorial protection as being necessary when the Association was in its early stages, but considered that that stage had passed and that these provisions were no longer indispensable. The Association appears to have accepted that view.

The Commission also made its extension of the exemption subject to five other requirements. There should be an annual report to the Commission, which should also be informed without delay of (a) any change in the Association agreement, (b) any decision by the Association's Board of Directors or under its arbitration provisions, (c) any change in the composition of its membership, and (d) any "links" between a member and any other concern in the paints field – "links" for this purpose including common directors or managers and any financial participation. In its *Third Report on Competition Policy*, the Commission explained that this requirement was intended to ensure that the autonomy of the parties was not compromised by outside links.[1]

The Association objected to (d) and appealed to the European Court. The Association argued that the Statement of Objections given to it by the Commission as part of the procedure under Regulation 99/63 (cf. 4-82) did not sufficiently particularise the Commission's proposals to allow the Association to comment adequately on those proposals. The Court annulled that portion of the Commission's decision relating to (d) and referred the issue

[1] Commission of the European Communities. *Third Report on Competition Policy*. Brussels 1974. p.57.

back to the Commission. The Court also ordered the Commission to pay the costs.

-09 In the *Papiers Peints de Belgique* case, the parties argued that their system of quality classification assisted the buyer. The parties were manufacturers of wallpaper. They argued that their classification system contributed to the improvement of distribution by making it easier for buyers to choose between hundreds of designs. While not denying that this might be the case, the Commission pointed out that the quality classification was only a small part of a restrictive arrangement prohibited by Article 85.1. If the parties wished to do so, there was nothing to stop them having a separate agreement relating to the quality classification scheme, without any reference to prices, which could be notified to the Commission to determine whether exemption could be granted under Article 85.3.

CHAPTER 12
Specialisation Agreements

2. Regulations and Notices

Regulation 2779/72

12–05A Council Regulation 2821/71 (Appendix K) gave the Commission power to grant block exemption to specialisation agreements (using that term to include decisions and concerted practices). As required, the Commission published a draft of the block exemption regulation it proposed to make (reproduced as Appendix O in the book). In due course the final regulation was issued as Commission Regulation 2779/72 – the English text is set out in Appendix Q, in this Supplement.

Scope

12–05B The scope of the block exemption is indicated by Article 1 of the Regulation (33-02). It extends to agreements by which the parties "mutually bind themselves":

(i) "not to manufacture certain products or cause them to be manufactured by other undertakings",

"and" (ii) "to leave it to the other contracting parties to manufacture such products or cause them to be manufactured by other undertakings".

The words "mutually" and "and" are significant. They suggest that the exemption is available only where *each* party renounces some freedom to manufacture. For example, an agreement between A, B, and C may provide that A and B will not manufacture, but will take all their supplies from C. By such an agreement, A and B "mutually bind themselves" not to manufacture, but C has not given up any freedom. It would seem that the block exemption applies only where, say, A will make product X for all three parties, B product Y, and C product Z, each binding himself not to make, or have made, the products which the other two are to produce. This interpretation is confirmed by the comment in the Commission's decision on the *Prym/Beka* agreement; the agreement did not qualify for exemption under Regulation 2779/72 "since there is no reciprocal commitment by each of the parties to refrain .... from the manufacture of certain products in order to entrust it to its partner, but only the unilateral commitment by Prym to cease its production of needles and transfer it to Beka".[1] Were it not for this requirement of reciprocity, the exemption would apply to an agreement under which only one party undertook to give up production, for example in return for a cash payment, without any corresponding restriction upon the other party's freedom to manufacture – a straight closing-down agreement. The obligation not to manufacture can run only "for the duration of the agreement" – it cannot extend beyond the life of the agreement (there is a fine academic point here – if the ban on manufacture is expressed to continue "for ten years after determination of the agreement", can the agreement be said to be determined if one of its terms is still operative?).

-05C It will be noted that Article 1 is confined to "manufacture". Consequently specialisation agreements relating to services do not benefit from the block exemption – for example, an agreement whereby A did the dry-cleaning for both parties and B the wet-cleaning.

-05D The Regulation distinguishes three levels of products:

(1) "the products which are the subject of specialisation",
(2) "identical products",
(3) "products considered by consumers to be similar by reason of their characteristics, price or use".

It would seem that (1) are the products made or supplied pursuant to the agreement – for example, Article 2 permits obligations as to minimum stocks and after-sales service. "Identical products" are the products in question, but made or supplied by a non-party. The expression in (3) appears elsewhere in

[1] Official Journal L296. 24.10.73. p.26.

Community competition law – in Regulation 2822/71 (28-02) and in the Notice Concerning Minor Agreements (26-06); it means, in effect, "substitutes".

12–05E By virtue of Article 7 (33-08), the exemption under Regulation 2779 extends also to decisions of associations of undertakings and to concerted practices. For convenience, in the following comments, "agreement" will be used to cover all three.

Permitted restrictions

12–05F Because of Article 2 (33-03), the benefit of the exemption is lost if the agreement contains any "other restrictions on competition" apart from those on production allowed in Article 1 and the four restrictions specified in paragraph 1 of Article 2 itself. Using the same lettering as in that paragraph, the four are:

(a) a ban on specialisation agreements with non-parties relating to identical products or substitutes, without the consent of the parties. Such a term is a reasonable safeguard for the other parties. It prevents party A, for example, who is obligated by the agreement not to make Y, going to a non-party and offering not to make Y if the other party will give up making Z. Equally, it prevents party B, who has to supply the other parties with X, from making a new specialisation agreement with a non-party under which the latter will be the manufacturer of X.

(b) the obligation to supply the other parties, and to meet minimum quality standards. In most instances, a party will accept an obligation not to manufacture a product only if another party has accepted an obligation to supply him with it, and to the requisite quality standards. It is significant that, whereas the draft regulation referred to "minimum quantities" (31-03 in the book), Article 2.1(b) does not allow an obligation as to quantities. This could be unfair. If A has to supply B with product X, and there is a sudden upsurge in demand, has A to supply all B's requirements even if this means A not being able to supply his own requirements? It would be normal in such agreements to provide some basis of allocation in such circumstances, but that seems to be ruled out by the terms of Article 2. It may be that A could put up his price to B, but the position as regards terms relating to prices is not clear – *v. infra* 12-05H.

(c) the obligation to buy solely from the other parties, except where they are not prepared to match more favourable terms available elsewhere. On the face of it, this seems reasonable, but it does not adequately protect the supplying party. The more favourable terms may be available from somebody who is supplying below cost to enter the market, or from somebody selling at a specially low price because of some exceptional factor, or from imports at dumped prices.

(d) the obligation to grant exclusive distribution rights, so long as parallel imports are not excluded.

-05G Although geographical area is not mentioned in sub-paragraph (d) of Article 2.1, presumably geographical exclusivity is allowed for by it. But what about industrial exclusivity (such as the right to supply industry X but not industry Y)? Division of customers had to be removed from the *Prym/Beka* agreement before individual exemption was accorded to it. If (d) was to be confined to geographical exclusivity, why does it not say so in terms? On the face of it, industrial exclusivity is not ruled out. However, the *acquiring* parties (the Regulation says "those parties" in Article 2.1(d)) must not be able to prevent parallel imports (or parallel supplies), in particular by the exercise of patent and other rights. The Regulation seems to assume that the manufacturing party should be free to exercise his patent and other intellectual-property rights, but not the acquiring parties. Is this fair? If manufacturer A, with patent rights to a medicament in, say, Holland, makes a specialisation agreement with B in Italy, under which B makes that medicament and supplies it to A, is it fair that A should lose the benefit of the block exemption if he seeks to use his patent rights in Holland to stop parallel imports from Italy (where patents are not available for medicaments)?

-05H The introductory words of paragraph 1 of Article 2 include the phrase "no other restriction on competition". Would a term in the specialisation agreement fixing the prices at which the specialisation goods were to be supplied be a "restriction on competition"? It would mean that the aquiring parties would not normally sell for less. But the acquiring parties would surely require some protection as regards price in return for giving up production, even if only a fixed discount below the supplier's published list price. In such agreements it would not be unusual to require that any more favourable price offered by the supplier to some non-party should also be offered to the acquiring parties. Would such terms be "restrictions on competition", and disallowed by the Regulation?

Permitted obligations

12–05I Paragraph 2 of Article 2 allows obligations to maintain stocks of the products and of spares, and to provide after-sales and guarantee services.

Quantitative limitations

12–05J These are contained in Articles 3 and 4. The exemption applies only if:

(a) the agreement products represent "in any member country" not more than 10% of the business in identical products and substitutes.

Prima facie, this suggests that the exemption is lost if in *any* Member State the market for the identical goods and substitutes is less than ten times the agreement products, even if none of the parties carry on business in that State. It would seem more likely, however, that the exemption is lost only if the agreement products supplied by any Member State in which the parties trade in those products exceed 10% of the market for identical goods and substitutes.

(b) the aggregate turnover of the parties (including associate undertakings brought in by Article 4) does not exceed 150 million units of account. In calculating turnover inter-party dealings are ignored (Article 4).

The exemption is not lost even if in two consecutive financial years *either* limit is exceeded by not more than 10%. Apparently it is *either* limit, but not *both* limits, because paragraph 3 of Article 3 uses the words "share of the market *or* the turnover" (emphasis added).

Control

12–05K Article 5 implements Article 7 of Regulation 2821/71. If the agreement in question has effects incompatible with Article 85.3 of the Treaty, the Commission may withdraw the exemption, in particular where the rationalisation which should follow specialisation is not yielding significant results, or consumers are not being given a fair share of the resulting benefits. In such circumstances, the Commission can exercise its powers under Articles 6 and 8 of Regulation 17, even though the agreement has not been notified (Article 7 of Regulation 2821/71 – 27-08); for example, it could issue an individual exemption to which special conditions were attached (e.g. as to passing on a share of the benefits to the consumers).

Time limits

-05L By Article 8, the Regulation came into force on 1st January, 1973 (the date of accession of the New Members – Denmark, Ireland, and United Kingdom) and, by Article 1, it applies until 31st December, 1977.

Account must be taken of Article 6, which provides that the exemption "shall have retroactive effect from the time" when the requisite conditions were satisfied. This patently does not mean what it says! It means that the block exemption has retroactive effect prior to 1st January, 1973 running back to the date when the requisite conditions were satisfied in respect of the particular agreement in question, i.e. "retroactive from" 1st January, 1973 and running forward from the date when an agreement in existence before 1973 complied with the requirements of the Regulation.

-05M The operation of the Regulation in relation to different classes of agreements may be summarised as follows:

(1) Accession agreements, i.e. agreements to which Article 85.1 applies by virtue of the accession of the New Members on 1st January 1973. As Community law did not apply to these agreements prior to that date, they benefit from the block exemption *ab initio*, i.e. from the time when Community law applies to them. (Reference should be made to paragraphs 4-35 – 4-40 where the problem as to what is an "accession agreement" is discussed.)

(2) Specialisation agreements in operation before 18th January, 1972. The 18th January, 1972 was the date on which Regulation 2822/71 came into force and sub-paragraph (c) added to paragraph 3 of Article 4 of Regulation 17. Prior to that date specialisation agreements falling within Article 85.1 were compulsorily notifiable, unless relieved from the obligation to notify under the other provisions of

Article 4. Consequently, in respect of any such agreement which was compulsorily notifiable, the benefit of the block exemption under Regulation 2779/72 is available only from the date the agreement was notified if that is later than the date when the agreement satisfied the requirements of the Regulation.

(3) Specialisation agreements in operation only on or after 18th January, 1972. Such an agreement benefits from the block exemption from the date it complies with the requirements of Regulation 2779/72. This includes agreements coming into operation after 1st January, 1973.

Conclusion

12–05N From the foregoing comments, it will be seen that Regulation 2779/72 suffers from drafting deficiencies. It is to be hoped that it will be clarified, and perhaps amended, at an early date. In the meantime, if parties wish to make a specialisation agreement which would appear to fall outside the Regulation on a strict interpretation, they may wish to consider consulting the Commission as to the possibility of obtaining individual exemption. It would be unwise to rely upon the block exemption and not notify, and then discover that the agreement fell outside the Regulation. Except for existing agreements and accession agreements, notified in due time, an individual exemption cannot apply to any period prior to notification.

3. Cases

12–10A *Papeteries Bolloré/Braunstein agreement* In October 1962, five French paper manufacturers notified their agreement made in 1960. That agreement was to promote collaboration between the parties, and provided for production quotas, with fines and compensation for excess production and under-production, and price co-ordination. The 1960 agreement was replaced by one made in 1970 which provided only for specialisation of production, each party to specialise on producing a different type of fine paper. The agreement, so the Commission found, improved production and technical progress by permitting long production runs and the adaptation of plant, with larger production units.

Costs and selling prices had been reduced, giving consumers a fair share of the benefits.

Exemption under Article 85.3 was given to the 1970 agreement, subject to three conditions: (a) any arbitration awards relating to the specialisation provisions in the agreement made under the arbitration clause were to be communicated to the Commission; (b) a report covering the first two years working of the agreement had to be submitted to the Commission; (c) any inter-locking management links between the parties and any changes in the ownership of the parties were to be communicated without delay to the Commission. The 1960 agreement did not qualify for exemption, but had been notified in due time; the Commission's decision, therefore, contained a declaration under Article 7 of Regulation 17 that the prohibition in Article 85.1 did not apply to that agreement for the period from 13th February, 1962 to 31st March, 1970 (the date of the 1970 agreement).

—10B *Prym/Beka agreement* Both parties, Prym, a German limited partnership, and Beka, a Belgian limited liability company, made needles for domestic sewing machines, the former representing about 3% of world output and the latter about 6%. They decided to concentrate production at Beka's factory in Belgium, Prym giving up production of the needles and transferring its plant to Beka's factory. In return, Prym received 25% of Beka's capital. In its final form, the agreement provided that Prym would not manufacture or have manufactured the needles in question, but would buy all its requirements from Beka, to whom it would send at the end of each year a statement of its requirements in the next year. Beka undertook to supply Prym's requirements at special prices calculated as set out in the agreement by reference to Prym's realised prices. In the event of Beka being unable to meet Prym's requirements, the latter could buy from third parties subject to its advising Beka of the name of the other supplier and of the quantities involved. Needles of standard quality were to be marked "555" whichever party sold them, but higher-quality needles were to be marked "Prym" or "Beka" according to the party selling them.

In its original form, the agreement provided for a division of customers, Prym supplying certain classes of outlets and Beka other classes, and Beka would supply outlets competing with certain of Prym's customers only with Prym's consent. In addition, exports to countries outside Europe were to be reserved to Prym, with some exceptions; but trade with Eastern countries was to be open to both parties. The Commission objected to the provisions relating to the division of customers, and these were annulled so far as concerned E.E.C. markets.

The parties had applied originally, on 9th April, 1970, for negative clearance. As the agreement clearly restricted competition (Prym could not manufacture and had to buy exclusively from Beka, the latter had to supply and at preferential prices) and affected inter-Member trade (a firm in one Member had the exclusive right to supply a firm in another Member) Article 85.1 applied, and negative clearance could not be given even to the agreement in its amended form. (The decision does not discuss the question of appreciable effect. Apparently the two parties together had about 10% of the E.E.C. market,[2] and it may have been thought that this was appreciable.)

The parties had also, on the 18th May, 1972, notified the agreement, seeking exemption under Article 85.3. The agreement had led to rationalisation of production, increasing output at Beka's factory by 50%, and making possible more intensive use of the existing plant and the adoption of production-line techniques. Costs of production had fallen, despite increases in wages and raw-material prices. There were also quality benefits. There remained keen competition within the Common Market from other sources. That competition would ensure that consumers would receive a fair share of the resulting benefits. And the amended agreement did not contain any inessential provisions. Individual exemption was granted as from 10th October, 1972, when the offending provisions as to market division were amended, until 31st December, 1984.

The agreement did not qualify for block exemption under Regulation 2779/72, because only one party – Prym – was to give up manufacture and draw from the other; there was no reciprocal obligation upon Beka to abandon some other product in favour of Prym. Where the specialisation is only unilateral, the Regulation does not apply.

4. Check List

12–11 Question 8. The relevant block exemption regulation is Regulation 2779/72 (Appendix Q).

[2] Commission of the European Communities. *Third Report on Competition Policy.* Brussels 1974. p.54.

CHAPTER 13
Exchange of Information Agreements

2. Regulations and Notices

3–13 The "Notice Concerning Co-operation between Enterprises" indicated that general clearance could not be given in respect of agreements to exchange four classes of information, i.e. orders, turnover, investment, and prices. In a number of recent cases, provisions to exchange information as to production and consumption, investment, and prices have been condemned. These cases are discussed in the next section of this Chapter.

3. Cases

Exchange of technical information

–16A The agreement in the *Rank/Sopelem* case provided for the parties to co-ordinate their research, development, and production activities, by continuous contact between them and by allocating projects to one or the other. This inevitably involved exchange of information, and the parties undertook to do all in their power to keep that information secret, even after the expiry of the agreement.

Exchange of price information

3–18A Exchange of price information was a feature of the *European Glass Manufacturers* case. Twenty-four concerns were party to the "International Fair Trade Practice Rules Administration" ("IFTRA") relating to glass bottles, jars, and flasks. The practical implementation of the IFTRA Rules was discussed at regular meetings of the parties, resulting in agreement on two points – prices in export markets, and exchange of price information. As to prices in export markets, it was considered that the major local producer who dominated the market would be the "natural price leader" – the producer who first raised his prices would be the price leader if the others followed. The price leader would fix his prices and inform the other parties. Any of the latter exporting to that market would then charge his prices when selling in that market. Information as to price lists, discounts, sales terms, etc., and as to any changes in them, was exchanged between the parties, sometimes directly, sometimes indirectly through national offices.

It is interesting to note that the Commission in its decision did not formally condemn the arrangements as regard export prices – it may be that the Commission considered the discussions at the meetings to be merely descriptive of what *would* happen, rather than normative, i.e. what *should* happen. Be that as it may, the Commission did condemn the arrangements to exchange price information. The parties had argued that supply of price information was not compulsory under the IFTRA Rules, and that in any event the information given was always historical, in the sense that it was not given to competitors before disclosure to the market. As to the first argument, the Commission pointed out that exchange of price information was inherent in the IFTRA Rules, being indispensable to the enforcement of certain of the Rules. As to the second argument, there was sufficient interval between publication of the price changes and their operative date for other suppliers to bring their prices, etc., into line. The reasoning upon which the Commission concluded that the exchange of price information was contrary to Article 85.1 was expressed in the decision as follows:

> "It is contrary to the provisions of Article 85 (1) of the EEC Treaty for a producer to communicate to his competitors the essential elements of his price policy such as price lists, the discounts and terms of trade he applies, the rates and date of any change to them and the special exceptions he grants to specific customers.
>
> An undertaking which informs its competitors of such elements of its price policy will only do so when certain that, in accordance with the agreement entered into with such competitors in pursuance of the IFTRA rules, they will pursue a similar price policy for deliveries to the market where the undertaking is a price leader. By such means the possibility of

unforeseen or unforeseeable reactions by competitors is sought to be eliminated, thus removing a large element of the risk normally attaching to any individual action in the market.

An undertaking which is informed by its competitors of the prices imposed by the latter, including special prices and discounts granted to particular customers in respect of certain goods, is placed in a position of precise knowledge of the current and future policy of its competitors in their respective markets, and consequently may adapt its own price policy for exports to such markets.

Considering the data already at their disposal, the information exchanged between the undertakings in question is of decisive importance for determining the price policy of each individual undertaking for exports to the other Member States concerned.

Therefore, the agreement to exchange information on prices has the object of restricting or distorting competition between the parties within the Common Market."[1]

–18B A somewhat different line of reasoning was adopted by the Commission in the *Dutch Sporting Cartridges* case. There were twelve manufacturers supplying 22LR calibre sporting ammunition to the Dutch market, one a Dutch manufacturer, the others manufacturers in other countries. Between them they had 90% of the Dutch market. There was an undertaking by each supplier to notify its individually-fixed price to a committee.

The Commission held the undertaking to be contrary to Article 85.1. Suppliers would be less inclined to change prices, knowing that competitors would be informed immediately and could react. The effect sought was to prevent unilateral price changes, eliminating price competition and making prices rigid.

Exchange of information as to costs

–18C In the *European Glass Manufacturers* case, the parties adopted a common method for calculating costs for the purpose of fixing prices. This was to eliminate, for pricing purposes, differences in costing methods – formerly some manufacturers had based costs on weight, others on complexity of manufacture, etc. The common standard method had to be used for pricing purposes, but not for internal management purposes (for which presumably each party could use its traditional methods). There does not

[1] Official Journal L160. 17.6.74. p.13.

appear to have been any provision for exchanging cost information.

The use of the common standard method of costing for pricing purposes was condemned as an infringement of Article 85.1. The Commission pointed out that the comment in the "Notice Concerning Co-operation between Enterprises" that agreements having as their sole object the joint preparation of standardised calculation systems were not considered to restrict competition did not apply in the *Glass Manufacturers* case. The agreement did not have the preparation of a standardised calculation model as its sole object – on the contrary, it was only one part of a series of agreements aimed at restricting competition as to prices, etc.

The Commission's decision in this case should be borne in mind in connection with any proposal to have an agreement for the exchange of cost information. In most cases, an essential part of such an agreement would be a requirement that the parties adopt a standardised calculation method. It would seem that if the sole object of the agreement is to achieve some object which is not incompatible with Article 85.1, the agreement will be permissible – for example, where the parties can show that the purpose of the exchange was to increase efficiency and reduce production costs. But if the information exchanged is used for pricing purposes, to arrive at common prices, the agreement will be outside the Notice, and will fall within Article 85.1.

Exchange of production information

13–18D In *Marketing of Potassium Salts*, the Commission found that the parties, the French concern S.C.P.A. and the German Kali und Salz, supplied each other with information regarding current production and production forecasts, and also the levels of stocks. As this exchange of information was to enable the parties to co-ordinate their deliveries, it was condemned. It gave them the means to concert their production policy.

Exchange of information as to orders

13–18E In its "Notice Concerning Co-operation between Enterprises" the Commission indicated that exchange of information as to orders was outside the general clearance. In the *Marketing of Potassium Salts* case, the Commission found that the parties supplied each other with information as to orders received and forecasts of trends in demand. This was to enable the parties to co-ordinate their deliveries and was condemned.

Exchange of information as to investment

3–18F In some industries the minimum economic size of plant is substantial in relation to the size of the market. These tend to be high-technology, capital-intensive industries. If competitors have to take their separate decisions in complete ignorance of their rivals' plans, considerable excess of capacity may result, with considerable waste of economic resources. On the other hand, if competitors are allowed to exchange information as to their investment plans, there may be restriction of competition.

The Commission acknowledged the existence of the problem in its *Second Report on Competition Policy* – "This problem is too delicate to afford grounds for hoping that it can be solved by a general approach. The method of case-by-case examination is unavoidable."[2] In its *Third Report on Competition Policy*, the Commission went a little further. It referred to two particular cases (*Cimbel* and *Polyester Fibres*) and commented:

> "However, this does not mean that, in exceptional circumstances and under conditions designed to ensure that the interests of the Community as a whole are respected, the Commission cannot organize for certain industries an improved system for exchanging forecasts of market trends and developments in production capacity, providing individual firms retain full control of their respective decision-making powers and full responsibility over their individual investments."[3]

3–18G In the *Cimbel* case, the Belgian cement manufacturers operated their agreements through a company called La Cimenterie belge SA. ("Cimbel"). Each party had undertaken to inform the others in writing of intentions to increase, replace, or modify production facilities. The Commission considered that this provision was intended to prevent one party achieving an advantage over its rivals by clandestine extension of capacity. By increasing total sales a party might procure a larger quota under the market-sharing provisions in the agreement. The undertaking was, in effect, a necessary safeguard to the quota agreement. In fact, the three largest manufacturers all extended their capacity at almost the same time after years of stagnation. The undertaking was condemned as contrary to Article 85.1. The agreement had not

[2] *Second Report on Competition Policy.* Brussels 1973. p.26.
[3] *Third Report on Competition Policy.* Brussels 1974. p.28.

solved the overcapacity problem – it had failed to prevent the creation and maintenance of excess capacity.[4]

13–18H In the *Polyester Fibres* case, the Commission accepted that the cut polyester fibre industry had considerable excess capacity, with pressure on prices because manufacturers sought to reduce their surpluses. But the notified agreement covered an area wider than investment projects, extending to production and selling policies. On receiving the Commission's views, the parties terminated the agreement and withdrew the notification.[5]

13–18I The Commission appears to have taken a different view in the *Cementregeling voor Nederland* case. After discussions with the Commission, the agreement had been substantially modified. In its final form it contained a provision that the parties would advise each other of any investment of importance in relation to supplies to the Dutch market. Certain other aspects of the agreement were condemned, but not that provision.

[4] *Second Report on Competition Policy.* Brussels 1974. p.291.
[5] *Ibid.* p.40.

CHAPTER 14
Other Forms of Co-operation

1. Introduction

-01 As an illustration of the point that competition law is not inimical to all forms of inter-firm co-operation, reference may be made to the Business Co-operation Centre established by the Community, which commenced operation in May 1973. Its tasks are:

> "(i) to forward general information to enterprises which request it;
>
> (ii) to establish contact between undertakings wishing to co-operate or to make approaches;
>
> (iii) to inform the Community institutions of barriers which hinder co-operation."[1]

It had 1,800 approaches in its first year. In the twelve months to 31st October, 1974, according to the Centre's second annual report, there were some 900 approaches, again mainly from Germany and the United Kingdom.

2. Regulations and Notices

-04 The comment that United Kingdom law does not extend to joint negotiation of wages and conditions of employment is no longer entirely correct. The Restrictive Trade Practices Acts, in essence the law relating to cartels, still exclude restrictions and information obligations relating to remuneration, conditions of employment, etc. But the law relating to monopolies and dominant positions, revised and consolidated in the Fair Trading Act 1973,

[1] *Seventh General Report on the Activities of the European Communities.* Brussels 1974. p.291.

no longer excludes agreements relating to such matters; in determining whether firms who by their conduct restrict competition between themselves have one-quarter or more of the market, agreements relating to labour-relations matters can now be taken into account.

3. Cases

14–08A *EUMAPRINT case* The European Committee of Printing and Papermaking Machinery Manufacturers (EUMAPRINT) had a regulation distinguishing between "international" and "national" exhibitions. The latter were confined to undertakings located in the organising country or having some connection there (a branch, agent, etc.). The Italians had issued invitations to firms in other Member States to take part in their 1973 exhibition, GRAFITALIA '73, but those invitations had subsequently been withdrawn for concerns located outside Italy who did not have a permanent connection there. The Commission regarded the regulation as discriminating against firms located in other Members who did not have a permanent connection with the organising country; in effect, small and medium-sized firms were denied the opportunity of making their wares better known and of meeting prospective agents or distributors. The regulation was, therefore, incompatible with Article 85. At the Commission's request EUMAPRINT discontinued the regulation, and the organising committee for GRAFITALIA '73 changed its rules to admit foreign firms.

14–08B *UNIDI case* UNIDI, the national association of the Italian dental industry, organised every eighteen months an exhibition under the title "Expo Dental". The rules for the exhibition prohibited exhibitors from taking part, in the nine months preceding each "Expo Dental", in any other exhibition of dental equipment, subject to certain exceptions. Exemption was justified by the nationalisation deriving from the concentration of exhibitors at one exhibition.

Transfer or creation of capacity

14–09A The Belgian cement manufacturers operated a trade organisation, Cimbel. The ownership or use of production facilities could be transferred within the Benelux area only if the transferee had previously undertaken to fulfil all the obligations of membership of the organisation. The transfer agreement had to be approved by the management committee of Cimbel, which also fixed the number of shares in Cimbel which the assignor had to transfer to the transferee. In the Commission's view these restraints on transfer restricted competition. Production facilities within Benelux could not be assigned without the transferee becoming contractually bound by the Cimbel arrangements, automatically excluding any stimulus to competition which the advent of a non-party might have brought. The transfer restraints were condemned as being contrary to Article 85.1.

There was also a provision in the Cimbel constitution binding its members not to create any new capacity without the approval of all other parties concerned. In the Commission's view, this prevented members from setting up capacity in any Member State of the E.E.C. without prior approval of the other parties, and so competing in other Member States. The provision was condemned.

*Fair Trading Rules**

-09B The *European Glass Manufacturers* case was concerned with the "International Fair Trade Practice Rules Administration", IFTRA for short. The IFTRA Rules governed a wide range of trading practices, and included the following:

A. Practices regarded as unfair and contrary to free competition.

A.1. Sales below cost and destructive competition

(a) Sales below cost to weaken or destroy a competitor are unfair.

(b) Use of financial strength to cut prices below cost in order to obtain a monopoly is unfair.

(c) Systematically undercutting a competitor's prices or systematically matching his offer is unfair if done to weaken or destroy the competitor.

A.2. Discrimination

(a) It is unfair to discriminate between customers by offering differing prices, etc., to customers of equivalent standing.

(b) It is unfair to grant to some customers special conditions, which are in effect price reductions, which are not granted to all customers.

(c) It is unfair to allow quantity discounts before the quantity has been reached.

(d) It is unfair to make unjustified payments to third parties in connection with the conclusion of a business transaction.

*See also 14–09R.

A.3. Tying contracts

A.4. Imitation of trade marks, trade names, etc., to mislead customers

A.5. Loss leaders

(a) It is unfair to sell goods below cost to suggest that the firm's normal price level is low.

(b) It is unfair to sell goods below cost as loss leaders.

A.6. Misrepresentation towards customers and competitors

(a) It is unfair to offer special prices, rebates, etc., in respect of conditions which cannot be met or which are not intended to be met.

It is unfair to deviate secretly from published list prices to obtain commercial advantage from abuse of the confidence of customers and competitors in the published prices.

(b) Deliberately to make out false invoices, etc., is unfair.

(c) It is unfair to make untrue statements as to the origin, composition or quality, or use of goods offered or sold.

A.7. Presumptions and rebuttals

An unfair trade practice will be presumed if an undertaking is shown to have applied prices, etc., which are discriminatory or deviate from published price lists. This presumption can be rebutted, e.g. by showing that the price reduction, etc., was caused by necessity, such as insolvency, or to meet a competitor's price. The evidence must show that the price reduction, etc., was no more than necessary to defend the firm's interest.

B. Rules and principles regarded as customary in the trade.

B.1. Fulfilment of contracts

Contracts are to be performed according to their letter and spirit.

B.2. Price lists

Publication and distribution of separate lists of gross prices showing discounts is the normal practice in the industry.

B.3. Predatory pricing

Prices should be calculated in such a way as to cover costs as determined by customary rules.

B.4. Files relating to costing and complaints

Files shall be opened and maintained for costing, and also for complaints.

B.5. Status of customer

To avoid unjustified discrimination, the status of a customer shall be checked before granting a discount or other terms.

B.6. Quality

Defective goods shall not be exported.

B.7. Contents

Prescribed standards shall be observed as a matter of normal practice.

C. Misrepresentation of prices

It is unfair for a person who has promised to give his competitors information as to his prices to charge different prices without informing those competitors.

D. Cessation and damages

Any signatory may require any other party to cease any unfair and anti-competitive practice under the Rules, and may claim damages. For violation of Group C, the damages will be presumed to be at least 30% of the turnover in question.

There was provision for arbitration in connection with disputes.

The minutes of the IFTRA meetings showed that the parties were concerned with other matters as well. Export prices were fixed on the basis of the domestic prices in the export country, usually the prices of the largest producer in that country as "price leader". Price lists were exchanged, either directly between the parties or indirectly. There was a common method for calculating prices. And prices were on a *delivered* basis, i.e. delivered customer's railhead or warehouse.

-09C When discussing in its decision whether the IFTRA Rules restricted competition, the Commission started by noting that there are differences, and in some respects great disparities, between the legislation in Member States relating to the suppression of unfair competition and to the protection of consumers. The selection of common rules to govern the conduct of undertakings in several Member States must, therefore, be arbitrary:

> "An agreement to observe such rules may thus lead the undertakings which are party to such an agreement to apply in their own country, or in the countries to which they export, rules more stringent than those in force in such countries. In the present decision, the Commission takes no view on the question whether the adoption, by national legislation or otherwise, of some of the rules set out [in the IFTRA Rules] is desirable or not."[2]

In other words, the decision in the *Glass Manufacturers* case should not be taken as indicating a view as to a *bona fide* attempt to lay down a fair basis on which firms in different Members will compete. (Perhaps the Commission has in mind some such distinction as that drawn by the U.S. courts in the *Chicago Board of Trade* case, between *restriction* of competition, which is not admissible, and *regulation* of competition, which may be permissible?) But:

> "The mere labelling of an agreement between undertakings as 'fair trading rules' does not suffice to remove the agreement from the ambit of Article 85(1) of the EEC Treaty."[3]

14–09D As to the provisions in the IFTRA Rules, some of them, although presented as attempts to prevent unfair trading, "in fact give the parties the opportunity to take joint action against normal methods of competition. Consequently, these clauses have as their real and principal object the restriction of competition between the parties to the detriment of users of glass containers." The provisions condemned by the Commission were (using the same lettering as in 14-09B):

A.1(c)	This provision, and also A.7, prevented the more efficient and viable firm from offering prices lower than its competitors' prices. Thus one party, when delivering into the territory of another party, would not disturb the local price level nor apply prices lower than those of the local "price leader". The Commission commented that the true purpose of the provisions

[2] Official Journal L160. 17.6.74. p.11.
[3] *Ibid.*

	was abundantly clear from the IFTRA minutes.
A.2(a) A.6(a)(second sentence) A.7.	These all had the same object, to suppress normal competitive behaviour, especially to restrict competition in prices, discounts, etc. The purpose of the provisions was all the more apparent when considered in the light of the arrangements between the parties to exchange price lists.
B.2.	This rule, relating to publication of price lists, had the object of enabling the application and enforcement of the provisions in A just noted.
B.6.	The prohibition on export of defective products (bottles with imperfect colouring) also had the object of complementing the A provisions – export of defective products at lower prices would have the same effect as under-cutting the prices of the local "price leader".
C.	"According to the parties, clause C prescribes as being unfair 'only the breach of a promise, where made to supply information, since price information which is incorrect, or not given, or supplied too late has the effect of misleading a competitor who may have acted on the faith of such a promise to supply information'. It was also maintained that clause C did not have 'as its object or effect that such a promise and the corresponding price information be given, but only presupposed that such would be provided'.

The reasoning is particularly specious in seeking to distinguish between a promise made, apparently outside the IFTRA agreement, by a manufacturer to supply information on prices to one or more of his competitors, and the obligation undertaken by the same manufacturer within the framework of the IFTRA agreement, to supply such information with speed, accuracy and candour. Whenever undertakings of the importance and renown as those presently concerned take the decision to supply such information to competitors, it is self evident that such information will be correct and complete. Consequently, clause C in fact seeks to establish the elaborate system of exchange of price information, ... between all the parties to the IFTRA agreement."[4]

These seven provisions – together with the agreements relating to exchange of price information, the price calculation scheme, and the adoption of delivered prices – were the aspects condemned by the Commission. This means that the parties were allowed to continue the other provisions in A, B, and C – for example, those relating to: sales below cost to attack a competitor (A.1(a)), some forms of discrimination (A.2(b), (c), (d)), tying contracts (A.3), loss leaders (A.5), preparation of false invoices, etc. (A.6), predatory pricing (B.3), status of customers (B.5), and observance of standards (B.7).

14–09E It would appear, therefore, that the door has not been closed on genuine attempts by enterprises in individual industries to achieve *bona fide* regulation of competition between them in different Member States, perhaps something on the lines of the codes of acceptable competitive practices adopted in some U.S. industries under the aegis of the Federal Trade Commission. But to defend

[4] *Ibid.* p.12.

successfully any such regulation adopted by agreement between the competitors, as distinct from regulation imposed by legislation, the parties will have to satisfy the Commission that their object is indeed *bona fide* regulation of competition and not a disguised suppression of competition.

Common methods for calculating costs and prices

-09F In the *European Glass Manufacturers* case, the parties had noted that differences in selling prices could result from differences in costing methods. They therefore decided to adopt a single method of calculation, i.e. a list, with definitions, of the various cost items. The system was . . . 'to be used for sales pricing and not for purposes of internal management'. Costs were to be worked out by traditional methods, and then compared with the standard method 'to avoid serious mistakes'.

The Commission held the standard method to be an adjunct to the IFTRA Rules and the price-exchange agreement. It enabled the parties more easily to compare their prices and co-ordinate their market activities. It was condemned as being contrary to Article 85.1.

The Commission referred to its 'Notice Concerning Co-operation between Enterprises', which indicates the Commission's view that agreements whose 'sole object is the joint preparation of calculation models' do not restrict competition. The *Glass Manufacturers* agreement was outside the view expressed in the Notice, because it did not have as its sole object the joint preparation of a calculation model – on the contrary, it was part of a series of agreements aimed at restricting competition as to prices, discounts, and conditions of sale.

Self-limitation agreements

-09G The expansion of Japanese exports and the strategy adopted by Japanese exporters, have aroused concern in Western industrialised countries. An article in *European Community* of April 1974[5] described the export strategy as concentration on markets where the home industries were weak or non-existent so as to obtain a position of strength through lower prices and discount schemes for retailers, etc. Instances cited were tape-recorders in Italy and cameras in France; in Britain, Japan had 75% of the market for imported motor-cycles, 90% for small computers and calculators,

[5] "Japan Talks to Europe" by David Perman. pp.6-7.

66% for transistor radios and cassettes, and 58% for binoculars. E.E.C. trade with Japan, which in 1968 showed a balance of $89 million in Japan's favour, by 1972 had reached a balance of $1,207 million in favour of the Japanese. In September 1970 the Community opened negotiations with Japan with a view to reaching some bilateral agreements, but the exchanges became bogged down over safe-guard clauses.

It was, no doubt, inevitable that individual industries would seek to protect themselves by direct discussions with their Japanese counterparts pending the outcome of official negotiations. In October 1972, the Commission published a statement giving its views.[6] It noted that instances had been observed of Japanese industries preparing measures aimed at limiting their exports to the Community or at regulating those exports in some other way, as regards quantity, price, quality, etc. – measures adopted by the Japanese industry unilaterally or in concert with the corresponding European industry. The Commission drew attention to Article 85.1 and advised notification of such agreements. The fact that some or all of the parties were located outside the E.E.C. did not, the Commission pointed out, exclude the operation of the Article if there were effects within the Common Market – a clear application of the "effects" principle (*v.* 3-91 *et seq.*) In his reply to a question in the European Parliament in May 1973,[7] M. Borschette, the Commissioner responsible for competition, referred to the Commission's statement, and indicated that at that date there had been no follow-up to it, as regards voluntary-restriction agreements between Japanese and European firms. He also drew attention to two other types of measures, restrictions imposed by the Japanese on themselves, and voluntary restrictions incorporated in trade agreements between governments. In the latter category, the Commission had decided that there was no objection to quota limitations on Japanese electronic equipment in an agreement between the French and Japanese governments. The Benelux countries and Italy were also operating import controls in respect of electronic equipment and tape recorders respectively.

14–09H The Commission re-stated its views in its *Third Report on Competition Policy:*

"Voluntary restraint provisions in trade agreements between

[6] Journal Officiel C111. 21.10.72. p.13.
[7] Official Journal 162. Annex. May 1973. pp.31-2.

> Community and non-Community countries, if they are acts of foreign trade policy which, provided that the quantities to which the restraint applies can be freely disposed of within the Community, are not as such caught by the competition rules. Likewise, Article 85 would not apply to export agreements imposed on firms in non-member countries by their governments, unless there was an agreement or concerted practice between the firms. The Community should seek to solve this situation by measures of official commercial policy.
>
> Auto-limitation agreements, whether concluded by firms in non-member countries alone or between such firms and corresponding European firms, are subject to Article 85 according to the notice published by the Commission on 21 October 1972 which calls for measures of competition policy."[8]

By the time the Report was written, a number of agreements had been notified.

-091 The Commission's first formal decision upon an inter-firm agreement has now been issued, the *Franco-Japanese Ballbearings Agreement.*

During 1972 there were meetings and correspondence between, on the one hand, two major French manufacturers of ballbearings and their Chambre Syndicale, and, on the other, the four major Japanese manufacturers and their Industrial Association. The main subjects covered were an increase in the prices of the Japanese exports, and limitations of their exports to France. As a result, there were increases in the prices of Japanese ballbearings exported to France.

The first issue was the question whether there was an agreement between the parties or not. The Commission pointed to (a) a letter dated 10th March, 1972, from the Japanese Association to the Chambre Syndicale in which the Japanese informed the French of price increases which had been made to take effect from 1st April, 1972, and also to (b) the French reply dated 27th April, 1972, noting the Japanese increases. The Commission held that the French and Japanese manufacturers, through the mediation of their trade associations, had "entered into an agreement in principle for the purpose of increasing the prices of Japanese ballbearings imported into France", and added:

[8] Brussels 1974. p.27.

> "Contrary to the arguments put forward by the parties in their reply to the statement of objections and at the hearing, for Article 85(1) of the EEC Treaty to apply it is not essential that this agreement should take the form of a contract having all the elements required by civil law: it is sufficient that one of the parties voluntarily undertakes to limit its freedom of action with regard to the other."[9]

The parties had argued that the exchange of letters did not constitute an agreement – the Japanese had raised their prices by unilateral decision. The Commission rejected the argument on the ground that, in the light of the negotiations, the exchange of letters formed "a consistent and explicit whole and is evidence of a common understanding by the parties that the prices of Japanese bearings would be increased". It was "therefore, an agreement between undertakings within the meaning of Article 85".

As the agreement was concerned with bringing the Japanese prices into line with the French prices, it had as its object the restriction of competition within the Common Market. As to the question whether the agreement might affect inter-Member trade, the French had drawn the attention of the Japanese at the beginning of the negotiations to the fact that some of the imports into France were made via Germany, Belgium, and the Netherlands. The Commission ruled that the agreement came within, and constituted an infringement of, Article 85.1.

14–09J There are four significant points to be noted regarding the Commission's conclusion.

(i) First, the interpretation of "agreement" in Article 85 to include an "understanding". It could be argued that what had happened was that the Japanese had listened to and considered the representations put forward by the French, and had then taken their own, unilateral, decision; and that, in those circumstances, there was no agreement. It would seem that the Commission is following a line of reasoning similar to United Kingdom law under the Restrictive Trade Practices Acts 1956 to 1973: "agreement" includes "arrangement", and "arrangement" includes communication between the parties resulting (in United Kingdom law) in restrictions or information obligations on at least two parties. In the Commission's view of Community law, it would seem, "agreement" includes the situation where there has been communication between the parties with the object or

[9] Official Journal L343. 21.12.74. p.24.

effect of restricting competition. No doubt at some stage the question will come before the European Court for a final ruling as to the extent of "agreement" for the purposes of Article 85.

(ii) Secondly, the Commission's decision, although it holds the agreement to be an infringement of Article 85.1, does not require the parties concerned to desist. This may arise from doubts as to the validity or practicability of requiring a party to reduce its prices. Presumably it would not have been a simple question of ordering the Japanese to lower their prices to the *status quo ante* the relevant increases. Subsequent changes in economic and financial conditions might have made some other price level appropriate – and to have investigated that may have meant the Commission acting as price-fixers for the Japanese. Or, there may have been considerations of extra-territorial jurisdiction and the validity or practicability, or perhaps wisdom, of issuing orders to foreign nationals not located within the Commission's jurisdiction. It appears that the parties had not been in touch with each other after the publication of the Commission's statement in October, 1972 (cf. 14-09G), as mentioned in the next paragraph, and on that account the Commission may have thought the infringement would have ceased.

(iii) In the third place, although there had been no notification, no fines were imposed. The Commission explained, in its *Fourth Report on Competition Policy,* that it had not fined the firms concerned because of the special circumstances of the case, in particular because the agreement had been entered into before the Commission's statement had been published and the firms had not been in contact with each other after its publication.

(iv) This decision does reflect upon the "effects" principle. Of course, in so far as any agreement there may have been was made within the Community (e.g. during the discussions in France) the territorial principle would apply. But in so far as any agreement there was was made outside the Community, in Japan, and in so far as any relevant actions were also taken in Japan, then for the Commission to have jurisdiction, the effects principle must apply.

–09K In conclusion, it is of interest to note the four categories of self-limitation measures identified by the Commission in its *Franco-Japanese Ballbearings* decision, and its comments on them:

(i) Measures taken in pursuance of trade agreements between the Community and Japan (and presumably those made by Member States, with

Commission approval, and Japan). These are "acts of external commercial policy" and as such are outside Article 85.

However, any agreements or concerted practices additional to such measures could come within the Article.

(ii) Measures imposed upon Japanese enterprises by Japanese authorities. These are also outside the scope of Article 85 (but any additional agreements or concerted practices could be within the Article).

(iii) "Measures resulting from agreements or concerted practices between undertakings which are merely authorized by the Japanese authorities under Japanese law." Article 85 could apply if the undertakings in question were free, under Japanese law, to refrain from participation in the agreement or concerted practice.

(iv) "Measures resulting solely from agreements, concerted practices, or decisions by associations of undertakings, entered into or engaged in either unilaterally by Japanese undertakings or in concert with the appropriate European undertakings."

These are private measures and may fall within Article 85.

Although these are worded in relation to Japan, the same principles apply as regards other countries. The agreement between the French and Taiwanese producers in *Preserved Mushrooms* is discussed in paragraph 14-09P.

Regulation of trade auctions

14–09L The *FRUBO* case concerned an agreement between the fruit Importers' Association and the Wholesalers' Association with regard to the regulation of the Rotterdam fruit auction. The agreement contained purely technical provisions relating to, for example, sampling and display of fruit, inspection to check quality and quantities, terms of delivery of goods sold, etc., and also enforcement provisions, including reprimands, fines, and exclusion from auctions. The agreement had been amended several times in response to the Commission's comments. The only term in the final version to which the Commission objected related to imports of fresh citrus fruit from outside the Common Market and of apples and pears from outside Europe for marketing in Holland. With certain insignificant exceptions, importers and wholesalers taking part in the Rotterdam market were prohibited from marketing such fruit in Holland except through the Rotterdam auctions.

The Commission held that this restricted competition within the Common Market. The wholesalers could not import themselves, and although they could buy in the other E.E.C. fruit import auctions (Antwerp and Hamburg), only small supplies were available there. Similarly, fruit importers in other Member States, although they could sell through the Rotterdam market, could not sell directly in Holland without going through that market. For the same reasons, trade between Member States was affected. The Commission required the parties to terminate the condemned provisions.

The Commission recognised that a system of sales by auction may have advantages. Concentration of supply and demand in one place may reduce transport and marketing costs. On the other hand, the obligation to pass through Rotterdam might increase transport costs. In any event, in so far as prices at the Rotterdam market were lower and the facilities there more advantageous, wholesalers would use that market in preference to alternative methods of supply, so that, to that extent, the prohibition on direct handling was not indispensable to the attainment of any advantages achieved by the agreement. Consequently, exemption under Article 85.3 could not be granted. Moreover, although the goods involved came within the term "agricultural products" in the E.E.C. Treaty, the agreement did not come within the special provisions relating to such products.

The two Associations appealed against the Commission's decision, but the Court rejected the appeal.

Collective boycott

09M The *Papiers Peints de Belgique* decision concerned four Belgian manufacturers of wallpaper selling something less than 50% of the wallpapers marketed in Belgium. They had a comprehensive agreement regulating most aspects of their trading activities, including a basis schedule of prices, ranges, and qualities, schedules of ex-factory and retail prices, standard conditions of sale, credit terms, opening and closing of the marketing year, supply of sample books, clearance sales, listing of wholesalers, joint advertising, etc. Their association had issued circulars providing for aggregated rebates calculated on the basis of the customer's purchases from all four members. The circulars also specified certain conditions to be imposed on customers, in particular an obligation to apply and display the prices fixed by the association (i.e. resale price maintenance), and also a prohibition on displaying lower prices or price reductions; the customers were required to impose the same obligations on their customers.

A Belgian wholesaler re-sold to a Belgian retailer some wallpaper bought from members of the association. The latter displayed the goods at prices which allowed for the discount customary in their self-service stores. In one such store, the wallpaper was being sold at prices higher than those permitted under the association price lists. From October 1971 onwards, the association members operated a collective boycott against the wholesaler.

14–09N The Commission held that the association agreement and the circulars were within Article 85.1. The circulars were decisions of an association, and when sales were made to customers incorporating their terms they became agreements between enterprises. They restricted competition in many directions, fixing prices, selling terms, etc. The aggregated rebates concentrated purchases on the association members; and also represented an element of discrimination between buyers in that, for a purchase of an identical quantity, the buyer with the greater total purchases from the members would get a better discount (unless both were within the same bracket).

The Commission also held that the agreements and the decisions of the association might affect inter-Member trade. In calculating purchases from members for the purposes of the aggregated rebate, wallpaper imported by a member and re-sold by him was included. Freedom of trade between Member States was affected. By its very nature, an agreement covering the whole of the territory of a Member State would have a compartmentalising effect at the national level.

The Commission having held that the agreement and circulars infringed Article 85.1 refused exemption under 85.3 (the agreement had been notified). In respect of the collective boycott, the Commission imposed on the four concerns fines totalling 358,500 units of account (say £150,000).

Although the Commission's decision discusses the application of Article 85.1 to the association agreement and decisions (the circulars), the decision does not explain how a boycott within

Belgium could affect inter-Member trade. The parties have appealed to the European Court.

Co-ordination of delivery programmes

–09O In its *Marketing of Potassium Salts* decision, the Commission dealt with the co-operation between the French Société Commerciale des Potasses et de l'Azote (S.C.P.A.) and the German Kali und Salz, both producers of potassium salts. The Commission found that there was an oral agreement between the two companies for co-ordinating their activities. As part of this co-operation, they co-ordinated their delivery programmes in the light of production capacity and stocks, and took joint decisions each year as to what tonnage each would export, including exports to other Member States, after meeting the requirements of their domestic markets. The Commission required the parties to terminate the co-operation agreement and also to bring to an end the ancillary exchange of information between them as to production and distribution. (The parties also had joint distributors in Holland and Italy, and S.C.P.A.'s sales in Germany were handled by a subsidiary of Kali und Salz, practices which the Commission also required to be terminated.)

–09P The monthly quantities which the parties could deliver were specified in *Preserved Mushrooms*. When investigating a complaint about the selling prices charged in Germany by French producers of preserved mushrooms, the Commission discovered an unnotified agreement with the Taiwanese producers, signed in January, 1973. On the French side, the agreement was made by the five principal French producers, acting as a group under the name Major French Mushroom Packers (M.F.M.P.) The Taiwanese Mushroom Packers United Export Corporation (T.M.P.U.E.C.) was the other party, representing all Taiwanese exporters. The agreement aimed at establishing co-operation between the parties by programming sales in Germany. For 1973, the French share of the German market was to be some 1,402,500 standard cartons, and the Taiwanese share some 1,350,000 standard cartons. The French were to deliver 116,875 cartons a month, the Taiwanese 112,500 cartons. Selling prices were to be fixed, and to be raised by 3% from 1st May, 1973. On request, either party would allow the other to check sales, production, and despatch documents; and a joint accounting organisation was to be set up. Taiwan was the world's largest producer of first-quality mushrooms, France the second largest.

Because of disturbance in the mushroom market, the Commission took protective action against imports of preserved mushrooms, in August, 1974 (in Regulation 2107/74). In fact, the downward trend of mushroom prices in Germany continued in 1973, and the parties did not put into effect the agreed 3% increase in May of that year. Nevertheless, the Commission held that the parties had implemented the agreement – contracts at prices similar to the Taiwanese prices were being made by the French at least until May, 1973 – and, even though the agreement may not have in fact had significant effects on the market, the intention was to divide up the German market between the parties. The Commission argued that, even if the French did have good reason to expect serious market disturbance such as was recognised by the Commission in Regulation 2107/74, it was not permissible for them to take the initiative by infringing the Treaty. As to the Taiwanese, the Commission regarded their blameworthiness as being less, in that they were hardly likely to have known, at the time the agreement was negotiated, of the statement issued by the Commission in October, 1972 of its views on agreements with foreign exporters. Fines amounting to 100,000 units of account (say £40,000) were imposed on the five French producers. No fines were imposed on the Taiwanese.

Mutual supply

14–09Q Under the *Bayer/Gist* agreement Gist increased its output of raw penicillin to supply Bayer. Bayer made penicillin derivatives for itself and Gist. The Commission proposed to grant exemption.

Fair Trading – Addendum

14-09R The *Aluminium Producers* had an International Fair Trade Practice Rules Administration (IFTRA), i.e. "Fair Trade Practice Rules" and "Contract of Commitment". The Rules identified as unfair practices: (a) destructive sales below cost, (b) dumping, (c) discrimination between customers contrary to declared policy, (d) failure to give price information contrary to declared policy, (e) agreements not to disclose deviations from published prices. The Rules encouraged published price lists, etc. The Contract set up procedures for investigation of contraventions. The parties terminated the agreements. Nevertheless the Commission issued a formal decision condemning the main provisions. The Commission regarded (c), (d), and (e) as discouraging sales below published prices, and inferred an obligation to exchange price information with competitors from the procedure for investigating contraventions.

PART 4
MERGERS AND ABUSES OF DOMINANT POSITIONS

CHAPTER 15
Mergers

1. Introduction

04 An instance of two companies setting up a joint company and transferring to it parts of their respective undertakings is the *SHV/Chevron* case. SHV was a Dutch company, Chevron Oil Europe an American company. They set up Calpam NV, a holding company, in Holland, and a series of subsidiary companies, also called Calpam, in Belgium, Holland, Luxembourg, Germany, and Denmark – in those countries SHV and Chevron had independent distribution networks for fuel oil, paraffin, lubricating oils, and asphalt. The agreement between SHV and Chevron provided for the two parties to transfer to the Calpam subsidiaries their distribution networks and related assets and plant in the countries in question for a period of at least fifty years. For a variety of reasons, the Commission held that the agreement did not infringe Article 85.1, and gave negative clearance; as neither party held a dominant position, the Commission held that the agreement did not fall within Article 86 either.

-07 The inherent dichotomy in merger policy has been evidenced by Community actions. On the one hand, there is the desire to see the creation of effective, viable undertakings of a European scale. The Commission itself has set up the Business Co-operation Centre, known as "The Marriage Bureau"; this started operation in May 1973, and in its first twelve months handled enquiries from over 1,800 firms. At their meeting in December 1973, representatives of the governments of Member States undertook "to do their utmost to complete promptly the work on the

Agreement on transnational mergers".[1] On the other hand, there is constant surveillance of the extent of industrial and commercial concentration. In its *Third Report on Competition Policy,* the Commission noted that in the six Original Members mergers (defined as acquisition of holdings in excess of 50%) rose from an annual figure of 173 in 1962 to 612 in 1970, the rate of increase being higher in the second five years, 1966 to 1970; between 1953 and 1970 the share of total sales held by the hundred largest manufacturing firms rose from 26% to 50% in the United Kingdom, and in Germany from 34% in 1954 to 50% in 1969; the results of studies into selected industries carried out as part of the Commission's research programme into concentration are also given in the Report.[2] The *Fourth Report on Competition Policy* has statistics for the enlarged Community for 1973, but in a different form. Of 1,638 "operations" in 1973, 138 (8%) were take-overs and mergers, 952 (58%) were acquisitions of participation, and 548 (34%) the setting up of joint subsidiaries – none of the take-overs or mergers involved companies in more than one country, but of the acquisitions of participation, only 40% were purely national, 60% being international, and of the joint subsidiaries only 22% were purely national, 78% being international, and of the international operations those within the E.E.C. predominated, 60% in the case of participations, 54% in the case of joint subsidiaries; the fifty largest European companies represented 17.1% of total industrial employment, and 25% of total sales. The *Fourth Report* gives some statistics of the number of firms with sales of more than 200 million units of account and of those with sales exceeding 1,000 million units, coinciding with the levels adopted in the draft mergers regulation (paragraph 15-26 below). In 1973, there were 332 firms in the E.E.C. with sales exceeding 200 million units, 116 in the United Kingdom, 92 in Germany, and 69 in France; 79 had sales exceeding 1,000 million units, 22 in the United Kingdom, 26 in Germany, and 15 in France. The *Fourth Report* also gives further information on the degree of concentration in various industries.[3]

The Commission, in an answer to a written question in the European Parliament, has indicated that it keeps a "systematic

[1] Official Journal C117. 31.12.73. p.15.

[2] *Third Report on Competition Policy.* Brussels 1974. pp.30-1, and pp.109 *et seq.*

[3] *Fourth Report on Competition Policy.* Brussels 1975. pp.114 *et seq,*

watch" on concentration in certain sectors, and a list is kept for this purpose. The object is to note any mergers which reduce consumers' freedom of choice and which are incompatible with the Treaty.

2. Application of Article 85 to mergers

—10 In the *SHV/Chevron* agreement, the two parties undertook not to compete in distribution of the agreement products, without the other's consent. The Commission noted that SHV, although it had interests in other fields, had no other interests in the petroleum products field, so that on the transfer of its distribution activities in that field to the joint Calpam companies, SHV disappeared as an independent wholesaler of petroleum products. So far as Chevron was concerned, it was part of the Standard Oil of California group, an integrated international group with activities covering crude-oil production and refining, and also distribution, as well as manufacture of petrochemicals. But there would be no incentive for Chevron to compete with Calpam in which it had a 50% interest. The Commission therefore concluded that there was no appreciable restriction of competition, and granted negative clearance under Article 85.1 (as neither party held a dominant position, Article 86 did not apply).

The Commission's decision in the *SHV/Chevron* case is dated December 1974, i.e. it is subsequent to Regulation 2779/72 (Appendix Q) giving block exemption to specialisation agreements. But as the decision accords negative clearance for the agreement, it remains uncertain whether the Regulation would apply to such a case. The Regulation, bearing in mind the *Prym/Beka* decision, would seem to require each party to give up a line of manufacture, and each to continue or undertake one, so that the obligations are mutual. In the *SHV/Chevron* situation, both parties gave up the activity, which was taken over by Calpam, a non-party. As neither party undertook an activity, the Regulation might not apply. But the Regulation does permit arrangements for manufacture by some other undertaking. It may be therefore, that renunciation of manufacture by both parties, with an arrangement to have manufacture undertaken by the joint company, may be accepted by the Commission as coming within the block exemption. The issue must remain in doubt until an appropriate case has arisen to test the point. (The *SHV/Chevron* agreement could not have benefited from the block exemption in any case because it was concerned, not with manufacture, but with distribution – the Regulation applies only to manufacture.)

3. Application of Article 86 to mergers

15–11 In view of the comments in the Court's judgment on the appeal in the *Continental Can* case, it may be doubtful that there must be abuse *of a* dominant position for Article 86 to apply to a merger. As the Court put it:

> "There may therefore be abusive behaviour if an undertaking in a dominant position strengthens that dominant position so that the degree of control achieved substantially obstructs competition, i.e. so that the only undertakings left in the market are those which are dependent on the dominant undertaking with regard to their market behaviour.
>
> Such being the meaning and the scope of **Article 86** of the EEC Treaty, the question raised by the applicant companies of the causal connection which in their view must exist between the dominant position and the abusive exploitation is irrelevant, for the strengthening of the position of an undertaking may be abusive and prohibited by **Article 86** of the Treaty, regardless of the means or the methods whereby it has been achieved, if it has the effects described above."[4]

The validity of this conclusion is discussed in paragraphs 15-32 *et seq.* below.

But from the *SHV/Chevron* decision, it is clear that the Commission's view is that if neither party has a dominant position, Article 86 does not apply.

15–12 As will be seen from the extract quoted in the preceding paragraph, the Court has followed the view expressed in the Study, *Le Problème de la concentration dans le Marché Commun*. In the Court's view, where a firm in a dominant position strengthens that position by a merger so that competition is obstructed substantially, there is an abuse within Article 86.

15–14 As noted in paragraph 15-11 above, the Court's decision on the *Continental Can* appeal was that Article 86 could apply to a merger involving a dominant firm provided that the strengthening of the dominant position substantially reduced competition. And this was so, in the Court's view, even though the merger took place without any improper or reprehensible exercise of the

[4] [1973] C.M.L.R. p.225.

economic power conferred by the dominant position, in order to procure or induce the merger. In the Court's words, any question of a "causal connection . . . between the dominant position and the abusive exploitation is irrelevant"! The validity of the Court's reasoning is discussed in paragraphs 15-32 *et seq*. below.

However, the Court allowed the appeal on purely factual grounds. The Commission had not established that light metal containers for meat and such containers for fish constituted separate markets distinct from each other and from containers for other products such as vegetables, fruit juices, etc. Nor had the necessity to exclude containers made of other materials been established. In effect, the Commission had not proved the existence of a dominant position.

Horizontal mergers

-16 — Some guidance may be obtained from the draft regulation on
-18 mergers issued by the Commission (Appendix T). Below a turnover of 200 million units of account, and a market share of 25% in any Member, the merger is considered to be outside the proposed control. The draft regulation is discussed in paragraphs 15-24 *et seq.* below.

Vertical mergers

-19 The emphasis in the draft mergers regulation is upon power to hinder effective competition. There is likely, therefore, to be less scope for it to apply in the case of vertical mergers. Its application to such mergers may not be completely ruled out, as, for example, where a buyer with say 50% of the market (in the materials purchased and perhaps in the resultant products) takes over a supplier with 40% of the market.

Conglomerate mergers

-21 As the emphasis in the draft mergers regulation is upon power to restrict effective competition, it is unlikely that conglomerate mergers will come within its scope, assuming that the Regulation when made is in its present form.

Limitation

-23 As regards infringements of Article 86, the regulation providing for limitation periods in the form in which it was made (Regulation 2988/74 – Appendix S), follows the draft. The limitation period is five years, running from the day the infringement was committed (Article 1.2). However, in the case of a continuing infringement, time runs from the day the infringement ceased. In the case of a merger which contravenes Article 86, the infringement is by its very nature a continuing one, and one which is not likely to cease. It is unlikely, therefore, that the limitation period will be of help in such cases. In the unlikely event of the merger being undone, the period would start to run. Presumably it would also start to run if the market situation were to change so that competition was no longer obstructed.

4. Mergers Regulation

15–24 In the course of his submissions on the appeal in *Continental Can*, the Advocate General pointed out that Article 86 does not provide any means for exempting activities which infringe it. To apply the Article to mergers might, therefore, result in undesirable consequences from the point of view of industrial policy. Putting the argument more generally, it might be said that merger control requires a more sophisticated instrument than the blunt prohibition in Article 86 – a totally inflexible weapon.

15–25 Within five months of the Court's judgment in *Continental Can*, the Commission had submitted to the Council a draft regulation providing for control of mergers in the Common Market (Appendix T). In its preamble, the draft points to deficiencies in the powers given by Article 86. The Article applies only in what might be called extreme cases – there ought to be power to act in respect of other mergers, and to prevent mergers. In some circumstances it might be desirable to permit mergers which might infringe the Article, i.e. there ought to be powers of exemption under conditions decided in the light of each case. There ought also to be provision for prior notification and suspension of implementation of mergers. The preamble envisages the exercise of the powers given by Article 235 of the Treaty, under which the Council, acting unanimously, adopts appropriate measures to make good any failure in the Treaty to provide powers necessary to achieve one of the objectives of the Community – a recognition that, *pace* the Court, the Treaty does not provide a system for controlling mergers.

15–26 The kernel of the draft lies in Article 1.1. A merger is incompatible with the Common Market if it confers or enhances the "power to hinder effective competition" in the Common Market or in a substantial part of it. To come within the Article, one of the parties to the merger must be "established" within the Market, and the merger must be capable of affecting inter-Member trade. The second sentence of Article 1.1 elaborates the meaning of "hinder effective competition".

Paragraph 3 of Article 1 would confer power to grant exemption. If the Commission finds that a merger is within Article 1.1, it must come to a decision, condemning or exempting the merger, within nine months (Article 17).

In effect, the draft divides mergers into three classes. Where the turnover of the parties does not exceed 200 million units of account (say £80 million) and the merged group would not account for more than 25% of the relevant market (in identical goods or services or acceptable substitutes) in any Member State, the merger is outside Article 1.1. Where the turnover of the parties amounts to 1,000 million units or more (say £400 million), Article 4 would call for prior notification, unless the undertaking to be taken over had a turnover of less than 30 million units (say £12 million). Consequently, parties to mergers falling between these two extremes would be free, but not obliged, to notify.

An extended definition of "merger" is given in Article 2.

-27 In February, 1974, the Economic and Social Committee accepted the idea of regulations to set up a system of merger control, based on a "case-by-case" approach and providing for exemption in appropriate cases. The Committee did, however, put forward some pertinent criticisms of the draft.

While turnover was an acceptable yardstick, consideration should be given to the relevance of any extra-Community turnover of the parties. Regard should also be had to adverse impact on multi-product concerns where turnover might not be indicative of market power. A more precise definition might be needed to deal with such things as indirect taxes, intra-group trading, etc.

The draft should also be amplifed to give more guidance to those undertakings it might affect. It might also be necessary to have regard to near-substitutes or the possibility of new entrants to the market.

As to the figure of 25% of the market in any Member State suggested for mergers excluded from control, this might discriminate against concerns in the smaller Members.

The figure of 1,000 million units as the level for compulsory notification should be reviewed at regular intervals. Again, there should be a fuller definition of turnover – allowance might have to be made for cases such as financial institutions.

15–28 No doubt it is indicative of the compexity of the problems involved that, to date, the final regulation has not been made.

Some indication of the scope of the proposed regulation is that in 1971 there were 57 industrial enterprises in the nine Member States with an annual turnover exceeding 1,000 million units, of which 18 were in Germany, 15 in the United Kingdom, and 13 in France; in addition, 1 was shared by the United Kingdom and Italy, and 2 by the United Kingdom and the Netherlands. In the same year there were 104 industrial enterprises with a turnover of 500 million units.[5]

[5] Answer to Written Question in European Parliament, 16th September, 1974. Official Journal C121. 11.10.74. p.5.

Annexe to Chapter 15

1. Introduction

–29 From the point of view of merger control under Community law, the prime interest of the appeal in the *Continental Can* case is the question whether Article 86 applies to a merger, given that there has been no reprehensible use of a dominant position to procure the merger. The Commission in its decision had, in effect, held that the Article did so apply:

> "For an undertaking in a dominant position to reinforce that position by means of merger with another undertaking with the consequence that the competition which would have existed actually or potentially in spite of the existence of the initial dominant position is in practice eliminated for the products in question in a substantial part of the Common Market constitutes behaviour which is incompatible with Article 86 of the Treaty."[6]

–30 In their appeal, Continental Can and Europemballage argued that this interpretation of the Article was erroneous – an attempt by the Commission to acquire powers to control mergers which it did not possess under the Treaty.

The companies pointed out that this interpretation was contrary to the clear wording of the Article. The Article applied only where the economic strength conferred by the dominant position was used, i.e. an abusive exploitation of the dominant position.

[6] [1972] C.M.L.R. p.D31.

2. Advocate General's Submissions

15–31 The Advocate General began his discussion of the point by stressing that Article 86 did not permit a 'blanket control' of mergers – a comparison with Article 66 of the European Coal and Steel Community Treaty, with its specific obligation to obtain prior authorisation for mergers and its detailed system, showed that that was not the draftsmen's intention. Nor could it be said that alteration of market structure by merger was completely outside the Article – pressure on a competitor to merge by cutting prices could fall within the Article, i.e. "unfair market conduct".[7] In the *Continental Can* case, such conduct was absent, so that the only question was:

> ". . . whether **Article 86** also applies where an enterprise in a dominant position strengthens its position in the market by the acquisition of another enterprise to such an extent that competition of economic significance no longer exists in practice."[8]

That was the basic argument of the Commission. But the words of Article 86 "to exploit in an improper manner a dominant position within the Common Market" implied that the Article applied only "where the market strength is used as an *instrument* and in a reprehensible manner, i.e. that these criteria must be fulfilled as conditions for the application of the law".[9] The Commission had sought to argue the contrary, pointing to the Preamble to the Treaty with its "guarantee. . . fair competition", to Article 3(f), and to Article 85.3(b) with its requirement that competition should not be substantially eliminated; and had relied on Article 86(b), suggesting that this did not require the use of market strength, only internal operations. The Advocate General doubted the "viability" of the Commission's argument. It involved a wide interpretation of Article 86, whereas, bearing in mind the penal consequences of an action being held to infringe the Article, general legal principles required a strict interpretation to be applied in areas of doubt. The Preamble and Article 3(f) were not "directly applicable" law. They were only general, imprecise, expressions of principle given concrete form by Articles 85 and 86. Article 86 permitted absence of all competition, a complete monopoly. Moreover, it was significant that

[7] [1973] C.M.L.R. p.206.
[8] *Ibid.*
[9] *Ibid.*

Article 86 did not contain any reference to preserving "genuine competition" as in Article 66 of the Coal and Steel Community Treaty nor anything comparable with Article 85.3(b) of the E.E.C. Treaty with its requirement that there should be no opportunity to eliminate competition in a substantial part of the Community. Finally, there were no exempting provisions in that Article, which could lead to undesirable consequences. And adoption of the Commission's argument would be dangerous, in that only the worst merger cases would be caught – it would be better to show that Article 86 did not apply, so that a proper system of merger control could be devised and adopted. The Advocate General concluded that, for Article 86 to apply, the market power given by the dominant position had to be "used in an unfair way".[10]

3. The Court's judgment

–32 The full ingenuity of the reasoning adopted by the Court can be appreciated only by reproducing the relevant passage:

> "**Article 86(1)** of the Treaty declares as 'incompatible with the Common Market and prohibited' the abusive exploitation of a 'dominant position within the Common Market or within a substantial part of it' by 'one or more undertakings . . . in so far as trade between member-States is liable to be affected by it'. It must be
> examined whether the term 'abusive exploitation' in (a)
> **Article 86** is only intended to cover behaviour on the part of undertakings which may have a direct effect on the market and is detrimental to production or marketing, buyers or consumers, or whether it also refers to
> alterations in the structure of an undertaking which lead (b)
> to serious impairment of competition in a substantial part of the Common Market.
>
> However, there can be no distinction between measures concerning the structure of an undertaking and
> practices that have an effect on the market, for any (c)
> structural measure may affect market conditions in so far as it makes the undertaking bigger and economically stronger.

[10] *Ibid.* p.209.

To resolve this problem it is necessary to resort to the spirit, structure and working of **Article 86** and to the system and aims of the Treaty. The problems in issue (d) here cannot therefore be solved by a comparison of this **Article** with certain provisions of the ECSC Treaty.

Article 86 forms part of the chapter devoted to the common rules for the policy of the Community in the sphere of competition. This policy is derived from **Article 3 (f)** of the Treaty whereby the activity of the (e) Community includes the establishment of a system to protect competition within the Common Market from distortion. The applicant companies' contention that this provision only contains a general programme that is not legally binding ignores the fact that **Article 3** regards (f) the pursuit of the aims that it lays down as indispensable for the achievement of the tasks of the Community. With regard to the aim mentioned in paragraph **(f)** in (g) particular, the Treaty provides greater detail on this question in several provisions the interpretation of which is governed by this purpose.

By providing for the establishment of a system that will protect competition within the Common Market (h) from distortion. **Article 3 (f)** demands *a fortiori* that competition must not be eliminated. This requirement is (i) so essential that if it did not exist numerous provisions of the Treaty would be futile. Moreover, it corresponds with the principles laid down in **Article 2** of the Treaty (j) whereby the task of the Community is 'to promote throughout the Community a harmonious development of economic activities'. Thus the restrictions on competition, that are permitted by the Treaty in certain circumstances because the various aims of the Treaty must be reconciled with one another, are limited by the (k) requirements of **Articles 2** and **3** since if these limits are exceeded there is a danger that a restriction of competition would be contrary to the aims of the Common Market.

The purpose of the general provisions applicable to undertakings contained in **Articles 85** to **90** is to (l) preserve the principles of **Articles 2** and **3** of the EEC Treaty and the achievement of the aims laid down in those **Articles. Article 85** concerns agreements between

undertakings, decisions by associations of undertakings and concerted practices, whereas **Article 86** covers (m)
unilateral activity on the part of one or several undertakings. **Articles 85** and **86** are intended to achieve the (n)
same aim on different levels – the maintenance of effective competition in the Common Market. The restriction of competition, which is prohibited if it is the result of behaviour coming within **Article 85**, cannot be (o)
allowed by virtue of the fact that this behaviour is successful under the influence of a dominant undertaking and results in a merger of the undertakings concerned. In the absence of express provisions, it cannot be supposed that the Treaty, which in **Article 85** prohibits certain decisions of normal associations of undertakings restricting but not eliminating competition, intended in **Article 86** to permit undertakings, by (p)
merging into an organic unit, to obtain such a dominant position that any serious possibility of competition is almost eliminated. Such a diversity of legal treatment would open a breach in the whole system of competition law that could jeopardise the proper functioning of the Common Market. If it were sufficent to avoid the prohibitions contained in **Article 85** to form the (q)
connections between undertakings so closely that they escaped the application of that **Article** without coming within the scope of **Article 86**, the partitioning of a substantial part of the Common Market would thus be permitted, contrary to its fundamental principles. The efforts of the authors of the Treaty to preserve actual or potential competition in the market, even in cases where (r)
restrictions on competition are permitted, have been expressly recorded in **Article 85 (3) (b)** of the Treaty. If **Article 86** does not contain the same express provision it (s)
is because the provision made there for dominant positions does not, unlike **Article 85 (3)**, permit any exceptions to the prohibition. In the case of such a system, the subjection to the fundamental objectives of (t)
the Treaty, in particular that of **Article 3 (f)**, follows from the compulsory nature of these aims. In any event, **Articles 85** and **86** cannot be interpreted in a mutually (u)
contradictory sense, since they are intended to achieve the same end.

It is in the light of these considerations that the decisive criterion laid down in **Article 86,** whereby the (v) exploitation of a dominant position must be abusive to come within the prohibition, must be interpreted. The provision enumerates a number of abusive practices which it prohibits. It merely gives examples, *i.e.*, not an exhaustive list of the kinds of abusive exploitation of a dominant position prohibited by the Treaty. As **Article 86 (2) (c)** and **(d)** further shows, the provision applies not only to practices that may cause a direct prejudice to consumers but also to those that cause a prejudice to (w) consumers through interference in the structure of actual competition, which is mentioned in **Article 3 (f)** of the Treaty. There may therefore be abusive behaviour if an undertaking in a dominant position strengthens that dominant position so that the degree of control achieved substantially obstructs competition, *i.e.*, so that the only undertakings left in the market are those which are dependent on the dominant undertaking with regard to their market behaviour.

Such being the meaning and the scope of **Article 86** of the EEC Treaty, the question raised by the applicant companies of the causal connection which in their view must exist between the dominant position and the abusive exploitation is irrelevant, for the strengthening (x) of the position of an undertaking may be abusive and prohibited by **Article 86** of the Treaty, regardless of the (y) means or the methods whereby it has been achieved, if it has the effects described above."[11]

15–33 It must be admitted that this is a masterly piece of verbal sleight-of-hand. It recognises at the start that it is dealing with "the abusive exploitation of a dominant position" but by the end it has reached the conclusion that any question of "causal connection . . . between the dominant position and the abusive exploitation" is "irrelevant", and that "the strengthening of the position of an undertaking may be abusive. . . regardless of the means or the methods whereby it has been achieved"! That strengthening need not be *via* an abusive exploitation of the dominant position!

The verbal prestidigitation is so well done that the fallacies in

[11] *Ibid.* pp.223-5.

the argument can be uncovered only by going through the passage almost sentence by sentence, examining and testing each in turn. To facilitate identification of the part of the passage under discussion, letters in parenthesis have been placed in the margin beside the relevant part of the passage and these letters are used for reference purposes in the discussion below.

–34 A diversion is always helpful as a means of confusing the issue. The passage begins with a monumental red herring. At (a) it claims that "it must be examined" whether "abusive exploitation" covers only external market behaviour or whether it includes internal alterations of structure. But at (c) it admits that there is no distinction between them!

And the diversion has achieved its aim – there is no reference at (b) to the requirement in Article 86 that the activity in question must be "abuse. . . of a dominant position", or in the more expressive words used by the Court itself "abusive exploitation of a dominant position". The suppression of that aspect of Article 86 has begun!

-35 Awkward comparisons with the Coal and Steel Community Treaty are dismissed very cavalierly, at (d). It is undeniable that interpretation of Article 86 may call for consideration of the object of that Article and of the aims and system of the Treaty, and cannot be established by comparison with provisions of the E.C.S.C. Treaty alone. But it does not necessarily follow that those provisions cannot throw light upon the meaning and intention of the Article. Indeed, as the Advocate General pointed out, comparison with Article 66 of the E.C.S.C. Treaty does throw aspects of Article 86 into relief. But of course, comparison with Article 66 is dangerous in that it leads to conclusions which the Court does not favour, so it must be dismissed out-of-hand, without running the risk of attempting to meet its all-too-cogent argument.

-36 At (e), (f), and (g), the Court seeks to brush aside clear words in Article 3, to read into that Article something which is not there, and to give it a role which it does not possess, to the prejudice of Article 86.

As to (e), the policy of the Community in relation to competition does indeed "derive" from Article 3(f), in the sense that 3(f) states the general purpose while Articles 85, 86, etc. represent the detailed measures to achieve that purpose. But Articles 85, 86, etc. are not mere subsidiary provisions, to be governed by 3(f). This is made clear by the introductory words of

Article 3: "For the purposes set out in Article 2, the activities of the Community shall include, *as provided in this Treaty . . .*" (emphasis added). In other words, Articles 85, 86, etc. show how the Article 3(f) objective is to be achieved – so that in so far as some competition measure does not appear in Articles 85, 86, etc., that measure is not part of the Treaty. Contrary to the Court's statement at (f), there is nothing in Article 3 to say that pursuit of its aims is indispensable to the achievement of the Community's tasks. Nor – and this the Court completely ignores – is there anything in the Article to say that, in so far as the Court considers the provisions of the Treaty, as expressed in the Treaty, are inadequate to achieve what the Court deems to be the objectives of the Treaty, the Court is free to impose something else on the Members and their peoples. Finally, is the Court suggesting that 3(f) is *legally binding* in every Member – so that, for example, Italy must introduce some internal competition law?

It is significant, as regards (g), that the Court does not attempt to say what those "several provisions" are whose interpretation is governed by Article 3(f) – the very precise words in the introductory part of the Article as quoted in italics above demonstrate that Article 3 is to be interpreted against the background and in the light of the implementing provisions which appear later in the Treaty.

15–37 Turning to (h), Article 3(f) does *not* provide for the establishment of a system to protect competition – that is the role of Articles 85 and, to some extent, 86. Consequently, Article 3(f) does not demand "that competition must not be eliminated". If 3(f) had so demanded, why do Articles 85, 86, etc. not say so *explicitly*? And if the non-elimination-of-competition requirement is so essential, why was it not incorporated in detail into the Treaty – why are there no specific implementing provisions? These comments also dispose of (i) of the extract in 15-32.

As to (j) of the extract, the "harmonious development of economic activities" certainly does not predicate solely a regime of competition. Harmonious development can be sought by other means, such as regulation – hence the provisions in the Treaty relating to agriculture and transport. Moreover, what is the position of monopolies existing when the Treaty was signed? There is nothing requiring them to be dismantled. In (k), the Court has attempted half-heartedly to deal with such points. But in (k), the Court again ignores the relationship of the Articles

– Article 3 expands on 2, but is subject to the later provisions of the Treaty and is, therefore, restricted to Articles 85, 86, etc. so far as competition is concerned.

-38 As to (l), the Court again refuses to recognise the implications of the words "as provided in this Treaty" in the introductory part of Article 3. The purpose of Articles 85, 86, *et seq.* is to spell out how Article 3(f) is to be implemented, not to "preserve the principles" in Articles 2 and 3.

Turning to (m), what is there in Article 86 to say that it is confined to "unilateral" activity? An agreement between firms could constitute a breach of Article 86, even if it were, or were not, also a breach of Article 85.

As to (n), it is blatant misrepresentation to say that Articles 85 and 86 are intended to achieve the same aim – maintenance of effective competition, at different levels. The former is concerned with preventing consensual restrictions on competition, the latter with abuse of dominant position – no more, no less. Abuse of dominant position can take a form unrelated to competition. If a monopoly charges excessive prices that may be abuse of dominant position, but it does not restrict competition! (On the contrary, by making the market more attractive, it might induce competition by attracting new entrants.)

As to (o) and (p), if mergers were so clearly contrary to Article 86, why does the Article not say so? This is precisely what Article 66 of the E.C.S.C. Treaty does. And comparison of Article 65 of that Treaty (which deals with inter-firm agreements, etc.) with Article 85 shows, from the similarity of wording, that the former was in the minds of the draftsmen of the latter – in fact, 85 seems to have been an improvement of 65. In that case, if Article 86 was intended to cover mergers, why did it not follow Article 66? This is the argument which the Advocate General adduced, and which the Court evaded.

At (q), the Court demonstrates a lack of awareness of real economic life. Human beings tend to prefer independence and liberty. This is particularly so in the case of the active, energetic, creative, individuals who either build up or manage successful enterprises. Such people do not wish to tie themselves up or subordinate themselves to others. Perhaps it is because the majority of the members of the Court come from countries which do not have a tradition or experience of widespread operations through a Stock Exchange – observation of the defensive action by the victims of take-over bids on the London Stock Exchange would have made the Court realise that businessmen do not lightly give up their independence (one of the main considerations in the United Kingdom Monopolies Commission report on the bid by Rank for De La Rue was that the senior management of the latter would leave if it were taken over).

The defect in the Court's argument at (r) is that paragraph (b) of Article 85.3 relates solely to that Article. If the same consideration were to be applicable in Article 86, why does that Article not provide for it? The purported answer at (s), that Article 86 does not need to provide for exemption, falls to the ground – one of the reasons for the draft regulation on mergers, as stated in the preamble (36-01), is the need to provide for exemption provisions in the draft regulation if it is made under not apply to mergers – if it did so apply, it would have contained provisions for exemption (as does Article 66 of the E.C.S.C. Treaty).

As to (t), this is typical of the Court's inability, or unwillingness, to express itself clearly. What system is it referring to? If the argument is that there could be no exemption provisions in Article 86 because Article 3(f) is mandatory, then why are there exemption provisions in the draft regulation if it is made under Article 86?

Finally, the comment at (u) ignores the fact that Articles 85 and 86 are *not* intended to achieve the same end. As explained above, the former deals with consensual restrictions on competition, the latter with abuse of dominant position.

15–39 It is interesting to note that, even as late as (v), the Court is still prepared to pay lip service to the objective interpretation of Article 86 – to come within the Article there has to be an "exploitation of a dominant position" which is "abusive".

At (w), we are back to the distinction which at the outset the Court said "must be examined" and then considered did not exist. What the Court carefully omits is that, to come within Article 86, the abusive behaviour must be an exploitation of a dominant position.

15–40 Having thus completely obscured the proper interpretation of Article 86, by introducing confusing diversions, by completely ignoring clear words in the Treaty, and by misrepresentation, the Court – like a conjuror – produces the rabbit out of the hat. At (x), there need be no causal connection between the dominant position and the abusive exploitation. The requirement of Article 86 that the abuse must be "of a dominant position" is ignored.

And at (y), a strengthening of a dominant position can be a breach of Article 86 regardless of how it is achieved!

-41 The utter falsity of the Court's reasoning can be easily demonstrated by applying it to a different situation. The Court, in essence, is saying that Article 3(f) requires the maintenance of effective competition, therefore, in so far as Articles 85 and 86 do not make specific provision for what the Court considers to be necessary, the language of the Articles must be enlarged to include that provision.

It is accepted that Article 85 does not apply to conscious parallelism. On analysis of the policy underlying competition law, it cannot. Competition policy requires each firm to determine its own industrial and commercial policy and its own actions by entirely separate and independent decision. But there is nothing to stop a firm deciding, by separate and independent decision, that a change introduced by a competitor – say a price rise – is right. The firm can, by its own separate decision, follow that price rise. The Court itself has recognised that conscious parallelism is outside Article 85 – *v.* paragraphs 3-12 *et seq.* If all the firms in the market follow a policy of conscious parallelism, of price leadership say, there will to that extent be no effective competition. But the Treaty – as the Court accepts – has no remedy.

If Article 3(f) is so mandatory, how can the Court accept conscious parallelism? If that parallelism is followed by a dominant firm, apparently Article 86 does not apply. Where then is all this argument about effective competition?

-42 The Court cannot reply that the firm would be ordered to follow non-parallel policies. That is impossible, for a variety of reasons. Who is to decide what the different policies are to be? Who is to tell which firm to follow which policy? That may mean putting some firms out of business. If the market contains only two firms, one dominant and one small, the dominant firm must be allowed to bring its price down to that of the smaller, otherwise it will go out of business. If the smaller introduces a market-winning innovation, the dominant firm must be allowed to match it. And so on.

The problem was recognised even before the Treaty was signed, in the United States in the *Report of the Attorney General's Committee to Study the Antitrust Laws:*

"To forbid a seller to meet his rival's price would involve a *reductio ad absurdum,* so long as the market structure itself is untouched. For example, in the case of homogeneous products, if A only partway meets B's price, it does A no good – he still cannot sell his goods – and if A more than meets B's price, then B cannot sell his goods, or not until he in turn has more than met A's price. Under these circumstances, in the absence of a change in demand, there is no place where competitive price can level off, and no adjustment permitting a number of competitors to remain in the market in question, unless a seller is permitted to meet his competitor's price. . . . But any rule, public or private, which forbade the meeting of prices, or one which forbade the undercutting of prices, would be a rule against workable competition."[12]

The United Kingdom Monopolies Commission faced the problem in its report on *Parallel Pricing:*

"Therefore, if the [Monopolies] Commission found that the practice operated against the public interest in a particular industry and had to consider how the damage might be limited, they might well conclude that this would need to be achieved by some direct supervision of prices (and in some cases, possibly, of costs) in the industry concerned. It could not be objected that such a remedy would destroy effective price competition since in the circumstances postulated such competition would not exist. The effect of the remedy would be to replace control of the price level by the sellers in the industry acting in their own interests by control from without aimed at safeguarding the public interest."[13]

In short, where competition does not exist, by virtue of practices outside the scope of competition law, the only remedy may be public operation and control, i.e. complete monopoly (and the experience of nationalised industries in the United Kingdom and elsewhere does not induce confidence as to the economic success of such public interference). Is the Court going to argue that the Treaty gives the Brussels Commission power to take over and operate individual enterprises?

4. Conclusion

5–43 To sum up – the Court's interpretation of Article 86 to cover mergers not involving abuse of a dominant position is fallacious

[12] At pp.331-2.

[13] At paragraph 112.

and unacceptable. Not only is its legal reasoning unsound, its economic analysis is non-existent.

This is not to say that some Community control of mergers is not required. On the contrary. It may be that the Court has fallen into the error of confusing the normative with the positive, of confusing what *ought to be* with what *is.* It is significant that the draft regulation on mergers does not claim to be made under Article 86, but under Article 235.

CHAPTER 16
Other Abuses of a Dominant Position

Imposing unfair prices or terms

16–01A In April 1973 the Commission issued a press release dealing with the first case in which the Commission had taken action under Article 86 against a dominant buyer. The undertaking in question was not identified by name in the release, but it is believed to be a joint company, Eurofima, set up by sixteen European railway administrations as a joint procuring agency. The case is reported under the name *Eurofima,* and additional particulars are to be found in the *Third Report on Competition Policy.*[1]

Acting on behalf of six national railway managements, Eurofima invited tenders for the development and delivery of a series of Europan standard passenger carriages for long-distance travel, the intention being that the carriages would be used by as many railway undertakings as possible. One of the terms upon which tenders were to be submitted was that Eurofima was to have unrestricted rights to use the designs, documents, patents and other rights arising from the execution of the contract.

The Commission found Eurofima to have a dominant position in the Common Market. Although its constituent railway undertakings were not obliged to procure all their requirements through it, the Commission considered that they were dependent on Eurofima for the construction of further rolling stock.

The Commission took the view that, having regard to the close technical co-operation between Eurofima and the successful tenderer, it was reasonable for Eurofima to have the right to use the patent and other rights for its own purposes. But the

[1] Brussels 1974. pp.60-1.

Commission also took the view that it was unreasonable for Eurofima to have the right to give licences to third parties without consulting or giving additional compensation to the successful tenderer. In the light of the Commission's attitude, the contract as negotiated between Eurofima and the successful tenderer, while giving the former the right to grant licences to third parties to promote standardisation of rolling stock, nevertheless stipulated that such licences could be given only with the agreement of the contractor and in return for adequate compensation negotiated in respect of each case.

Unfortunately, the press release and the comments in the *Third Report* do not give all the information necessary to assess the propriety and implications of the Commission's attitude. It may have been that the contract was such that the contractor was to be paid only for the rolling stock accepted and delivered, i.e. he had to undertake the development and design work as a commercial venture. In such circumstances, the Commission's view would seem to be justified. But if the basis of the contract was that Eurofima would finance the development work and also pay for the rolling stock delivered, then it would seem proper that *all* the rights in the development should belong to Eurofima.

Without further information on these points, all that can be done is to note the view taken by the Commission.

-01B Unfair terms were held by the Commission to have been imposed by suppliers, in the *European Sugar Cartel* case. That decision involved sugar producers in France, Italy, West Germany, Belgium, and Holland, but the Article 86 aspects concerned only those in Belgium, Holland, and southern Germany.

In Belgium, Raffinerie Tirlemontoise owned or controlled about 85% of the sugar output. It exercised influence over other Belgian producers, and had influence in the sugar markets in other Member States, particularly France because of its financial holdings in French producers. In effect, Tirlemontoise could act independently. The Commission therefore held Tirlemontoise to have a dominant position in the Belgian and Luxembourg sugar markets (there was no producer in Luxembourg, its needs being supplied by the Belgian producers particularly Tirlemontoise), which constituted a substantial part of the Common Market. After strong competitive pressure on the Dutch market, Tirlemontoise and the Dutch producers decided to regulate the activities of the wholesalers. For its part, Tirlemontoise gave two Belgian wholesalers, Exportation de Sucre and Hottelet, the exclusive right to handle its exports to Holland. But that exclusive right was subject to two conditions: first, that the wholesalers would supply only those customers or users approved by the two Dutch producers, and second, that the two wholesalers would no longer export to Holland sugar from the Belgian producers independent of Tirlemontoise. The Commission held that the economic pressure brought by Tirlemontoise to bear on the two wholesalers consisted in refusing to supply sugar to them – particularly for export to non-Member countries, which constituted a large proportion of their turnover – if the sugar was re-sold for non-approved uses. This abusive exploitation by Tirlemontoise of its dominant position was capable of affecting inter-Member trade, because sales in other Member States were either restricted or prevented. For all its activities condemned in the decision, Tirlemontoise was fined 1,500,000 units of account (say £625,000).

The two Dutch producers, Suiker Unie and Centrale Suiker, produced the whole of the Dutch sugar output and controlled almost the whole of the imports, which accounted for 10% – 15% of the Dutch market. They also co-operated closely in their activities, to the extent, in the Commission's view, of appearing to other firms and particularly the three Dutch wholesalers as being a single entity. They had joint buying of raw materials, a quota system for production, collaboration in the use of by-products, pooling of research, co-operation in market research and marketing, and also unified ex-works prices and sales conditions. The Commission held that they had a dominant position in the Dutch sugar market, which constituted a substantial part of the Common Market. They had abused that dominant position by forcing on the three Dutch wholesalers an agreement under which the wholesalers undertook, (a) not to sell certain imports of French sugar at prices appreciably lower than the Dutch prices, (b) to sell some of their French imports to the two Dutch producers so that the latter could sell it under their own marks and at their own prices, and (c) not to import further quantities into Holland without the consent of the two producers. Part of the economic pressure brought by the two producers upon the wholesalers was the threat to curtail the freedom to sell to the Dutch dairy industry, a significant part of the wholesalers' trade. Inter-Member trade was affected by the restrictions of imports into Holland of sugar from other Member States. The fine imposed on Suiker Unie was 800,000 units (say

£330,000) and on Centrale Suiker 600,000 units (say £250,000).

In the southern part of Federal Germany, the producers' organisation was Südzucker Verkaufs. Südzucker was estimated to have 90% – 95% of the market. It was able to act independently and had a dominant position. The Commission considered that it had abused its position in two ways. First, it had compelled its distributors not to handle sugar from the other sources without its consent – consent being given only for special qualities and sugar for processing. This effectively prevented imports, despite the higher prices in southern Germany. Secondly, Südzucker granted a loyalty discount, in the form of an additional quantity discount of 0.30 marks per 100 kilos if the distributor took all his requirements from Südzucker. Because the distributor was dependent at least partly on Südzucker, purchase of even small quantities from other sources could mean a substantial loss – on an average turnover of 30,000 tonnes the loyalty discount would amount to 90,000 DM. Both practices were likely to affect inter-Member trade. The fine imposed on Südzucker was 200,000 units (say £80,000).

The parties concerned in the *Sugar Cartel* case appealed, and the Court's decision is awaited.

-01C In its *GEMA (No. 1)* decision, the Commission held that the imposition by the association of non-essential obligations on its members was an abuse within Article 86. The European Court took a similar view in the *SABAM* case. SABAM was a co-operative association established in Belgium to manage copyrights and kindred rights on behalf of its members. Almost all authors in Belgium used its services. SABAM's standard form of agreement with its members required the author to assign all his present and future rights in his present and future works to SABAM, and upon the author withdrawing from SABAM, the association could, without giving reasons, retain the assigned rights for five years.

A lyric writer and a composer both became members of SABAM on the standard terms. Some time later B.R.T., the Belgian broadcasting and television body, decided to see whether suitable promotion could make a commercial success of a nonsense song. It commissioned the lyric writer and the composer to compose such a song, which they did, their rights being assigned to B.R.T. The song was broadcast, and eventually records were marketed by Fonior under an agreement with the agency employed by SABAM to deal with mechanical-production rights. In the ensuing litigation in the Belgian courts one issue was whether the rights in the song belonged to SABAM or to B.R.T. The validity of the SABAM standard agreement with its members was attacked, on the ground that some of the terms constituted abuse of dominant position within Article 86. The Belgian court sought a ruling from the European Court.

The questions put to the European Court asked whether a body set up to manage copyrights, holding a dominant position, would abuse that position (a) if it demanded from its members the global assignment of all copyrights without distinguishing between different categories of rights, and (b) if it required the assignment of all present and future rights with the right to use the assigned rights for five years after the member's withdrawal. The Court, in its judgment, explained that it was for the national court to decide whether the provisions in question were inequitable. The Court ruled that the imposition on its members by a body entrusted with the management of copyrights and having a dominant position within Article 86 of "obligations which are not absolutely necessary for the attainment of its object and which thus encroach unfairly upon a member's freedom to exercise his copyright" could constitute an abuse.

16–01D One of the abuses found by the Commission in *General Motors Continental* was charging excessive prices. In five instances, the company charged B.fr. 5,000 plus B.fr.900 VAT, as against B.fr.1,000 including tax in other cases. In two of the five cases, the company later re-imbursed B.fr.4,900, and in the other three cases B.fr.4,425. A fine of 100,000 units of account (say £40,000) was imposed.

Discrimination

16–04A The charging of excessive prices was held to be a form of discrimination in *General Motors Continental,* in so far as independent dealers, importing on their own account, would have had to pay the higher charges.

A possible form of discrimination is refusal to supply undertakings in another Member State, or giving them less favourable treatment than undertakings in the home market, for example by giving them lower allocations of scarce materials. The point was brought up in a question in the European Parliament. It was suggested that an Italian supplier was meeting the full demands of the Italian customers while refusing any supplies to a Dutch concern, and that a German supplier had cut its allocation to the Dutch by 50% whereas German customers suffered only a

20% reduction. In its reply, the Commission pointed out that discrimination on grounds of nationality would infringe Article 7 of the Rome Treaty, and where it derived from agreement between undertakings or from abuse of a dominant position there could be infringement of Article 85 or Article 86.[2]

Price cutting

-04B One of the possible abuses mentioned in Study No. 3 was price cutting to eliminate a weaker competitor, or perhaps to impose a merger.[3] Action against a firm for *reducing* prices may seem paradoxical, and could possibly lead to reaction from consumers. Firms in Holland and Ireland complained that United Brands, an American food firm, was cutting its prices for bananas to drive them out of the market – the Irish complained that United Brands' prices in Ireland were much lower than in England. Even if it could be demonstrated that United Brands had a dominant position and had reduced prices for that purpose, would it be politic for the Commission to act?[4]

Refusal to supply – Zoja case

04C Zoja, an Italian manufacturer of medicaments, included in its products pharmaceutical specialities based upon ethambutol, a compound used in treating pulmonary tuberculosis. Ethambutol was derived from aminobutanol, which in turn was made from nitropropane, a product resulting from the nitration of paraffin. In addition to being a source of aminobutanol, nitropropane was used as an emulsifier in paint manufacture. Zoja bought aminobutanol, and made its own ethambutol. From 1966 onwards it drew its supplies of aminobutanol from Istituto Chemioterapico, being Istituto's main customer. Istituto was a subsidiary of the American company, Commercial Solvents Corporation. The Commission's decision found that Commercial Solvents had a world monopoly in products derived from the nitration of paraffin, including nitropropane and aminobutanol. In 1968 and 1969 there were merger talks between Istituto and Zoja, but these came to nothing.

In late 1969 and early 1970, Zoja found that it could buy aminobutanol from other, independent, distributors, and by

[2] Official Journal C61. 29.5.74. p.6.

[3] European Economic Community. Série Concurrence 3. *Le Problème de la Concentration dans le Marché Commun.* Brussels 1966.

[4] *Financial Times.* 3.12.74.

agreement cancelled its contract with Istituto – up to that date, it had bought substantial quantities from Istituto under annual contracts and separate orders, and had been Istituto's main customer.

At the beginning of 1970, Commercial Solvents changed its policy, so that its supplies to Istituto were in the form of aminobutanol for processing into ethambutol which Istituto then sold or used for making its own ethambutol specialties (Istituto having entered that field). In 1970, Istituto bought nitropropane from a producer of ethambutol, which it re-sold to small paint manufacturers as an emulsifier, on condition that they did not re-sell it for pharmaceutical use. There were some five producers of ethambutol in the E.E.C. then, three of them large producers, i.e. Istituto, American Cyanamid, and Zoja.

In the first half of 1970, Zoja was able to buy large quantities of aminobutanol at prices lower than those charged by Istituto, but in the second half of that year, supplies of aminobutanol and nitropropane began to dry up. Zoja applied to suppliers in the E.E.C. and outside, but with no success. Either the suppliers were themselves without supplies because Commercial Solvents had stopped delivery, or they were bound not to export or to re-sell for pharmaceutical use. In April 1971, Zoja complained to the Commission. The Commission held that Commercial Solvents and Istituto had abused their dominant position by refusing supplies to Zoja; a fine was imposed on both companies, and they were required to recommence supplies. On appeal, the Court in effect upheld the Commission's conclusions, although it reduced the fine.

A number of issues arose in the case, which can best be discussed separately.

16–04D The first of the issues is the question of enterprise entity. Commercial Solvents had 51% of Istituto's share capital, three representatives on Istituto's executive committee of six, and five on its board of ten directors including the chairman who had a casting vote. In Commercial Solvents' report for 1972 Istituto was described as "our subsdiary". It was unlikely that Commercial Solvents would not have been involved in the merger proposals with Zoja, and the prohibition on other distributors of the raw materials exporting or selling for pharmaceutical use indicated an intention to prevent Zoja from obtaining supplies, at a time when Istituto was developing its own production and sales of ethambutol. The Commission concluded that "in their relations with Zoja and for the purposes of application of Article 86" Commercial Solvents and Istituto "should be treated as forming . . . only one single and identical undertaking or economic entity".[5] As the Court put it:

> "As regards the market in nitropropane and its derivatives the conduct of Commercial Solvents Corp. and Istituto has thus been characterised by an obviously united action, which, taking account of the power of control of Commercial Solvents Corp. over Istituto, confirms the conclusions in the decision that as regards their relations with Zoja the two companies must be deemed an economic unit and that they are jointly and severally responsible for the conduct complained of. In these circumstances the argument of Commercial Solvents Corp. that it did not do business within the Community and that therefore the Commission lacked competence to apply Regulation 17 to it must likewise be rejected."[6]

-04E Did the group formed by Commercial Solvents and Istituto have a dominant position? The Commission pointed to Commercial Solvents' world monopoly in the production and sale of nitropropane and aminobutanol, and concluded that that concern had a dominant position both in the world and in the Common Market. Before the Court, Commercial Solvents argued that there were other methods of producing, and another producer of, nitropropane, and also other methods of producing and also other producers of both aminobutanol and ethambutol. The Court did not accept these arguments. The other methods of production suggested were experimental or too vague, the other producers manufactured only on a modest scale and for their own needs. The Commission's conclusion that in the circumstances it was not possible to have recourse on an industrial scale to other methods of making ethambutol was justified, as Commercial Solvents did have a dominant position on the world market.

-04F As to the relevant *market*, the appellants had argued that there was not a separate market for ethambutol, that product being part of the larger market for anti-tuberculosis drugs, and since there was no separate market for ethambutol, there could not be a separate market for the raw material for making ethambutol. The Court rejected the argument. In fact, it was possible to

[5] [1973] C.M.L.R. p.D57.
[6] [1974] 1 C.M.L.R. p.344.

distinguish the market for the raw material from the market for the product. However, abuse of a dominant position in the market for the raw material might restrict competition in the market for the product, and the effects in the latter market must be taken into account when considering the effects of the infringement of Article 86 even though the market for the product was not a self-contained market.

16–04G The Commission in its decision took the view that refusal to supply a customer was an abuse under Article 86 both because it eliminated one of the principal producers (of ethambutol) and so reduced competition, and also because it limited production and outlets contrary to paragraph (b) of the Article. The Court emphasised the elimination of competition:

> "However, an undertaking being in a dominant position as regards the production of raw material and therefore able to control the supply to manufacturers of derivatives cannot, just because it decides to start manufacturing these derivatives (in competition with its former customers), act in such a way as to eliminate their competition which, in the case in question, would have amounted to eliminating one of the principal manufacturers of ethambutol in the Common Market. Since such conduct is contrary to the objectives expressed in **Article 3 (f)** of the Treaty and set out in greater detail in **Articles 85** and **86**, it follows that an undertaking which has a dominant position in the market in raw materials and which, with the object of reserving such raw material for manufacturing its own derivatives, refuses to supply a customer which is itself a manufacturer of these derivatives, and therefore risks eliminating all competition on the part of this customer, is abusing its dominant position within the meaning of **Article 86.** In this context it does not matter that the undertaking ceased to supply in the spring of 1970 because of the cancellation of the purchases by Zoja, because it appears from the applicants' own statement that, when the supplies provided for in the contract had been completed, the sale of aminobutanol would have stopped in any case."[7]

16–04H As to *effect on inter-Member trade,* the Commission pointed to the growth in demand for ethambutol in the Common Market countries, particularly France and Germany in addition to Italy. Zoja exported to France and had begun to supply the German

[7] *Ibid.* pp.340-1.

market. Elimination of Zoja would thus affect both actual and potential trade. The appellants argued before the Court that Zoja sold 90% of its production outside the Common Market, as the developing countries were the main market, tuberculosis having largely disappeared in the then Common Market countries. The Court rejected these points, not only on the ground relied upon by the Commission (effect on actual and potential trade) but because:

> "When an undertaking in a dominant position within the Common Market abusively exploits its position in such a way that a competitor in the Common Market is likely to be eliminated, it does not matter whether the conduct relates to the latter's exports or its trade within the Common Market, once it has been established that this elimination will have repercussions on the competitive structure within the Common Market."[8]

Effect on "competitive structure" is a very wide construction of "may affect trade between Member States"!

041 The Commission ordered Commercial Solvents and Istituto to make immediate deliveries of raw material to Zoja, and also to submit proposals within two months as regards subsequent supplies – with penalties of 1,000 units per day (say £400) in the event of failure, in respect of both. A fine of 200,000 units (say £80,000) was also imposed.

Commercial Solvents and Istituto suggested that the Commission had no power to order supplies to be made and further that, even if it had such power, the order should relate only to Zoja's Common Market trade, and not to its export trade. As to the first point, the Court ruled:

> "As to the first submission, according to the wording of Article 3 of Regulation 17, where the Commission finds that there is an infringement of **Article 86**, 'it may by decision require the undertakings. . . concerned to bring such infringement to an end'. This provision must be applied in relation to the infringement which has been established and may include an order to do certain acts or provide certain advantages which have been wrongfully withheld as well as prohibiting the continuation of certain action, practices or situations which are contrary to the Treaty. For this purpose the Commission may, if necessary, require the undertaking concerned to

[8] *Ibid.* p.342.

submit to it proposals with a view to bringing the situation into conformity with the requirements of the Treaty."[9]

As to the second point, the Court's remarks are worth quoting in full:

"As to the second submission, it has been established above that it cannot be inferred from the expression 'in so far as it may affect trade between member-States' that only the effects of a possible infringement on trade within the Community must be taken into account when it is a question of defining the infringement and its consequences. Moreover the rather limited measure that the applicants suggested would have resulted in the production and sales outlets of Zoja being controlled by Commercial Solvents Corp.-Istituto and in Zoja being in a position where its cost price would have been affected to such an extent that its production of ethambutol would have been in danger of being unmarketable. In these circumstances the Commission could well consider that the maintenance of an effective competitive structure necessitated the measures in question.

Although in the disputed decision and during the course of the present proceedings the Commission has constantly avoided meeting the complaint in the way that the applicants argued it, it has on the other hand ever since the Notice of Objections maintained that, since the conduct complained of aimed at eliminating one of the principal competitors within the Common Market, it was above all necessary to prevent such an infringement of Community competition by adequate measures. Both in the disputed decision and in the written procedure the measures taken were justified by the necessity of preventing the conduct of Commercial Solvents Corp. and Istituto having the effect referred to and eliminating Zoja as one of the principal manufacturers of ethambutol in the Community. This reasoning is at the root of the litigation and cannot therefore be considered as insufficient.

This submission, therefore also fails."[10]

In other words, if the export trade is necessary to maintain the firm's competitive strength within the Common Market, the order can extend to supplies required for the export component. It will normally be only where the export trade is being carried on at a

[9] *Ibid.* pp.344-5.
[10] *Ibid.* p.345.

loss that it can be considered dispensable – and even then, only when the loss is as great as or greater than the increase in overheads per unit of production if the export trade is discontinued.

–04J The fine imposed by the Commission was 200,000 units of account. The Court recognised that the seriousness of the infringement justified a heavy fine. But the Court also felt that the duration of the infringement might have been shorter if the Commission had acted more speedily. Moreover, Commercial Solvents and Istituto had provided the supplies ordered. The Court therefore reduced the fine to 100,000 units.

–04K As will have been gathered from the above account, the *Zoja* case opens up wide possibilities, and it may well be some time before its full implications become apparent. Some points certainly call for clarification.

First, although Zoja had been a customer of Istituto, it was no longer a customer when supplies were refused, and the break in the customer/supplier relationship was at Zoja's instigation. The Court's comment that, even if the supply contract between Istituto and Zoja had been allowed to run the full course, supplies would have been stopped thereafter, does not answer the point. Once a customer has been supplied, can he never thereafter be refused supplies, except for some such reason as credit risk? Or how long must elapse before he can be refused?

Does the obligation to supply exist only in relation to an existing customer, so that an approach from a firm which has not been supplied before – at least with that product? – can be refused?

Many firms have a policy of not relying on one source for supplies. Zoja does not seem to have had such a policy. Moreover, it is commercially short-sighted to fall out with one's main, or only, supplier!

The order requiring Commercial Solvents and Istituto to submit proposals as regards future supplies to Zoja contained no time limit. Does this mean that Zoja are now guaranteed supplies in perpetuity, provided they can pay? They will have no incentive to seek other sources of supply.

These are not mere academic points. The policy underlying competition law is the maintenance of economic and commercial freedom – society benefits from ensuring that firms are free to modify their conduct to exploit circumstances, to innovate. It is desirable that businessmen be stimulated to build up strong, healthy enterprises, for example by identifying areas of weakness and taking appropriate action. The competitive struggle is justifiable only as a means of allowing the fittest to survive. It will be paradoxical, to say the least, if the law, in the name of competition policy, introduces rigidities into the economic system – supports for firms which have got themselves into difficulties. It may be that Zoja was not in that category, but some of the Court's reasoning does smack more of a corporatist approach to commercial matters than a competitive, *laissez-faire*, approach. If the line of reasoning in the *Zoja* case is widely followed, large groups may find it safer to expand forwards so as to keep all their activities under their own control rather than start supplying outsiders and be bound to go on doing so. Rigid adherence to the *Zoja* line might defeat the very object of competition policy and law.

Private suit

16–06 The *SABAM* case illustrates the "directly applicable" nature of Article 86. It is open to the national civil court to find the action complained of an infringement of the Article. In that case, the Article was being used to resolve a dispute as to the ownership of legal rights – did the right to reproduce the song vest in SABAM or B.R.T.? In other words, infringement of Article 86 would mean a defect in SABAM's title so as to validate B.R.T.'s title. But could Article 86 be used to obtain a positive order, such as the Commission's order in the *Zoja* case, from the civil courts?

APPENDICES

APPENDIX A

EXTRACTS FROM THE ROME TREATY*

PART ONE: PRINCIPLES

·01 *ARTICLE 1*

By this Treaty, the High Contracting Parties establish among themselves a EUROPEAN ECONOMIC COMMUNITY.

·02 *ARTICLE 2*

The Community shall have as its task, by establishing a common market and progressively approximating the economic policies of Member States, to promote throughout the Community a harmonious development of economic activities, a continuous and balanced expansion, an increase in stability, an accelerated raising of the standard of living and closer relations between the States belonging to it.

·03 *ARTICLE 3*

For the purposes set out in Article 2, the activities of the Community shall include, as provided in this Treaty and in accordance with the timetable set out therein:

(a) the elimination, as between Member States, of customs duties and of quantitative restrictions on the import and export of goods, and of all other measures having equivalent effect;

(b) the establishment of a common customs tariff and of a common commercial policy towards third countries;

* H. M. Stationery Office. London. 1972. Cmnd. 4864.

(c) the abolition, as between Member States, of obstacles to freedom of movement for persons, services and capital;
(d) the adoption of a common policy in the sphere of agriculture;
(e) the adoption of a common policy in the sphere of transport;
(f) the institution of a system ensuring that competition in the common market is not distorted;
(g) the application of procedures by which the economic policies of Member States can be coordinated and disequilibria in their balances of payments remedied;
(h) the approximation of the laws of Member States to the extent required for the proper functioning of the common market;
(i) the creation of a European Social Fund in order to improve employment opportunities for workers and to contribute to the raising of their standard of living;
(j) the establishment of a European Investment Bank to facilitate the economic expansion of the Community by opening up fresh resources;
(k) the association of the overseas countries and territories in order to increase trade and to promote jointly economic and social development.

17–04 *ARTICLE 4*

1. The tasks entrusted to the Community shall be carried out by the following institutions:

—an ASSEMBLY,
—a COUNCIL,
—a COMMISSION,
—a COURT OF JUSTICE

Each institution shall act within the limits of the powers conferred upon it by this Treaty.

2. The Council and the Commission shall be assisted by an Economic and Social Committee acting in an advisory capacity.

17–05 *ARTICLE 5*

Member States shall take all appropriate measures, whether general or particular, to ensure fulfilment of the obligations arising out of this Treaty or resulting from action taken by the institutions of the Community. They shall facilitate the achievement of the Community's tasks.

They shall abstain from any measure which could jeopardise the attainment of the objectives of this Treaty.

–05A *ARTICLE 7*

Within the scope of application of this Treaty, and without prejudice to any special provisions contained therein, any discrimination on grounds of nationality shall be prohibited.

The Council may, on a proposal from the Commission and after consulting the Assembly, adopt, by a qualified majority, rules designed to prohibit such discrimination.

. . . .

PART TWO: FOUNDATIONS OF THE COMMUNITY

TITLE I – FREE MOVEMENT OF GOODS

–05B *ARTICLE 9*

1. The Community shall be based upon a customs union which shall cover all trade in goods and which shall involve the prohibition between Member States of customs duties on imports and exports and of all charges having equivalent effect, and the adoption of a common customs tariff in their relations with third countries.

2. The provisions of Chapter 1, Section 1, and of Chapter 2 of this Title shall apply to products originating in Member States and to products coming from third countries which are in free circulation in Member States.

–05C *ARTICLE 10*

1. Products coming from a third country shall be considered to be in free circulation in a Member State if the import formalities have been complied with and any customs duties or charges having equivalent effect which are payable have been levied in that Member State, and if they have not benefited from a total or partial drawback of such duties or charges.

2. The Commission shall, before the end of the first year after the entry into force of this Treaty, determine the methods of administrative co-operation to be adopted for the purpose of applying Article 9(2), taking into account the need to reduce as much as possible formalities imposed on trade.

Before the end of the first year after the entry into force of this Treaty, the Commission shall lay down the provisions applicable, as regards trade between Member States, to goods originating in another Member State in whose manufacture products have been used on which the exporting Member State has not levied the appropriate customs duties or charges having equivalent effect, or which have benefited from a total or partial drawback of such duties or charges.

In adopting these provisions, the Commission shall take into account the rules for the elimination of customs duties within the Community and for the progressive application of the common customs tariff.

17–05D *ARTICLE 11*

Member States shall take all appropriate measures to enable Governments to carry out, within the periods of time laid down, the obligations with regard to customs duties which devolve upon them pursuant to this Treaty.

. . . .

CHAPTER 2 – ELIMINATION OF QUANTITATIVE RESTRICTIONS BETWEEN MEMBER STATES

17–06 *ARTICLE 30*

Quantitative restrictions on imports and all measures having equivalent effect shall, without prejudice to the following provisions, be prohibited between Member States.

17–07 *ARTICLE 34*

1. Quantitative restrictions on exports, and all measures having equivalent effect, shall be prohibited between Member States.
2. Member States shall, by the end of the first stage at the latest, abolish all quantitative restrictions on exports and any measures having equivalent effect which are in existence when this Treaty enters into force.

17–08 *ARTICLE 36*

The provisions of Articles 30 to 34 shall not preclude prohibitions or restrictions on imports, exports or goods in transit justified on grounds of public morality, public policy or public security; the protection of health and life of humans, animals or plants; the protection of national treasures possessing artistic, historic or archaeological value; or the protection of industrial and commercial property. Such prohibitions or restrictions shall not, however, constitute a means of arbitrary discrimination or a disguised restriction on trade between Member States.

. . . .

TITLE III – FREE MOVEMENT OF PERSONS, SERVICES AND CAPITAL

. . . .

CHAPTER 2 – RIGHT OF ESTABLISHMENT

. . . .

–08A *ARTICLE 57*

1. In order to make it easier for persons to take up and pursue activities as self-employed persons, the Council shall, on a proposal from the Commission and after consulting the Assembly, acting unanimously during the first stage and by a qualified majority thereafter, issue directives for the mutual recognition of diplomas, certificates and other evidence of formal qualifications.

2. For the same purpose, the Council shall, before the end of the transitional period, acting on a proposal from the Commission and after consulting the Assembly, issue directives for the coordination of the provisions laid down by law, regulation or administrative action in Member States concerning the taking up and pursuit of activities as self-employed persons. Unanimity shall be required on matters which are the subject of legislation in at least one Member State and measures concerned with the protection of savings, in particular the granting of credit and the exercise of the banking profession, and with the conditions governing the exercise of the medical and allied, and pharmaceutical professions in the various Member States. In other cases, the

Council shall act unanimously during the first stage and by a qualified majority thereafter.

3. In the case of the medical and allied, and pharmaceutical professions, the progressive abolition of restrictions shall be dependent upon coordination of the conditions for their exercise in the various Member States.

. . . .

PART THREE: POLICY OF THE COMMUNITY
TITLE I – COMMON RULES
CHAPTER 1 – RULES ON COMPETITION
SECTION 1 – RULES APPLYING TO UNDERTAKINGS

17–09 *ARTICLE 85*

1. The following shall be prohibited as incompatible with the common market: all agreements between undertakings, decisions by associations of undertakings and concerted practices which may affect trade between Member States and which have as their object or effect the prevention, restriction or distortion of competition within the common market, and in particular those which:

(a) directly or indirectly fix purchase or selling prices or any other trading conditions;

(b) limit or control production, markets, technical development, or investment;

(c) share markets or sources of supply;

(d) apply dissimilar conditions to equivalent transactions with other trading parties, thereby placing them at a competitive disadvantage;

(e) make the conclusion of contracts subject to acceptance by the other parties of supplementary obligations which, by their nature or according to commercial usage, have no connection with the subject of such contracts.

2. Any agreements or decisions prohibited pursuant to this Article shall be automatically void.

3. The provisions of paragraph 1 may, however, be declared inapplicable in the case of:

– any agreement or category of agreements between undertakings;

– any decision or category of decisions by associations of undertakings;
– any concerted practice or category of concerted practices;

which contributes to improving the production or distribution of goods or to promoting technical or economic progress, while allowing consumers a fair share of the resulting benefit, and which does not:

(a) impose on the undertakings concerned restrictions which are not indispensable to the attainment of these objectives;
(b) afford such undertakings the possibility of eliminating competition in respect of a substantial part of the products in question.

–10 *ARTICLE 86*

Any abuse by one or more undertakings of a dominant position within the common market or in a substantial part of it shall be prohibited as incompatible with the common market in so far as it may affect trade between Member States. Such abuse may, in particular, consist in:

(a) directly or indirectly imposing unfair purchase or selling prices or other unfair trading conditions;
(b) limiting production, markets or technical development to the prejudice of consumers;
(c) applying dissimilar conditions to equivalent transactions with other trading parties, thereby placing them at a competitive disadvantage;
(d) making the conclusion of contracts subject to acceptance by the other parties of supplementary obligations which, by their nature or according to commercial usage, have no connection with the subject of such contracts.

–11 *ARTICLE 87*

1. Within three years of the entry into force of this Treaty the Council shall, acting unanimously on a proposal from the Commission and after consulting the Assembly, adopt any appropriate regulations or directives to give effect to the principles set out in Articles 85 and 86.

If such provisions have not been adopted within the period mentioned, they shall be laid down by the Council, acting by a qualified majority on a proposal from the Commission and after consulting the Assembly.

2. The regulations or directives referred to in paragraph 1 shall be designed; in particular:

(a) to ensure compliance with the prohibitions laid down in Article 85 (1) and in Article 86 by making provision for fines and periodic penalty payments;

(b) to lay down detailed rules for the application of Article 85 (3), taking into account the need to ensure effective supervision on the one hand, and to simplify administration to the greatest possible extent on the other;

(c) to define, if need be, in the various branches of the economy, the scope of the provisions of Articles 85 and 86;

(d) to define the respective functions of the Commission and of the Court of Justice in applying the provisions laid down in this paragraph;

(e) to determine the relationship between national laws and the provisions contained in this Section or adopted pursuant to this Article.

17–12 *ARTICLE 88*

Until the entry into force of the provisions adopted in pursuance of Article 87, the authorities in Member States shall rule on the admissibility of agreements, decisions and concerted practices and on abuse of a dominant position in the common market in accordance with the law of their country and with the provisions of Article 85, in particular paragraph 3, and of Article 86.

17–13 *ARTICLE 89*

1. Without prejudice to Article 88, the Commission shall, as soon as it takes up its duties, ensure the application of the principles laid down in Articles 85 and 86. On application by a Member State or on its own initiative, and in co-operation with the competent authorities in the Member States, who shall give it their assistance, the Commission shall investigate cases of suspected infringement of these principles. If it finds that there has been an infringement, it shall propose appropriate measures to bring it to an end.

2. If the infringement is not brought to an end, the Commission shall record such infringement of the principles in a reasoned

decision. The Commission may publish its decision and authorise Member States to take the measures, the conditions and details of which it shall determine, needed to remedy the situation.

–14 *ARTICLE 90*

1. In the case of public undertakings and undertakings to which Member States grant special or exclusive rights, Member States shall neither enact nor maintain in force any measure contrary to the rules contained in this Treaty, in particular to those rules provided for in Article 7 and Articles 85 to 94.

2. Undertakings entrusted with the operation of services of general economic interest or having the character of a revenue-producing monopoly shall be subject to the rules contained in this Treaty, in particular to the rules on competition, in so far as the application of such rules does not obstruct the performance, in law or in fact, of the particular tasks assigned to them. The development of trade must not be affected to such an extent as would be contrary to the interests of the Community.

3. The Commission shall ensure the application of the provisions of this Article and shall, where necessary, address appropriate directives or decisions to Member States.

. . . .

SECTION 3 – AIDS GRANTED BY STATES

–15 *ARTICLE 92*

1. Save as otherwise provided in this Treaty, any aid granted by a Member State or through State resources in any form whatsoever which distorts or threatens to distort competition by favouring certain undertakings or the production of certain goods shall, in so far as it affects trade between Member States, be incompatible with the common market.

2. The following shall be compatible with the common market:

(a) aid having a social character, granted to individual consumers, provided that such aid is granted without discrimination related to the origin of the products concerned;

(b) aid to make good the damage caused by natural disasters or other exceptional occurrences;

(c) aid granted to the economy of certain areas of the

Federal Republic of Germany affected by the division of Germany, in so far as such aid is required in order to compensate for the economic disadvantages caused by that division.

3. The following may be considered to be compatible with the common market:

(a) aid to promote the economic development of areas where the standard of living is abnormally low or where there is serious underemployment;

(b) aid to promote the execution of an important project of common European interest or to remedy a serious disturbance in the economy of a Member State;

(c) aid to facilitate the development of certain economic activities or of certain economic areas, where such aid does not adversely affect trading conditions to an extent contrary to the common interest. However, the aids granted to shipbuilding as of 1 January 1957 shall, in so far as they serve only to compensate for the absence of customs protection, be progressively reduced under the same conditions as apply to the elimination of customs duties, subject to the provisions of this Treaty concerning common commercial policy towards third countries;

(d) such other categories of aid as may be specified by decision of the Council acting by a qualified majority on a proposal from the Commission.

. . . .

CHAPTER 3 – APPROXIMATION OF LAWS

17–15A *ARTICLE 100*

The Council shall, acting unanimously on a proposal from the Commission, issue directives for the approximation of such provisions laid down by law, regulation or administrative action in Member States as directly affect the establishment or functioning of the common market.

The Assembly and the Economic and Social Committee shall be consulted in the case of directives whose implementation would, in one or more Member States, involve the amendment of legislation.

. . . .

TITLE III – SOCIAL POLICY
CHAPTER 1 – SOCIAL PROVISIONS

15B *ARTICLE 117*

Member States agree upon the need to promote improved working conditions and an improved standard of living for workers, so as to make possible their harmonisation while the improvement is being maintained.

They believe that such a development will ensue not only from the functioning of the common market, which will favour the harmonisation of social systems, but also from the procedures provided for in this Treaty and from the approximation of provisions laid down by law, regulation or administrative action.

. . . .

PART FIVE: INSTITUTIONS OF THE COMMUNITY
TITLE 1 – PROVISIONS GOVERNING THE INSTITUTIONS
CHAPTER 1 – THE INSTITUTIONS

. . . .

SECTION 4 – THE COURT OF JUSTICE

15C *ARTICLE 164*

The Court of Justice shall ensure that in the interpretation and application of this Treaty the law is observed.

15D *ARTICLE 172*

Regulations made by the Council pursuant to the provisions of this Treaty may give the Court of Justice unlimited jurisdiction in regard to the penalties provided for in such regulations.

16 *ARTICLE 173*

The Court of Justice shall review the legality of acts of the Council and the Commission other than recommendations or opinions. It shall for this purpose have jurisdiction in actions brought by a Member State, the Council or the Commission on grounds of lack of competence, infringement of an essential procedural requirement, infringement of this Treaty or of any rule of law relating to its application, or misuse of powers.

Any natural or legal person may, under the same conditions, institute proceedings against a decision addressed to that person or against a decision which, although in the form of a regulation or a decision addressed to another person, is of direct and individual concern to the former.

The proceedings provided for in this Article shall be instituted within two months of the publication of the measure, or of its notification to the plaintiff, or, in the absence thereof, of the day on which it came to the knowledge of the latter, as the case may be.

17–17 *ARTICLE 177*

The Court of Justice shall have jurisdiction to give preliminary rulings concerning:

(a) the interpretation of this Treaty;

(b) the validity and interpretation of acts of the institutions of the Community;

(c) the interpretation of the statutes of bodies established by an act of the Council, where those statutes so provide.

Where such a question is raised before any court or tribunal of a Member State, that court or tribunal may, if it considers that a decision on the question is necessary to enable it to give judgment, request the Court of Justice to give a ruling thereon.

Where any such question is raised in a case pending before a court or tribunal of a Member State, against whose decisions there is no judicial remedy under national law, that court or tribunal shall bring the matter before the Court of Justice.

17–18 *ARTICLE 184*

Notwithstanding the expiry of the period laid down in the third paragraph of Article 173, any party may, in proceedings in which a regulation of the Council or of the Commission is in issue, plead the grounds specified in the first paragraph of Article 173, in order to invoke before the Court of Justice the inapplicability of that regulation.

17–18A *ARTICLE 185*

Actions brought before the Court of Justice shall not have

suspensory effect. The Court of Justice may, however, if it considers that circumstances so require, order that application of the contested act be suspended.

. . . .

CHAPTER 2 – PROVISIONS COMMON TO SEVERAL INSTITUTIONS

-18B *ARTICLE 189*

In order to carry out their task the Council and the Commission shall, in accordance with the provisions of this Treaty, make regulations, issue directives, take decisions, make recommendations or deliver opinions.

A regulation shall have general application. It shall be binding in its entirety and directly applicable in all Member States.

A directive shall be binding, as to the result to be achieved, upon each Member State to which it is addressed, but shall leave to the national authorities the choice of form and methods.

A decision shall be binding in its entirety upon those to whom it is addressed.

Recommendations and opinions shall have no binding force.

·18C *ARTICLE 190*

Regulations, directives and decisions of the Council and of the Commission shall state the reasons on which they are based and shall refer to any proposals or opinions which were required to be obtained pursuant to this Treaty.

·19 *ARTICLE 191*

Regulations shall be published in the Official Journal of the Community. They shall enter into force on the date specified in them or, in the absence thereof, on the twentieth day following their publication.

Directives and decisions shall be notified to those to whom they are addressed and shall take effect upon such notification.

19A *ARTICLE 192*

Decisions of the Council or of the Commission which impose a pecuniary obligation on persons other than States shall be enforceable.

Enforcement shall be governed by the rules of civil procedure in force in the State in the territory of which it is carried out. The order for its enforcement shall be appended to the decision, without other formality than verification of the authenticity of the decision, by the national authority which the Government of each Member State shall designate for this purpose and shall make known to the Commission and to the Court of Justice.

When these formalities have been completed on application by the party concerned, the latter may proceed to enforcement in accordance with the national law, by bringing the matter directly before the competent authority.

Enforcement may be suspended only by a decision of the Court of Justice. However, the courts of the country concerned shall have jurisdiction over complaints that enforcement is being carried out in an irregular manner.

. . . .

PART SIX: GENERAL AND FINAL PROVISIONS

. . . .

17–20 *ARTICLE 222*

This Treaty shall in no way prejudice the rules in Member States governing the system of property ownership.

17–21 *ARTICLE 227*[1]

1. This Treaty shall apply to the Kingdom of Belgium, the Kingdom of Denmark, the Federal Republic of Germany, the French Republic, Ireland, the Italian Republic, the Grand Duchy of Luxembourg, the Kingdom of the Netherlands, the Kingdom of Norway and the United Kingdom of Great Britain and Northern Ireland.

2. With regard to Algeria and the French overseas departments, the general and particular provisions of this Treaty relating to:

- the free movement of goods;
- agriculture, save for Article 40(4);
- the liberalisation of services;

[1] As amended by Article 26 of the Act annexed to the Treaty of Accession. Accession.

- the rules on competition;
- the protective measures provided for in Articles 108, 109 and 226;
- the institutions;

shall apply as soon as this Treaty enters into force.

The conditions under which the other provisions of this Treaty are to apply shall be determined, within two years of the entry into force of this Treaty, by decisions of the Council, acting unanimously on a proposal from the Commission.

The institutions of the Community will, within the framework of the procedures provided for in this Treaty, in particular Article 226, take care that the economic and social development of these areas is made possible.

3. The special arrangements for association set out in Part Four of this Treaty shall apply to the overseas countries and territories listed in Annex IV to this Treaty.

This Treaty shall not apply to those overseas countries and territories having special relations with the United Kingdom of Great Britain and Northern Ireland which are not included in the aforementioned list.

4. The provisions of this Treaty shall apply to the European territories for whose external relations a Member State is responsible.

5. Notwithstanding the preceding paragraphs:

(a) This Treaty shall not apply to the Faroe Islands. The Government of the Kingdom of Denmark may, however, give notice, by a declaration deposited by 31 December 1975 at the latest with the Government of the Italian Republic, which shall transmit a certified copy thereof to each of the Governments of the other Member States, that this Treaty shall apply to those Islands. In that event, this Treaty shall apply to those Islands from the first day of the second month following the deposit of the declaration.

(b) This Treaty shall not apply to the Sovereign Base Areas of the United Kingdom of Great Britain and Northern Ireland in Cyprus.

(c) This Treaty shall apply to the Channel Islands and the Isle of Man only to the extent necessary to ensure the implementation of the arrangements for those islands set out in the Treaty concerning the accession of the Kingdom of Denmark, Ireland, the Kingdom of

Norway and the United Kingdom of Great Britain and Northern Ireland to the European Economic Community and to the European Atomic Energy Community.

APPENDIX B

REGULATION NO 17/62/EEC OF THE COUNCIL

First Regulation Implementing Articles 85 and 86 of the Treaty

8–01 THE COUNCIL OF THE EUROPEAN ECONOMIC COMMUNITY,

HAVING REGARD to the Treaty establishing the European Economic Community, and in particular Article 87 thereof;

HAVING REGARD to the proposal from the Commission;

HAVING REGARD to the Opinion of the Economic and Social Committee;

HAVING REGARD to the Opinion of the European Parliament;

WHEREAS, in order to establish a system ensuring that competition shall not be distorted in the common market, it is necessary to provide for balanced application of Articles 85 and 86 in a uniform manner in the Member States;

WHEREAS in establishing the rules for applying Article 85(3) account must be taken of the need to ensure effective supervision and to simplify administration to the greatest possible extent;

WHEREAS it is accordingly necessary to make it obligatory, as a general principle, for undertakings which seek application of Article 85(3) to notify to the Commission their agreements, decisions and concerted practices;

WHEREAS, on the one hand, such agreements, decisions and concerted practices are probably very numerous and cannot

* Published in the Journal Officiel 21st February, 1962, English text Official Journal Special Edition 1959-1962 p.87.

therefore all be examined at the same time and, on the other hand, some of them have special features which may make them less prejudicial to the development of the common market;

WHEREAS there is consequently a need to make more flexible arrangements for the time being in respect of certain categories of agreement, decision and concerted practice without prejudging their validity under Article 85;

WHEREAS it may be in the interest of undertakings to know whether any agreements, decisions or practices to which they are party, or propose to become party, may lead to action on the part of the Commission pursuant to Article 85(1) or Article 86;

WHEREAS, in order to secure uniform application of Articles 85 and 86 in the common market, rules must be made under which the Commission, acting in close and constant liaison with the competent authorities of the Member States, may take the requisite measures for applying those Articles;

WHEREAS for this purpose the Commission must have the co-operation of the competent authorities of the Member States and be empowered, throughout the common market, to require such information to be supplied and to undertake such investigations as are necessary to bring to light any agreement, decision or concerted practice prohibited by Article 85(1) or any abuse of a dominant position prohibited by Article 86:

WHEREAS, in order to carry out its duty of ensuring that the provisions of the Treaty are applied, the Commission must be empowered to address to undertakings or associations of undertakings recommendations and decisions for the purpose of bringing to an end infringements of Articles 85 and 86;

WHEREAS compliance with Articles 85 and 86 and the fulfilment of obligations imposed on undertakings and associations of undertakings under this Regulation must be enforceable by means of fines and periodic penalty payments;

WHEREAS undertakings concerned must be accorded the right to be heard by the Commission, third parties whose interests may be affected by a decision must be given the opportunity of submitting their comments beforehand, and it must be ensured that wide publicity is given to decisions taken;

WHEREAS all decisions taken by the Commission under this Regulation are subject to review by the Court of Justice under the conditions specified in the Treaty; whereas it is moreover desirable to confer upon the Court of Justice, pursuant to Article 172, unlimited jurisdiction in respect of decisions under which the Commission imposes fines or periodic penalty payments;

WHEREAS this Regulation may enter into force without prejudice to any other provisions that may hereafter be adopted pursuant to Article 87;

HAS ADOPTED THIS REGULATION:

–02 *ARTICLE 1*

Basic provision

Without prejudice to Articles 6, 7 and 23 of this Regulation, agreements, decisions and concerted practices of the kind described in Article 85 (1) of the Treaty and the abuse of a dominant position in the market, within the meaning of Article 86 of the Treaty, shall be prohibited, no prior decision to that effect being required.

–03 *ARTICLE 2*

Negative clearance

Upon application by the undertakings or associations of undertakings concerned, the Commission may certify that, on the basis of the facts in its possession, there are no grounds under Article 85(1) or Article 86 of the Treaty for action on its part in respect of an agreement, decision or practice.

–04 *ARTICLE 3*

Termination of infringements

1. Where the Commission, upon application or upon its own initiative, finds that there is infringement of Article 85 or Article 86 of the Treaty, it may by decision require the undertakings or associations of undertakings concerned to bring such infringement to an end.

2. Those entitled to make application are:
   (a) Member States;
   (b) natural or legal persons who claim a legitimate interest.

3. Without prejudice to the other provisions of this Regulation, the Commission may, before taking a decision under paragraph 1, address to the undertakings or associations of undertakings concerned recommendations for termination of the infringement.

–05 *ARTICLE 4 (as amended by Regulation 2822/71 – Appendix L)*

Notification of new agreements, decisions and practices

1. Agreements, decisions and concerted practices of the kind described in Article 85 (1) of the Treaty which come into existence after the entry into force of this Regulation and in

respect of which the parties seek application of Article 85 (3) must be notified to the Commission. Until they have been notified, no decision in application of Article 85(3) may be taken.

2. Paragraph 1 shall not apply to agreements, decisions or concerted practices where:

(1) the only parties thereto are undertakings from one Member State and the agreements, decisions or practices do not relate either to imports or to exports between Member States;

(2) not more than two undertakings are party thereto, and the agreements only:

(a) restrict the freedom of one party to the contract in determining the prices or conditions of business upon which the goods which he has obtained from the other party to the contract may be resold; or

(b) impose restrictions on the exercise of the rights of the assignee or user of industrial property rights – in particular patents, utility models, designs or trade marks – or of the person entitled under a contract to the assignment, or grant, of the right to use a method of manufacture or knowledge relating to the use and to the application of industrial processes;

(3) they have as their sole object:

(a) the development or uniform application of standards or types; or

(b) *joint research and development;*

(c) *specialisation in the manufacture of products, including agreements necessary for achieving this,*

– *where the products which are the subject of specialisation do not, in a substantial part of the common market, represent more than 15% of the volume of business done in identical products or those considered by consumers to be similar by reason of their characteristics, price and use,*

and

– *where the total annual turnover of the participating undertakings does not exceed 200 million units of account.*

These agreements, decisions and practices may be notified to the Commission.

–06 *ARTICLE 5 (as amended by Regulation 59/62)*

Notification of existing agreements, decisions and practices

1. Agreements, decisions and concerted practices of the kind described in Article 85(1) of the Treaty which are in existence at the date of entry into force of this Regulation and in respect of which the parties seek application of Article 85(3) shall be notified to the Commission before *1 November* 1962.

However, notwithstanding the foregoing provisions, any agreements, decisions and concerted practices to which not more than two undertakings are party shall be notified before 1 February 1963.

2. Paragraph 1 shall not apply to agreements, decisions or concerted practices falling within Article 4(2); these may be notified to the Commission.

–07 *ARTICLE 6*

Decisions pursuant to Article 85(3)

1. Whenever the Commission takes a decision pursuant to Article 85(3) of the Treaty, it shall specify therein the date from which the decision shall take effect. Such date shall not be earlier than the date of notification.

2. The second sentence of paragraph 1 shall not apply to agreements, decisions or concerted practices falling within Article 4(2) and Article 5(2), nor to those falling within Article 5(1) which have been notified within the time limit specified in Article 5(1).

–08 *ARTICLE 7*

Special provisions for existing agreements, decisions and practices

1. Where agreements, decisions and concerted practices in existence at the date of entry into force of this Regulation and notified *within the time limits specified in Article 5(1)*[1] do not satisfy the requirements of Article 85(3) of the Treaty and the undertakings or associations of undertakings concerned cease to give effect to them or modify them in such manner that they no longer fall within the prohibition contained in Article 85(1) or that they satisfy the requirements of Article 85(3), the prohibition contained in Article 85(1) shall apply only for a period fixed by the Commission. A decision by the Commission pursuant to the foregoing sentence shall not apply as against undertakings and

[1] Amendment made by Regulation 59/62.

associations of undertakings which did not expressly consent to the notification.

2. Paragraph 1 shall apply to agreements, decisions and concerted practices falling within Article 4(2) which are in existence at the date of entry into force of this Regulation if they are notified before 1 January *1967*.[2]

18–09 *ARTICLE 8*

Duration and revocation of decisions under Article 85(3)

1. A decision in application of Article 85(3) of the Treaty shall be issued for a specified period and conditions and obligations may be attached thereto.

2. A decision may on application be renewed if the requirements of Article 85(3) of the Treaty continue to be satisfied.

3. The Commission may revoke or amend its decision or prohibit specified acts by the parties:

(a) where there has been a change in any of the facts which were basic to the making of the decision;

(b) where the parties commit a breach of any obligation attached to the decision;

(c) where the decision is based on incorrect information or was induced by deceit;

(d) where the parties abuse the exemption from the provisions of Article 85(1) of the Treaty granted to them by the decision.

In cases to which subparagraphs (b), (c) or (d) apply, the decision may be revoked with retroactive effect.

18–10 *ARTICLE 9*

Powers

1. Subject to review of its decision by the Court of Justice, the Commission shall have sole power to declare Article 85(1) inapplicable pursuant to Article 85(3) of the Treaty.

2. The Commission shall have power to apply Article 85(1) and Article 86 of the Treaty; this power may be exercised notwithstanding that the time limits specified in Article 5(1) and in Article 7(2) relating to notification have not expired.

3. As long as the Commission has not initiated any procedure under Articles 2, 3 or 6, the authorities of the Member States shall remain competent to apply Article 85(1) and Article 86 in

[2] Amendment made by Regulation 118/63.

accordance with Article 88 of the Treaty; they shall remain competent in this respect notwithstanding that the time limits specified in Article 5(1) and in Article 7(2) relating to notification have not expired.

11 *ARTICLE 10*

Liaison with the authorities of the Member States

1. The Commission shall forthwith transmit to the competent authorities of the Member States a copy of the applications and notifications together with copies of the most important documents lodged with the Commission for the purpose of establishing the existence of infringements of Articles 85 and 86 of the Treaty or of obtaining negative clearance or a decision in application of Article 85(3).

2. The Commission shall carry out the procedure set out in paragraph 1 in close and constant liaison with the competent authorities of the Member States; such authorities shall have the right to express their views upon that procedure.

3. An Advisory Committee on Restrictive Practices and Monopolies shall be consulted prior to the taking of any decision following upon a procedure under paragraph 1, and of any decision concerning the renewal, amendment or revocation of a decision pursuant to Article 85(3) of the Treaty.

4. The Advisory Committee shall be composed of officials competent in the matter of restrictive practices and monopolies. Each Member State shall appoint an official to represent it, who, if prevented from attending, may be replaced by another official.

5. The consultation shall take place at a joint meeting convened by the Commission; such meeting shall be held not earlier than fourteen days after dispatch of the notice convening it. The notice shall, in respect of each case to be examined, be accompanied by a summary of the case together with an indication of the most important documents, and a preliminary draft decision.

6. The Advisory Committee may deliver an opinion notwithstanding that some of its members or their alternates are not present. A report of the outcome of the consultative proceedings shall be annexed to the draft decision. It shall not be made public.

12 *ARTICLE 11*

Requests for information

1. In carrying out the duties assigned to it by Article 89 and by

provisions adopted under Article 87 of the Treaty, the Commission may obtain all necessary information from the Governments and competent authorities of the Member States and from undertakings and associations of undertakings.
2. When sending a request for information to an undertaking or association of undertakings, the Commission shall at the same time forward a copy of the request to the competent authority of the Member State in whose territory the seat of the undertaking or association of undertakings is situated.
3. In its request the Commission shall state the legal basis and the purpose of the request and also the penalties provided for in Article 15(1)(b) for supplying incorrect information.
4. The owners of the undertakings or their representatives and, in the case of legal persons, companies or firms, or of associations having no legal personality, the persons authorised to represent them by law or by their constitution shall supply the information requested.
5. Where an undertaking or association of undertakings does not supply the information requested within the time limit fixed by the Commission, or supplies incomplete information, the Commission shall by decision require the information to be supplied. The decision shall specify what information is required, fix an appropriate time limit within which it is to be supplied and indicate the penalties provided for in Article 15(1)(b) and Article 16(1)(c) and the right to have the decision reviewed by the Court of Justice.
6. The Commission shall at the same time forward a copy of its decision to the competent authority of the Member State in whose territory the seat of the undertaking or association of undertakings is situated.

18–13 *ARTICLE 12*

Inquiry into sectors of the economy

1. If in any sector of the economy the trend of trade between Member States, price movements, inflexibility of prices or other circumstances suggest that in the economic sector concerned competition is being restricted or distorted within the common market, the Commission may decide to conduct a general inquiry into that economic sector and in the course thereof may request undertakings in the sector concerned to supply the information necessary for giving effect to the principles formulated in Articles 85 and 86 of the Treaty and for carrying out the duties entrusted to the Commission.

2. The Commission may in particular request every undertaking or association of undertakings in the economic sector concerned to communicate to it all agreements, decisions and concerted practices which are exempt from notification by virtue of Article 4(2) and Article 5(2).
3. When making inquiries pursuant to paragraph 2, the Commission shall also request undertakings or groups of undertakings whose size suggests that they occupy a dominant position within the common market or a substantial part thereof to supply to the Commission such particulars of the structure of the undertakings and of their behaviour as are requisite to an appraisal of their position in the light of Article 86 of the Treaty.
4. Article 10(3) to (6) and Articles 11, 13 and 14 shall apply correspondingly.

14 *ARTICLE 13*

Investigations by the authorities of the Member States

1. At the request of the Commission, the competent authorities of the Member States shall undertake the investigations which the Commission considers to be necessary under Article 14(1), or which it has ordered by decision pursuant to Article 14(3). The officials of the competent authorities of the Member States responsible for conducting these investigations shall exercise their powers upon production of an authorisation in writing issued by the competent authority of the Member State in whose territory the investigation is to be made. Such authorisation shall specify the subject matter and purpose of the investigation.
2. If so requested by the Commission or by the competent authority of the Member State in whose territory the investigation is to be made, the officials of the Commission may assist the officials of such authorities in carrying out their duties.

-15 *ARTICLE 14*

Investigating powers of the Commission

1. In carrying out the duties assigned to it by Article 89 and by provisions adopted under Article 87 of the Treaty, the Commission may undertake all necessary investigations into undertakings and associations of undertakings. To this end the officials authorised by the Commission are empowered:
   - (a) to examine the books and other business records;
   - (b) to take copies of or extracts from the books and business records;
   - (c) to ask for oral explanations on the spot;

(d) to enter any premises; land and means of transport of undertakings.

2. The officials of the Commission authorised for the purpose of these investigations shall exercise their powers upon production of an authorisation in writing specifying the subject matter and purpose of the investigation and the penalties provided for in Article 15(1)(c) in cases where production of the required books or other business records is incomplete. In good time before the investigation, the Commission shall inform the competent authority of the Member State in whose territory the same is to be made of the investigation and of the identity of the authorised officials.

3. Undertakings and associations of undertakings shall submit to investigations ordered by decision of the Commission. The decision shall specify the subject matter and purpose of the investigation, appoint the date on which it is to begin and indicate the penalties provided for in Article 15(1)(c) and Article 16(1)(d) and the right to have the decision reviewed by the Court of Justice.

4. The Commission shall take decisions referred to in paragraph 3 after consultation with the competent authority of the Member State in whose territory the investigation is to be made.

5. Officials of the competent authority of the Member State in whose territory the investigation is to be made may, at the request of such authority or of the Commission, assist the officials of the Commission in carrying out their duties.

6. Where an undertaking opposes an investigation ordered pursuant to this Article, the Member State concerned shall afford the necessary assistance to the officials authorised by the Commission to enable them to make their investigation. Member States shall, after consultation with the Commission, take the necessary measures to this end before 1 October 1962.

18–16 *ARTICLE 15*

Fines

1. The Commission may by decision impose on undertakings or associations of undertakings fines of from 100 to 5000 units of account where, intentionally or negligently:

(a) they supply incorrect or misleading information in an application pursuant to Article 2 or in a notification pursuant to Articles 4 or 5; or

(b) they supply incorrect information in response to a request made pursuant to Article 11(3) or (5) or to Article 12, or do not supply information within the time limit fixed by a decision taken under Article 11(5); or

(c) they produce the required books or other business records in incomplete form during investigations under Article 13 or 14, or refuse to submit to an investigation ordered by decision issued in implementation of Article 14(3).

2. The Commission may by decision impose on undertakings or associations of undertakings fines of from 1000 to 1 000 000 units of account, or a sum in excess thereof but not exceeding 10% of the turnover in the preceding business year of each of the undertakings participating in the infringement where, either intentionally or negligently:

(a) they infringe Article 85(1) or Article 86 of the Treaty; or

(b) they commit a breach of any obligation imposed pursuant to Article 8(1).

In fixing the amount of the fine, regard shall be had both to the gravity and to the duration of the infringement.

3. Article 10(3) to (6) shall apply.

4. Decisions taken pursuant to paragraphs 1 and 2 shall not be of a criminal law nature.

5. The fines provided for in paragraph 2(a) shall not be imposed in respect of acts taking place:

(a) after notification to the Commission and before its decision in application of Article 85(3) of the Treaty, provided they fall within the limits of the activity described in the notification;

(b) before notification and in the course of agreements, decisions or concerted practices in existence at the date of entry into force of this Regulation, provided that notification was effected within the time limits specified in Article 5(1) and Article 7(2).

6. Paragraph 5 shall not have effect where the Commission has informed the undertakings concerned that after preliminary examination it is of opinion that Article 85(1) of the Treaty applies and that application of Article 85(3) is not justified.

17 *ARTICLE 16*

Periodic penalty payments

1. The Commission may by decision impose on undertakings or associations of undertakings periodic penalty payments of from

50 to 1000 units of account per day, calculated from the date appointed by the decision, in order to compel them:

(a) to put an end to an infringement of Article 85 or 86 of the Treaty, in accordance with a decision taken pursuant to Article 3 of this Regulation;

(b) to refrain from any act prohibited under Article 8(3);

(c) to supply complete and correct information which it has requested by decision taken pursuant to Article 11(5);

(d) to submit to an investigation which it has ordered by decision taken pursuant to Article 14(3).

2. Where the undertakings or associations of undertakings have satisfied the obligation which it was the purpose of the periodic penalty payment to enforce, the Commission may fix the total amount of the periodic penalty payment at a lower figure than that which would arise under the original decision.

3. Article 10(3) to (6) shall apply.

18–18 *ARTICLE 17*

Review by the Court of Justice

The Court of Justice shall have unlimited jurisdiction within the meaning of Article 172 of the Treaty to review decisions whereby the Commission has fixed a fine or periodic penalty payment; it may cancel, reduce or increase the fine or periodic penalty payment imposed.

18–19 *ARTICLE 18*

Unit of account

For the purposes of applying Articles 15 to 17 the unit of account shall be that adopted in drawing up the budget of the Community in accordance with Articles 207 and 209 of the Treaty.

18–20 *ARTICLE 19*

Hearing of the parties and of third persons

1. Before taking decisions as provided for in Articles 2, 3, 6, 7, 8, 15 and 16, the Commission shall give the undertakings or associations of undertakings concerned the opportunity of being heard on the matters to which the Commission has taken objection.

2. If the Commission or the competent authorities of the Member States consider it necessary, they may also hear other natural or legal persons. Applications to be heard on the part of

such persons shall, where they show a sufficient interest, be granted.

3. Where the Commission intends to give negative clearance pursuant to Article 2 or take a decision in application of Article 85(3) of the Treaty, it shall publish a summary of the relevant application or notification and invite all interested third parties to submit their observations within a time limit which it shall fix being not less than one month. Publication shall have regard to the legitimate interest of undertakings in the protection of their business secrets.

-21 *ARTICLE 20*

Professional secrecy

1. Information acquired as a result of the application of Articles 11, 12, 13 and 14 shall be used only for the purpose of the relevant request or investigation.

2. Without prejudice to the provisions of Articles 19 and 21, the Commission and the competent authorities of the Member States, their officials and other servants shall not disclose information acquired by them as a result of the application of this Regulation and of the kind covered by the obligation of professional secrecy.

3. The provisions of paragraphs 1 and 2 shall not prevent publication of general information or surveys which do not contain information relating to particular undertakings or associations of undertakings.

-22 *ARTICLE 21*

Publication of decisions

1. The Commission shall publish the decisions which it takes pursuant to Articles 2, 3, 6, 7 and 8.

2. The publication shall state the names of the parties and the main content of the decision; it shall have regard to the legitimate interest of undertakings in the protection of their business secrets.

23 *ARTICLE 22*

Special provisions

1. The Commission shall submit to the Council proposals for making certain categories of agreement, decision and concerted practice falling within Article 4(2) or Article 5(2) compulsorily notifiable under Article 4 or 5.

2. Within one year from the date of entry into force of this

Regulation, the Council shall examine, on a proposal from the Commission, what special provisions might be made for exempting from the provisions of this Regulation agreements, decisions and concerted practices falling within Article 4(2) or Article 5(2).

18–24 *ARTICLE 23*

Transitional provisions applicable to decisions of authorities of the Member States

1. Agreements, decisions and concerted practices of the kind described in Article 85(1) of the Treaty to which, before the entry into force of this Regulation, the competent authority of a Member State has declared Article 85(1) to be inapplicable pursuant to Article 85(3) shall not be subject to compulsory notification under Article 5. The decision of the competent authority of the Member State shall be deemed to be a decision within the meaning of Article 6; it shall cease to be valid upon expiration of the period fixed by such authority but in any event not more than three years after the entry into force of this Regulation. Article 8(3) shall apply.

2. Applications for renewal of decisions of the kind described in paragraph 1 shall be decided upon by the Commission in accordance with Article 8(2).

18–25 *ARTICLE 24*

Implementing provisions

The Commission shall have power to adopt implementing provisions concerning the form, content and other details of applications pursuant to Articles 2 and 3 and of notifications pursuant to Articles 4 and 5, and concerning hearings pursuant to Article 19(1) and (2).

18–26 *ARTICLE 25 (added by the Treaty of Accession)*

1. As regards agreements, decisions and concerted practices to which Article 85 of the Treaty applies by virtue of accession, the date of accession shall be substituted for the date of entry into force of this Regulation in every place where reference is made in this Regulation to this latter date.

2. Agreements, decisions and concerted practices existing at the date of accession to which Article 85 of the Treaty applies by virtue of accession shall be notified pursuant to Article 5(1) or Article 7(1) and (2) within six months from the date of accession.

3. Fines under Article 15(2)(a) shall not be imposed in respect of any act prior to notification of the agreements, decisions and practices to which paragraph 2 applies and which have been notified within the period therein specified.

4. *New Member States shall take the measures referred to in Article 14(6) within six months from the date of accession after consulting the Commission.*

–27 This Regulation shall be binding in its entirety and directly applicable in all Member States.

Done at Brussels, 6 February 1962.

For the Council
The President
M. COUVE DE MURVILLE

APPENDIX E

REGULATION NO 99/63/EEC OF THE COMMISSION

On the Hearings Provided For in Article 19(1) and (2) of Council Regulation no 17

21–01 THE COMMISSION OF THE EUROPEAN ECONOMIC COMMUNITY,

HAVING REGARD to the Treaty establishing the European Economic Community, and in particular Articles 87 and 155 thereof;

HAVING REGARD to Article 24 of Council Regulation No 17 of 6 February 1962 (First Regulation implementing Articles 85 and 86 of the Treaty);

WHEREAS the Commission has power under Article 24 of Council Regulation No 17 to lay down implementing provisions concerning the hearings provided for in Article 19(1) and (2) of that Regulation;

WHEREAS in most cases the Commission will in the course of its inquiries already be in close touch with the undertakings or associations of undertakings which are the subject thereof and they will accordingly have the opportunity of making known their views regarding the objections raised against them;

WHEREAS, however, in accordance with Article 19(1) of Regulation No 17 and with the rights of defence, the undertakings and associations of undertakings concerned must have the right on conclusion of the inquiry to submit their comments on

* Published in the Journal Officiel 20th August, 1963, English text Official Journal Special Edition 1963-1964. p.47.

the whole of the objections raised against them which the Commission proposes to deal with in its decisions;

WHEREAS persons other than the undertakings or associations of undertakings which are the subject of the inquiry may have an interest in being heard; whereas, by the second sentence of Article 19(2) of Regulation No 17, such persons must have the opportunity of being heard if they apply and show that they have a sufficient interest;

WHEREAS it is desirable to enable persons who, pursuant to Article 3(2) of Regulation No 17, have applied for an infringement to be terminated to submit their comments where the Commission considers that on the basis of the information in its possession there are insufficient grounds for granting the application;

WHEREAS the various persons entitled to submit comments must do so in writing, both in their own interest and in the interests of good administration, without prejudice to oral procedure where appropriate to supplement the written evidence;

WHEREAS it is necessary to define the rights of persons who are to be heard, and in particular the conditions upon which they may be represented or assisted and the setting and calculation of time limits;

WHEREAS the Advisory Committee on Restrictive Practices and Monopolies delivers its Opinion on the basis of a preliminary draft decision; whereas it must therefore be consulted concerning a case after the inquiry in respect thereof has been completed; whereas such consultation does not prevent the Commission from re-opening an inquiry if need be;

HAS ADOPTED THIS REGULATION:

-02 *ARTICLE 1*

Before consulting the Advisory Committee on Restrictive Practices and Monopolies, the Commission shall hold a hearing pursuant to Article 19(1) of Regulation No 17.

-03 *ARTICLE 2*

1. The Commission shall inform undertakings and associations of undertakings in writing of the objections raised against them. The communication shall be addressed to each of them or to a joint agent appointed by them.

2. The Commission may inform the parties by giving notice in the *Official Journal of the European Communities,* if from the

circumstances of the case this appears appropriate, in particular where notice is to be given to a number of undertakings but no joint agent has been appointed. The notice shall have regard to the legitimate interest of the undertakings in the protection of their business secrets.

3. A fine or a periodic penalty payment may be imposed on an undertaking or association of undertakings only if the objections were notified in the manner provided for in paragraph 1.

4. The Commission shall when giving notice of objections fix a time limit up to which the undertakings and associations of undertakings may inform the Commission of their views.

21–04 *ARTICLE 3*

1. Undertakings and associations of undertakings shall, within the appointed time limit, make known in writing their views concerning the objections raised against them.

2. They may in their written comments set out all matters relevant to their defence.

3. They may attach any relevant documents in proof of the facts set out. They may also propose that the Commission hear persons who may corroborate those facts.

21–05 *ARTICLE 4*

The Commission shall in its decisions deal only with those objections raised against undertakings and associations of undertakings in respect of which they have been afforded the opportunity of making known their views.

21–06 *ARTICLE 5*

If natural or legal persons showing a sufficient interest apply to be heard pursuant to Article 19(2) of Regulation No 17, the Commission shall afford them the opportunity of making known their views in writing within such time limit as it shall fix.

21–07 *ARTICLE 6*

Where the Commission, having received an application pursuant to Article 3(2) of Regulation No 17, considers that on the basis of the information in its possession there are insufficient grounds for granting the application, it shall inform the applicants of its reasons and fix a time limit for them to submit any further comments in writing.

–08 *ARTICLE 7*

1. The Commission shall afford to persons who have so requested in their written comments the opportunity to put forward their arguments orally, if those persons show a sufficient interest or if the Commission proposes to impose on them a fine or periodic penalty payment.

2. The Commission may likewise afford to any other person the opportunity of orally expressing his views.

–09 *ARTICLE 8*

1. The Commission shall summon the persons to be heard to attend on such date as it shall appoint.

2. It shall forthwith transmit a copy of the summons to the competent authorities of the Member States, who may appoint an official to take part in the hearing.

–10 *ARTICLE 9*

1. Hearings shall be conducted by the persons appointed by the Commission for that purpose.

2. Persons summoned to attend shall appear either in person or be represented by legal representatives or by representatives authorised by their constitution. Undertakings and associations of undertakings may moreover be represented by a duly authorised agent appointed from among their permament staff.

Persons heard by the Commission may be assisted by lawyers or university teachers who are entitled to plead before the Court of Justice of the European Communities in accordance with Article 17 of the Protocol on the Statute of the Court, or by other qualified persons.

3. Hearings shall not be public. Persons shall be heard separately or in the presence of other persons summoned to attend. In the latter case, regard shall be had to the legitimate interest of the undertakings in the protection of their business secrets.

4. The essential content of the statements made by each person heard shall be recorded in minutes which shall be read and approved by him.

–11 *ARTICLE 10*

Without prejudice to Article 2(2), information and summonses from the Commission shall be sent to the addressees by registered letter with acknowledgement of receipt, or shall be delivered by hand against receipt.

21–12 *ARTICLE 11*

1. In fixing the time limits provided for in Articles 2, 5 and 6, the Commission shall have regard both to the time required for preparation of comments and to the urgency of the case. The time limit shall be not less than two weeks; it may be extended.

2. Time limits shall run from the day following receipt of a communication or delivery thereof by hand.

3. Written comments must reach the Commission or be dispatched by registered letter before expiry of the time limit. Where the time limit would expire on a Sunday or public holiday, it shall be extended up to the end of the next following working day. For the purpose of calculating this extension, public holidays shall, in cases where the relevant date is the date of receipt of written comments, be those set out in the Annex to this Regulation, and in cases where the relevant date is the date of dispatch, those appointed by law in the country of dispatch.

21–13 This Regulation shall be binding in its entirety and directly applicable in all Member States.

Done at Brussels, 25 July 1963.

For the Commission
The President
WALTER HALLSTEIN

21–14 *ANNEX*

Referred to in the third sentence of Article 11(3)

(List of public holidays)

New Year	1 Jan
Good Friday	
Easter Saturday	
Easter Monday	
Labour Day	1 May
Schuman Plan Day	9 May
Ascension Day	
Whit Monday	
Belgian National Day	21 July
Assumption	15 Aug
All Saints	1 Nov
All Souls	2 Nov
Christmas Eve	24 Dec
Christmas Day	25 Dec
The day following Christmas Day	26 Dec
New Year's Eve	31 Dec

APPENDIX F

REGULATION NO 19/65/EEC OF THE COUNCIL

On Application of Article 85(3) of the Treaty to Certain Categories of Agreements and Concerted Practices

–01 THE COUNCIL OF THE EUROPEAN ECONOMIC COMMUNITY,

HAVING REGARD to the Treaty establishing the European Economic Community, and in particular Article 87 thereof;

HAVING REGARD to the proposal from the Commission;

HAVING REGARD to the Opinion of the European Parliament;

HAVING REGARD to the Opinion of the Economic and Social Committee;

WHEREAS Article 85(1) of the Treaty may in accordance with Article 85(3) be declared inapplicable to certain categories of agreements, decisions and concerted practices which fulfil the conditions contained in Article 85(3);

WHEREAS the provisions for implementation of Article 85(3) must be adopted by way of regulation pursuant to Article 87;

WHEREAS in view of the large number of notifications submitted in pursuance of Regulation No 17 it is desirable that in order to facilitate the task of the Commission it should be enabled to declare by way of regulation that the provisions of Article 85(1) do not apply to certain categories of agreements and concerted practices;

* Published in the Journal Officiel 6th March, 1965, English text Official Journal Special Edition 1965-1966 p.35.

WHEREAS it should be laid down under what conditions the Commission, in close and constant liaison with the competent authorities of the Member States, may exercise such powers after sufficient experience has been gained in the light of individual decisions and it becomes possible to define categories of agreements and concerted practices in respect of which the conditions of Article 85(3) may be considered as being fulfilled;

WHEREAS the Commission has indicated by the action it has taken, in particular by Regulation No 153, that there can be no easing of the procedures prescribed by Regulation No 17 in respect of certain types of agreements and concerted practices that are particularly liable to distort competition in the common market;

WHEREAS under Article 6 of Regulation No 17 the Commission may provide that a decision taken pursuant to Article 85(3) of the Treaty shall apply with retroactive effect; whereas it is desirable that the Commission be also empowered to adopt, by regulation, provisions to the like effect;

WHEREAS under Article 7 of Regulation No 17 agreements, decisions and concerted practices may, by decision of the Commission, be exempted from prohibition in particular if they are modified in such manner that they satisfy the requirements of Article 85(3); whereas it is desirable that the Commission be enabled to grant like exemption by regulation to such agreements and concerted practices if they are modified in such manner as to fall within a category defined in an exempting regulation;

WHEREAS, since there can be no exemption if the conditions set out in Article 85(3) are not satisfied, the Commission must have power to lay down by decision the conditions that must be satisfied by an agreement or concerted practice which owing to special circumstances has certain effects incompatible with Article 85(3);

HAS ADOPTED THIS REGULATION:

22–02 *ARTICLE 1*

1. Without prejudice to the application of Council Regulation No 17 and in accordance with Article 85(3) of the Treaty the Commission may by regulation declare that Article 85(1) shall not apply to categories of agreements to which only two undertakings are party and:

(a) – whereby one party agrees with the other to supply only to that other certain goods for resale within a defined area of the common market; or

– whereby one party agrees with the other to purchase only from that other certain goods for resale; or

– whereby the two undertakings have entered into obligations, as in the two preceding sub-paragraphs, with each other in respect of exclusive supply and purchase for resale;

(b) which include restrictions imposed in relation to the acquisition or use of industrial property rights – in particular of patents, utility models, designs or trade marks – or to the rights arising out of contracts for assignment of, or the right to use, a method of manufacture or knowledge relating to the use or to the application of industrial processes.

2. The regulation shall define the categories of agreements to which it applies and shall specify in particular:

(a) the restrictions or clauses which must not be contained in the agreements;

(b) the clauses which must be contained in the agreements, or the other conditions which must be satisfied.

3. Paragraphs 1 and 2 shall apply by analogy to categories of concerted practices to which only two undertakings are party.

–03 *ARTICLE 2*

1. A regulation pursuant to Article 1 shall be made for a specified period.

2. It may be repealed or amended where circumstances have changed with respect to any factor which was basic to its being made; in such case, a period shall be fixed for modification of the agreements and concerted practices to which the earlier regulation applies.

–04 *ARTICLE 3*

A regulation pursuant to Article 1 may stipulate that it shall apply with retroactive effect to agreements and concerted practices to which, at the date of entry into force of that regulation, a decision issued with retroactive effect in pursuance of Article 6 of Regulation No 17 would have applied.

22–05 *ARTICLE 4*

1. A regulation pursuant to Article 1 may stipulate that the prohibition contained in Article 85(1) of the Treaty shall not apply, for such period as shall be fixed by that regulation, to agreements and concerted practices already in existence *at the date of accession to which Article 85 applies by virtue of accession and*[1] which do not satisfy the conditions of Article 85(3), where:

– within three months from the entry into force of the Regulation, they are so modified as to satisfy the said conditions in accordance with the provisions of the regulation; and

– the modifications are brought to the notice of the Commission within the time limit fixed by the regulation.

2. *Paragraph 1 shall not apply to agreements and concerted practices to which Article 85(1) of the Treaty applies by virtue of accession and which must be notified before 1 July 1973, in accordance with Articles 5 and 25 of Regulation No 17, unless they have been so notified before that date.*[2]

3. The benefit of the provisions laid down pursuant to paragraph 1 may not be claimed in actions pending at the date of entry into force of a regulation adopted pursuant to Article 1; neither may it be relied on as grounds for claims for damages against third parties.

22–06 *ARTICLE 5*

Before adopting a regulation, the Commission shall publish a draft thereof and invite all persons concerned to submit their comments within such time limit, being not less than one month, as the Commission shall fix.

22–07 *ARTICLE 6*

1. The Commission shall consult the Advisory Committee on Restrictive Practices and Monopolies:

[1] Amendment made by the Treaty of Accession, substituting the words in italics for "on 13 March 1962".

[2] Amendment made by the Treaty of Accession. Article 4(2) formerly read: "2. Paragraph 1 shall apply to agreements and concerted practices which had to be notified before 1 February 1963, in accordance with Article 5 of Regulation No17, only where they have been so notified before that date."

(a) before publishing a draft regulation;
(b) before adopting a regulation.

2. Article 10(5) and (6) of Regulation No 17, relating to consultation with the Advisory Committee, shall apply by analogy, it being understood that joint meetings with the Commission shall take place not earlier than one month after dispatch of the notice convening them.

-08 *ARTICLE 7*

Where the Commission, either on its own initiative or at the request of a Member State or of natural or legal persons claiming a legitimate interest, finds that in any particular case agreements or concerted practices to which a regulation adopted pursuant to Article 1 of this Regulation applies have nevertheless certain effects which are incompatible with the conditions laid down in Article 85(3) of the Treaty, it may withdraw the benefit of application of that regulation and issue a decision in accordance with Articles 6 and 8 of Regulation No 17, without any notification under Article 4(1) of Regulation No 17 being required.

-09 *ARTICLE 8*

The Commission shall, before 1 January 1970, submit to the Council a proposal for a Regulation for such amendment of this Regulation as may prove necessary in the light of experience.

-10 This Regulation shall be binding in its entirety and directly applicable in all Member States.

Done at Brussels, 2 March 1965.

For the Council
The President
M. COUVE DE MURVILLE

APPENDIX G

REGULATION NO 67/67/EEC OF THE COMMISSION of 22 March 1967

On the Application of Article 85(3) of the Treaty to Certain Categories of Exclusive Dealing Agreements

23–01 THE COMMISSION OF THE EUROPEAN ECONOMIC COMMUNITY,

HAVING REGARD to the Treaty establishing the European Economic Community, and in particular Articles 87 and 155 thereof;

HAVING REGARD to Article 24 of Regulation No 17 of 6 February 1962;

HAVING REGARD to Regulation No 19/65/EEC of 2 March 1965 on the application of Article 85(3) of the Treaty to certain categories of agreements and concerted practices;

HAVING REGARD to the Opinions delivered by the Advisory Committee on Restrictive Practices and Monopolies in accordance with Article 6 of Regulation No 19/65/EEC;

WHEREAS under Regulation No 19/65/EEC the Commission has power to apply Article 85(3) of the Treaty by regulation to certain categories of bilateral exclusive dealing agreements and concerted practices coming within Article 85;

WHEREAS the experience gained up to now, on the basis of individual decisions, makes it possible to define a first category of agreements and concerted practices which can be accepted as normally satisfying the conditions laid down in Article 85(3);

* Published in the Journal Officiel 25th March, 1967, English text Official Journal Special Edition 1967. p.10.

WHEREAS, since adoption of such a regulation would not conflict with the application of Regulation No 17, the right of undertakings to request the Commission, on an individual basis, for a declaration under Article 85(3) of the Treaty would not be affected;

WHEREAS exclusive dealing agreements of the category defined in Article 1 of this Regulation may fall within the prohibition contained in Article 85(1) of the Treaty; whereas since it is only in exceptional cases that exclusive dealing agreements concluded within a Member State affect trade between Member States, there is no need to include them in this Regulation;

WHEREAS it is not necessary expressly to exclude from the category as defined those agreements which do not fulfil the conditions of Article 85(1) of the Treaty;

WHEREAS in the present state of trade exclusive dealing agreements relating to international trade lead in general to an improvement in distribution because the entrepreneur is able to consolidate his sales activities; whereas he is not obliged to maintain numerous business contacts with a large number of dealers, and whereas the fact of maintaining contacts with only one dealer makes it easier to overcome sales difficulties resulting from linguistic, legal, and other differences; whereas exclusive dealing agreements facilitate the promotion of the sale of a product and make it possible to carry out more intensive marketing and to ensure continuity of supplies, while at the same time rationalising distribution; whereas, moreover, the appointment of an exclusive distributor or of an exclusive purchaser who will take over, in place of the manufacturer, sales promotion, after-sales service and carrying of stocks, is often the sole means whereby small and medium-size undertakings can compete in the market; whereas it should be left to the contracting parties to decide whether and to what extent they consider it desirable to incorporate in the agreements terms designed to promote sales; whereas there can only be an improvement in distribution if dealing is not entrusted to a competitor;

WHEREAS as a rule such exclusive dealing agreements also help to give consumers a proper share of the resulting benefit as they gain directly from the improvement in distribution, and their economic or supply position is thereby improved as they can obtain products manufactured in other countries more quickly and more easily;

WHEREAS this Regulation must determine the obligations restricting competition which may be included in an exclusive dealing agreement; whereas it may be left to the contracting parties to decide which of those obligations they include in exclusive dealing agreements in order to draw the maximum advantages from exclusive dealing;

WHEREAS any exemption must be subject to certain conditions; whereas it is in particular advisable to ensure through the possibility of parallel imports that consumers obtain a proper share of the advantages resulting from exclusive dealing; whereas it is therefore not possible to allow industrial property rights and other rights to be exercised in an abusive manner in order to create absolute territorial protection; whereas these considerations do not prejudice the relationship between the law of competition and industrial property rights, since the sole object here is to determine the conditions for exemption of certain categories of agreements under this Regulation;

WHEREAS competition at the distribution stage is ensured by the possibility of parallel imports, whereas, therefore, the exclusive dealing agreements covered by this Regulation will not normally afford any possibility of preventing competition in respect of a substantial part of the products in question;

WHEREAS it is desirable to allow contracting parties a limited period of time within which they may, in accordance with Article 4 of Regulation No 19/65/EEC, modify their agreements and practices so as to satisfy the conditions laid down in this Regulation, without it being possible, under Article 4(3) of Regulation No 19/65/EEC, to rely thereon in actions which are pending at the time of entry into force of this Regulation, or as grounds for claims for damages against third parties;

WHEREAS agreements and concerted practices which satisfy the conditions set out in this Regulation need no longer be notified; whereas Article 4(2)(a) of Regulation No 27, as amended by Regulation No 153, can be repealed, since agreements which it was possible to notify on Form B 1 would normally come within the scope of the exemption;

WHEREAS agreements notified on Form B 1 and not amended so as to satisfy the conditions of this Regulation should be made subject to the normal notification procedure, in order that they may be examined individually;

HAS ADOPTED THIS REGULATION:

–02 *ARTICLE 1*

1. Pursuant to Article 85(3) of the Treaty and subject to the provisions of this Regulation it is hereby declared that until 31 December *1982*[1] Article 85(1) of the Treaty shall not apply to agreements to which only two undertakings are party and whereby:

(a) one party agrees with the other to supply only to that other certain goods for resale within a defined area of the common market; or

(b) one party agrees with the other to purchase only from that other certain goods for resale; or

(c) the two undertakings have entered into obligations, as in (a) and (b) above, with each other in respect of exclusive supply and purchase for resale.

2. Paragraph 1 shall not apply to agreements to which undertakings from one Member State only are party and which concern the resale of goods within that Member State.

–03 *ARTICLE 2*

1. Apart from an obligation falling within Article 1, no restriction on competition shall be imposed on the exclusive dealer other than:

(a) the obligation not to manufacture or distribute, during the duration of the contract or until one year after its expiration, goods which compete with the goods to which the contract relates;

(b) the obligation to refrain, outside the territory covered by the contract, from seeking customers for the goods to which the contract relates, from establishing any branch, or from maintaining any distribution depot.

2. Article 1(1) shall apply notwithstanding that the exclusive dealer undertakes all or any of the following obligations:

(a) to purchase complete ranges of goods or minimum quantities;

(b) to sell the goods to which the contract relates under trade marks or packed and presented as specified by the manufacturer;

[1] As amended by Commission Regulation No. 2591/72.

(c) To take measures for promotion of sales, in particular:
- to advertise;
- to maintain a sales network or stock of goods;
- to provide after-salc and guarantee services;
- to employ staff having specialised or technical training.

23–04 *ARTICLE 3*

Article 1(1) of this Regulation shall not apply where:

(a) manufacturers of competing goods entrust each other with exclusive dealing in those goods;

(b) the contracting parties make it difficult for intermediaries or consumers to obtain the goods to which the contract relates from other dealers within the common market, in particular where the contracting parties:

(1) exercise industrial property rights to prevent dealers or consumers from obtaining from other parts of the common market or from selling in the territory covered by the contract goods to which the contract relates which are properly marked or otherwise properly placed on the market;

(2) exercise other rights or take other measures to prevent dealers or consumers from obtaining from elsewhere goods to which the contract relates or from selling them in the territory covered by the contract.

23–05 *ARTICLE 4*

1. As regards agreements which were in existence on 13 March 1962 and were notified before 1 February 1963, the declaration contained in Article 1(1) of inapplicability of Article 85(1) of the Treaty shall have retroactive effect from the time when the conditions of application of this Regulation were fulfilled.

2. As regards all other agreements notified before the entry into force of this Regulation, the declaration contained in Article 1(1) of inapplicability of Article 85(1) of the Treaty shall have retroactive effect from the time when the conditions of application of this Regulation were fulfilled, but not earlier than the day of notification.

3–06 *ARTICLE 5*

As regards agreements, decisions or concerted practices for exclusive dealing already in existence at the date of accession to which Article 85(1) applies by virtue of accession, the prohibition in Article 85(1) of the Treaty shall not apply where they are modified within six months from the date of accession so as to fulfil the conditions contained in this Regulation.[2] The notification shall take effect from the time of receipt thereof by the Commission. Where the notification is sent by registered post, it shall take effect from the date on the postmark of the place of dispatch.

3–07 *ARTICLE 6*

The Commission shall examine whether Article 7 of Regulation No 19/65/EEC applies in individual cases, in particular when there are grounds for believing that:

(a) the goods to which the contract relates are not subject, in the territory covered by the contract, to competition from goods considered by the consumer as similar goods in view of their properties, price and intended use;

(b) it is not possible for other manufacturers to sell, in the territory covered by the contract, similar goods at the same stage of distribution as that of the exclusive dealer;

(c) the exclusive dealer has abused the exemption:

  (1) by refusing, without objectively valid reasons, to supply in the territory covered by the contract categories of purchasers who cannot obtain supplies elsewhere, on suitable terms, of the goods to which the contract relates;

  (2) by selling the goods to which the contract relates at excessive prices.

[2] As amended by the Treaty of Accession. The first sentence of Article 5 formerly read: "As regards agreements which were in existence on 13 March 1962, notified before 1 February 1963 and amended before 2 August 1967 so as to fulfil the conditions of application of this Regulation, the prohibition in Article 85(1) of the Treaty shall not apply in respect of the period prior to the amendment, where such amendment is notified to the Commission before 3 October 1967."

23–08 *ARTICLE 7*

1. Article 4(2)(a) of Regulation No 27 of 3 May 1962, as amended by Regulation No 153, is hereby repealed.

2. Notification, on Form B 1, on an exclusive dealing agreement which does not fulfil the conditions contained in Articles 1 to 3 of this Regulation shall, if such agreement is not amended so as to satisfy those conditions, be effected before 3 October 1967, by submission of Form B, with annexes, in accordance with the provisions of Regulation No 27.

23–09 *ARTICLE 8*

Articles 1 to 7 of this Regulation shall apply by analogy to the category of concerted practices defined in Article 1(1).

23–10 *ARTICLE 9*

This Regulation shall enter into force on 1 May 1967.

23–11 This Regulation shall be binding in its entirety and directly applicable in all Member States.

Done at Brussels, 16 June 1967.

For the Commission
The President
WALTER HALLSTEIN

APPENDIX I

PART I

REGULATION (EEC) NO 1133/68 OF THE COMMISSION of 26 July 1968*

Amending Commission Regulation no 27 of 3 May 1962

-01 THE COMMISSION OF THE EUROPEAN COMMUNITIES,

HAVING REGARD to the Treaty establishing the European Economic Community, and in particular Article 85 thereof;

HAVING REGARD to Council Regulation No 17 of 6 February 1962, and in particular Article 24 thereof;

WHEREAS under Article 24 of Regulation No 17 the Commission has power to adopt implementing provisions concerning the form, content and other details of applications pursuant to Articles 2 and 3 and of notifications pursuant to Articles 4 and 5;

WHEREAS Regulation No 27 adopted by the Commission pursuant to Article 24 of Regulation No 17 lays down, in particular, in Article 4(1) and (2) thereof that Form A must be used for applications for negative clearance under Article 2 of Regulation No 17 and Form B for notifications under Articles 4 or 5 of Regulation No 17, with a view to exemption pursuant to Article 85(3) of the Treaty;

WHEREAS it is advisable, in view of the general preference of undertakings to have the two alternatives open to them, to provide for the use of a single form for applications for negative clearance and for notification in order to simplify the procedure for all parties to an agreement and for the competent departments;

* Published in the Journal Officiel 1st August, 1968, English text Official Journal Special Edition 1968(II) p.400.

WHEREAS negative clearance and exemption pursuant to Article 85(3) of the Treaty have different consequences and whereas the single form must leave it open to undertakings to apply either for negative clearance or for a declaration of non-applicability;

HAS ADOPTED THIS REGULATION:

25–02 *Sole Article*

Article 4 of Regulation 27 shall be amended to read as follows:

"Content of applications and notifications

1. Applications under Article 2 of Regulation No 17 relating to the applicability of Article 85(1) of the Treaty and notifications under Article 4 or Article 5(2) of Regulation No 17 shall be submitted on Form A/B as shown in the Annex to this Regulation.

2. Applications and notifications shall contain the information asked for in Form A/B.

3. Several participating undertakings may submit an application or notification on a single form.

4. Applications under Article 2 of Regulation No 17 relating to the applicability of Article 86 of the Treaty shall contain a full statement of the facts, specifying, in particular, the practice concerned and the position of the undertaking or undertakings within the common market or a substantial part thereof in regard to products or services to which the practice relates."

25–03 This Regulation shall be binding in its entirety and directly applicable in all Member States.

Done at Brussels, 26 July 1968.

For the Commission
The President
JEAN REY

25–04 This form and the supporting documents should be forwarded in seven copies together with proof in duplicate of the representative's authority to act.

If the space opposite each question is insufficient, please use extra pages, specifying to which item on the form they relate.

FORM A/B

–05 TO THE COMMISSION OF THE EUROPEAN COMMUNITIES
Directorate General for Competition
170, rue de la Loi, Brussels 4

A. Application for negative clearance pursuant to Article 2 of Council Regulation No 17 of 6 February 1962 relating to implementation of Article 85(1) of the Treaty

B. Notification of an agreement, decision or concerted practice under Articles 4 and 5 of Council Regulation No 17 of 6 February 1962.

–06 I. *Information regarding parties*

1. Name, forenames and address of person submitting the application or notification. If such person is acting as representative, state also the name and address of the undertaking or association of undertakings represented and the name, forenames and address of the proprietors or partners or, in the case of legal persons, of their legal representatives.

Proof of representative's authority to act must be supplied.

If the application or notification is submitted by a number of persons or on behalf of a number of undertakings, the information must be given in respect of each person or undertaking.

---

2. Name and address of the undertakings which are parties to the agreement, decision or concerted practice and name, forenames and address of the proprietors or partners or, in the case of legal persons, of their legal representatives (unless this information has been given under 1(1)).

If the undertakings which are parties to the agreement are not all associated in submitting the application or notification, state what steps have been taken to inform the other undertakings.

This information is not necessary in respect of standard contracts (see Section II 1 (b) below).

3. If a firm or joint agency has been formed in pursuance of the agreement, state the name and address of such firm or agency and the names, forenames and addresses of its legal or other representatives.

4. If a firm or joint agency is responsible for operating the agreement, state the name and address of such firm or agency and the names, forenames and addresses of its legal or other representatives.

Attach a copy of the statutes.

5. In the case of a decision of an association of undertakings, state the name and address of the association and the names, forenames and addresses of its legal representatives.

Attach a copy of the statutes.

---

6. If the undertakings are established or have their seat outside the territory of the common market (Article 227(1) and (2) of the Treaty), state the name and address of a representative or branch established in the territory of the common market.

25–07 II. *Information regarding contents of agreement, decision or concerted practice:*

1. If the contents were reduced to writing, attach a copy of the full text unless (a), (b) or (c) below provides otherwise.

   (a) Is there only an outline agreement or outline decision?

   If so, attach also copy of the full text of the individual agreements and implementing provisions.

(b) Is there a standard contract, i.e., a contract which the undertaking submitting the notification regularly concludes with particular persons or groups of persons (e.g., a contract restricting the freedom of action of one of the contracting parties in respect of resale prices or terms of business for goods supplied by the other contracting party)?

If so, only the text of the standard contract need be attached.

(c) If there is a licensing agreement of the type covered by Article 4(2) (2b) of Regulation No 17, it is not necessary to submit those clauses of the contract which only describe a technical manufacturing process and have no connection with the restriction of competition; in such cases, however, an indication of the parts omitted from the text must be given.

2. If the contents were not, or were only partially, reduced to writing, state the contents in the space opposite.

3. In all cases give the following additional information:

(a) Date of agreement, decision or concerted practice.

(b) Date when it came into force and, where applicable, proposed period of validity.

(c) Subject: exact description of the goods or services involved.

(d) Aims of the agreement, decision or concerted practice.

(e) Terms of adherence, termination or withdrawal.

(f) Sanctions which may be taken against participating undertakings (penalty clause, expulsion, withholding of supplies, etc.).

25–08 III. *Means of achieving the aims of the agreement, decision or concerted practice:*

1. State whether and how far the agreement, decision or concerted practice relates to:

- adherence to certain buying or selling prices, discounts or other trading conditions

- restriction or control of production, technical development or investment

- sharing of markets or sources of supply

- restrictions on freedom to purchase from, or resell to, third parties (exclusive contracts)

- application of different terms for supply of equivalent goods or services

2. Is the agreement, decision or concerted practice concerned with supply of goods or services

(a) within one Member State only?

(b) between a Member State and third States?

(c) between Member States?

—09 IV. *If you consider Article 85(1) to be inapplicable and are notifying the agreement, decision or concerted practice as a precaution only:*

(a) Please attach a statement of the relevant facts and reasons as to why you consider Article 85(1) to be inapplicable, e.g., that the agreement, decision or concerted practice

1. does not have the object or effect of preventing, restricting or distorting competition; or

2. is not one which may affect trade between Member States.

(b) Are you asking for a negative clearance pursuant to Article 2 of Regulation No 17?

25–10 V. *Are you notifying the agreement, decision or concerted practice, even if only as a precaution, in order to obtain a declaration of applicability under Article 85(3)?*

If so, explain to what extent

1. the agreement, decision or concerted practice contributes towards

- improving production or distribution, or
- promoting technical or economic progress;

---

2. a proper share of the benefits arising from such improvement or progress accrues to the consumers;

---

3. the agreement, decision or concerted practice is essential for realising the aims set out under 1 above; and

---

4. the agreement, decision or concerted practice does not eliminate competition in respect of a substantial part of the goods concerned.

5–11 VI. *State whether you intend to produce further supporting arguments and, if so, on which points.*

The undersigned declare that the information given above and in the .... annexes attached hereto is correct. They are aware of the provisions of Article 15(1)(a) of Regulation No 17.

.... date ....

Signatures:

....

....

....

25–12 EUROPEAN COMMUNITIES
COMMISSION

Brussels, (date) . . . .

Directorate General for Competition 170, rue de la Loi

To

Acknowledgement of receipt

(This form will be returned to the address inserted above if completed in a single copy by the person lodging it).

Your application for negative clearance dated . . . .

Your notification dated . . . .

concerning:

(a) Parties:

1 . . . .

2 . . . . and others

(There is no need to name the other undertakings party to the arrangement)

(b) Subject . . . .

. . . .

. . . .

(brief description of the restriction on competition)

was received on . . . .

and registered under No IV . . . .

<u>Please quote the above number in all correspondence.</u>

PART II

FORM C

5–21 This form and the supporting documents should be forwarded in seven copies together with proof in duplicate of the representative's authority to act.

If the space opposite each question is insufficient, please use extra pages, specifying to which item on the form they relate.

–14 To the
COMMISSION OF THE EUROPEAN COMMUNITIES
Directorate-General for Competition
rue de la Loi 200 – 1040 Brussels

5–15 Application for initiation of procedure to establish the existence of an infringement of Articles 85 or 86 of the Treaty, submitted by natural or legal persons pursuant to Article 3 of Council Regulation No 17 of 6 February 1962

5–16 I. *Information regarding parties concerned:*

1. Name, forenames and address of person submitting the application. If such person is acting as a

representative, state also the name and address of his principal; for an undertaking, or association of undertakings or persons, state the name, forenames and address of the proprietors or members; for legal persons, state the name, forenames and address of their legal representatives.

Proof of representative's authority to act must be supplied.

If the application is submitted by a number of persons or on behalf of a number of persons, the information must be given in respect of each applicant or principal.

2. Name and address of persons to whom the application relates.

5–17 II. *Details of the alleged infringement:*

Set out in detail, in an Annex, the facts from which, in your opinion, it appears that there is infringement of Articles 85 or 86 of the Treaty.

Indicate in particular:

1. The practices of the undertakings or associations of undertakings to which this application relates which have as their object or effect the prevention, restriction or distortion of competition or constitute an abuse of a dominant position within the common market; and

---

2. To what extent trade between Member States may be affected.

–18 III. *Existence of legitimate interest:*

Set out – if necessary in an Annex – the grounds on which you claim a legitimate interest in the initiation by the Commission of the procedure provided for in Article 3 of Regulation No 17.

25–19 IV. *Evidence:*

1. State the names and addresses of persons able to testify to the facts set out, and in particular of persons affected by the alleged infringement.

2. Submit all documentation relating to or directly connected with the facts set out (for example, texts of agreements, minutes of negotiations or meetings, terms of transactions, business documents, circulars).

3. Submit statistics or other data relating to the facts set out (and relating, for example, to price trends, formation of prices, terms of transactions, terms of supply or sale, boycotting, discrimination).

4. Where appropriate, give any necessary technical details relating to production, sales, etc., or name experts able to do so.

5. Indicate any other evidence of the existence of the alleged infringement.

25–20 V. Indicate all approaches made, and all steps taken, prior to this application, by you or any other person affected by the practice described above, with a view to terminating the alleged infringement (Proceedings commenced before national judicial or administrative bodies, stating in particular the reference numbers of the cases and the results thereof).

5–21 We, the undersigned, declare that the information given in this form and in the . . . . Annexes thereto is given entirely in good faith.

At . . . .

Signed:

. . . .

. . . .

. . . .

. . . .

. . . .

. . . .

. . . .

. . . .

25–22 COMMISSION OF THE
EUROPEAN COMMUNITIES
Directorate-General for Competition

Brussels . . . .
200, rue de la Loi

To

Acknowledgement of Receipt

(This form will be returned to the address inserted above if one copy thereof is completed by the applicant)

Your application for a finding of infringement of Articles 85 or 86 of the Treaty, dated . . . .

(a) Applicant:

. . . .

. . . .

(b) Infringing parties

. . . .

. . . .

was received on . . . .

and registered under No. IV . . . .

Please quote the above number in all correspondence.

APPENDIX K

REGULATION (EEC) NO 2821/71 OF THE COUNCIL of 20 December 1971

On Application of Article 85(3) of the Treaty to Categories of Agreements, Decisions and Concerted Practices

7–01 THE COUNCIL OF THE EUROPEAN COMMUNITIES,

HAVING REGARD to the Treaty establishing the European Economic Community, and in particular Article 87 thereof;

HAVING REGARD to the proposal from the Commission;

HAVING REGARD to the Opinion of the European Parliament;

HAVING REGARD to the Opinion of the Economic and Social Committee;

WHEREAS Article 85(1) of the Treaty may in accordance with Article 85(3) be declared inapplicable to categories of agreements, decisions and concerted practices which fulfil the conditions contained in Article 85(3);

WHEREAS the provisions for implementation of Article 85(3) must be adopted by way of regulation pursuant to Article 87;

WHEREAS the creation of a common market requires that undertakings be adapted to the conditions of the enlarged market and whereas co-operation between undertakings can be a suitable means of achieving this;

WHEREAS agreements, decisions and concerted practices for co-operation between undertakings which enable the undertakings to work more rationally and adapt their productivity and

* Published in the Journal Officiel 29th December, 1971, English text Official Journal Special Edition 1971 (III) p.1032.

competitiveness to the enlarged market may, in so far as they fall within the prohibition contained in Article 85(1), be exempted therefrom under certain conditions; whereas this measure is necessary in particular as regards agreements, decisions and concerted practices relating to the application of standards and types, research and development of products or processes up to the stage of industrial application, exploitation of the results thereof and specialisation;

WHEREAS it is desirable that the Commission be enabled to declare by way of regulation that the provisions of Article 85(1) do not apply to those categories of agreements, decisions and concerted practices, in order to make it easier for undertakings to co-operate in ways which are economically desirable and without adverse effect from the point of view of competition policy;

WHEREAS it should be laid down under what conditions the Commission, in close and constant liaison with the competent authorities of the Member States, may exercise such powers;

WHEREAS under Article 6 of Regulation No 17 the Commission may provide that a decision taken in accordance with Article 85(3) of the Treaty shall apply with retroactive effect; whereas it is desirable that the Commission be empowered to issue regulations whose provisions are to the like effect;

WHEREAS under Article 7 of Regulation No 17 agreements, decisions and concerted practices may by decision of the Commission be exempted from prohibition, in particular if they are modified in such manner that Article 85(3) applies to them; whereas it is desirable that the Commission be enabled to grant by regulation like exemption to such agreements, decisions and concerted practices if they are modified in such manner as to fall within a category defined in an exempting regulation;

WHEREAS the possibility cannot be excluded that, in a specific case, the conditions set out in Article 85(3) may not be fulfilled; whereas the Commission must have power to regulate such a case in pursuance of Regulation No 17 by way of decision having effect for the future;

HAS ADOPTED THIS REGULATION:

27–02 *ARTICLE 1*

1. Without prejudice to the application of Regulation No 17 the Commission may, by regulation and in accordance with Article 85(3) of the Treaty, declare that Article 85(1) shall not apply to categories of agreements between undertakings, decisions of

associations of undertakings and concerted practices which have as their object:

(a) the application of standards or types;

(b) the research and development of products or processes up to the stage of industrial application, and exploitation of the results, including provisions regarding industrial property rights and confidential technical knowledge;

(c) specialisation, including agreements necessary for achieving it.

2. Such regulation shall define the categories of agreements, decisions and concerted practices to which it applies and shall specify in particular:

(a) the restrictions or clauses which may, or may not, appear in the agreements, decisions and concerted practices;

(b) the clauses which must be contained in the agreements, decisions and concerted practices or the other conditions which must be satisfied.

–03 *ARTICLE 2*

1. Any regulation pursuant to Article 1 shall be made for a specified period.

2. It may be repealed or amended where circumstances have changed with respect to any of the facts which were basic to its being made; in such case, a period shall be fixed for modification of the agreements, decisions and concerted practices to which the earlier regulation applies.

–04 *ARTICLE 3*

A regulation pursuant to Article 1 may provide that it shall apply with retroactive effect to agreements, decisions and concerted practices to which, at the date of entry into force of that regulation, a decision issued with retroactive effect in pursuance of Article 6 of Regulation No 17 would have applied.

-05 *ARTICLE 4 (as amended by Regulation 2743/72 – Appendix P)*

1. A regulation pursuant to Article 1 may provide that the prohibition contained in Article 85(1) of the Treaty shall not apply, for such period as shall be fixed by that regulation, to agreements, decisions and concerted practices already in existence on 13 March 1962 which do not satisfy the conditions of Article

85(3), where:

- within six months from the entry into force of the regulation, they are so modified as to satisfy the said conditions in accordance with the provisions of the regulation; and
- the modifications are brought to the notice of the Commission within the time limit fixed by the regulation.

A Regulation adopted pursuant to Article 1 may lay down that the prohibition referred to in Article 85(1) of the Treaty shall not apply, for the period fixed in the same Regulation, to agreements and concerted practices which existed at the date of accession and which, by virtue of accession, come within the scope of Article 85 and do not fulfil the conditions set out in Article 85(3).

2. Paragraph 1 shall apply to agreements, decisions and concerted practices which had to be notified before 1 February 1963, in accordance with Article 5 of Regulation No 17, only where they have been so notified before that date.

Paragraph 1 shall be applicable to those agreements and concerted practices which, by virtue of the accession, come within the scope of Article 85(1) of the Treaty and for which notification before 1 July 1973 is mandatory, in accordance with Articles 5 and 25 of Regulation No 17, only if notification was given before that date.

3. The benefit of the provisions laid down pursuant to paragraph 1 may not be claimed in actions pending at the date of entry into force of a regulation adopted pursuant to Article 1; neither may it be relied on as grounds for claims for damages against third parties.

27–06 *ARTICLE 5*

Before making a regulation, the Commission shall publish a draft thereof to enable all persons and organisations concerned to submit their comments within such time limit, being not less than one month, as the Commission shall fix.

27–07 *ARTICLE 6*

1. The Commission shall consult the Advisory Committee on Restrictive Practices and Monopolies:

(a) before publishing a draft regulation;
(b) before making a regulation.

2. Paragraphs 5 and 6 of Article 10 of Regulation No 17, relating to consultation with the Advisory Committee, shall apply by analogy, it being understood that joint meetings with the Commission shall take place not earlier than one month after dispatch of the notice convening them.

7–08 *ARTICLE 7*

Where the Commission, either on its own initiative or at the request of a Member State or of natural or legal persons claiming a legitimate interest, finds that in any particular case agreements, decisions or concerted practices to which a regulation made pursuant to Article 1 of this Regulation applies have nevertheless certain effects which are incompatible with the conditions laid down in Article 85(3) of the Treaty, it may withdraw the benefit of application of that regulation and take a decision in accordance with Articles 6 and 8 of Regulation No 17, without any notification under Article 4(1) of Regulation No 17 being required.

7–09 This Regulation shall be binding in its entirety and directly applicable in all Member States.

Done at Brussels, 20 December 1971.

For the Council
The President
M. PEDINI

APPENDIX L

REGULATION (EEC) NO 2822/71 OF THE COUNCIL of 20 December 1971

Supplementing the Provisions of Regulation no 17 Implementing Articles 85 and 86 of the Treaty

28–01 THE COUNCIL OF THE EUROPEAN COMMUNITIES,

HAVING REGARD to the Treaty establishing the European Economic Community, and in particular Article 87 thereof;

HAVING REGARD to the proposal from the Commission;

HAVING REGARD to the Opinion of the European Parliament;

HAVING REGARD to the Opinion of the Economic and Social Committee;

WHEREAS Article 4(2) of Regulation No 17 exempts a number of agreements, decisions and concerted practices from the requirement of notification under Article 4(1);

WHEREAS the creation of a common market requires that undertakings be adapted to the conditions of the enlarged market and whereas co-operation between undertakings can be a suitable means of achieving this; whereas it is in particular advisable to encourage co-operation in the field of research and development and the conclusion of specialisation agreements which do not affect competition;

WHEREAS such co-operation would be facilitated if notification of the agreements, decisions and concerted practices in question were no longer required;

WHEREAS, in introducing exemption from notification, account must be taken on the one hand of the desire on the part of undertakings that co-operation between them be made easier and on the other of the need for effective supervision;

WHEREAS agreements, decisions and concerted practices relating only to joint research and development, in so far as they restrict competition, do not as a rule present such dangers as to make notification necessary;

WHEREAS specialisation agreements may make for improvement in the production and distribution of products; whereas generally there is no reason to fear that competition will be affected provided the participating undertakings do not exceed a certain size and their share of the market in the specialised products does not exceed a given limit; whereas as a general rule agreements of this kind may, pursuant to Article 85(3) of the Treaty, be exempted from the prohibition imposed by Article 85(1) thereof;

WHEREAS, therefore, Article 4(2) of Regulation No 17 should be supplemented and agreements, decisions and concerted practices for joint research and development, in so far as they restrict competition, and certain specialisation agreements, should be exempted from compulsory notification;

HAS ADOPTED THIS REGULATION:

2 *Sole Article*

Article 4(2) of Regulation No 17 shall be supplemented as follows:

"2 Paragraph 1 shall not apply to agreements, decisions and concerted practices where:

(1) . . . . . . (unchanged)

(2) . . . . . . (unchanged)

(3) they have as their sole object:

(a) . . . . . . (unchanged)

(b) joint research and development;

(c) specialisation in the manufacture of products, including agreements necessary for achieving this,

— where the products which are the subject of specialisation do not, in a substantial part of the common market, represent more than 15% of the volume of business done in identical products or those considered by consumers to be similar by reason of their characteristics, price and use,

and

where the total annual turnover of the participating undertakings does not exceed 200 million units of account.

These agreements, decisions and practices may be notified to the Commission."

28–03 This Regulation shall be binding in its entirety and directly applicable in all Member States.

Done at Brussels, 20 December 1971.

For the Council

The President

M. PEDINI

APPENDIX P

REGULATIONS (EEC) NO 2743/72 OF THE COUNCIL of 19 December 1972

Amending Regulation (EEC) no 2821/71 on the Application of Article 85(3) of the Treaty to Categories of Agreements, Decisions and Concerted Practices

–01 THE COUNCIL OF THE EUROPEAN COMMUNITIES,

HAVING REGARD to the Treaty concerning the Accession of new Member States to the European Economic Community and the European Atomic Energy Community, signed on 22 January 1972, and in particular Article 153 of the Act annexed thereto;

HAVING REGARD to the proposal from the Commission;

WHEREAS Council Regulation (EEC) No 2821/71 of 20 December 1971, on the application of Article 85(3) of the Treaty to categories of agreements, decisions and concerted practices requires amendments corresponding to those made to Regulation No 19/65/EEC, the amendments to which are set out in Annex I to the Act of Accession, so that the agreements which, by virtue of accession, come within the scope of Article 85 of the Treaty establishing the European Economic Community may benefit from exemption from the prohibition laid down in paragraph 1 of the said Article;

HAS ADOPTED THIS REGULATION:

–02 *ARTICLE 1*

Article 4 of Regulation (EEC) No 2821/71 shall be amended as

* Published in the Journal Officiel 28th December, 1972, English text Official Journal Special Edition 1972 (28-30 December) p.60.

follows:

1. The following is inserted at the end of paragraph 1:
"A Regulation adopted pursuant to Article 1 may lay down that the prohibition referred to in Article 85(1) of the Treaty shall not apply, for the period fixed in the same Regulation, to agreements and concerted practices which existed at the date of accession and which, by virtue of accession, come within the scope of Article 85 and do not fulfil the conditions set out in Article 85(3)."
2. Paragraph 2 shall be supplemented by the following:
"Paragraph 1 shall be applicable to those agreements and concerted practices which, by virtue of the accession, come within the scope of Article 85(1) of the Treaty and for which notification before 1 July 1973 is mandatory, in accordance with Articles 5 and 25 of Regulation No 17, only if notification was given before that date."

32–03 *ARTICLE 2*

This Regulation shall enter into force upon accession.

32–04 This Regulation shall be binding in its entirety and directly applicable in all Member States.

Done at Brussels, 19 December 1972.

For the Council
The President
T. WESTERTERP

APPENDIX Q

REGULATION (EEC) NO 2779/72 OF THE COMMISSION of 21 December 1972*

On the Application of Article 85(3) of the Treaty to Categories of Specialisation Agreements

01 THE COMMISSION OF THE EUROPEAN COMMUNITIES,

HAVING REGARD to the Treaty establishing the European Economic Community, and in particular Articles 87 and 155 thereof;

HAVING REGARD to Council Regulation (EEC) No 2821/71 of 20 December 1971 on application of Article 85(3) of the Treaty to categories of agreements, decisions and concerted practices;

HAVING REGARD to the Opinions of the Advisory Committee on Restrictive Practices and Monopolies delivered pursuant to Article 6 of Regulation (EEC) No 2821/71;

WHEREAS under Regulation (EEC) No 2821/71 the Commission has power to apply Article 85(3) of the Treaty by regulation to certain categories of agreements, decisions and concerted practices relating to specialisation, including agreements necessary for achieving it, which fall within Article 85(1);

WHEREAS, since the adoption of such a Regulation would not conflict with the application of Regulation No 17, the right of undertakings to apply in individual cases to the Commission for a declaration under Article 85(3) of the Treaty would not thereby be affected;

* Published in the Journal Officiel 29th December, 1972, English text Official Journal Special Edition 1972 (28-30 December) p.80.

WHEREAS agreements for the specialisation of production may fall within the prohibition contained in Article 85(1);

WHEREAS agreements for the specialisation of production lead in general to an improvement in the production or distribution of goods, because the undertakings can concentrate on the manufacture of certain products, thus operate on a more rational basis and offer these products at more favourable prices; whereas it is to be anticipated that, with effective competition, consumers will receive a fair share of the profit resulting therefrom;

WHEREAS this Regulation must determine what restrictions on competition may be included in a specialisation agreement; whereas the restrictions on competition provided for in this Regulation are, in general, indispensable for the purpose of ensuring that the desired benefits accrue to undertakings and consumers; whereas it may be left to the contracting parties to decide which of these provisions they include in their agreements;

WHEREAS in order to ensure that competition is not eliminated in respect of a substantial part of the goods in question, this Regulation applies only if the share of the market held by the participating undertakings and the size of the undertakings themselves do not exceed a specified limit;

WHEREAS this Regulation should also apply to specialisation agreements made prior to its entry into force;

HAS ADOPTED THIS REGULATION:

33–02 *ARTICLE 1*

Pursuant to Article 85(3) it is hereby declared that, subject as provided in this Regulation, until 31 December 1977 Article 85(1) of the Treaty shall not apply to agreements whereby, with the object of specialisation, undertakings mutually bind themselves for the duration of the agreements not to manufacture certain products or cause them to be manufactured by other undertakings, and to leave it to the other contracting parties to manufacture such products or cause them to be manufactured by other undertakings.

33–03 *ARTICLE 2*

1. Apart from the obligation referred to in Article 1, no other restriction on competition shall be imposed on the contracting parties save the following:

(a) the obligation not to conclude with other undertakings specialisation agreements relating to identical products or to products considered by consumers to be similar by reason of their characteristics, price or use, except with the consent of the other contracting parties;

(b) the obligation to supply the other contracting parties with the products which are the subject of specialisation, and in so doing to observe minimum standards of quality;

(c) the obligation to purchase products which are the subject of specialisation solely from the other contracting parties, except where more favourable terms of purchase are available elsewhere and the other contracting parties are not prepared to offer the same terms;

(d) the obligation to grant to the other contracting parties the exclusive right to distribute the products which are the subject of specialisation so long as those parties do not – in particular by the exercise of industrial property rights or of other rights and measures – limit the opportunities, for intermediaries or consumers, of purchasing the products to which the agreement relates from other dealers within the common market.

2. Article 1 shall apply notwithstanding that the following obligations are imposed:

(a) the obligation to maintain minimum stocks of the products which are the subject of specialisation and of replacement parts for them;

(b) the obligation to provide after-sale and guarantee services for the products which are the subject of specialisation.

)4 *ARTICLE 3*

1. Article 1 shall apply only:

(a) if the products which are the subject of specialisation represent in any member country not more than 10 per cent of the volume of business done in identical products or in products considered by consumers to be similar by reason of their characteristics, price or use; and

(b) if the aggregate annual turnover of the participating undertakings does not exceed 150 million units of account.

2. For purposes of applying paragraph 1 the unit of account shall be that adopted in drawing up the budget of the Community in accordance with Articles 207 and 209 of the Treaty.

3. Article 1 of this Regulation shall continue to apply notwithstanding that in any two consecutive financial years the share of the market or the turnover is greater than as specified in paragraph 1, provided the excess is not more than 10%.

33–05 *ARTICLE 4*

The aggregate turnover within the meaning of Article 3(1) (b) shall be calculated by adding together the turnover achieved during the last financial year in respect of all products and services:

1. by the undertakings which are parties to the agreement;
2. by undertakings in respect of which the undertakings which are parties to the agreement hold:
   - at least 25% of the capital or of the working capital whether directly or indirectly; or
   - at least half the voting rights; or
   - the power to appoint at least half the members of the supervisory board, board of management or bodies legally representing the undertaking; or
   - the right to manage the affairs of the undertaking;
3. by undertakings which hold in an undertaking which is a party to the agreement:
   - at least 25% of the capital or of the working capital whether directly or indirectly; or
   - at least half the voting rights; or
   - the power to appoint at least half the members of the supervisory board, board of management or bodies legally representing the undertaking; or
   - the right to manage the affairs of the undertaking.

In calculating aggregate turnover no account shall be taken of dealings between the undertakings which are parties to the agreement.

–06 *ARTICLE 5*

The Commission shall examine whether Article 7 of Regulation (EEC) No 2821/71 applies in any specific case, in particular where there is reason to believe that rationalisation is not yielding significant results or that consumers are not receiving a fair share of the resulting profit.

–07 *ARTICLE 6*

The non-applicability of Article 85(1) provided for in Article 1 of this Regulation shall have retroactive effect from the time when the conditions requisite for the application of this Regulation were satisfied. In the case of agreements which, prior to 18 January 1972, were compulsorily notifiable, the time aforesaid shall not be earlier than the day of notification.

–08 *ARTICLE 7*

Articles 1 to 6 of this Regulation shall apply by analogy to decisions by associations of undertakings and to concerted practices.

–09 *ARTICLE 8*

This Regulation shall enter into force on 1 January 1973.

–10 This Regulation shall be binding in its entirety and directly applicable in all Member States.

Done at Brussels, 21 December 1972.

For the Commission
The President
S. L. MANSHOLT

APPENDIX R

REGULATION (EEC) NO 2591/72 OF THE COMMISSION of 8 December 1972*

Amending Regulation No 67/67/EEC of 22 March 1967 Concerning Application of Article 85(3) of the Treaty to Certain Categories of Concerted Practices

34–01 THE COMMISSION OF THE EUROPEAN COMMUNITIES,

HAVING REGARD to the Treaty establishing the European Economic Community, and in particular Articles 87 and 155 thereof;

HAVING REGARD to Article 24 of Regulation No 17 of 6 February 1962;

HAVING REGARD to Regulation No 19/65/EEC of 2 March 1965 on the application of Article 85(3) of the Treaty to certain categories of agreements and concerted practices;

HAVING REGARD to the Opinions delivered by the Advisory Committee on Restrictive Practices and Monopolies in accordance with Article 6 of Regulation No 19/65/EEC;

WHEREAS under Regulation No 19/65/EEC the Commission has power to apply Article 85(3) of the Treaty by regulation to certain categories of bilateral exclusive dealing agreements and concerted practices coming within Article 85(1);

WHEREAS Commission Regulation No 67/67/EEC on the application of Article 85(3) of the Treaty to certain categories of exclusive dealing agreements is valid only until 31 December 1972;

* Published in the Journal Officiel 9th December, 1972, English text Official Journal Special Edition 1972 (9-28 December) p.7.

WHEREAS the experience gained in connection with Regulation No 67/67/EEC shows that the rule under this Regulation whereby Article 85(1) of the Treaty is declared inapplicable to certain categories of exclusive dealing agreements, subject to the provisions of that Regulation, has proved its value.

WHEREAS it is therefore expedient to extend the validity of Regulation No 67/67/EEC; whereas it appears desirable, for the sake of certainty in the law, to extend the period of validity of the Regulation for ten years and so enable undertakings to plan for a long period ahead;

WHEREAS such extension also appears unobjectionable since under Article 7 of Regulation No 19/65/EEC in conjunction with Article 6 of Regulation No 67/67/EEC the Commission may at any time intervene if it finds that the agreements falling within the Regulation have effects that are incompatible with the conditions contained in Article 85(3) of the Treaty;

HAS ADOPTED THIS REGULATION:

·02 *ARTICLE 1*

In Article 1(1) of Regulation No 67/67/EEC the date '31 December 1982' shall be substituted for the date '31 December 1972'.

·03 *ARTICLE 2*

This Regulation shall enter into force on the day of its publication in the *Official Journal of the European Communities.*

·04 This Regulation shall be binding in its entirety and directly applicable in all Member States.

Done at Brussels, 8 December 1972.

For the Commission
The President
S. L. MANSHOLT

APPENDIX S

REGULATION (EEC) NO 2988/74 OF THE COUNCIL of 26 November 1974

Concerning Limitation Periods in Proceedings and the Enforcement of Sanctions under the Rules of the European Economic Community Relating to Transport and Competition

35–01 THE COUNCIL OF THE EUROPEAN COMMUNITIES,

HAVING REGARD to the Treaty establishing the European Economic Community, and in particular Articles 75, 79 and 87 thereof;

HAVING REGARD to the proposal from the Commission;

HAVING REGARD to the Opinion of the European Parliament;

HAVING REGARD to the Opinion of the Economic and Social Committee;

WHEREAS under the rules of the European Economic Community relating to transport and competition the Commission has the power to impose fines, penalties and periodic penalty payments on undertakings or associations of undertakings which infringe Community law relating to information or investigation, or to the prohibition on discrimination, restrictive practices and abuse of dominant position; whereas those rules make no provision for any limitation period;

WHEREAS it is necessary in the interests of legal certainty that the principle of limitation be introduced and that implementing rules be laid down; whereas, for the matter to be covered

* Published in the Official Journal 29th November 1974, No.L.319. p.1.

fully, it is necessary that provision for limitation be made not only as regards the power to impose fines or penalties, but also as regards the power to enforce decisions, imposing fines, penalties or periodic penalty payments; whereas such provisions should specify the length of limitation periods, the date on which time starts to run and the events which have the effect of interrupting or suspending the limitation period; whereas in this respect the interests of undertakings and associations of undertakings on the one hand, and the requirements imposed by administrative practice, on the other hand, should be taken into account;

WHEREAS this Regulation must apply to the relevant provisions of Regulation No 11 concerning the abolition of discrimination in transport rates and conditions, in implementation of Article 79(3) of the Treaty establishing the European Economic Community, of Regulation No 17, first Regulation implementing Articles 85 and 86 of the Treaty, and of Council Regulation (EEC) No 1017/68 of 19 July 1968 applying rules of competition to transport by rail, road and inland waterway; whereas it must also apply to the relevant provisions of future regulations in the fields of European Economic Community law relating to transport and competition,

HAS ADOPTED THIS REGULATION:

-02 *ARTICLE 1*

Limitation periods in proceedings

1. The power of the Commission to impose fines or penalties for infringements of the rules of the European Economic Community relating to transport or competition shall be subject to the following limitation periods:

(a) three years in the case of infringements of provisions concerning applications or notifications of undertakings or associations of undertakings, requests for information, or the carrying out of investigations;

(b) five years in the case of all other infringements.

2. Time shall begin to run upon the day on which the infringement is committed. However, in the case of continuing or repeated infringements, time shall begin to run on the day on which the infringement ceases.

-03 *ARTICLE 2*

Interruption of the limitation period in proceedings

1. Any action taken by the Commission, or by any Member

State, acting at the request of the Commission, for the purpose of the preliminary investigation or proceedings in respect of an infringement shall interrupt the limitation period in proceedings. The limitation period shall be interrupted with effect from the date on which the action is notified to at least one undertaking or association of undertakings which have participated in the infringement.

Actions which interrupt the running of the period shall include in particular the following:

(a) written requests for information by the Commission, or by the competent authority of a Member State acting at the request of the Commission; or a Commission decision requiring the requested information;

(b) written authorizations to carry out investigations issued to their officials by the Commission or by the competent authority of any Member State at the request of the Commission; or a Commission decision ordering an investigation;

(c) the commencement of proceedings by the Commission;

(d) notification of the Commission's statement of objections.

2. The interruption of the limitation period shall apply for all the undertakings or associations of undertakings which have participated in the infringement.

3. Each interruption shall start time running afresh. However, the limitation period shall expire at the latest on the day on which a period equal to twice the limitation period has elapsed without the Commission having imposed a fine or a penalty; that period shall be extended by the time during which limitation is suspended pursuant to Article 3.

35–04 *ARTICLE 3*

Suspension of the limitation period in proceedings

The limitation period in proceedings shall be suspended for as long as the decision of the Commission is the subject of proceedings pending before the Court of Justice of the European Communities.

35–05 *ARTICLE 4*

Limitation period for the enforcement of sanctions

1. The power of the Commission to enforce decisions imposing fines, penalties or periodic payments for infringements of the rules of the European Economic Community relating to transport or competition shall be subject to a limitation period of five years.
2. Time shall begin to run on the day on which the decision becomes final.

–06 *ARTICLE 5*

Interruption of the limitation period for the enforcement of sanctions

1. The limitation period for the enforcement of sanctions shall be interrupted:

(a) by notification of a decision varying the original amount of the fine, penalty or periodic penalty payments or refusing an application for variation;

(b) by any action of the Commission, or of a Member State at the request of the Commission, for the purpose of enforcing payments of a fine, penalty or periodic penalty payment.

2. Each interruption shall start time running afresh.

-07 *ARTICLE 6*

Suspension of the limitation period for the enforcement of sanctions

The limitation period for the enforcement of sanctions shall be suspended for so long as:

(a) time to pay is allowed; or

(b) enforcement of payment is suspended pursuant to a decision of the Court of Justice of the European Communities.

-08 *ARTICLE 7*

Application to transitional cases

This Regulation shall also apply in respect of infringements committed before it enters into force.

-09 *ARTICLE 8*

Entry into force

This Regulation shall enter into force on 1 January 1975.

35–10 This Regulation shall be binding in its entirety and directly applicable in all Member States.

Done at Brussels, 26 November 1974.

For the Council
The President
J. LECANUET

APPENDIX T

DRAFT MERGERS REGULATION

Proposal for a Regulation (EEC) of the Council on the Control of Concentrations Between Undertakings

(Submitted to the Council by the Commission on 20 July 1973)

-01 THE COUNCIL OF THE EUROPEAN COMMUNITIES,

HAVING REGARD to the Treaty establishing the European Economic Community and in particular to Articles 87 and 235 thereof;

HAVING REGARD to the proposal from the Commission;

HAVING REGARD to the Opinion of the European Parliament;

HAVING REGARD to the Opinion of the Economic and Social Committee;

WHEREAS, for the achievement of the objectives of the Treaty establishing the European Economic Community, Article 3(f) requires the Community to institute 'a system ensuring that competition in the common market is not distorted';

WHEREAS analysis of market structures in the Community shows that the concentration process is becoming faster and that the degree of concentration is growing in such manner that the preservation of effective competition in the common market and the objective set out in Article 3(f) could be jeopardized;

WHEREAS concentration must therefore be made subject to a systematic control arrangement;

* Published in the Official Journal C92, 31st October, 1973, p.1.

WHEREAS the Treaty already provides some powers of action of the Community to this end;

WHEREAS Article 86 applies to concentrations effected by undertakings holding a dominant position in the common market or in a substantial part of it which strengthen such position to such an extent that the resulting degree of dominance would substantially restrict competition;

WHEREAS the power of action aforesaid extends only to such concentrations, as would result in only undertakings remaining in the market whose conduct depended on the undertaking which had effected the concentration; whereas it does not extend to the prevention of such concentrations;

WHEREAS additional powers of action must be provided for to make it possible to act against other concentrations which may distort competition in the common market and to establish arrangements for controlling them before they are effected;

WHEREAS under Article 235 of the Treaty the Community may give itself the powers of action necessary for the attainment of its objectives;

WHEREAS, to institute a system ensuring that competition in the common market is not distorted, it is necessary, in so far as trade between Member States may be affected, to submit to control arrangements such concentrations which give undertakings the power to prevent effective competition in the common market or in a substantial part of it, or which strengthen such a power;

WHEREAS the power to prevent effective competition must be appraised by reference, in particular, to the scope for choice available to suppliers and consumers, the economic and financial power of the undertakings concerned, the structure of the markets affected and supply and demand trends for the relevant goods or services;

WHEREAS concentrations which, by reason of the small significance of turnover and market share of the undertakings concerned, are not likely to impede the preservation of effective competition in the common market may be excluded from this Regulation;

WHEREAS it may be found necessary, for the purpose of reconciling objectives to be attained in the common interest of the Community, especially within the frame of common policies, to exempt certain concentrations from incompatibility, under conditions and obligations to be determined case by case;

WHEREAS the Commission should be entitled to take decisions to prevent or terminate concentrations which are incompatible with the common market, decisions designed to re-establish conditions of effective competition and decisions declaring that a particular concentration may be considered to be compatible with the common market; whereas the Commission should be given exclusive jurisdiction in this matter, subject to review by the Court of Justice;

WHEREAS, to ensure effective supervision, prior notification of major concentrations and the suspension of concentrations by undertakings should be made obligatory;

WHEREAS a time limit within which the Commission must commence proceedings in respect of a concentration notified to it and a time-limit within which it must give a final decision on the incompatibility of a concentration with the common market should be laid down;

WHEREAS undertakings concerned must be accorded the right to be heard by the Commission as soon as proceedings have commenced, and third parties showing a sufficient interest must be given the opportunity of submitting their comments;

WHEREAS the Commission must have the assistance of the Member States and must also be empowered to require information to be given and to carry out the necessary investigations in order to examine concentrations in the light of provisions of this Regulation;

WHEREAS compliance with this Regulation must be enforceable by means of fines and periodic penalty payments; whereas it is desirable to confer upon the Court of Justice, pursuant to Article 172, unlimited jurisdiction to that extent;

WHEREAS this Regulation should extend both to concentrations which constitute abuses of dominant positions and to concentrations which give the undertakings concerned the power to prevent effective competition in the common market; whereas it should therefore be stipulated that Regulations (EEC) Nos 17 and 1017/68 no longer apply to concentrations from the date of entry into force of the present Regulation,

HAS ADOPTED THIS REGULATION:

Basic provisions

-02 ***ARTICLE 1***

1. Any transaction which has the direct or indirect effect of bringing about a concentration between undertakings or groups

of undertakings, at least one of which is established in the common market, whereby they acquire or enhance the power to hinder effective competition in the common market or in a substantial part thereof, is incompatible with the common market in so far as the concentration may affect trade between Member States.

The power to hinder effective competition shall be appraised by reference in particular to the extent to which suppliers and consumers have a possibility of choice, to the economic and financial power of the undertakings concerned, to the structure of the markets affected, and to supply and demand trends for the relevant goods or services.

2. Paragraph 1 shall not apply where:

- the aggregate turnover of the undertakings participating in the concentration is less than 200 million units of account and
- the goods or services concerned by [sic] the concentration do not account in any Member State for more than 25% of the turnover in identical goods or services or in goods or services which, by reason of their characteristics, their price and the use for which they are intended, may be regarded as similar by the consumer.

3. Paragraph 1 may, however, be declared inapplicable to concentrations which are indispensable to the attainment of an objective which is given priority treatment in the common interest of the Community.

36–03 *ARTICLE 2*

Definition of concentration

1. The concentrations referred to in Article 1 are those whereby a person or an undertaking or a group of persons or undertakings, acquires control of one or several undertakings.

2. Control is constituted by rights or contracts which, either, separately or jointly, and having regard to the considerations of fact or law involved, make it possible to determine how an undertaking shall operate, and particularly by:

(1) Ownership or the right to use all or part of the assets of an undertaking;

(2) Rights or contracts which confer power to influence the composition, voting or decisions of the organs of an undertaking;

(3) Rights or contracts which make it possible to manage the business of an undertaking;

(4) Contracts made with an undertaking concerning the computation or appropriation of its profits;

(5) Contracts made with an undertaking concerning the whole or an important part of supplies or outlets, where the duration of these contracts or the quantities to which they relate exceed what is usual in commercial contracts dealing with those matters.

3. Control is acquired by persons, undertakings or groups of persons or undertakings who:

(1) Are holders of the rights or entitled to rights under the contracts concerned;

(2) While not being holders of such rights or entitled to rights under such contracts, have power to exercise the rights deriving therefrom;

(3) In a fiduciary capacity own assets of an undertaking or shares in an undertaking, and have power to exercise the rights attaching thereto.

4. Control of an undertaking is not constituted where, upon formation of an undertaking or increase of its capital, banks or financial institutions acquire shares in that undertaking with a view to selling them on the market, provided that they do not exercise voting rights in respect of those shares.

–04 *ARTICLE 3*

Powers of decision of the Commission

1. When the Commission finds that a concentration is caught by Article 1(1) and that the conditions laid down in Article 1(3) are not satisfied, it shall issue a decision declaring the concentration to be incompatible with the common market.

2. The decision by which the Commission declares a concentration to be incompatible within the meaning of paragraph 1 shall not automatically render null and void the legal transactions relating to such operation.

3. Where a concentration has already been put into effect, the Commission may require, by decision taken under paragraph 1 or by a separate decision, the undertakings, or assets acquired or concentrated to be separated or the cessation of common control or any other action that may be appropriate in order to restore conditions of effective competition.

4. When the Commission finds that a concentration is caught by

Article 1(1) and that the conditions laid down in Article 1(3) are satisfied, it shall issue a decision declaring Article 1(1) to be inapplicable; conditions and obligations may be attached thereto.
5. Subject to review by the Court of Justice, the Commission shall have sole power to take the decisions provided for in this Article.

36–05 *ARTICLE 4*

Prior notifications of concentrations

1. Concentrations shall be notified to the Commission before they are put into effect, where the aggregate turnover of the undertakings concerned is not less than one thousand million units of account.
2. Where concentrations proposed by an undertaking or a group of undertakings have already reached or exceeded the amounts referred to in paragraph 1, they shall be exempted from the obligation of prior notification, if the turnover of the undertaking, the control of which they propose to acquire is less than 30 million units of account.
3. The obligation to notify shall be discharged by the person or undertaking or the group of persons or undertakings which proposes to acquire control within the meaning of Article 2.
4. Concentrations which are not caught by paragraph 1 may nevertheless be notified to the Commission before they are put into effect.

36–06 *ARTICLE 5*

Detailed rules for calculating turnover and market shares

1. (a) The aggregate turnover specified in Articles 1(2) and 4(1) shall be obtained by adding together the turnover for the last financial year for all goods and services of:
   - (i) the undertakings participating in the concentration;
   - (ii) the undertakings and groups of undertakings which control the undertakings participating in the concentration within the meaning of Article 2;
   - (iii) the undertakings or groups of undertakings controlled within the meaning of Article 2 by the undertakings participating in the concentration.

(b) The market shares referred to in Article 1(2) near [sic] those held in the last financial year by all the undertakings listed in subparagraph (a) above.

2. In place of turnover as specified in Articles 1(2) and 4(1) and in paragraph 1 of this Article, the following shall be used:

– for banking and financial institutions: one tenth of their assets;
– for insurance companies: the value of the premiums received by them.

—07 *ARTICLE 6*

Commencement of proceedings

1. Where the Commission considers that a concentration is likely to become the subject of a decision under Article 1(1) or (3), it shall commence proceedings and so inform the undertakings in question and the competent authorities in the Member States.
2. As regards concentrations notified to it, the Commission shall commence proceedings within a period not exceeding 3 months unless the relevant undertakings agree to extend that period. The period of 3 months shall commence on the day following receipt of the notification, or if the information to be supplied with the notification is incomplete, on the day following the receipt of the complete information.
3. The Commission may commence proceedings after the expiry of the 3 months period where the information supplied by the undertakings in the notification is false or misleading.
4. Without prejudice to paragraph 3 a concentration notified to the Commission shall be presumed to be compatible with the common market if the Commission does not commence proceedings before expiration of the period specified in paragraph 2.

—08 *ARTICLE 7*

Suspension of the effecting of the concentration

1. Undertakings shall not put into effect a concentration notified to the Commission before the end of the time limit provided for in Article 6(2) unless the Commission informs them before the end of the time limit that it is not necessary to commence proceedings.
2. Where the Commission commences proceedings it may by decision require the undertakings to suspend the concentration until it has decided whether the concentration is compatible with the common market or has closed the proceedings.

36–09 *ARTICLE 8*

Communications of objections and hearings

1. Before taking decisions as provided for in Articles 3, 7, 13 and 14, the Commission shall give the undertakings concerned the opportunity of being heard on the matters to which the Commission has taken objection. The same opportunity shall be given to associations of undertakings concerned before decisions before being taken as provided for in Articles 13 and 14. [sic].

2. If the Commission or the competent authorities of the Member States consider it necessary, the Commission may also hear other natural or legal persons. Applications to be heard on the part of such persons shall, where they show a sufficient interest, be granted.

3. Articles 2, 3, 4, 7, 8, 9, 10 and 11 of Regulation No 99/63/EEC shall be applied.

36–10 *ARTICLE 9*

Closure of proceedings

If, after having commenced proceedings, the Commission considers that there are no grounds for action against a concentration, it shall close the proceedings and so inform the undertakings concerned and the competent authorities of the Member States.

36–11 *ARTICLE 10*

Requests for information

1. In carrying out the duties assigned to it by this Regulation, the Commission may obtain all necessary information from the governments and competent authorities of the Member States and from undertakings and associations of undertakings.

2. When sending a request for information to an undertaking or association of undertakings, the Commission shall at the same time forward a copy of the request to the competent authority of the Member State in whose territory the seat of the undertaking or association of undertakings is situated.

3. In its request the Commission shall state the legal basis and the purpose of the request and also the penalties provided for in Article 13(1)(b) for supplying incorrect information.

4. The owners of the undertakings or their representatives and, in the case of legal persons, companies or firms, or of associations having no legal personality, the persons authorized to represent

them by law or by their constitution, shall supply the information requested.

5. Where an undertaking or association of undertakings does not supply the information requested within the time limit fixed by the Commission, or supplies incomplete information, the Commission shall by decision require the information to be supplied. The decision shall specify what information is required, fix an appropriate time limit within which it is to be supplied and mention the penalties provided for in Article 13(1)(b) and Article 14(1)(a) and the right to have the decision reviewed by the Court of Justice.

6. The Commission shall at the same time forward a copy of its decision to the competent authority of the Member State in whose territory the seat of the undertaking or association of undertakings is situated.

6–12 *ARTICLE 11*

Investigations by the authorities of the Member States

1. At the request of the Commission, the competent authorities of the Member States shall undertake the investigations which the Commission considers to be necessary under Article 12(1), or which it has ordered by decision pursuant to Article 12(3). The officials of the competent authorities of the Member States responsible for conducting these investigations shall exercise their powers upon production of an authorization in writing issued by the competent authority of the Member State in whose territory the investigation is to be made. Such authorization shall specify the subject matter and purpose of the investigation.

2. If so requested by the Commission or by the competent authority of the Member State in whose territory the investigation is to be made, officials of the Commission may assist the officials of such authority in carrying out their duties.

–13 *ARTICLE 12*

Investigating powers of the Commission

1. In carrying out the duties assigned to it by this Regulation, the Commission may undertake all necessary investigations into undertakings and associations of undertakings.

To this end the officials authorized by the Commission are empowered:

(a) to examine the books and other business records;

(b) to take or demand copies of or extracts from the books and business records;
(c) to ask for oral explanations on the spot;
(d) to enter any premises, land and means of transport of undertakings.

2. The officials of the Commission authorized to carry out these investigations shall exercise their powers upon production of an authorization in writing specifying the subject matter and purpose of the investigation and the penalties provided for in Article 13(1)(c) in cases where production of the required books or other business records is incomplete. In good time before the investigation, the Commission shall inform the competent authority of the Member State in whose territory the investigation is to be made of the investigation and of the identity of the authorized officials.

3. Undertakings and associations of undertakings shall submit to investigations ordered by decision of the Commission. The decision shall specify the subject matter and purpose of the investigation, appoint the date on which it is to begin and indicate the penalties provided for in Article 13(1)(c) and Article 14(1)(b) and the right to have the decision reviewed by the Court of Justice.

4. The Commission shall take decisions referred to in paragraph 3 after consultation with the competent authority of the Member State in whose territory the investigation is to be made.

5. Officials of the competent authority of the Member State in whose territory the investigation is to be made may, at the request of such authority or of the Commission, assist the officials of the Commission in carrying out their duties.

6. Where an undertaking opposes an investigation ordered pursuant to this Article, the Member State concerned shall afford the necessary assistance to the officials authorized by the Commission to enable them to make their investigation. Member States shall, after consultation with the Commission, take the necessary measures to this end before. . . . .

36–14 *ARTICLE 13*

Fines

1. The Commission may by decision impose on undertakings and associations of undertakings fines of from 1 000 to 50 000 units of account where intentionally or negligently:

(a) they supply incorrect or misleading information in a notification pursuant to Article 4;

(b) they supply incorrect information in response to a request made pursuant to Article 10 or fail to supply information within the time limit fixed by a decision taken pursuant to Article 10,

(c) they produce the required books or other business records in incomplete form during investigations under Article 11 or 12, or refuse to submit to an investigation ordered by decision taken pursuant to Article 12.

2. The Commission may by decision impose on natural or legal persons fines of from 1 000 to 1 000 000 units of account where, either intentionally or negligently, they commit a breach of the obligation to notify under Article 4.

3. The Commission may by decision impose fines not exceeding 10% of the value of the reorganized assets where undertakings either intentionally or negligently, conclude an unlawful concentration before the end of the time limit provided for in Article 6(2) or in spite of a decision taken by the Commission under Articles 3(1) or 7(2).

–15 *ARTICLE 14*

Periodic penalty payments

1. The Commission may by decision impose on undertakings or associations of undertakings periodic penalty payments up to 25 000 units of account for each day of the delay calculated from the date appointed by the decision, in order to compel them:

(a) to supply complete and correct information which it has requested by decision taken pursuant to Article 10;

(b) to submit to an investigation which it has ordered by decision taken pursuant to Article 12.

2. The Commission may by decision impose on such undertakings periodic penalty payments up to 50 000 units of account for each day of the delay, calculated from the day appointed by the decision, in order to compel them to apply the measures resulting from a decision taken pursuant to Article 3(3).

–16 *ARTICLE 15*

Review by the Court of Justice

The Court of Justice shall have unlimited jurisdiction within the meaning of Article 172 of the Treaty to review decisions whereby the Commission has fixed a fine or periodic penalty payment; it may cancel, reduce or increase the fine or periodic penalty payment imposed.

36–17 *ARTICLE 16*

Professional secrecy

1. Information acquired as a result of the application of Articles 10, 11 and 12 shall be used only for the purpose of the relevant request or investigation.
2. The Commission and the competent authorities of the Member States, their officials and other servants shall not disclose information acquired by them as a result of the application of this Regulation and of the kind covered by the obligation of professional secrecy.
3. The provisions of paragraphs 1 and 2 shall not prevent publication of general information or surveys which do not contain information relating to particular undertakings or associations of undertakings.

36–18 *ARTICLE 17*

Time limits and publication of decisions

1. (a) Decisions under Article 3(1) and (4) shall be taken within 9 months following the date of commencement of proceedings, save where there is agreement with the relevant undertakings to extend that period.
   (b) The period of 9 months shall not apply where the Commission is obliged to request information by decision taken pursuant to Article 10 or require an investigation by decision taken pursuant to Article 12.
2. The Commission shall publish the decisions which it takes pursuant to Article 3.
3. The publication shall state the names of the parties and the main content of the decision; it shall have regard to the legitimate interest of undertakings in the protection of their business secrets.

36–19 *ARTICLE 18*

Unit of account

For the purpose of this Regulation the unit of account shall be that used in drawing up the budget of the Community in accordance with Articles 207 and 209 of the Treaty.

–20 *ARTICLE 19*

Liaison with the authorities of the Member States

1. The Commission shall forthwith transmit to the competent authorities of the Member States a copy of the notifications together with the most important documents lodged with the Commission pursuant to this Regulation.

2. The Commission shall carry out the procedure set out in this Regulation in close and constant cooperation with the competent authorities of the Member States; such authorities shall have the right to express their views upon that procedure, and in particular to request the Commission to commence proceedings under Article 6.

3. The Advisory Committee on Restrictive Practices and Monopolies shall be consulted prior to the taking of any decision under Articles 3, 13, and 14.

4. The Advisory Committee shall consist of officials having responsibility for restrictive practices and monopolies. Each Member State shall appoint an official to represent it; he may be replaced by another official where he is unable to act.

5. Consultation shall take place, at a meeting convened at the invitation of the Commission, not earlier than fourteen days following dispatch of the invitation. A summary of the facts together with the most important documents and a preliminary draft of the decision to be taken, shall be sent with the invitation.

6. The Committee may deliver an opinion even if certain members are absent and unrepresented. The outcome of the consultation shall be annexed to the draft decision. The minutes shall not be published.

–21 *ARTICLE 20*

Exclusive application of this Regulation

Regulations (EEC) No 17 and 1017/68 shall not apply to the concentrations covered by this Regulation.

–22 *ARTICLE 21*

Implementing provisions

The Commission shall have power to adopt implementing provisions concerning the form, content and other details of notifications pursuant to Article 4 of this Regulation.

36–23 *ARTICLE 22*

This Regulation shall enter into force. . . . . .

This Regulation shall be binding in its entirety and directly applicable in all Member States.

APPENDIX U

REGULATION NO 27 OF THE COMMISSION

(Form, Content and Other Details Concerning Applications and Notifications)

-01 THE COMMISSION OF THE EUROPEAN ECONOMIC COMMUNITY,

HAVING REGARD to the provisions of the Treaty establishing the European Economic Community, and in particular Articles 87 and 155 thereof;

HAVING REGARD to Article 24 of Council Regulation No 17 of 6 February 1962 (First Regulation implementing Articles 85 and 86 of the Treaty);

WHEREAS under Article 24 of Council Regulation No 17 the Commission is authorised to adopt implementing provisions concerning the form, content and other details of applications under Articles 2 and 3 and of notifications under Articles 4 and 5 of that Regulation;

WHEREAS the submission of such applications and notifications may have important legal consequences for each of the undertakings which is party to an agreement, decision or concerted practice; whereas every undertaking should accordingly have the right to submit an application or a notification to the Commission; whereas, furthermore, an undertaking exercising this right must inform the other undertakings which are parties to the

* Published in the Journal Officiel 10th May, 1962, English text Official Journal Special Edition 1959-62. p.132.

agreement, decision or concerted practice in order to enable them to protect their interests;

WHEREAS it is for the undertakings and associations of undertakings to transmit to the Commission information as to facts and circumstances in support of applications under Article 2 and of notifications under Articles 4 and 5;

WHEREAS it is desirable to prescribe forms for use in applications for negative clearance relating to implementation of Article 85(1) and for notifications relating to implementation of Article 85(3) of the Treaty, in order to simplify and accelerate consideration by the competent departments, in the interests of all concerned;

HAS ADOPTED THIS REGULATION:

37–02 *ARTICLE 1*

Persons entitled to submit applications and notifications

1. Any undertaking which is party to agreements, decisions or practices of the kind described in Articles 85 and 86 of the Treaty may submit an application under Article 2 or a notification under Articles 4 and 5 of Regulation No 17. Where the application or notification is submitted by some, but not all, of the undertakings concerned, they shall give notice to the others.

2. Where applications and notifications under Articles 2, 3(1), 3(2)(b), 4 and 5 of Regulation No 17 are signed by representatives of undertakings, associations of undertakings, or natural or legal persons, such representatives shall produce written proof that they are authorised to act.

3. Where a joint application or notification is submitted, a joint representative should be appointed.

37–03 *ARTICLE 2*

Submission of applications and notifications

1. *Ten*[1] copies of each application and notification and of the supporting documents shall be submitted to the Commission.

2. The supporting documents shall be either originals or copies. Copies must be certified as true copies of the original.

3. Applications and notifications shall be in one of the official languages of the Community. Supporting documents shall be submitted in their original language. Where the original language is not one of the official languages, a translation in one of the official languages shall be attached.

[1] Amendment made by Regulation 1699/75. (*v.* Appendix V.)

04 *ARTICLE 3*

Effective date of submission of applications and registrations

The date of submission of an application or notification shall be the date on which it is received by the Commission. Where, however, the application or notification is sent by registered post, it shall be deemed to have been received on the date shown on the postmark of the place of posting.

05 *ARTICLE 4*

Content of applications and notifications

1. Applications under Article 2 of Regulation No 17, relating to Article 85(1) of the Treaty, shall be submitted on Form A as shown in the Annex to this Regulation.
2. Notifications under Article 4 or Article 5 of Regulation No 17 shall be submitted on Form B as shown in the Annex to this Regulation.
3. Applications and notifications shall contain the information asked for in the forms.
4. Several participating undertakings may submit an application or notification on a single form.
5. Applications under Article 2 of Regulation No 17, relating to Article 86 of the Treaty, shall include a full statement of the facts, specifying, in particular, the practice concerned and the position of the undertaking or undertakings within the common market or a substantial part thereof in regard to products or services to which the practice relates.

06 *ARTICLE 5*

Transitional provisions

1. Applications and notifications submitted prior to the date of entry into force of this Regulation otherwise than on the prescribed forms shall be deemed to comply with Article 4 of this Regulation.
2. The Commission may require a duly completed form to be submitted to it within such time as it shall appoint. In that event, applications and notifications shall be treated as properly made only if the forms are submitted within the prescribed period and in accordance with the provisions of this Regulation.

07 *ARTICLE 6*

This Regulation shall enter into force on the day following its publication in the *Official Journal of the European Communities.*

37–08 This Regulation shall be binding in its entirety and directly applicable in all Member States.

Done at Brussels, 3 May 1962.

For the Commission
The President
W. HALLSTEIN

Note: Regulation 1133/68 combined the two Forms into Form A/B, *v.* Appendix I Part I.

APPENDIX V

REGULATION (EEC) NO 1699/75 OF THE COMMISSION of 2 July 1975*

Amending Commission Regulation no 27 of 3 May 1962

–01 THE COMMISSION OF THE EUROPEAN COMMUNITIES,

HAVING REGARD to the Treaty establishing the European Economic Community, and in particular Articles 87 and 155 thereof;

HAVING REGARD to Article 24 of Council Regulation No 17 of 6 February 1962;

WHEREAS Regulation No 27, adopted by the Commission pursuant to Article 24 of Regulation No 17, provides at Article 2(1) that applications and notifications and their supporting documents must be submitted to the Commission in seven copies;

WHEREAS the number of copies to be submitted was determined by reference to the number of Member States, with a view to the transmission of the documents to the competent authorities of the Member States pursuant to Article 10 of Regulation No 17;

WHEREAS the number of copies to be submitted should be adjusted to the present number of Member States so as to accelerate, in the interests of all parties concerned, the examination of applications and notifications,

HAS ADOPTED THIS REGULATION:

–02 *Sole Article*

Article 2(1) of Regulation No 27 is amended as follows:

* Published in the Official Journal L172. 3rd July 1975, p.11.

"10 copies of each application and notification and of the supporting documents shall be submitted to the Commission."

38–03 This Regulation shall be binding in its entirety and directly applicable in all Member States.

Done at Brussels, 2 July 1975.

For the Commission
The President
Francois-Xavier ORTOLI

INDEX